CRITICAL PRAISE FOR
THE SHERIFF OF BABYLON

"One of the best comics being published today. I'd probably even go as far as calling it the best."
—MATT SANTORI-GIFFITH, COMICOSITY.COM

"Incredible...reading THE SHERIFF OF BABYLON is like watching a big budget Iraq crime movie. Mitch Gerads draws this beauty in an engrossing and cinematic style...Tom King's writing is equally cinematic. His truncated scenes, fast moving plot, and compelling large cast are all superbly handled in this book that truly has a unique voice and style."
—LEVI HUNT, IGN.COM

"King's terse writing captures the volatility and cynical realpolitik of post-invasion Baghdad... will appeal to fans of *Homeland* and *The Honourable Woman*."
—GRAEME VIRTUE, *THE GUARDIAN*

"Highly ambitious...King's work stands out because he makes bold, sophisticated choices informed by a comprehensive understanding of how to use the comic book medium. He knows when to effectively use a nine-panel grid versus a widescreen layout, and he makes smart structural decisions in THE SHERIFF OF BABYLON #1 that provide a sturdy foundation for artist Mitch Gerads to build on with his meticulously detailed linework and rich, textured coloring."
—OLIVER SAVA, THEAVCLUB.COM

"Fearless...the creators of THE SHERIFF OF BABYLON are striving for nuance and complexity in relating and relying upon the delicate political realities of the day, factors still influencing the world today, while still working to build a narratively rich world that serves the story."
—MIKE RE, *ASBURY PARK PRESS*

"Superb...a complex depiction of a country very different from the foreign country invading it in the particulars, yet helplessly influenced by how that country sees it, and how that perception drives money and power."
—DAN SEITZ, UPROXX.COM

"This book is perfect...The setting is both familiar and yet entirely foreign, creating a world of realism that still manages to capture the imagination with gruesome truth...Mitch Gerads' gritty pencils and analogous color scheme vividly capture the brutal desert metropolis in a way worthy of the big screen."
—PATRICK HEALY, EXAMINER.COM

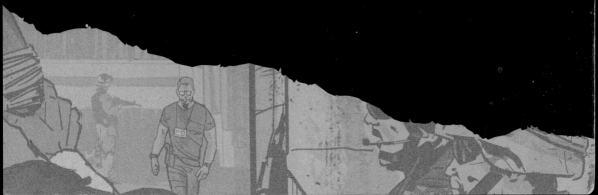

THE SHE
BABY

RIFF OF LION

BANG. BANG. BANG.

TOM KING
WRITER

MITCH GERADS
ART AND COLORS

NICK J. NAPOLITANO (ISSUES #1-2)
TRAVIS LANHAM (ISSUES #3-6)
LETTERING

JOHN PAUL LEON
COVER ART AND ORIGINAL SERIES COVERS

THE SHERIFF OF BABYLON CREATED BY
TOM KING **AND** MITCH GERADS

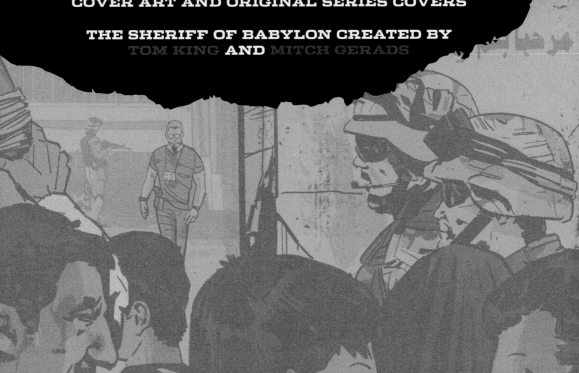

JAMIE S. RICH Editor – Original Series
MOLLY MAHAN Associate Editor – Original Series
JEB WOODARD Group Editor – Collected Editions
SCOTT NYBAKKEN Editor – Collected Edition
STEVE COOK Design Director – Books
DAMIAN RYLAND Publication Design

SHELLY BOND VP & Executive Editor – Vertigo

DIANE NELSON President
DAN DIDIO AND JIM LEE Co-Publishers
GEOFF JOHNS Chief Creative Officer
AMIT DESAI Senior VP – Marketing & Global Franchise Management
NAIRI GARDINER Senior VP – Finance
SAM ADES VP – Digital Marketing
BOBBIE CHASE VP – Talent Development
MARK CHIARELLO Senior VP – Art, Design & Collected Editions
JOHN CUNNINGHAM VP – Content Strategy
ANNE DEPIES VP – Strategy Planning & Reporting
DON FALLETTI VP – Manufacturing Operations
LAWRENCE GANEM VP – Editorial Administration & Talent Relations
ALISON GILL Senior VP – Manufacturing & Operations
HANK KANALZ Senior VP – Editorial Strategy & Administration
JAY KOGAN VP – Legal Affairs
DEREK MADDALENA Senior VP – Sales & Business Development
JACK MAHAN VP – Business Affairs
DAN MIRON VP – Sales Planning & Trade Development
NICK NAPOLITANO VP – Manufacturing Administration
CAROL ROEDER VP – Marketing
EDDIE SCANNELL VP – Mass Account & Digital Sales
COURTNEY SIMMONS Senior VP – Publicity & Communications
JIM (SKI) SOKOLOWSKI VP – Comic Book Specialty & Newsstand Sales
SANDY YI Senior VP – Global Franchise Management

Logo design by **MITCH GERADS**

THE SHERIFF OF BABYLON: BANG. BANG. BANG.

DC Comics
2900 West Alameda Avenue
Burbank, CA 91505
Printed in the USA. First Printing.
ISBN: 978-1-4012-6466-6

Library of Congress Cataloging-in-Publication Data is available.

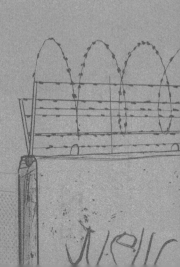

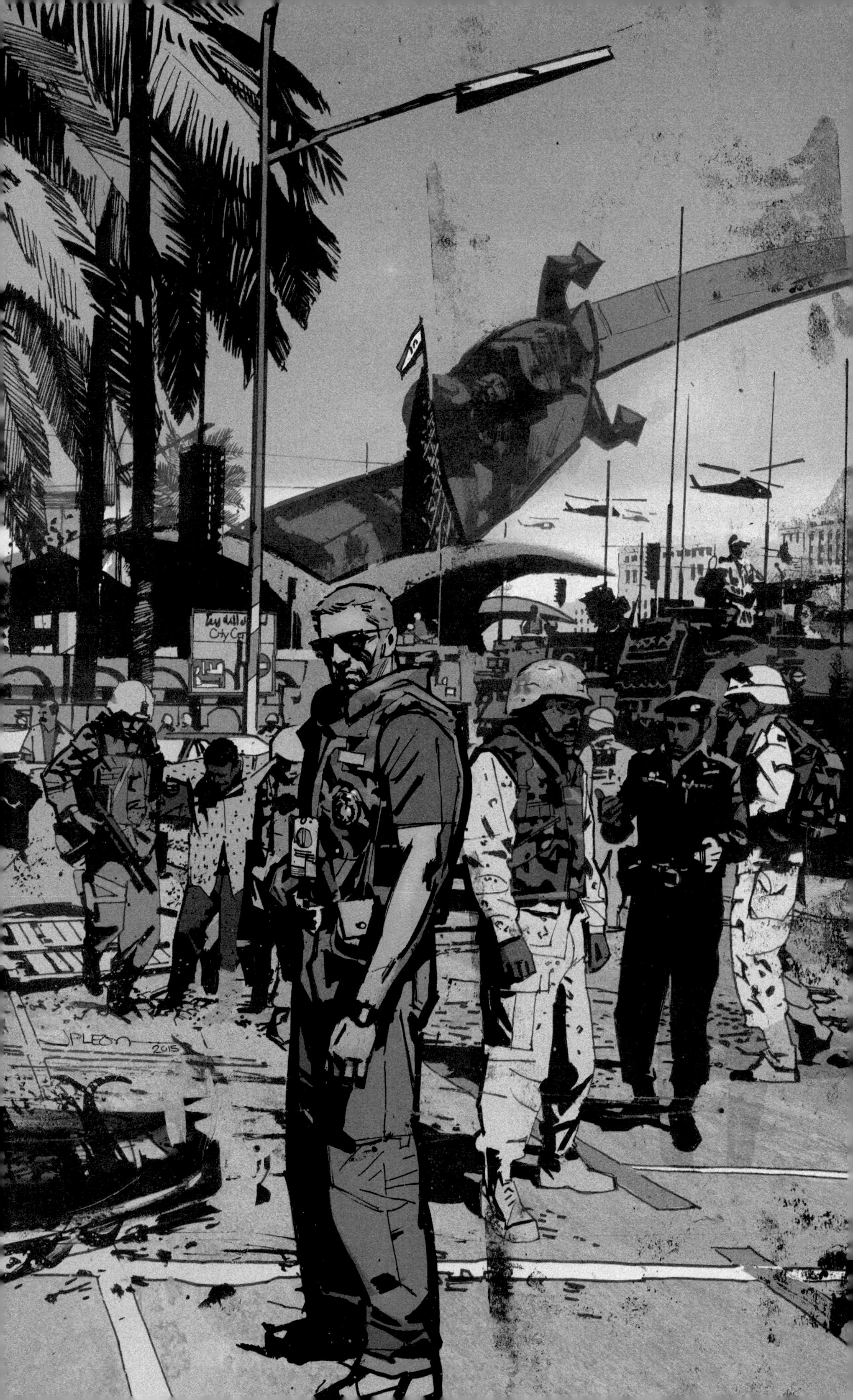
JPLEON
2015

PART ONE

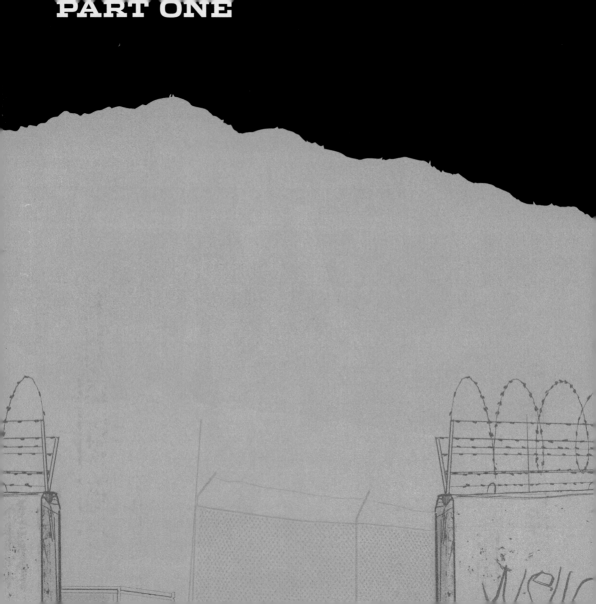

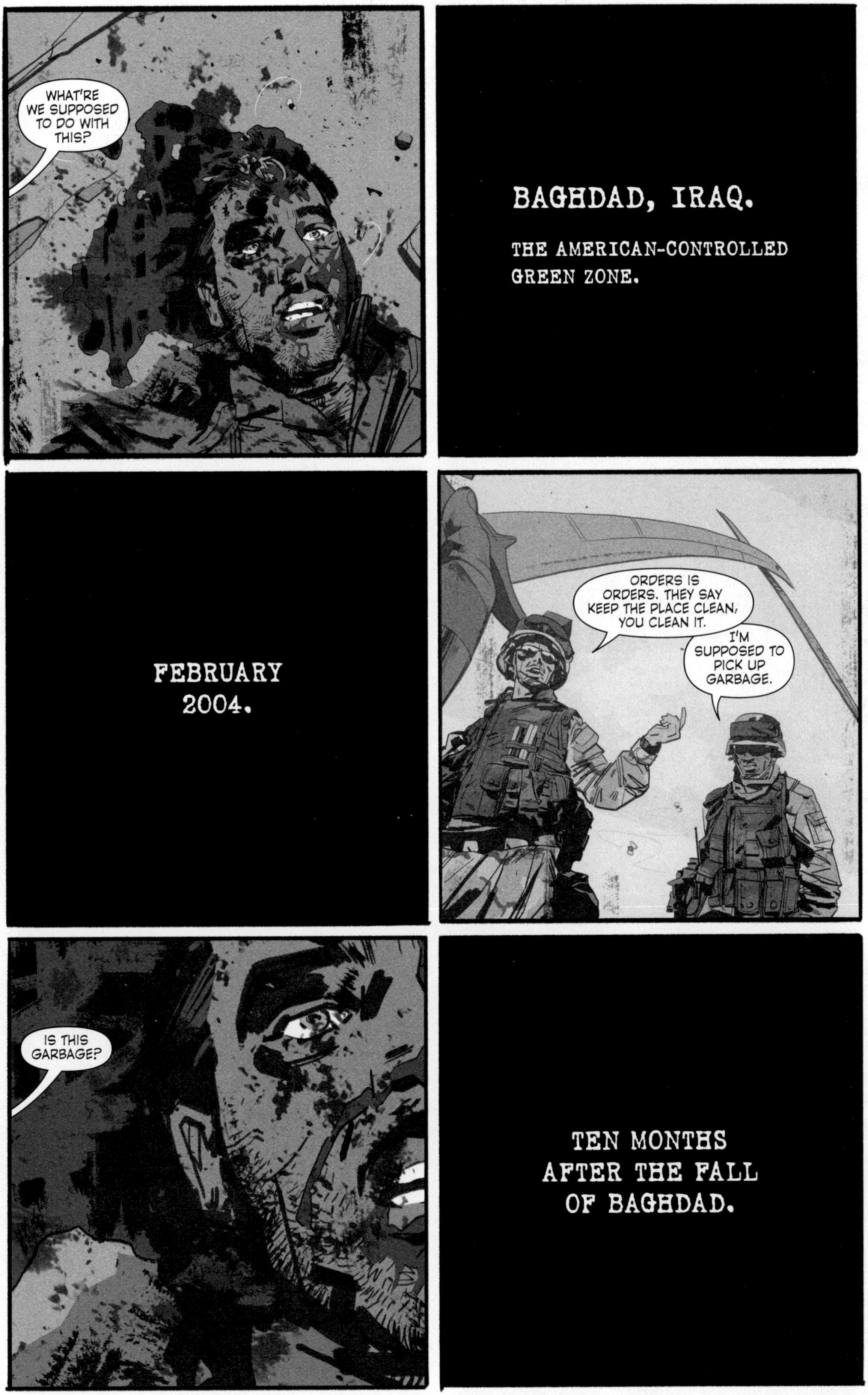
WHAT'RE WE SUPPOSED TO DO WITH THIS?
BAGHDAD, IRAQ.
THE AMERICAN-CONTROLLED GREEN ZONE.
FEBRUARY 2004.
ORDERS IS ORDERS. THEY SAY KEEP THE PLACE CLEAN, YOU CLEAN IT.
I'M SUPPOSED TO PICK UP GARBAGE.
IS THIS GARBAGE?
TEN MONTHS AFTER THE FALL OF BAGHDAD.

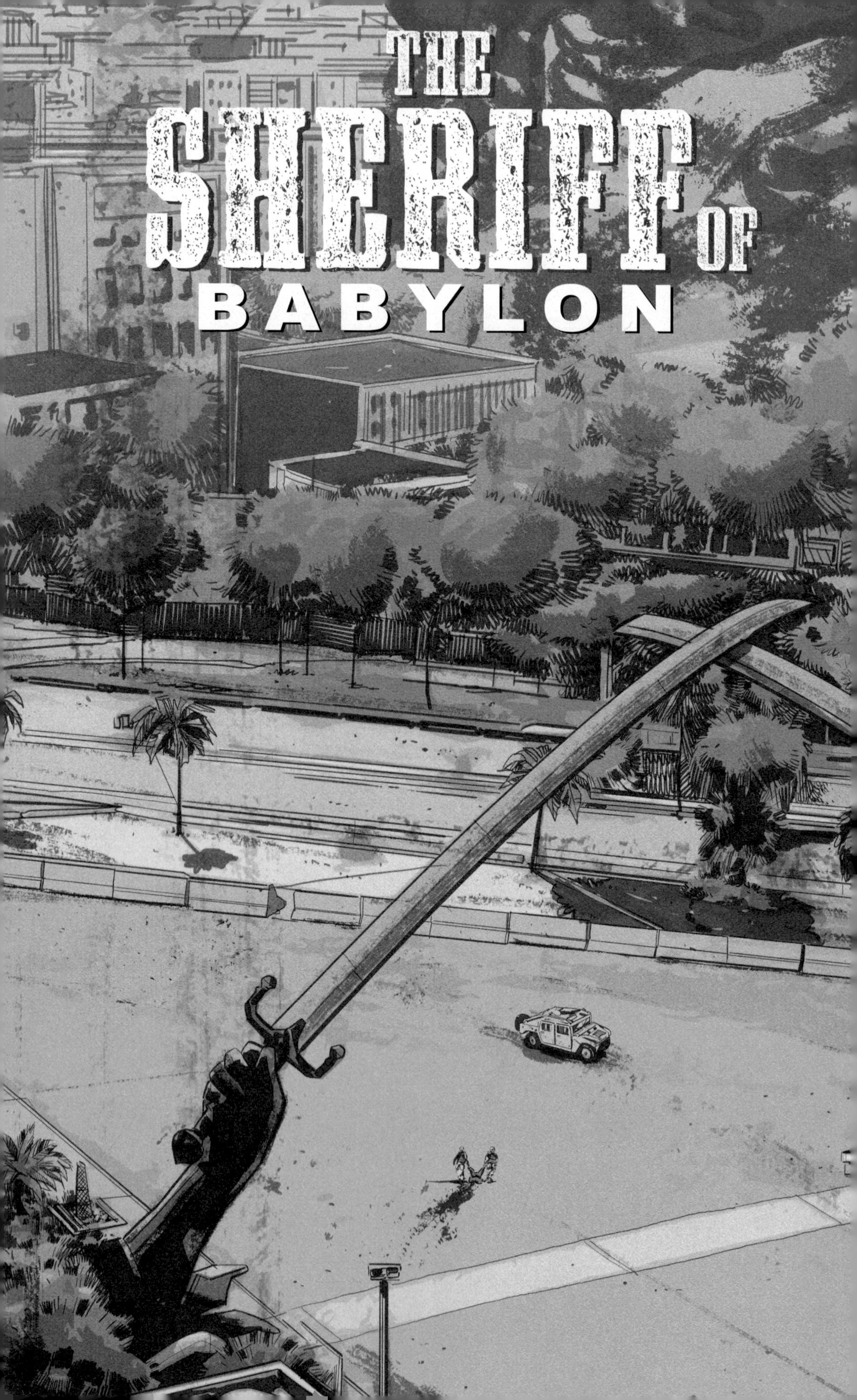
THE SHERIFF OF BABYLON

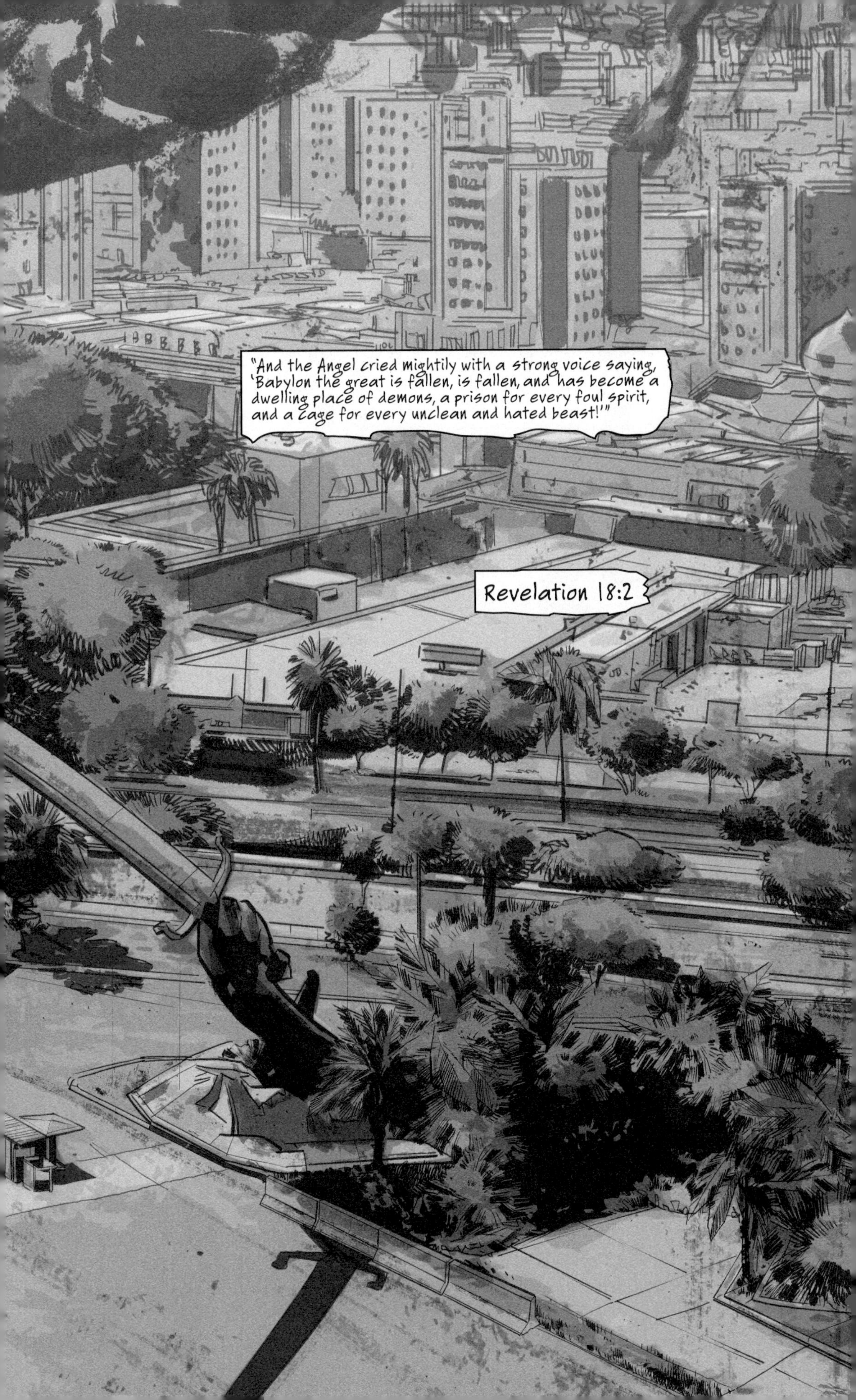
"And the Angel cried mightily with a strong voice saying, 'Babylon the great is fallen, is fallen, and has become a dwelling place of demons, a prison for every foul spirit, and a cage for every unclean and hated beast!'"
Revelation 18:2

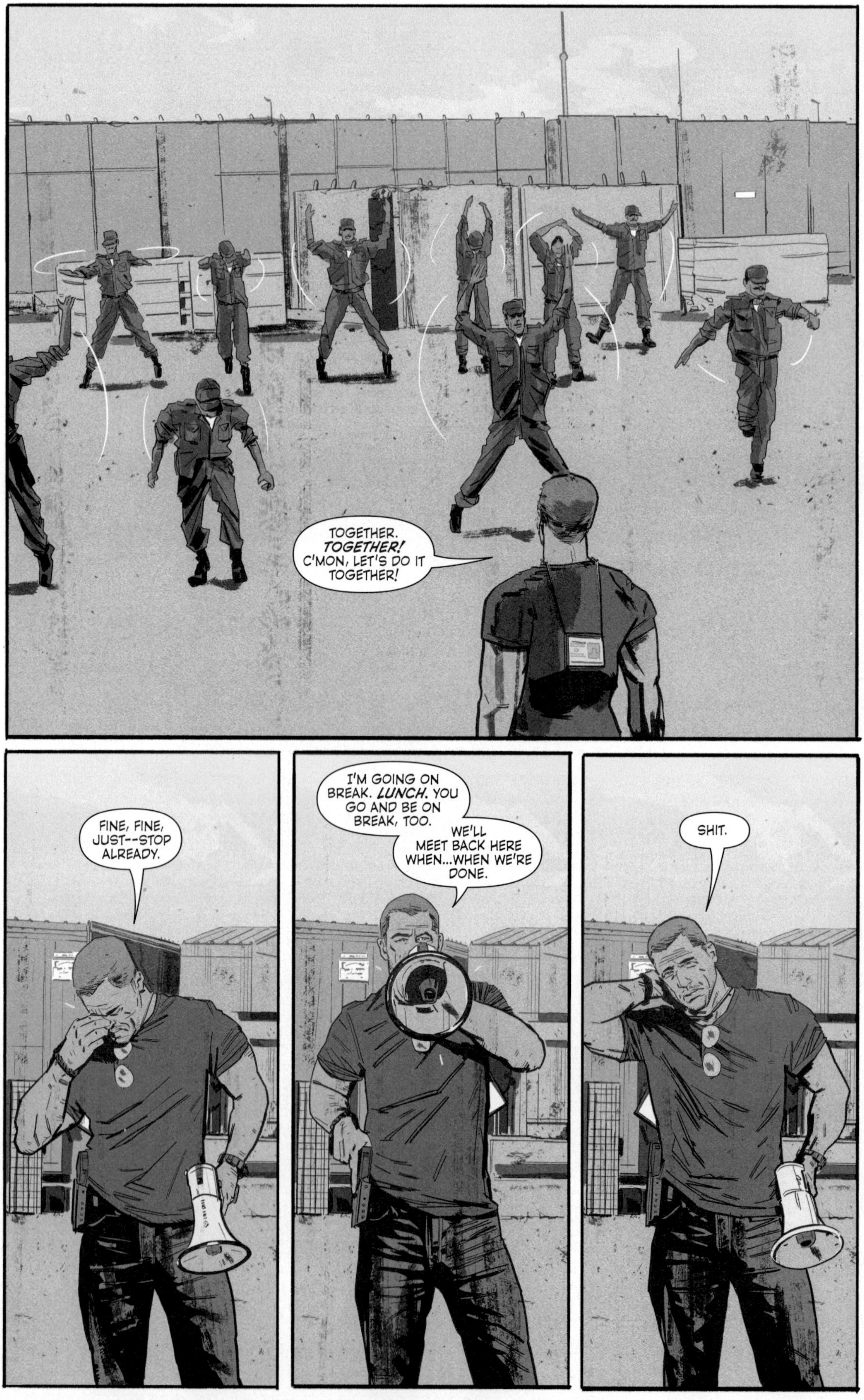
TOGETHER. ***TOGETHER!*** C'MON, LET'S DO IT TOGETHER!
FINE, FINE, JUST--STOP ALREADY.
I'M GOING ON BREAK. ***LUNCH.*** YOU GO AND BE ON BREAK, TOO.
WE'LL MEET BACK HERE WHEN...WHEN WE'RE DONE.
SHIT.

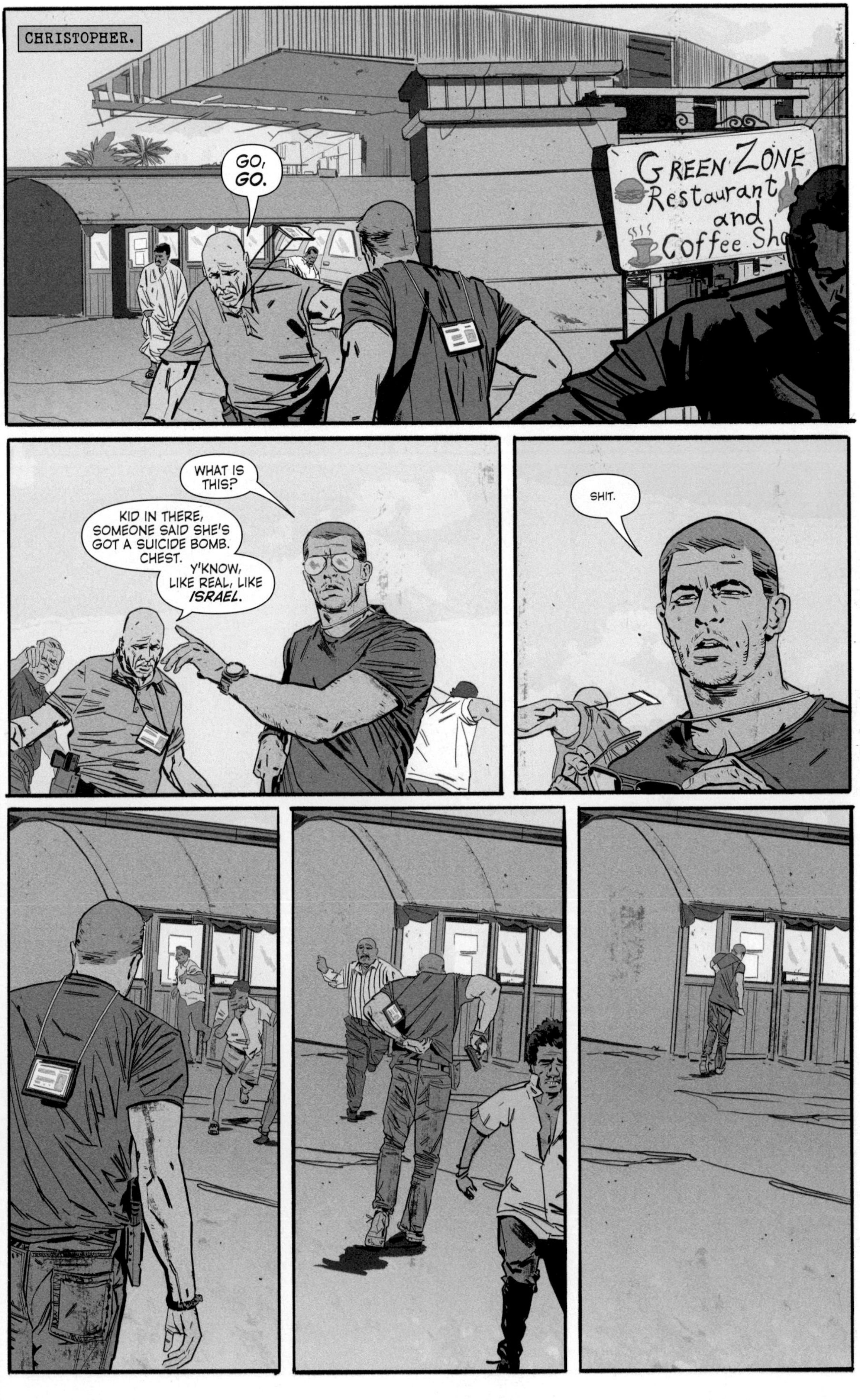
CHRISTOPHER.
GO, GO.
GREEN ZONE Restaurant and Coffee Sho
WHAT IS THIS?
KID IN THERE, SOMEONE SAID SHE'S GOT A SUICIDE BOMB. CHEST.
Y'KNOW, LIKE REAL, LIKE ISRAEL.
SHIT.

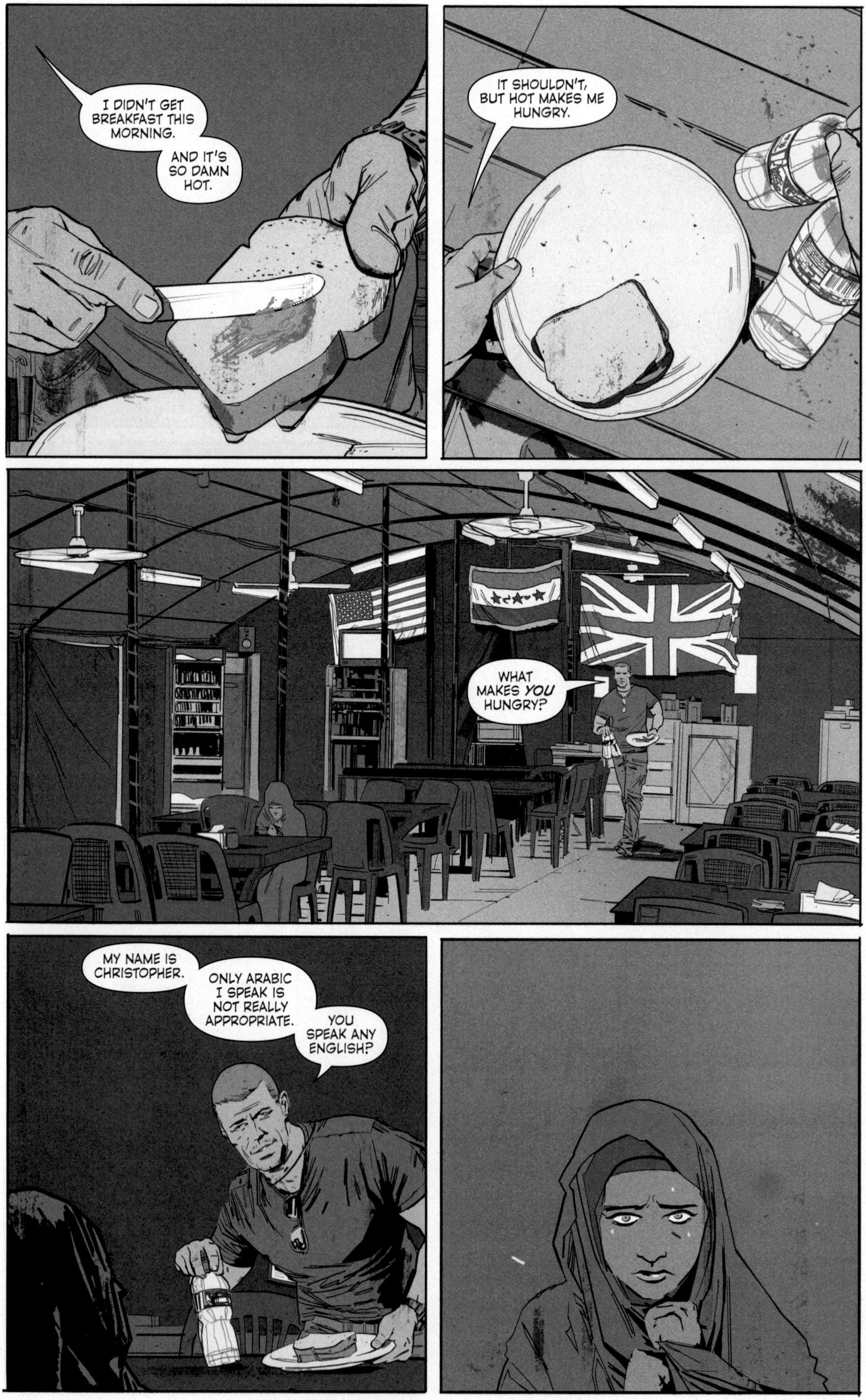
I DIDN'T GET BREAKFAST THIS MORNING.
AND IT'S SO DAMN HOT.
IT SHOULDN'T, BUT HOT MAKES ME HUNGRY.
WHAT MAKES *YOU* HUNGRY?
MY NAME IS CHRISTOPHER.
ONLY ARABIC I SPEAK IS NOT REALLY APPROPRIATE.
YOU SPEAK ANY ENGLISH?

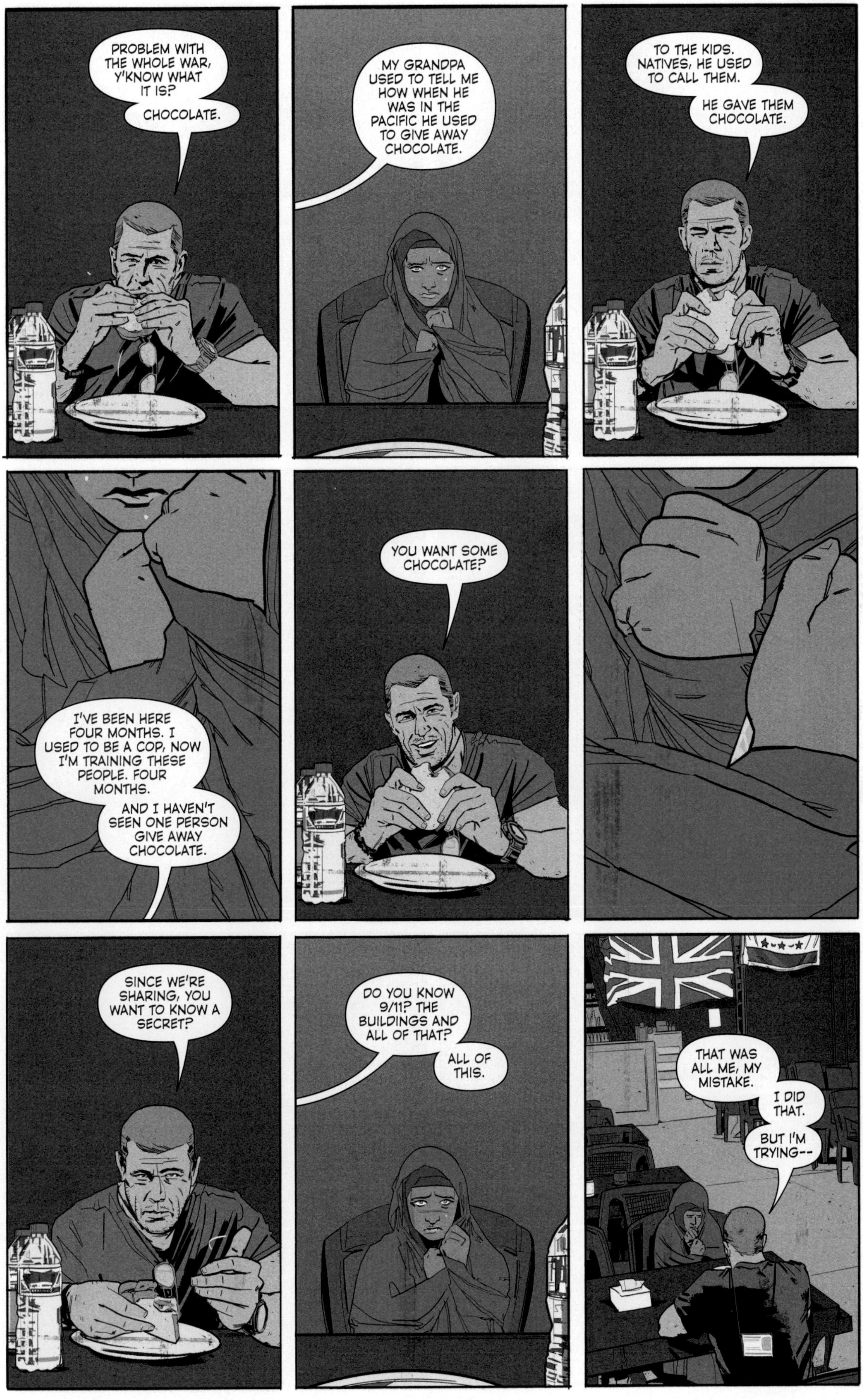
PROBLEM WITH THE WHOLE WAR, Y'KNOW WHAT IT IS?
CHOCOLATE.
MY GRANDPA USED TO TELL ME HOW WHEN HE WAS IN THE PACIFIC HE USED TO GIVE AWAY CHOCOLATE.
TO THE KIDS. NATIVES, HE USED TO CALL THEM.
HE GAVE THEM CHOCOLATE.
I'VE BEEN HERE FOUR MONTHS. I USED TO BE A COP, NOW I'M TRAINING THESE PEOPLE. FOUR MONTHS.
AND I HAVEN'T SEEN ONE PERSON GIVE AWAY CHOCOLATE.
YOU WANT SOME CHOCOLATE?
SINCE WE'RE SHARING, YOU WANT TO KNOW A SECRET?
DO YOU KNOW 9/11? THE BUILDINGS AND ALL OF THAT?
ALL OF THIS.
THAT WAS ALL ME, MY MISTAKE.
I DID THAT.
BUT I'M TRYING--

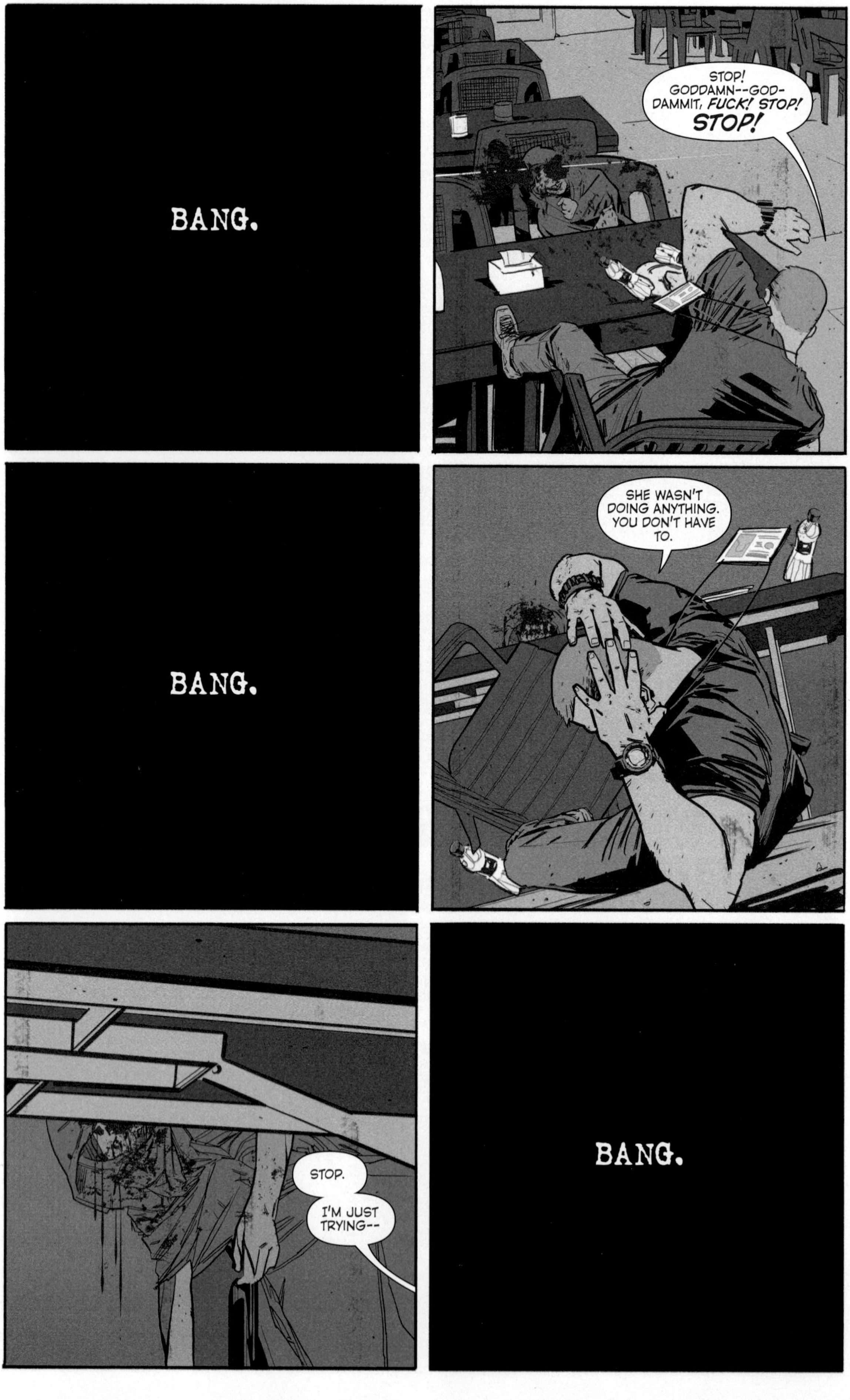
BANG.
STOP! GODDAMN--GOD-DAMMIT, FUCK! STOP! STOP!
BANG.
SHE WASN'T DOING ANYTHING. YOU DON'T HAVE TO.
STOP.
I'M JUST TRYING--
BANG.

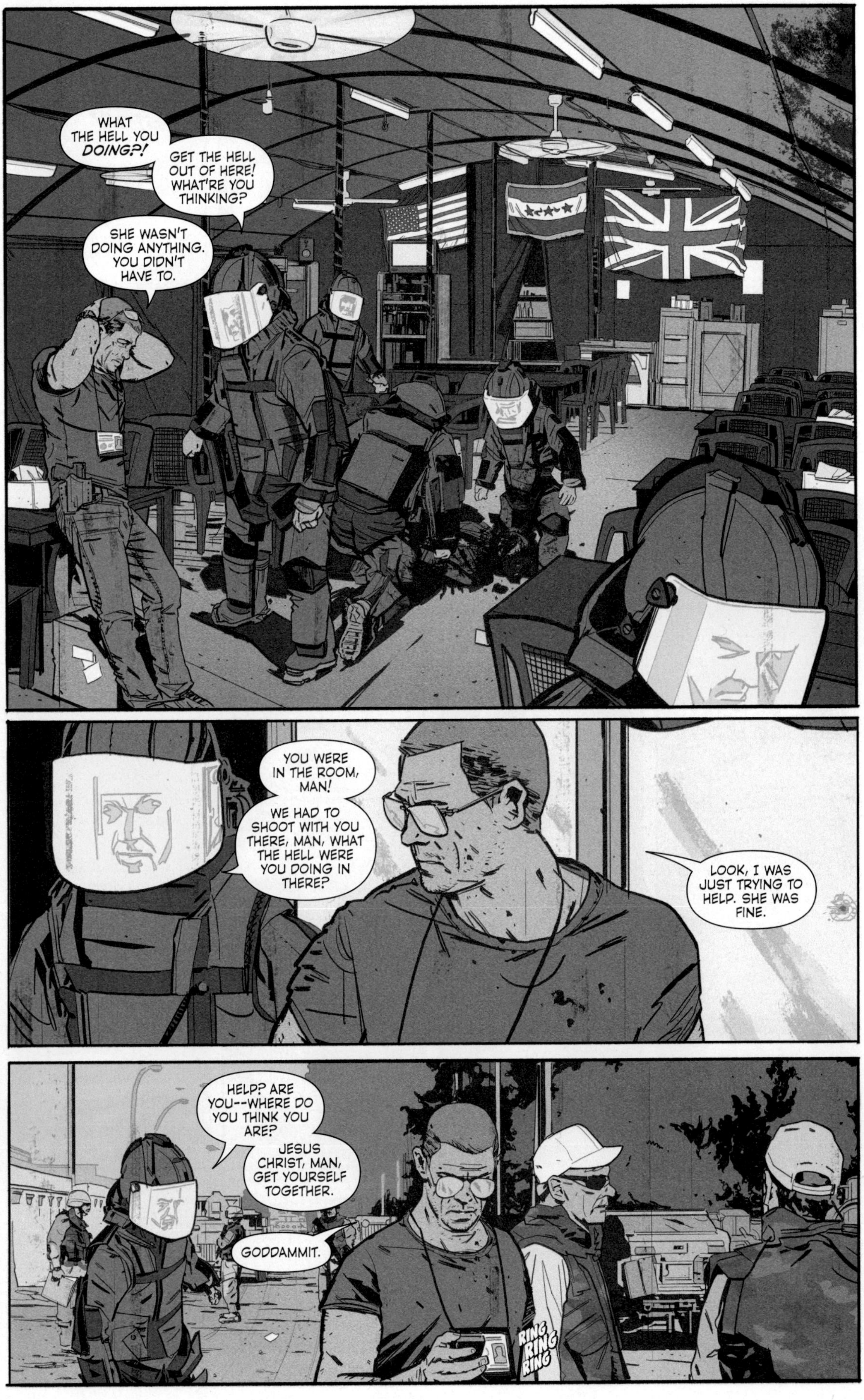
WHAT THE HELL YOU *DOING?!*
GET THE HELL OUT OF HERE! WHAT'RE YOU THINKING?
SHE WASN'T DOING ANYTHING. YOU DIDN'T HAVE TO.
YOU WERE IN THE ROOM, MAN!
WE HAD TO SHOOT WITH YOU THERE, MAN, WHAT THE HELL WERE YOU DOING IN THERE?
LOOK, I WAS JUST TRYING TO HELP. SHE WAS FINE.
HELP? ARE YOU--WHERE DO YOU THINK YOU ARE?
JESUS CHRIST, MAN, GET YOURSELF TOGETHER.
GODDAMMIT.
RING RING RING

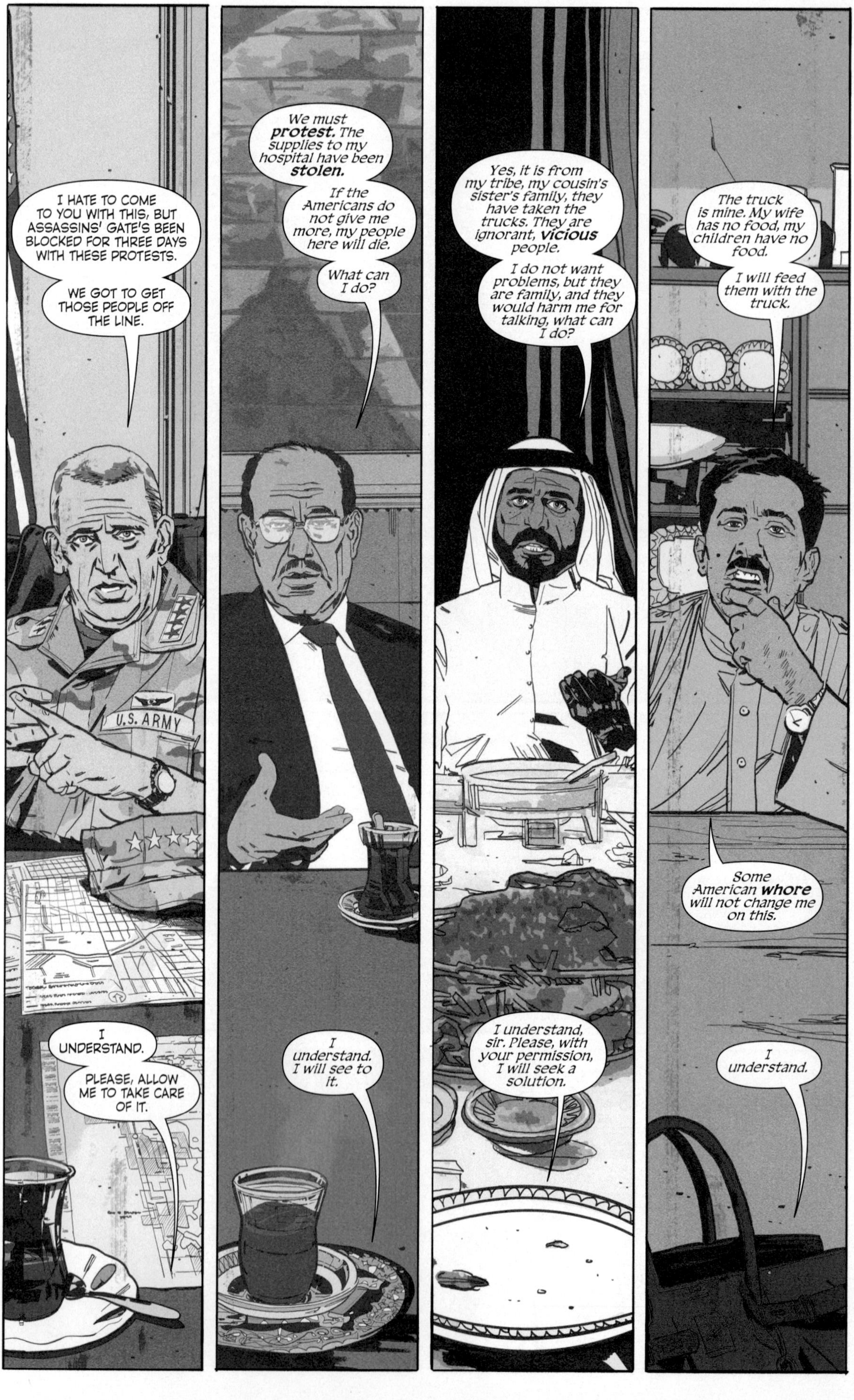
I HATE TO COME TO YOU WITH THIS, BUT ASSASSINS' GATE'S BEEN BLOCKED FOR THREE DAYS WITH THESE PROTESTS.
WE GOT TO GET THOSE PEOPLE OFF THE LINE.
U.S. ARMY
I UNDERSTAND.
PLEASE, ALLOW ME TO TAKE CARE OF IT.
We must protest. The supplies to my hospital have been stolen.
If the Americans do not give me more, my people here will die.
What can I do?
I understand. I will see to it.
Yes, it is from my tribe, my cousin's sister's family, they have taken the trucks. They are ignorant, vicious people.
I do not want problems, but they are family, and they would harm me for talking, what can I do?
I understand, sir. Please, with your permission, I will seek a solution.
The truck is mine. My wife has no food, my children have no food.
I will feed them with the truck.
Some American whore will not change me on this.
I understand.

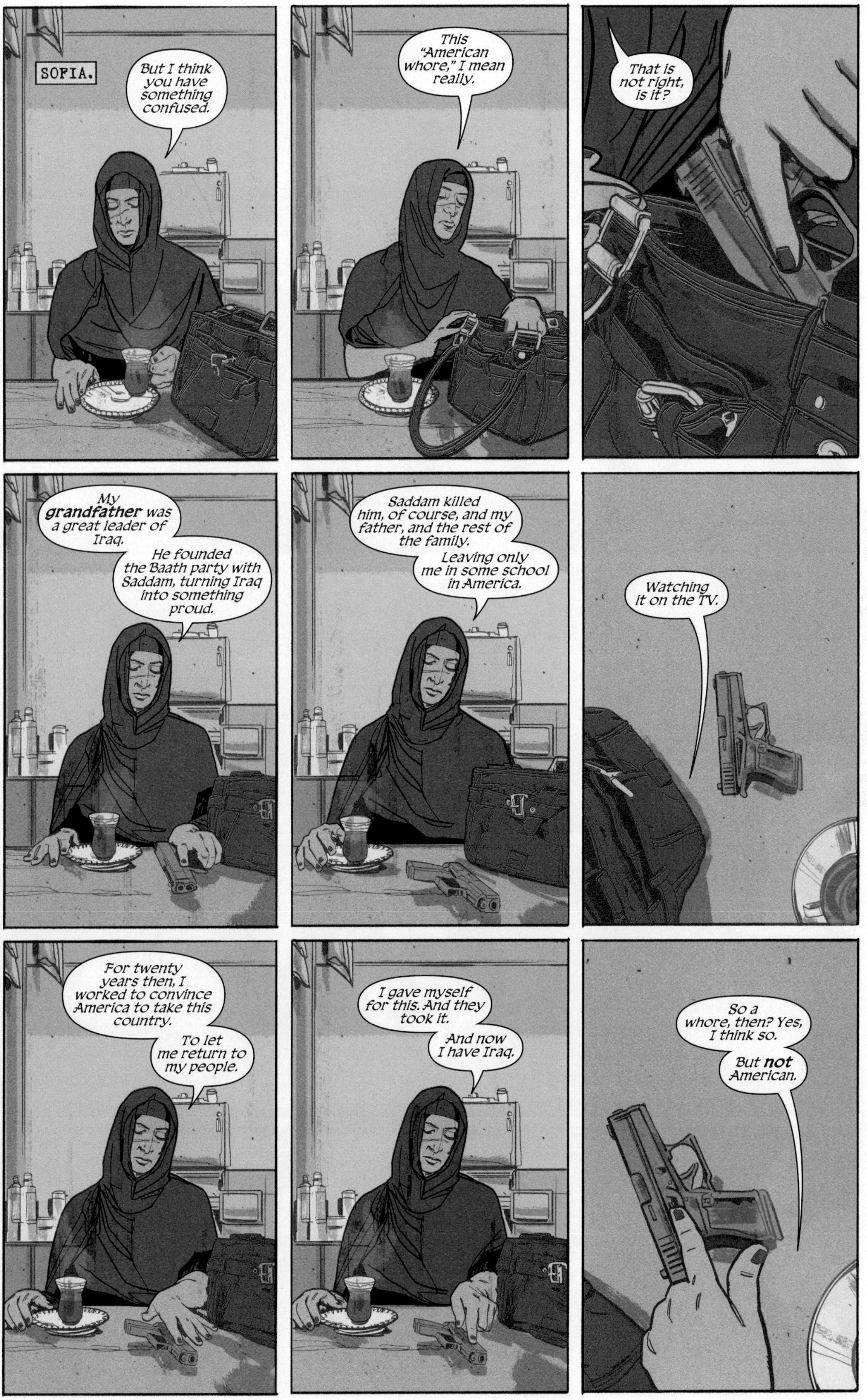
SOFIA.
But I think you have something confused.
This "American whore," I mean really.
That is not right, is it?
My **grandfather** was a great leader of Iraq.
He founded the Baath party with Saddam, turning Iraq into something proud.
Saddam killed him, of course, and my father, and the rest of the family.
Leaving only me in some school in America.
Watching it on the TV.
For twenty years then, I worked to convince America to take this country.
To let me return to my people.
I gave myself for this. And they took it.
And now I have Iraq.
So a whore, then? Yes, I think so.
But **not** American.

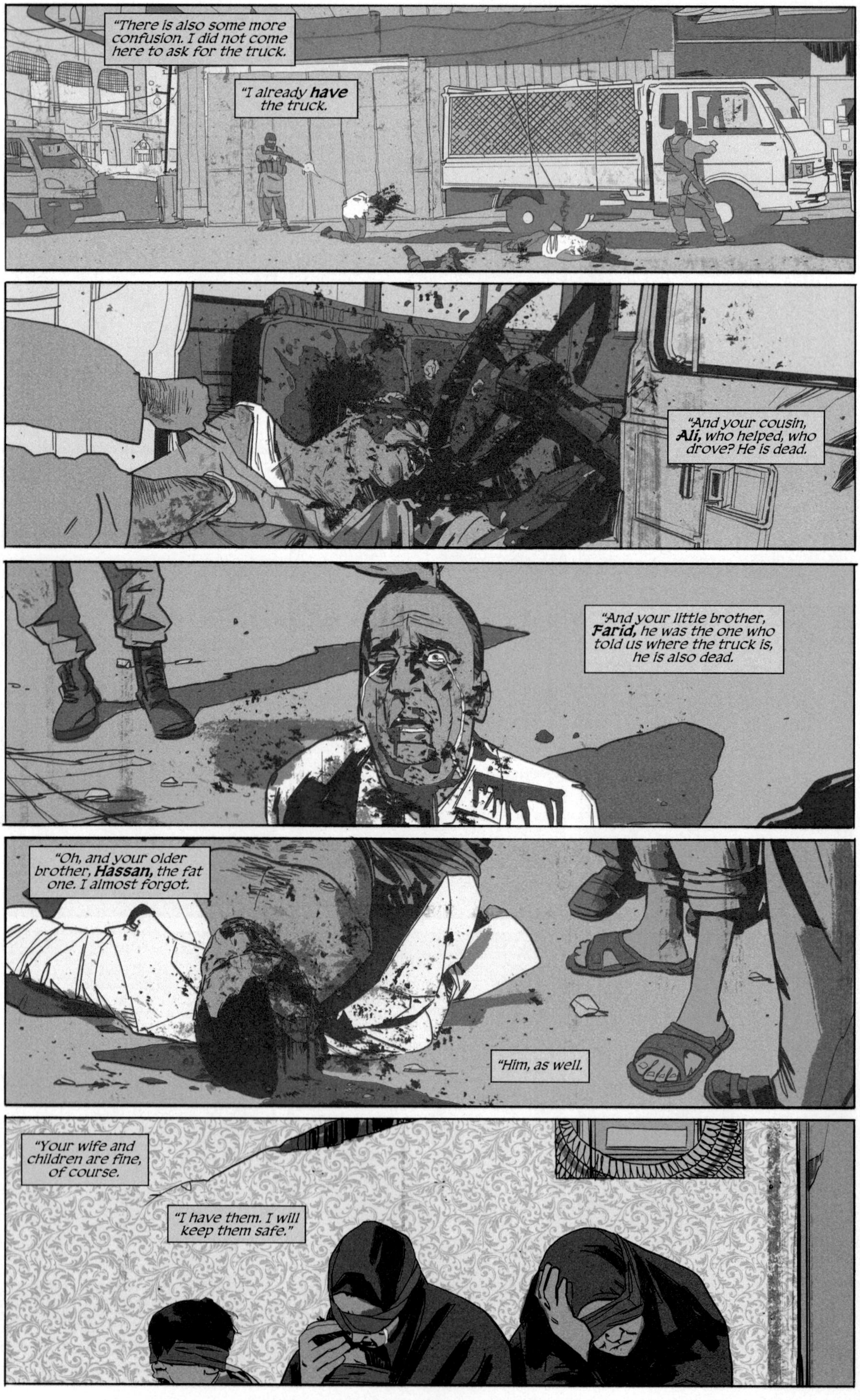
"There is also some more confusion. I did not come here to ask for the truck.
"I already **have** the truck.
"And your cousin, **Ali,** who helped, who drove? He is dead.
"And your little brother, **Farid,** he was the one who told us where the truck is, he is also dead.
"Oh, and your older brother, **Hassan,** the fat one. I almost forgot.
"Him, as well.
"Your wife and children are fine, of course.
"I have them. I will keep them safe."

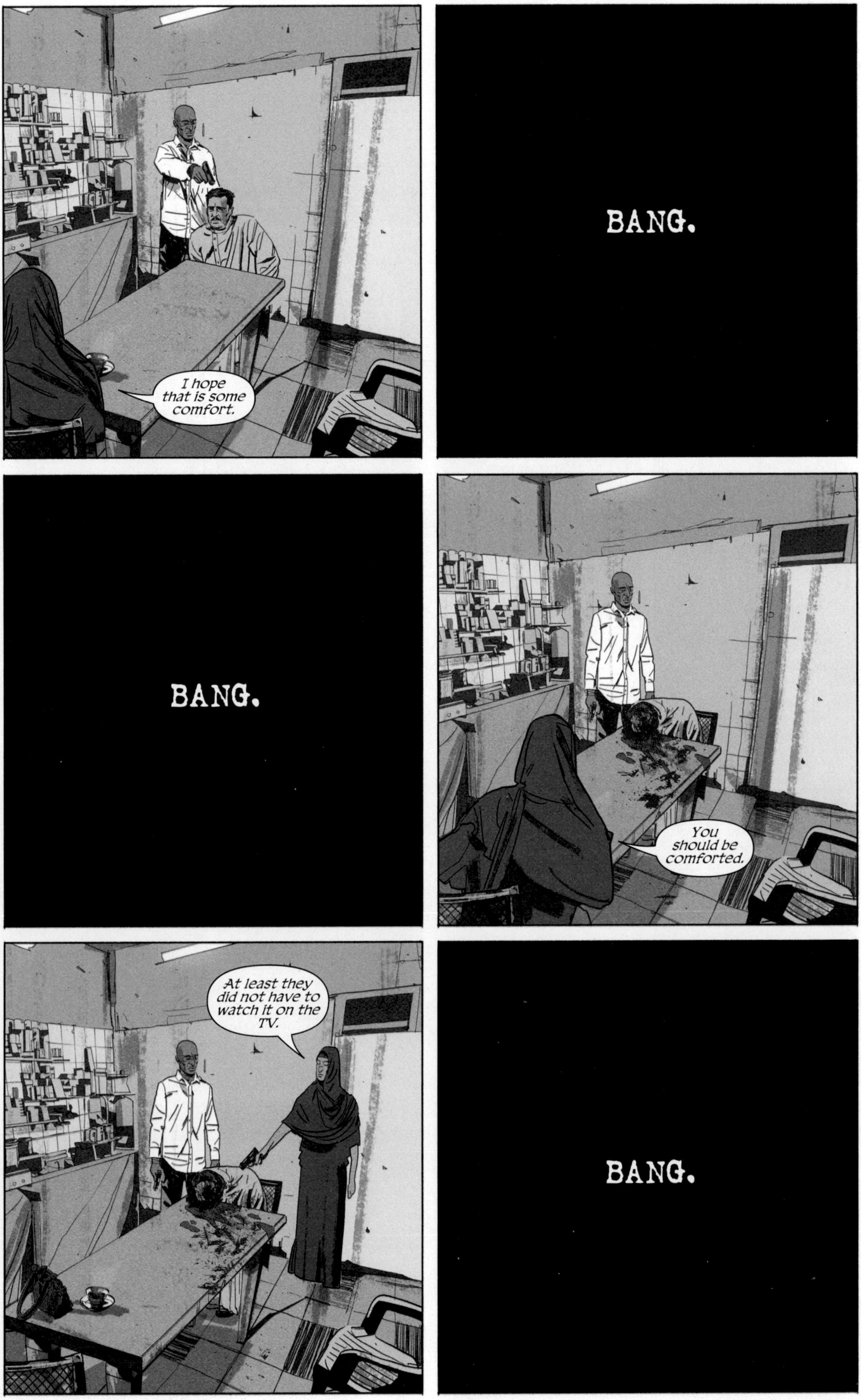
I hope that is some comfort.
BANG.
BANG.
You should be comforted.
At least they did not have to watch it on the TV.
BANG.

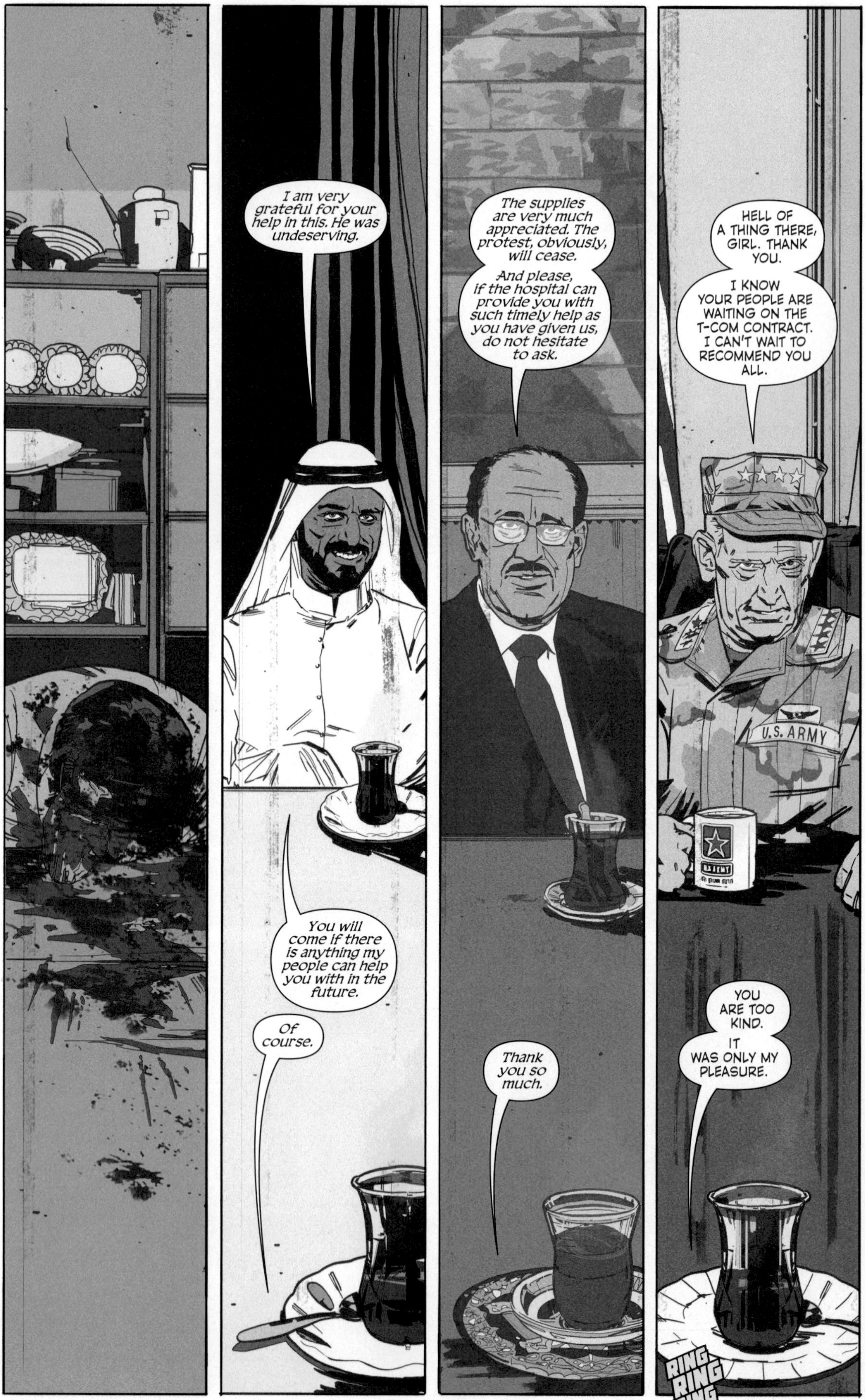
I am very grateful for your help in this. He was undeserving.
You will come if there is anything my people can help you with in the future.
Of course.
The supplies are very much appreciated. The protest, obviously, will cease.
And please, if the hospital can provide you with such timely help as you have given us, do not hesitate to ask.
Thank you so much.
HELL OF A THING THERE, GIRL. THANK YOU.
I KNOW YOUR PEOPLE ARE WAITING ON THE T-COM CONTRACT. I CAN'T WAIT TO RECOMMEND YOU ALL.
U.S. ARMY
YOU ARE TOO KIND.
IT WAS ONLY MY PLEASURE.
RING RING RING

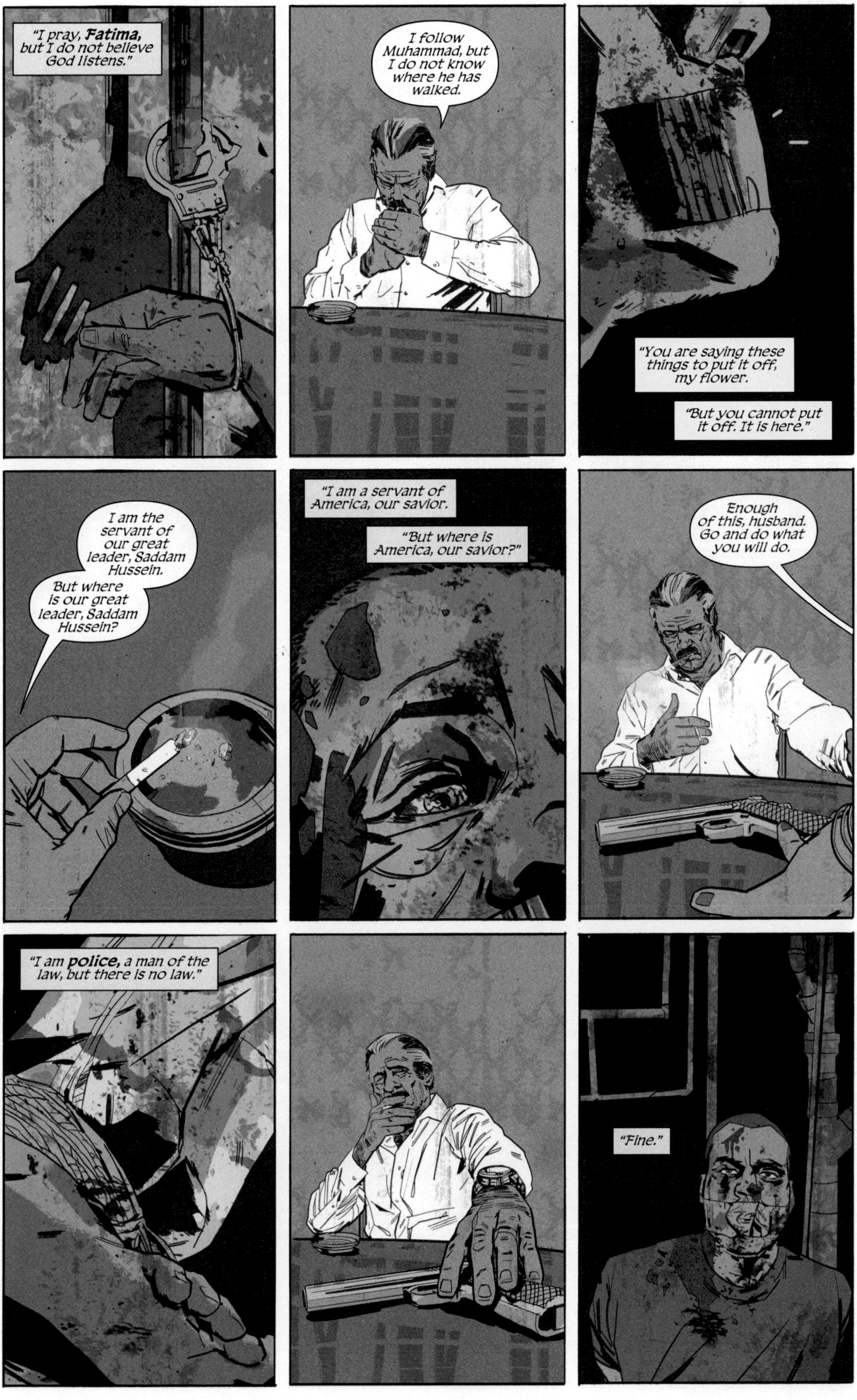
"I pray, **Fatima,** but I do not believe God listens."
I follow Muhammad, but I do not know where he has walked.
"You are saying these things to put it off, my flower.
"But you cannot put it off. It is here."
I am the servant of our great leader, Saddam Hussein.
But where is our great leader, Saddam Hussein?
"I am a servant of America, our savior.
"But where is America, our savior?"
Enough of this, husband. Go and do what you will do.
"I am **police,** a man of the law, but there is no law."
"Fine."

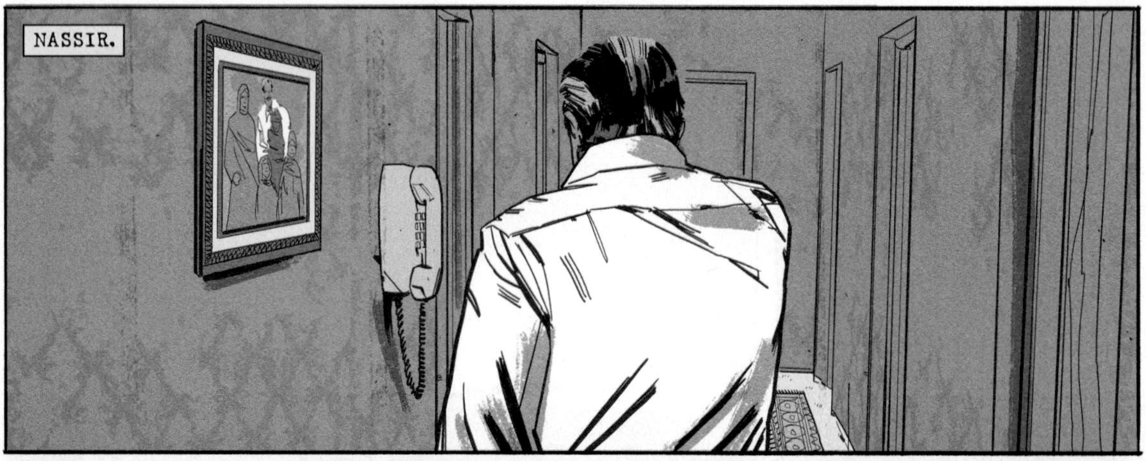
NASSIR.
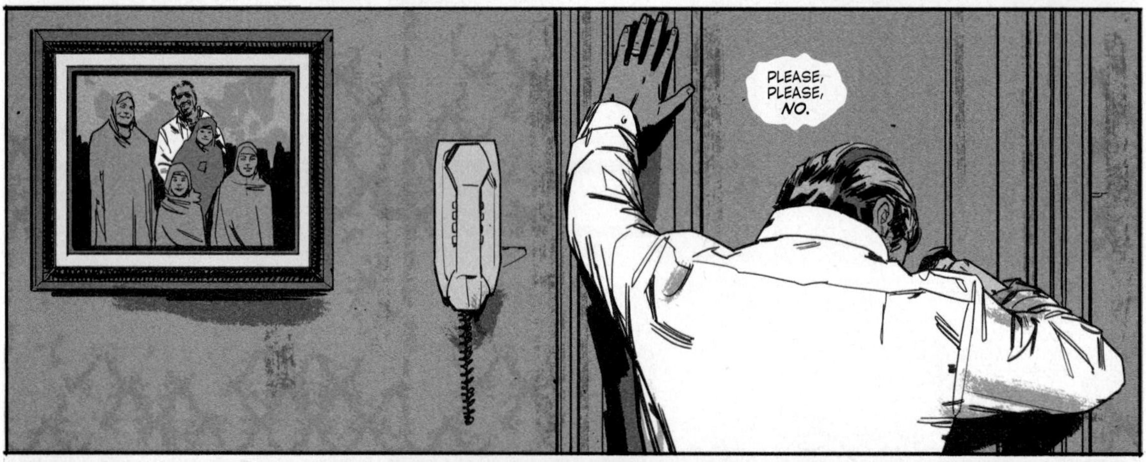
PLEASE, PLEASE, NO.
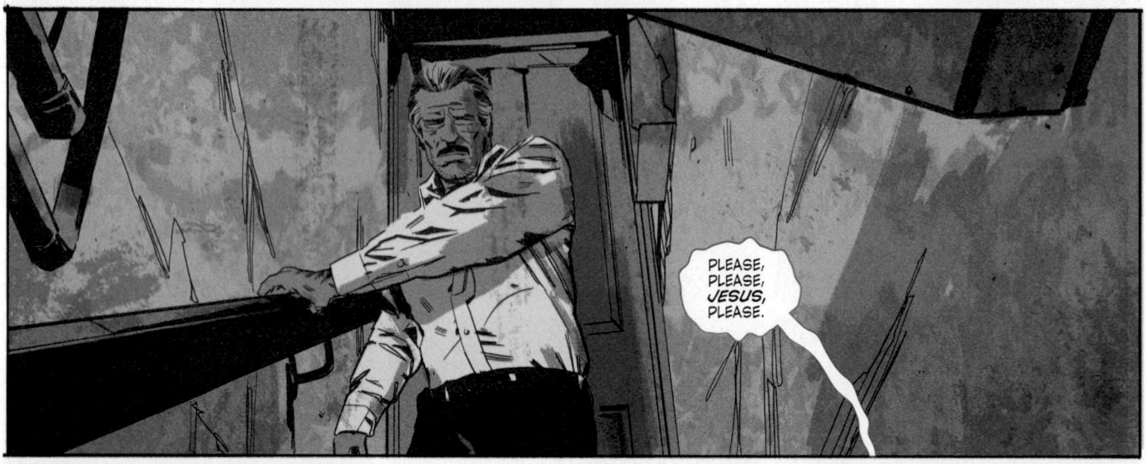
PLEASE, PLEASE, JESUS, PLEASE.
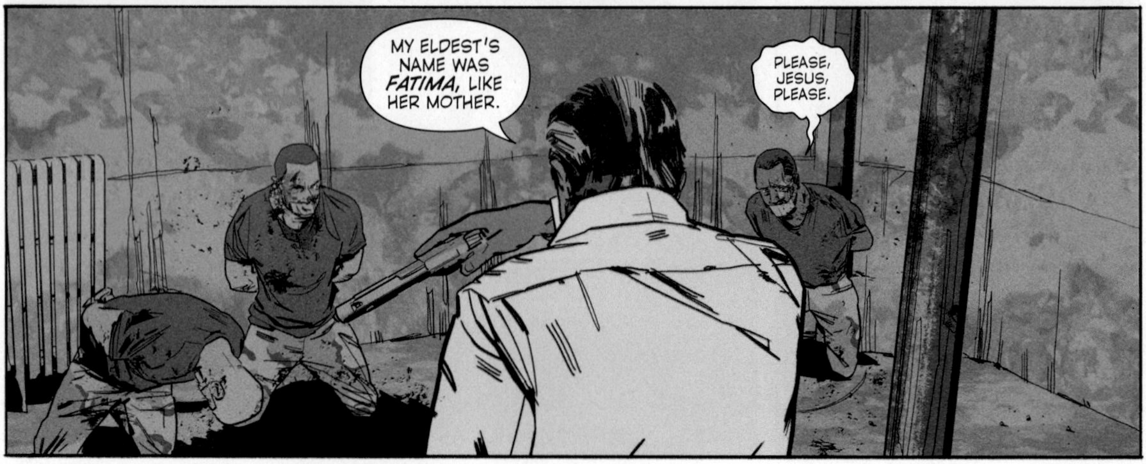
MY ELDEST'S NAME WAS FATIMA, LIKE HER MOTHER.
PLEASE, JESUS, PLEASE.

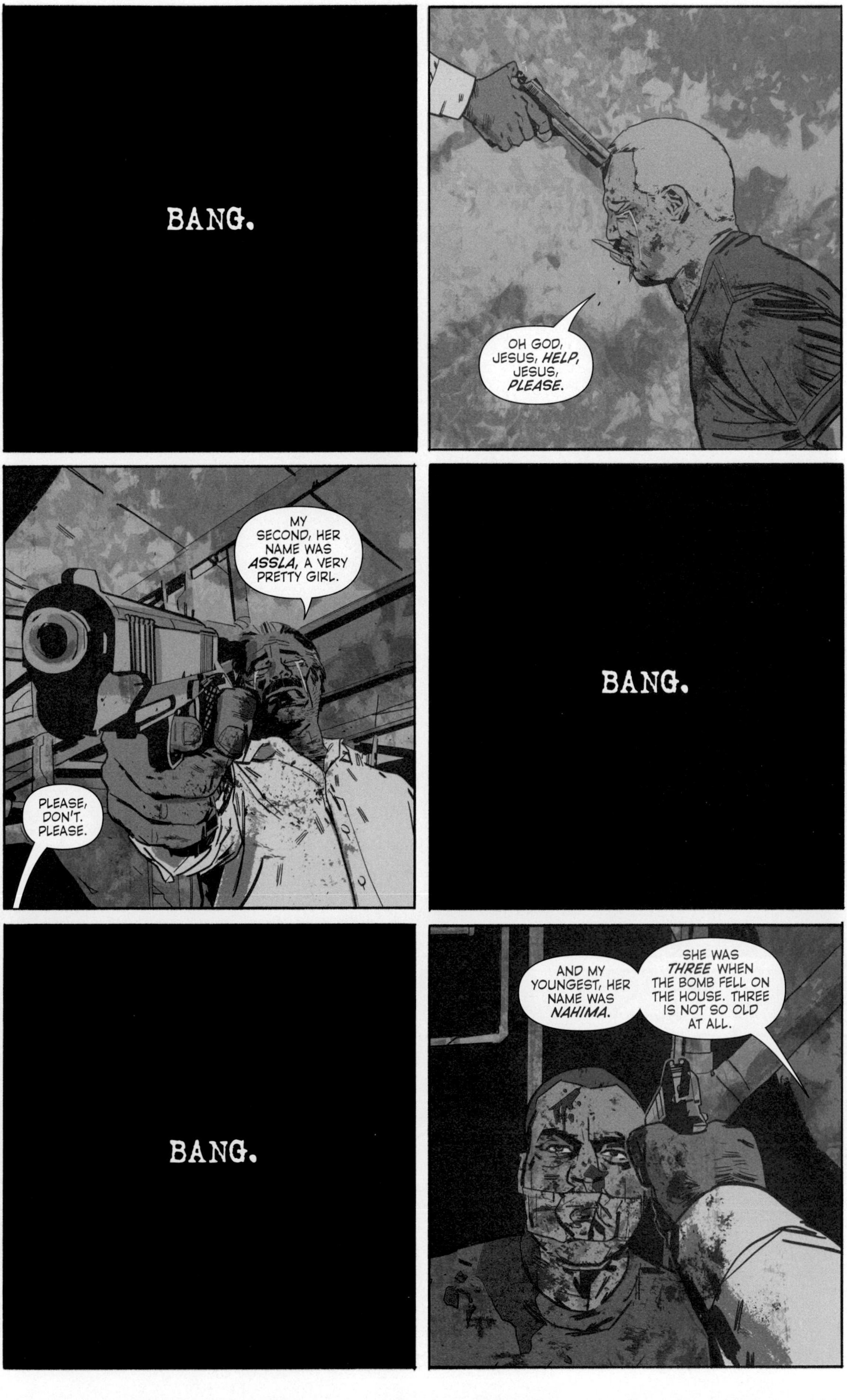
BANG.
OH GOD, JESUS, *HELP*, JESUS, *PLEASE*.
MY SECOND, HER NAME WAS *ASSLA*, A VERY PRETTY GIRL.
PLEASE, DON'T. PLEASE.
BANG.
BANG.
AND MY YOUNGEST, HER NAME WAS *NAHIMA*.
SHE WAS *THREE* WHEN THE BOMB FELL ON THE HOUSE. THREE IS NOT SO OLD AT ALL.

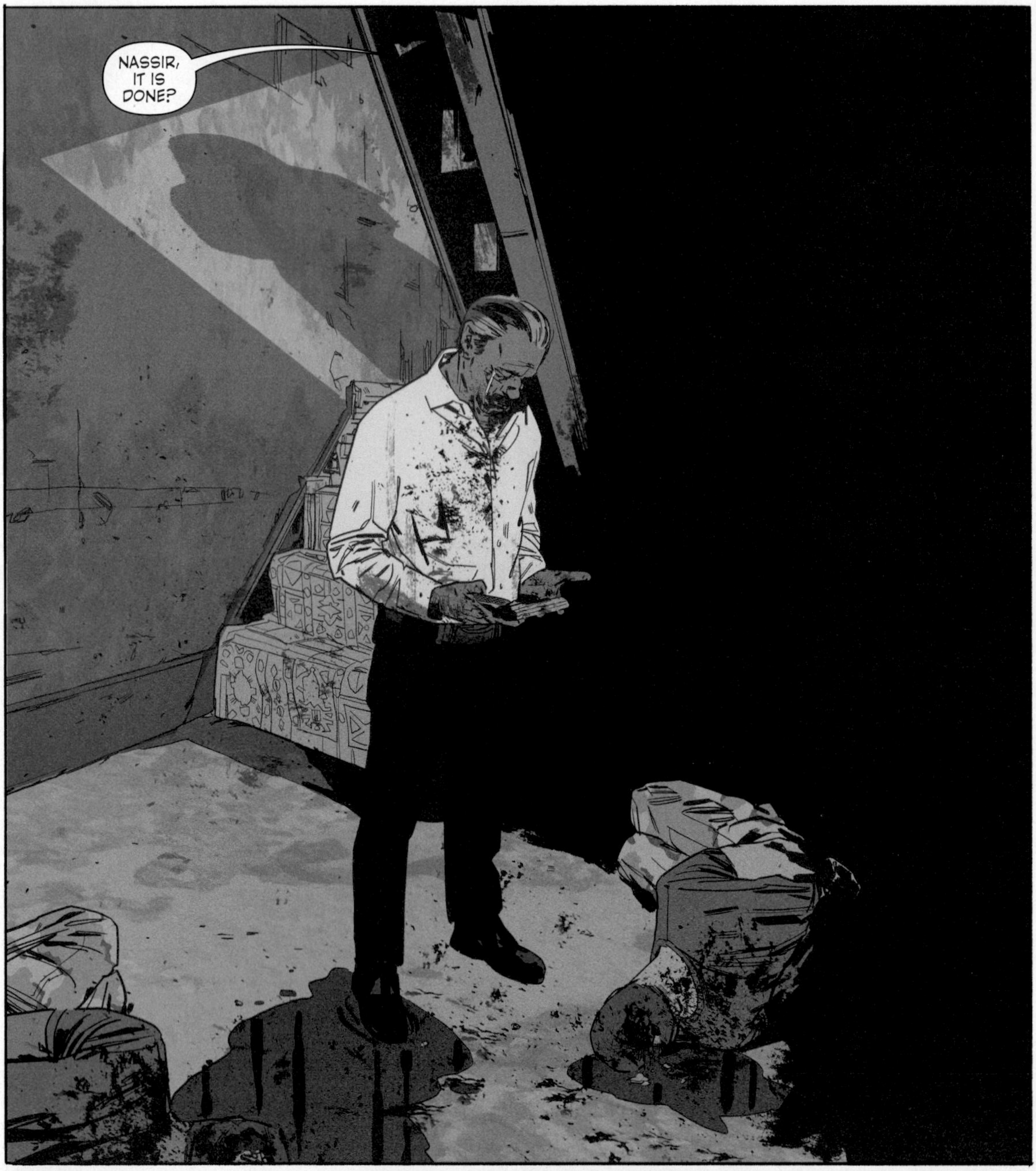
NASSIR, IT IS DONE?

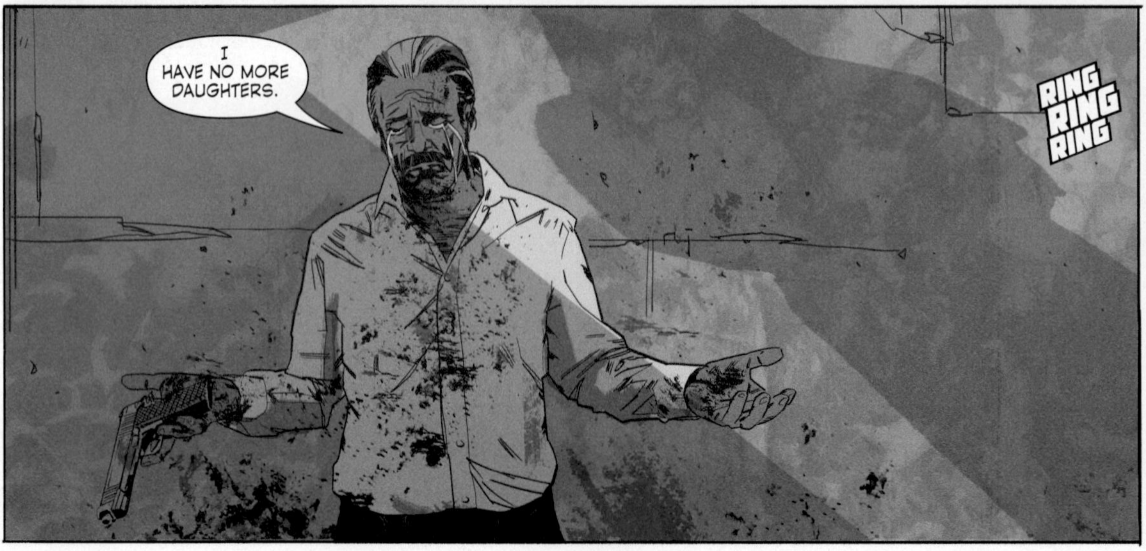
I HAVE NO MORE DAUGHTERS.
RING RING RING

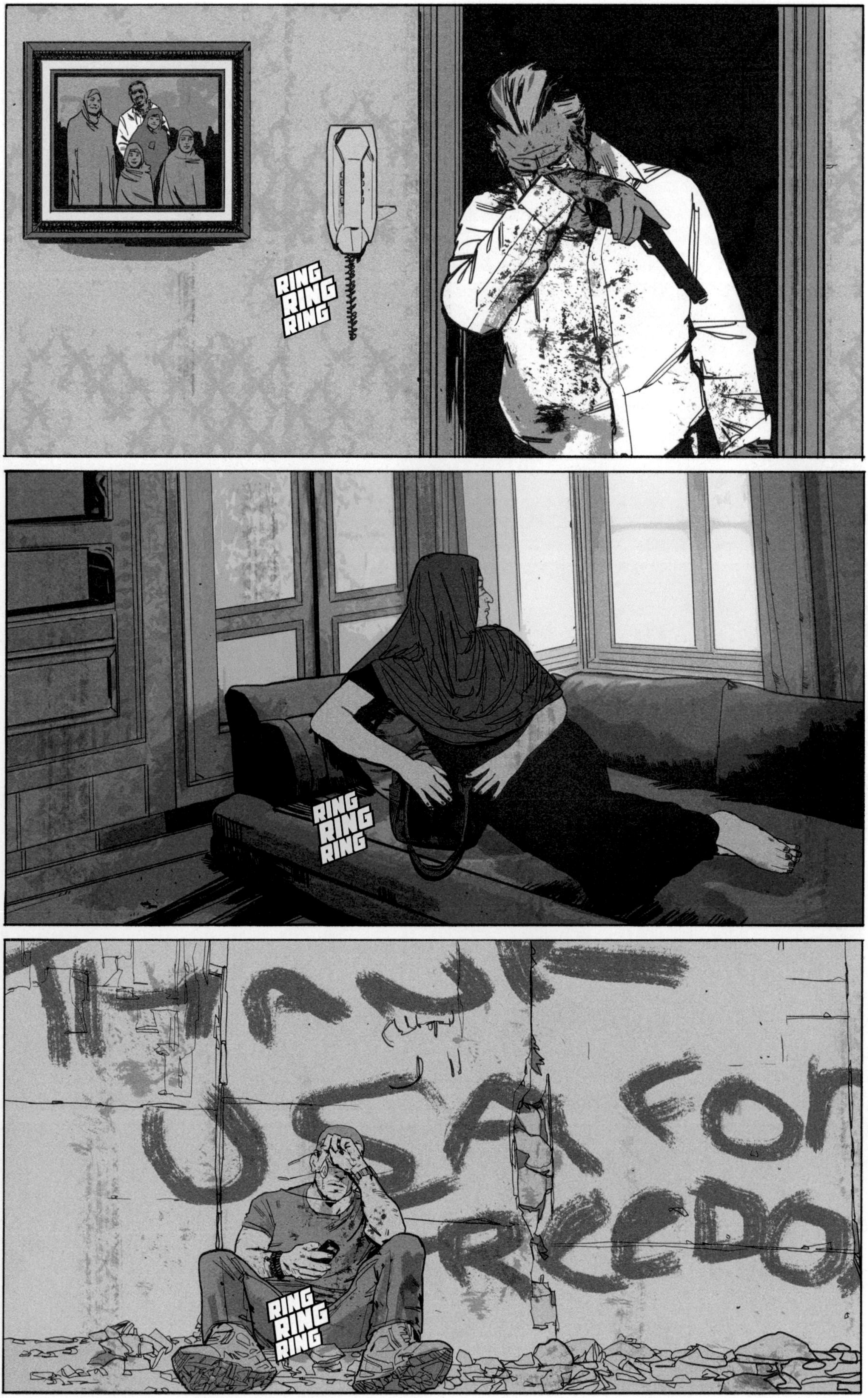
RING RING RING
RING RING RING
RING RING RING

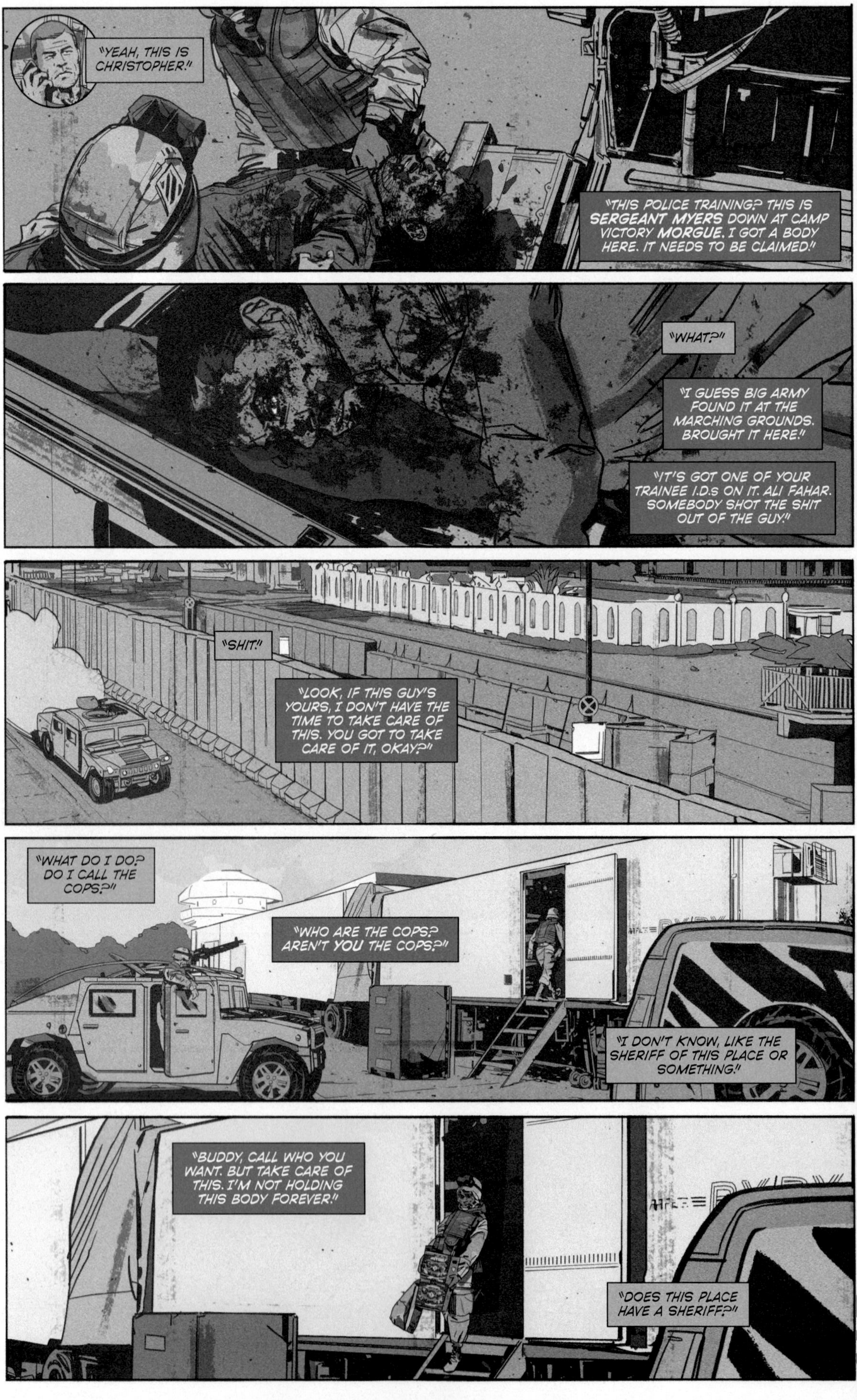
"YEAH, THIS IS CHRISTOPHER."
"THIS POLICE TRAINING? THIS IS **SERGEANT MYERS** DOWN AT CAMP VICTORY **MORGUE**. I GOT A BODY HERE. IT NEEDS TO BE CLAIMED."
"WHAT?"
"I GUESS BIG ARMY FOUND IT AT THE MARCHING GROUNDS. BROUGHT IT HERE."
"IT'S GOT ONE OF YOUR TRAINEE I.D.s ON IT. ALI FAHAR. SOMEBODY SHOT THE SHIT OUT OF THE GUY."
"SHIT."
"LOOK, IF THIS GUY'S YOURS, I DON'T HAVE THE TIME TO TAKE CARE OF THIS. YOU GOT TO TAKE CARE OF IT, OKAY?"
"WHAT DO I DO? DO I CALL THE COPS?"
"WHO ARE THE COPS? AREN'T **YOU** THE COPS?"
"I DON'T KNOW, LIKE THE SHERIFF OF THIS PLACE OR SOMETHING."
"BUDDY, CALL WHO YOU WANT. BUT TAKE CARE OF THIS. I'M NOT HOLDING THIS BODY FOREVER."
"DOES THIS PLACE HAVE A SHERIFF?"

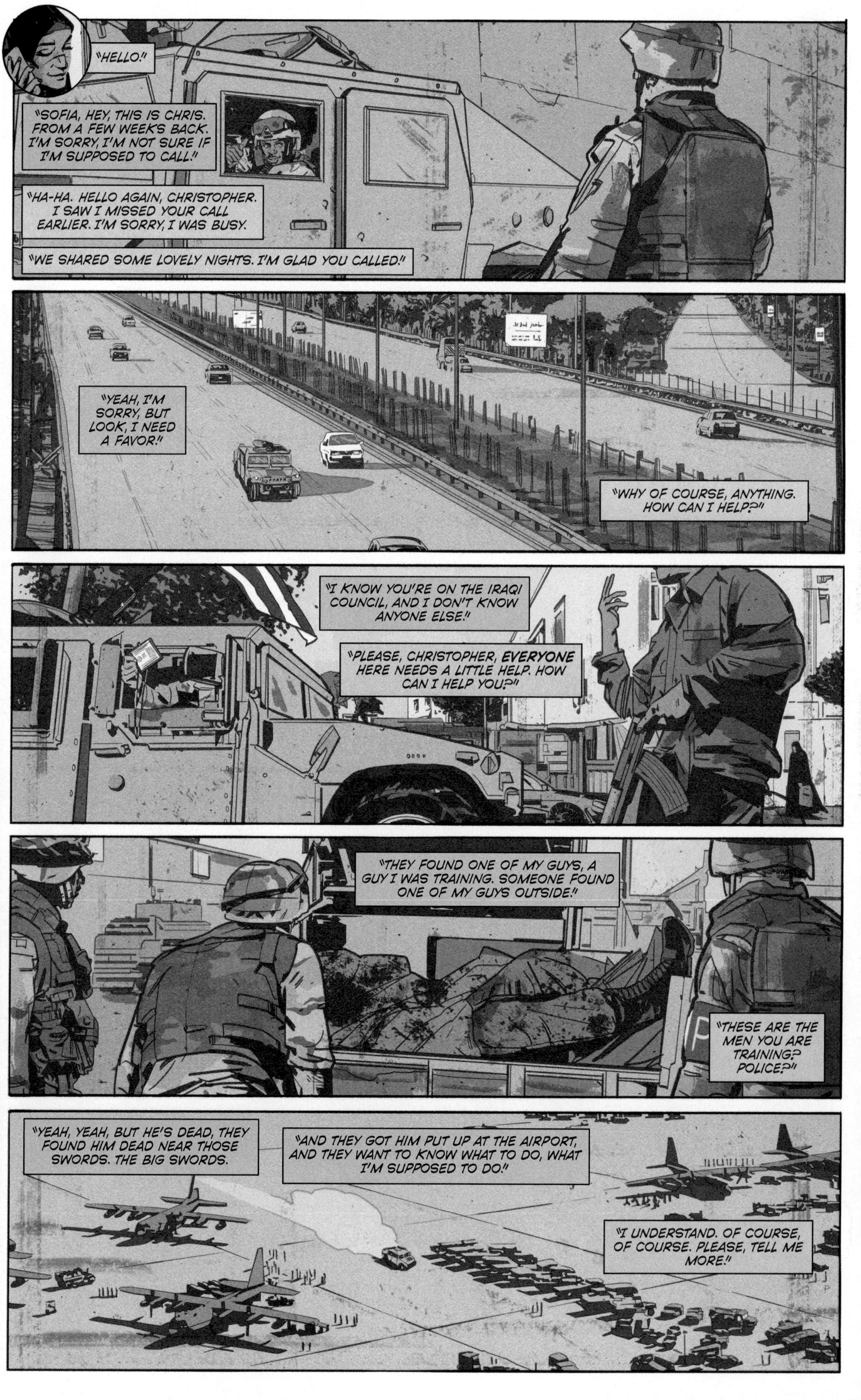
"HELLO."
"SOFIA, HEY, THIS IS CHRIS. FROM A FEW WEEKS BACK. I'M SORRY, I'M NOT SURE IF I'M SUPPOSED TO CALL."
"HA-HA. HELLO AGAIN, CHRISTOPHER. I SAW I MISSED YOUR CALL EARLIER. I'M SORRY, I WAS BUSY.
"WE SHARED SOME LOVELY NIGHTS. I'M GLAD YOU CALLED."
"YEAH, I'M SORRY, BUT LOOK, I NEED A FAVOR."
"WHY OF COURSE, ANYTHING. HOW CAN I HELP?"
"I KNOW YOU'RE ON THE IRAQI COUNCIL, AND I DON'T KNOW ANYONE ELSE."
"PLEASE, CHRISTOPHER, EVERYONE HERE NEEDS A LITTLE HELP. HOW CAN I HELP YOU?"
"THEY FOUND ONE OF MY GUYS, A GUY I WAS TRAINING. SOMEONE FOUND ONE OF MY GUYS OUTSIDE."
"THESE ARE THE MEN YOU ARE TRAINING? POLICE?"
"YEAH, YEAH, BUT HE'S DEAD, THEY FOUND HIM DEAD NEAR THOSE SWORDS. THE BIG SWORDS.
"AND THEY GOT HIM PUT UP AT THE AIRPORT, AND THEY WANT TO KNOW WHAT TO DO, WHAT I'M SUPPOSED TO DO."
"I UNDERSTAND. OF COURSE, OF COURSE. PLEASE, TELL ME MORE."

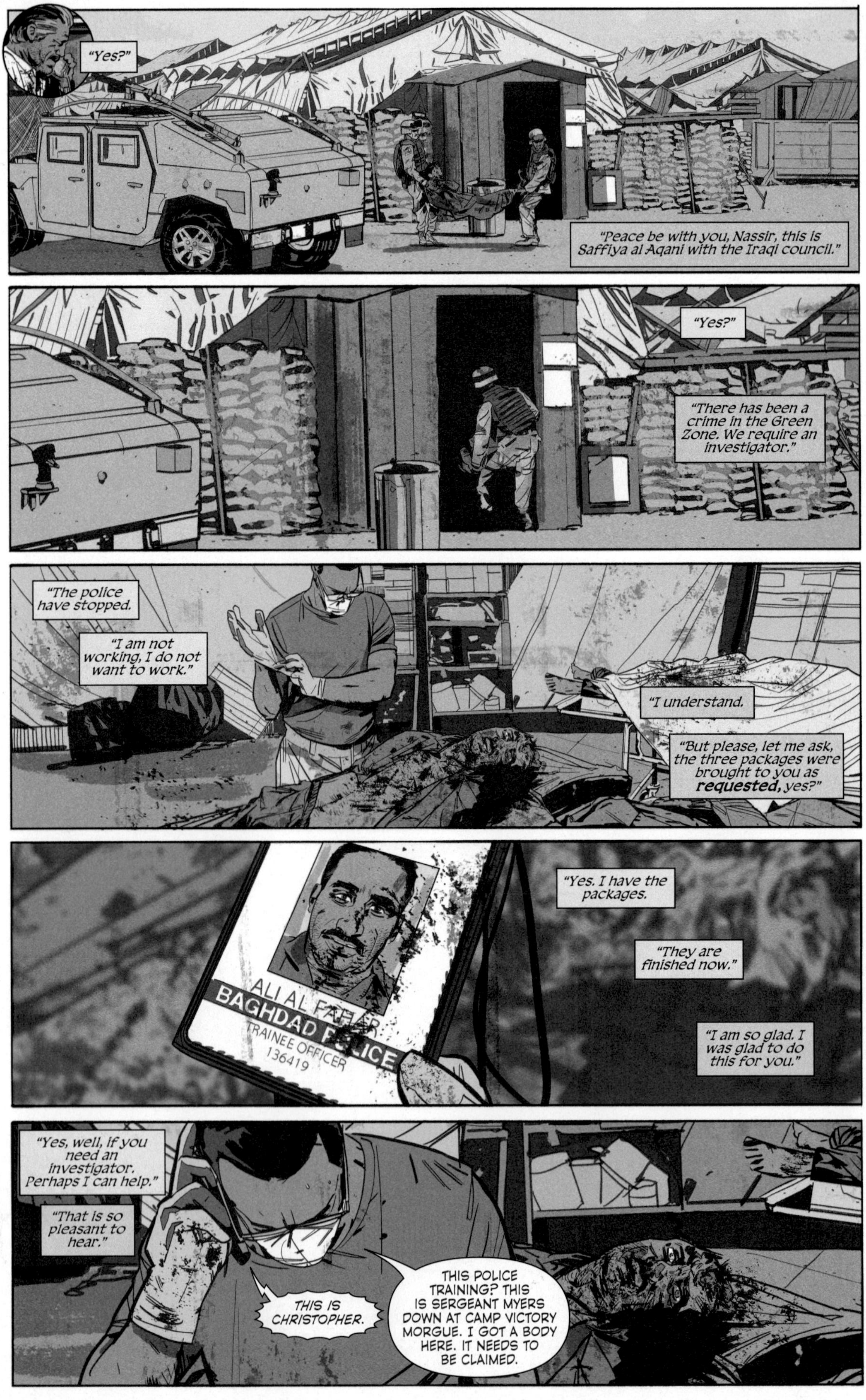
"Yes?"
"Peace be with you, Nassir, this is Saffiya al Aqani with the Iraqi council."
"Yes?"
"There has been a crime in the Green Zone. We require an investigator."
"The police have stopped.
"I am not working, I do not want to work."
"I understand.
"But please, let me ask, the three packages were brought to you as **requested,** yes?"
ALI AL FAHAR
BAGHDAD POLICE
TRAINEE OFFICER
136419
"Yes. I have the packages.
"They are finished now."
"I am so glad. I was glad to do this for you."
"Yes, well, if you need an investigator. Perhaps I can help."
"That is so pleasant to hear."
THIS IS CHRISTOPHER.
THIS POLICE TRAINING? THIS IS SERGEANT MYERS DOWN AT CAMP VICTORY MORGUE. I GOT A BODY HERE. IT NEEDS TO BE CLAIMED.

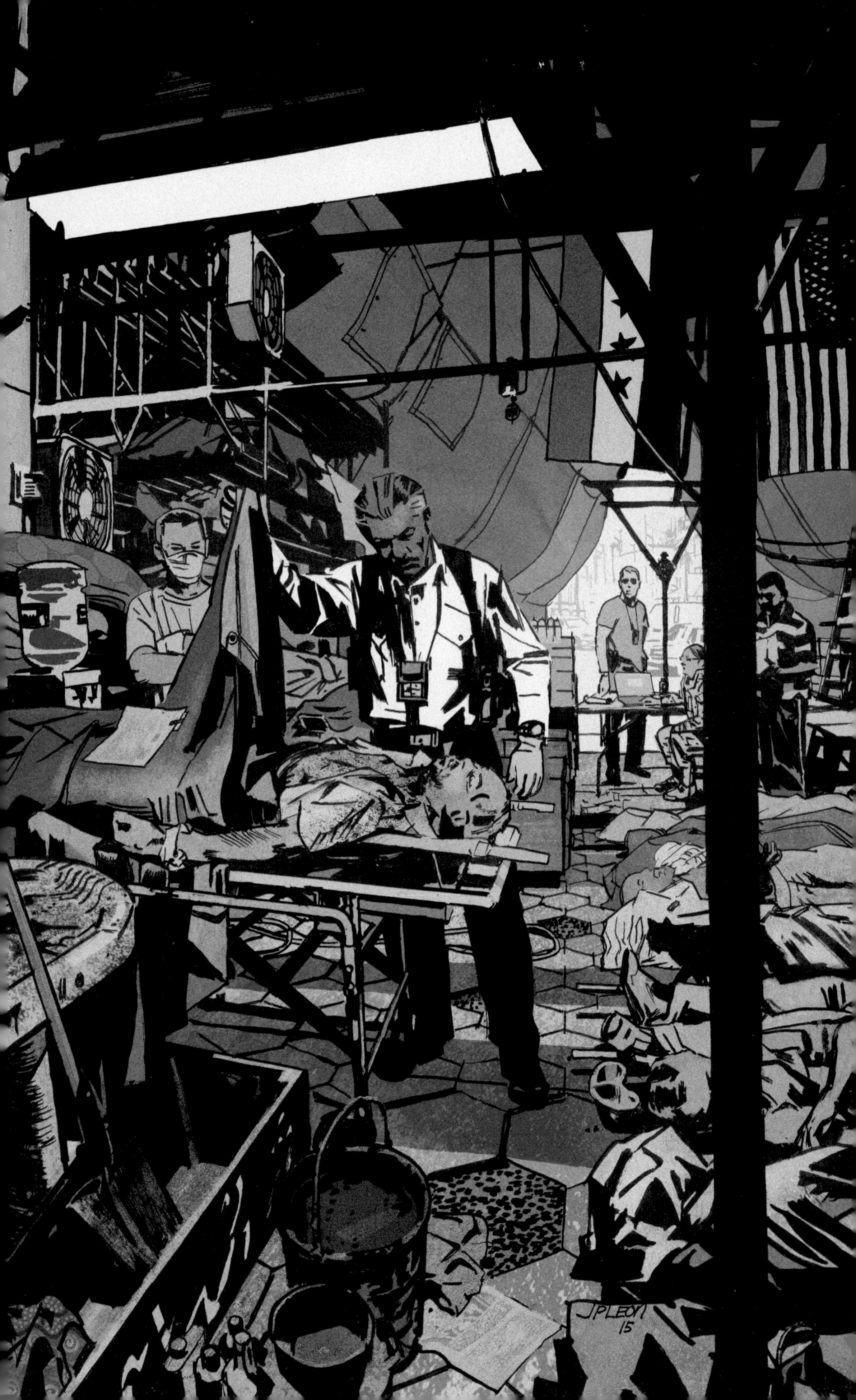
JPLEON
15

PART TWO

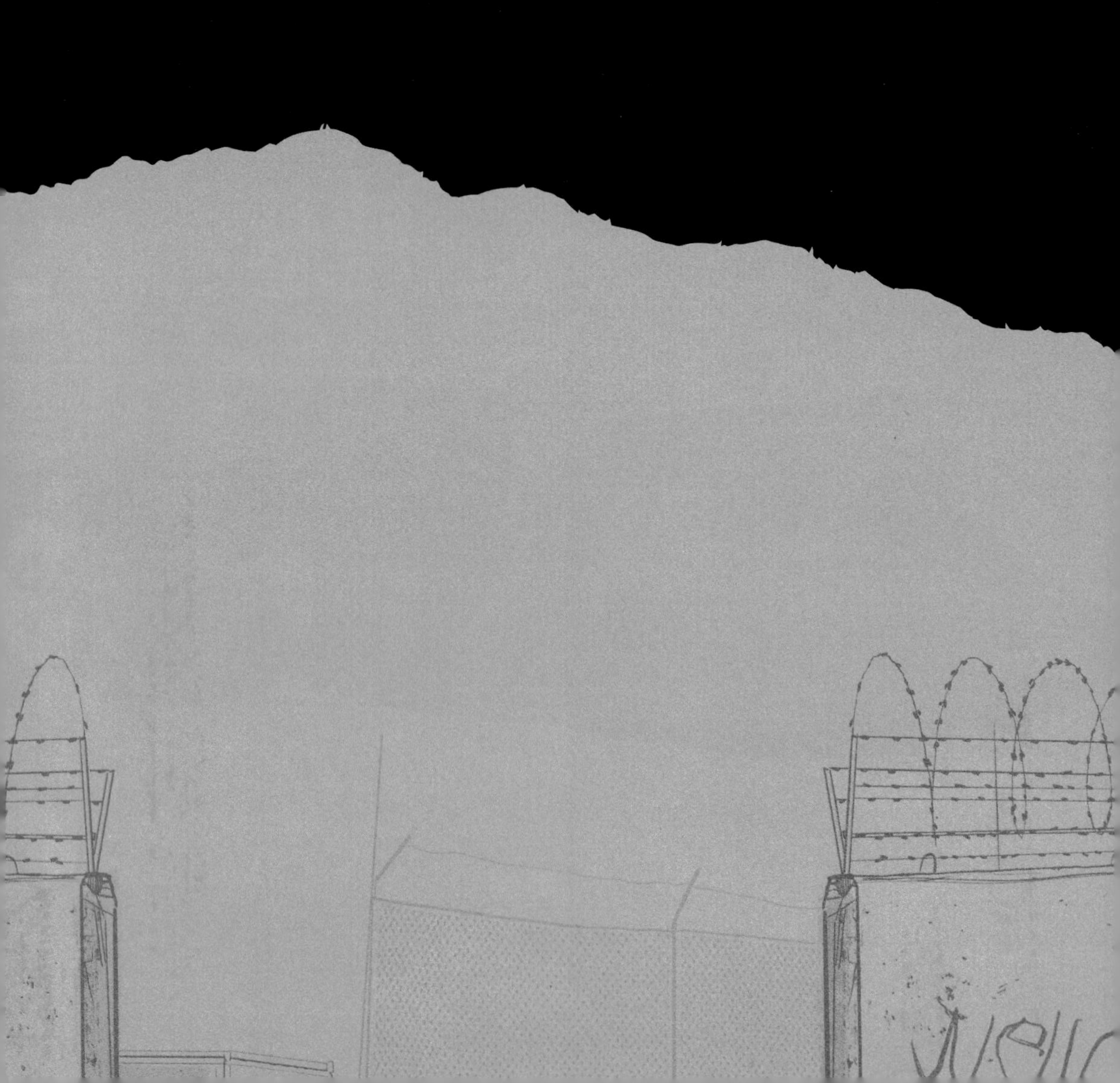

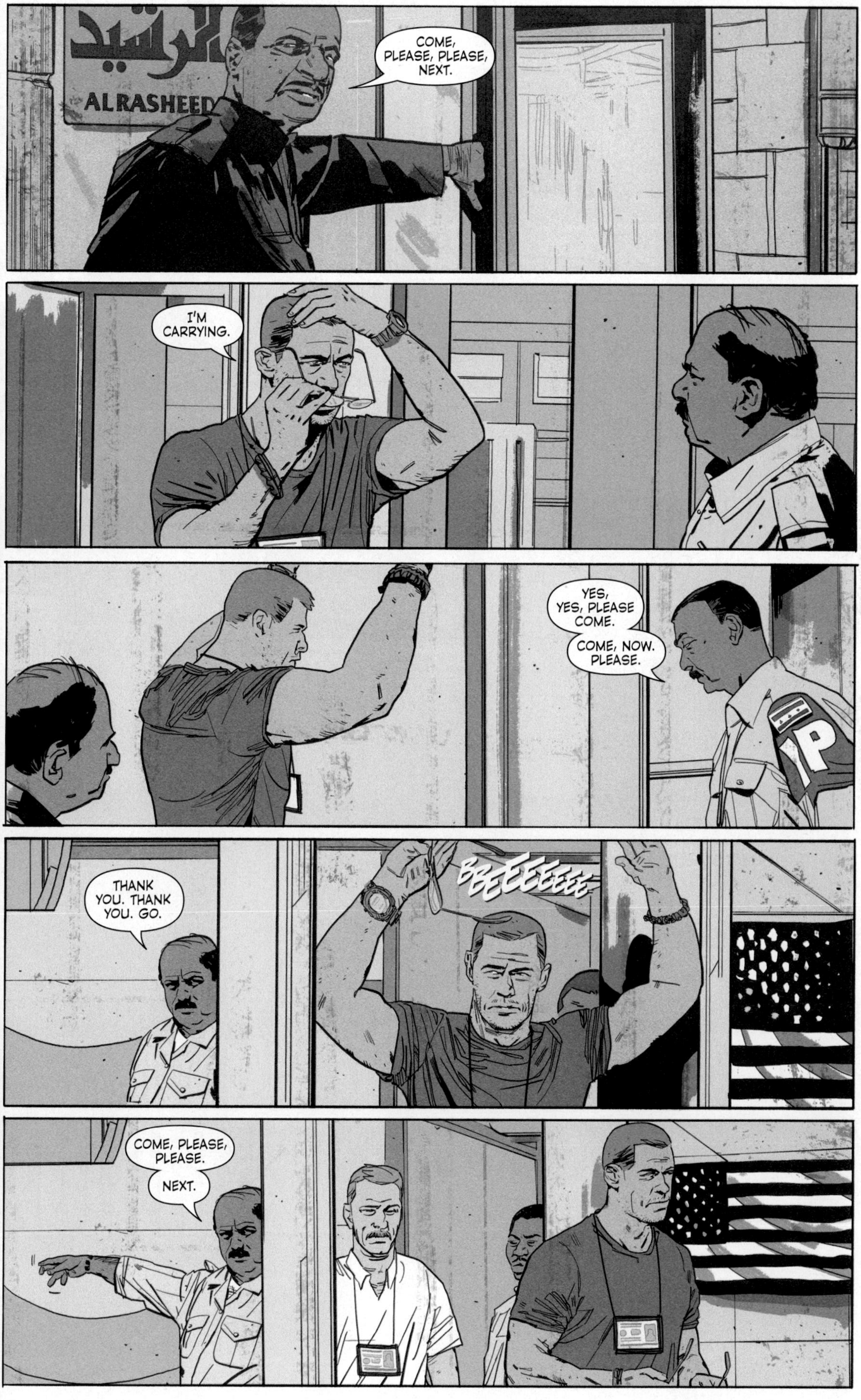

الرشيد
ALRASHEED
COME, PLEASE, PLEASE, NEXT.
I'M CARRYING.
YES, YES, PLEASE COME.
COME, NOW. PLEASE.
IP
THANK YOU. THANK YOU. GO.
BBEEEEEEEE
COME, PLEASE, PLEASE.
NEXT.

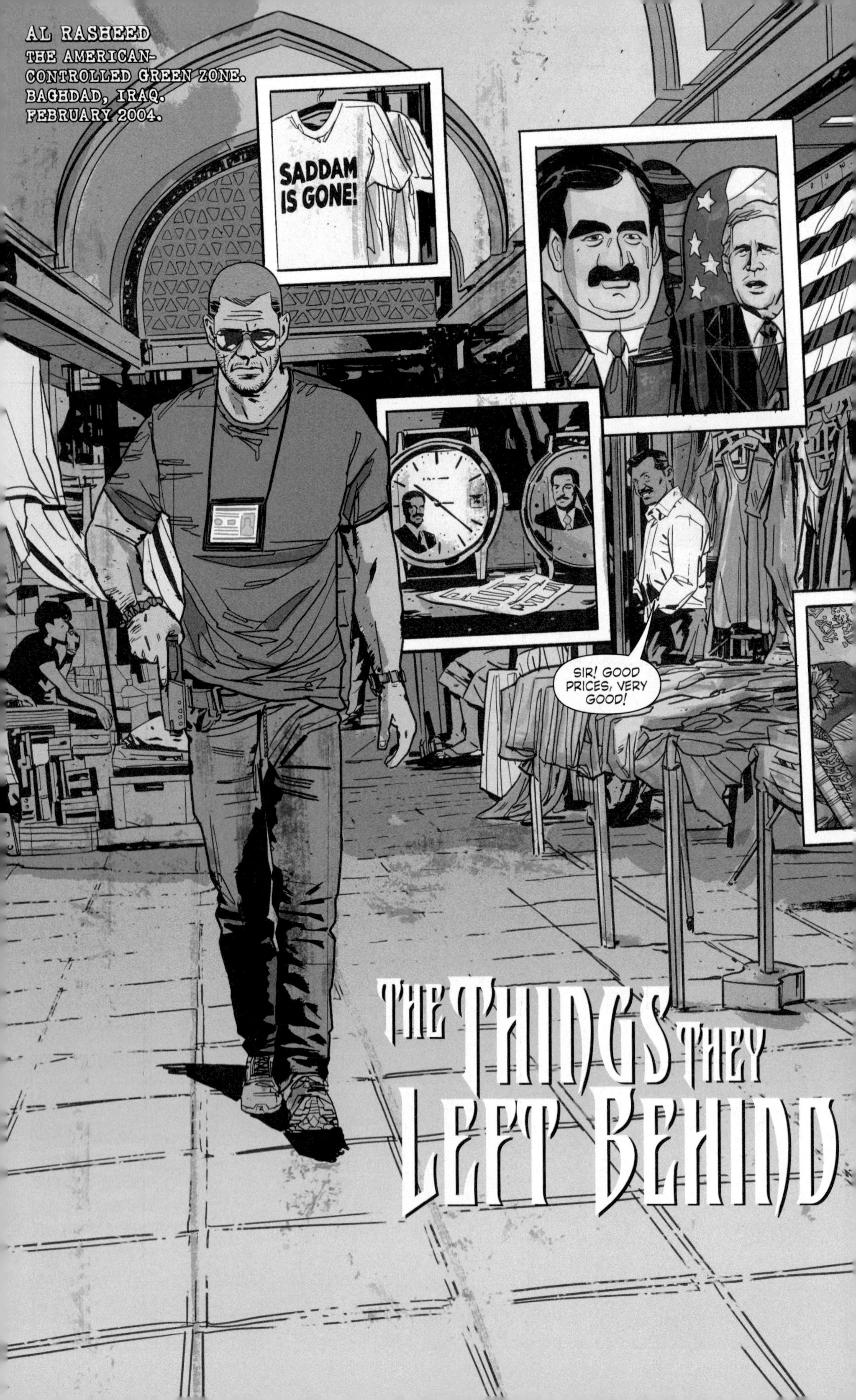
AL RASHEED
THE AMERICAN-CONTROLLED GREEN ZONE. BAGHDAD, IRAQ. FEBRUARY 2004.
SADDAM IS GONE!
SIR! GOOD PRICES, VERY GOOD!
THE THINGS THEY LEFT BEHIND

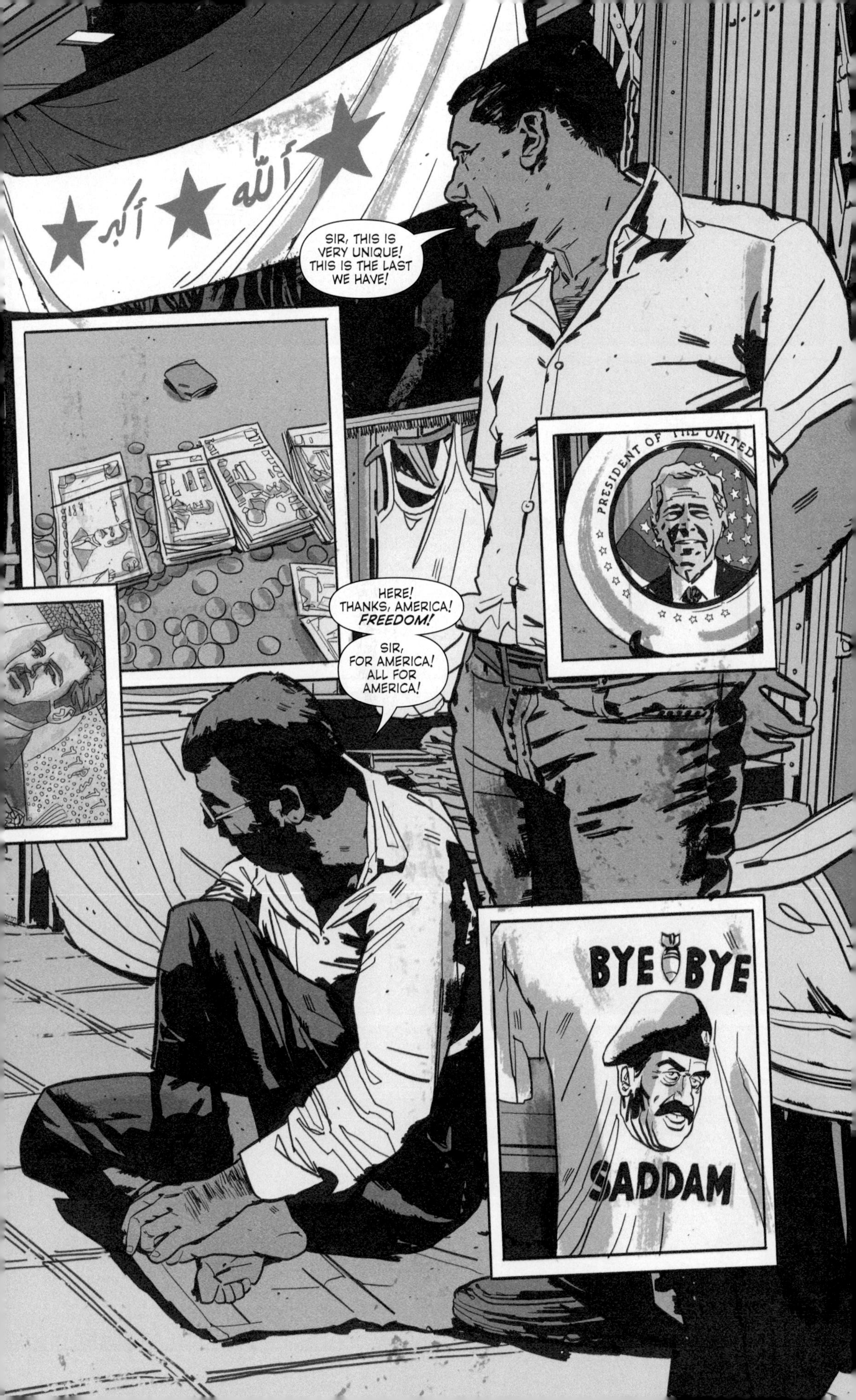
الله أكبر
SIR, THIS IS VERY UNIQUE! THIS IS THE LAST WE HAVE!
PRESIDENT OF THE UNITED
HERE! THANKS, AMERICA! *FREEDOM!*
SIR, FOR AMERICA! ALL FOR AMERICA!
BYE BYE
SADDAM

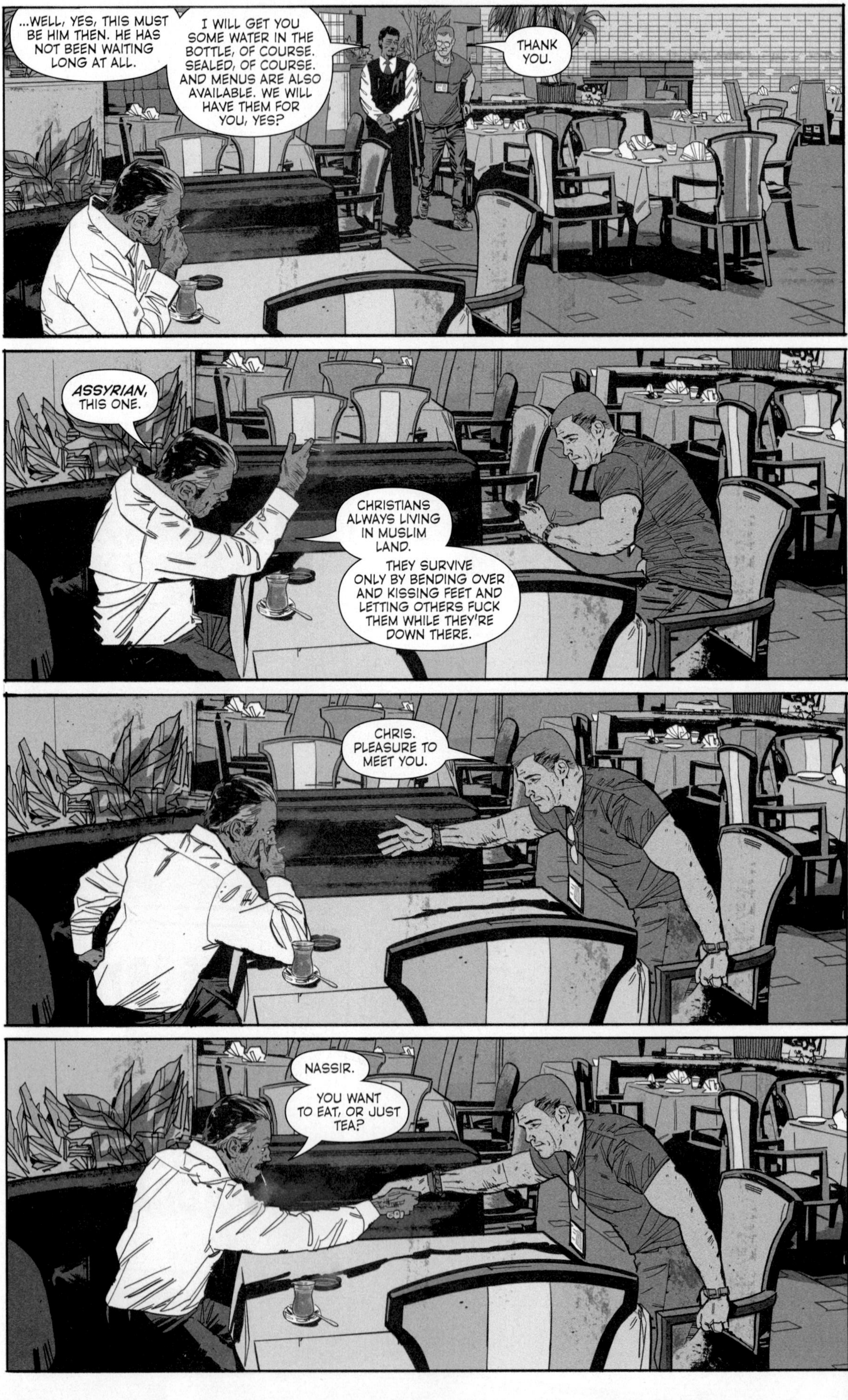
...WELL, YES, THIS MUST BE HIM THEN. HE HAS NOT BEEN WAITING LONG AT ALL.
I WILL GET YOU SOME WATER IN THE BOTTLE, OF COURSE. SEALED, OF COURSE. AND MENUS ARE ALSO AVAILABLE. WE WILL HAVE THEM FOR YOU, YES?
THANK YOU.
ASSYRIAN, THIS ONE.
CHRISTIANS ALWAYS LIVING IN MUSLIM LAND.
THEY SURVIVE ONLY BY BENDING OVER AND KISSING FEET AND LETTING OTHERS FUCK THEM WHILE THEY'RE DOWN THERE.
CHRIS. PLEASURE TO MEET YOU.
NASSIR.
YOU WANT TO EAT, OR JUST TEA?

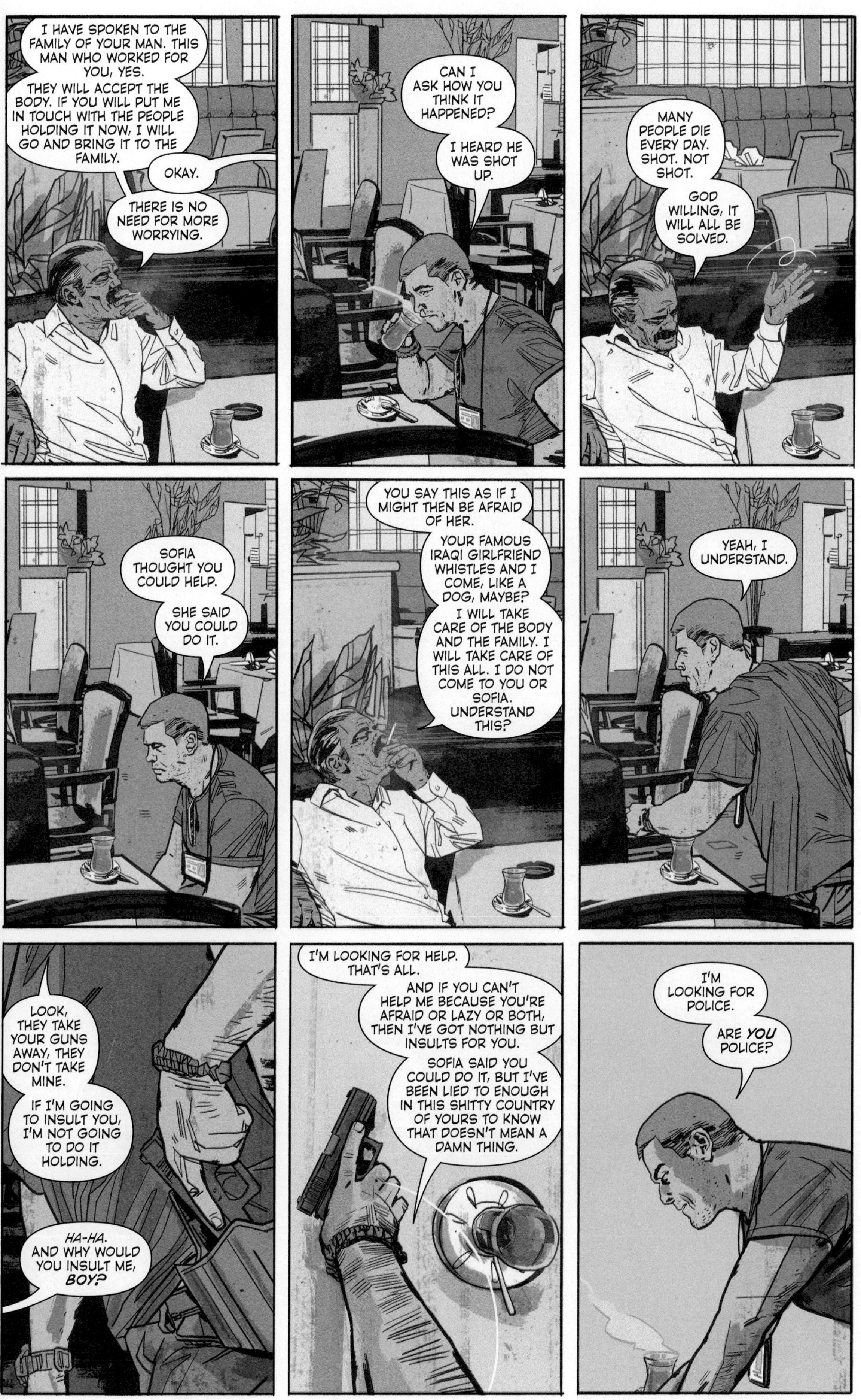
I HAVE SPOKEN TO THE FAMILY OF YOUR MAN. THIS MAN WHO WORKED FOR YOU, YES.
THEY WILL ACCEPT THE BODY. IF YOU WILL PUT ME IN TOUCH WITH THE PEOPLE HOLDING IT NOW, I WILL GO AND BRING IT TO THE FAMILY.
OKAY.
THERE IS NO NEED FOR MORE WORRYING.
CAN I ASK HOW YOU THINK IT HAPPENED?
I HEARD HE WAS SHOT UP.
MANY PEOPLE DIE EVERY DAY. SHOT. NOT SHOT.
GOD WILLING, IT WILL ALL BE SOLVED.
SOFIA THOUGHT YOU COULD HELP.
SHE SAID YOU COULD DO IT.
YOU SAY THIS AS IF I MIGHT THEN BE AFRAID OF HER.
YOUR FAMOUS IRAQI GIRLFRIEND WHISTLES AND I COME, LIKE A DOG, MAYBE?
I WILL TAKE CARE OF THE BODY AND THE FAMILY. I WILL TAKE CARE OF THIS ALL. I DO NOT COME TO YOU OR SOFIA. UNDERSTAND THIS?
YEAH, I UNDERSTAND.
LOOK, THEY TAKE YOUR GUNS AWAY, THEY DON'T TAKE MINE.
IF I'M GOING TO INSULT YOU, I'M NOT GOING TO DO IT HOLDING.
HA-HA. AND WHY WOULD YOU INSULT ME, ***BOY?***
I'M LOOKING FOR HELP. THAT'S ALL.
AND IF YOU CAN'T HELP ME BECAUSE YOU'RE AFRAID OR LAZY OR BOTH, THEN I'VE GOT NOTHING BUT INSULTS FOR YOU.
SOFIA SAID YOU COULD DO IT, BUT I'VE BEEN LIED TO ENOUGH IN THIS SHITTY COUNTRY OF YOURS TO KNOW THAT DOESN'T MEAN A DAMN THING.
I'M LOOKING FOR POLICE.
ARE ***YOU*** POLICE?

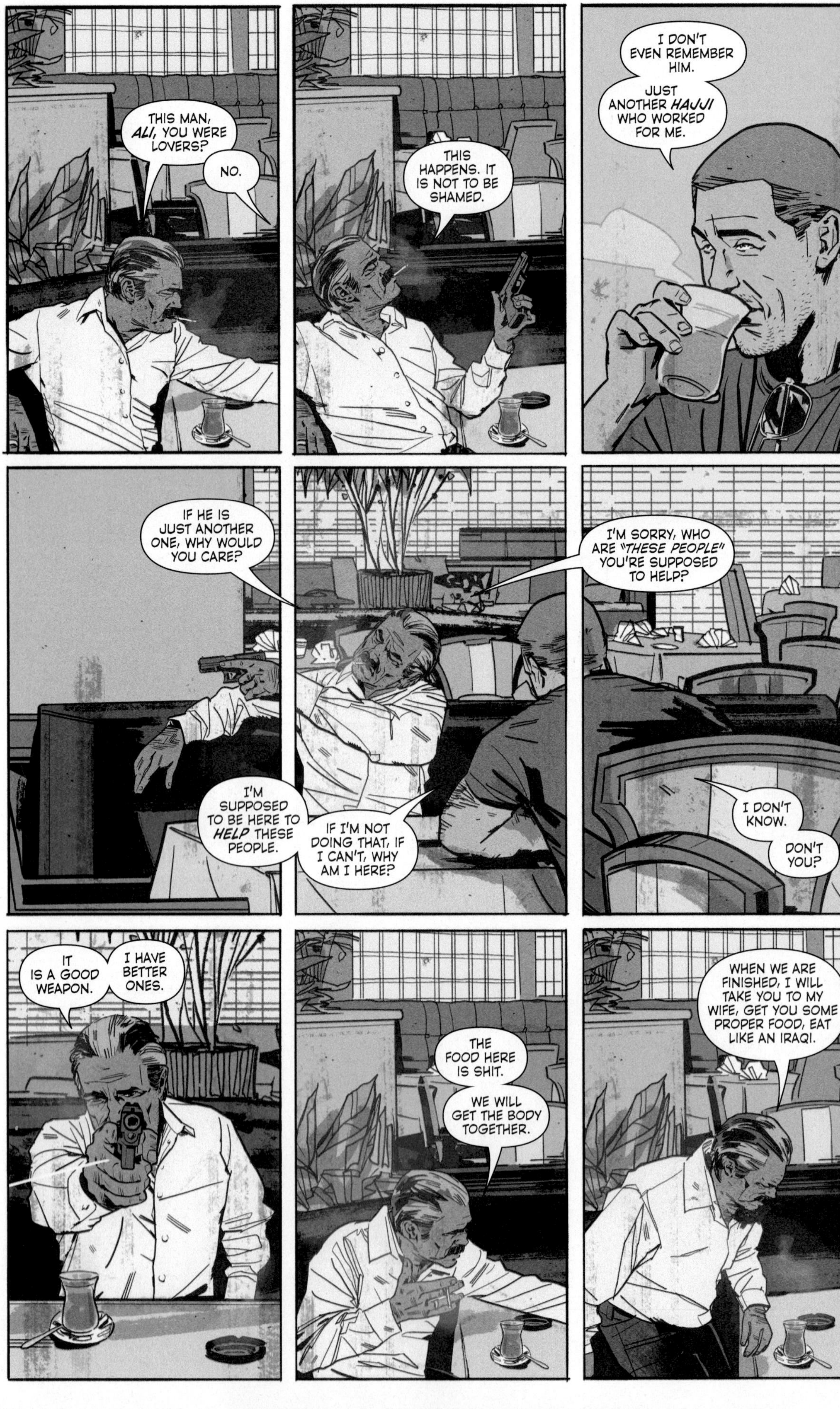
THIS MAN, *ALI*, YOU WERE LOVERS?
NO.
THIS HAPPENS. IT IS NOT TO BE SHAMED.
I DON'T EVEN REMEMBER HIM.
JUST ANOTHER *HAJJI* WHO WORKED FOR ME.
IF HE IS JUST ANOTHER ONE, WHY WOULD YOU CARE?
I'M SUPPOSED TO BE HERE TO *HELP* THESE PEOPLE.
IF I'M NOT DOING THAT, IF I CAN'T, WHY AM I HERE?
I'M SORRY, WHO ARE *"THESE PEOPLE"* YOU'RE SUPPOSED TO HELP?
I DON'T KNOW.
DON'T YOU?
IT IS A GOOD WEAPON.
I HAVE BETTER ONES.
THE FOOD HERE IS SHIT.
WE WILL GET THE BODY TOGETHER.
WHEN WE ARE FINISHED, I WILL TAKE YOU TO MY WIFE, GET YOU SOME PROPER FOOD, EAT LIKE AN IRAQI.

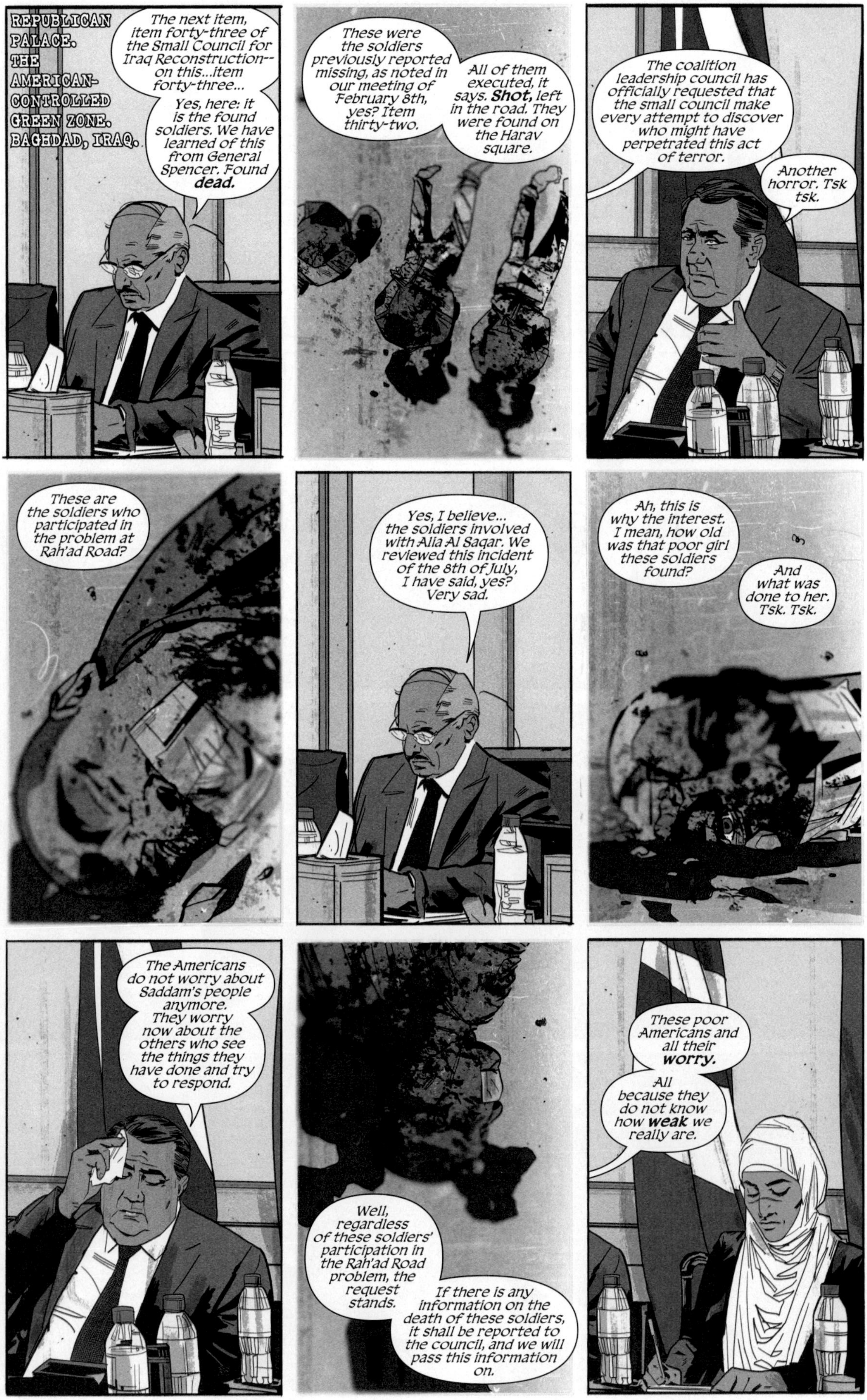
REPUBLICAN PALACE. THE AMERICAN-CONTROLLED GREEN ZONE. BAGHDAD, IRAQ.
The next item, item forty-three of the Small Council for Iraq Reconstruction--on this...item forty-three...
Yes, here: it is the found soldiers. We have learned of this from General Spencer. Found **dead.**
These were the soldiers previously reported missing, as noted in our meeting of February 8th, yes? Item thirty-two.
All of them executed, it says. **Shot,** left in the road. They were found on the Harav square.
The coalition leadership council has officially requested that the small council make every attempt to discover who might have perpetrated this act of terror.
Another horror. Tsk tsk.
These are the soldiers who participated in the problem at Rah'ad Road?
Yes, I believe... the soldiers involved with Alia Al Saqar. We reviewed this incident of the 8th of July, I have said, yes? Very sad.
Ah, this is why the interest. I mean, how old was that poor girl these soldiers found?
And what was done to her. Tsk. Tsk.
The Americans do not worry about Saddam's people anymore. They worry now about the others who see the things they have done and try to respond.
Well, regardless of these soldiers' participation in the Rah'ad Road problem, the request stands.
If there is any information on the death of these soldiers, it shall be reported to the council, and we will pass this information on.
These poor Americans and all their **worry.**
All because they do not know how **weak** we really are.

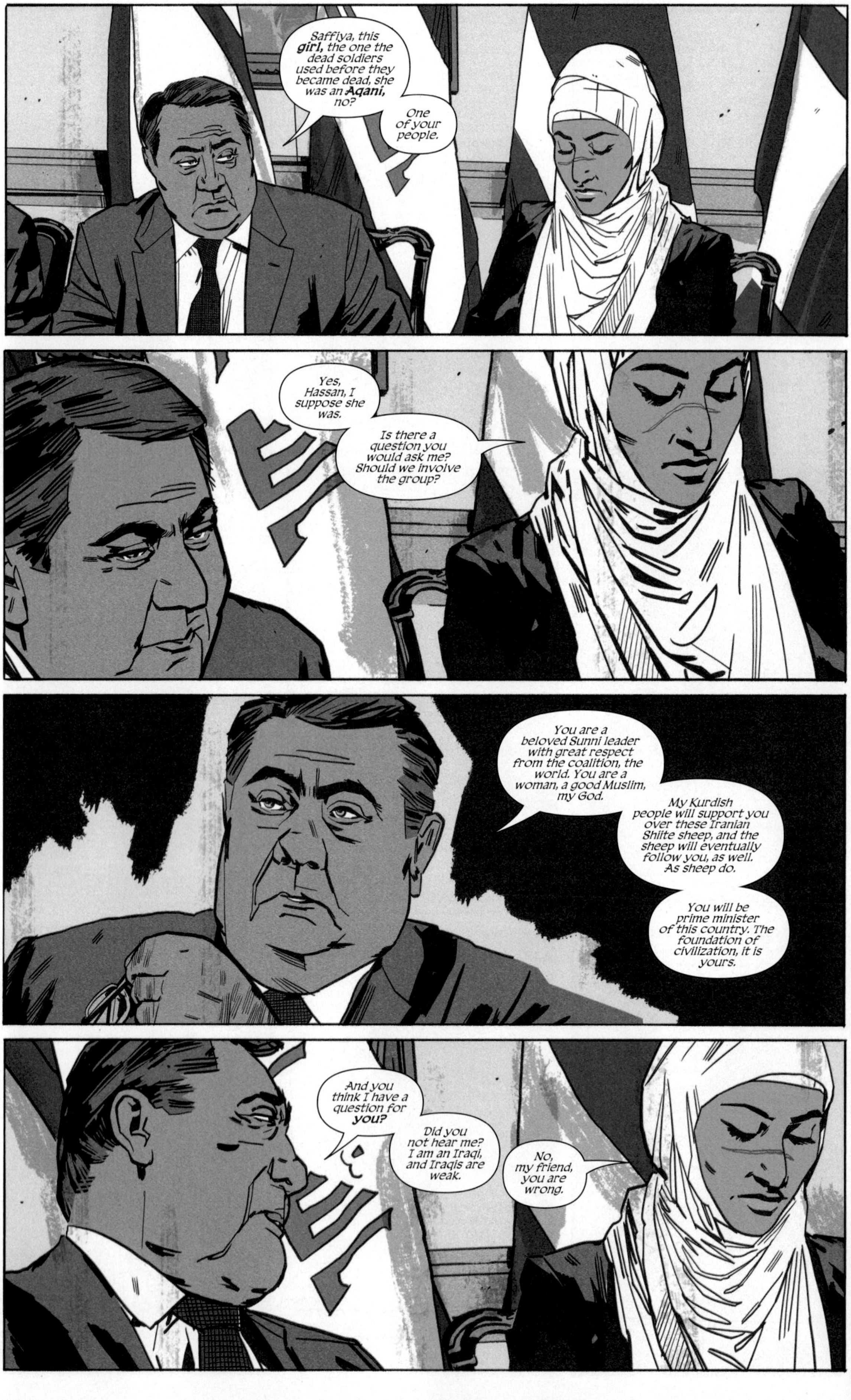
Saffiya, this girl, the one the dead soldiers used before they became dead, she was an Aqani, no?
One of your people.
Yes, Hassan, I suppose she was.
Is there a question you would ask me? Should we involve the group?
You are a beloved Sunni leader with great respect from the coalition, the world. You are a woman, a good Muslim, my God.
My Kurdish people will support you over these Iranian Shiite sheep, and the sheep will eventually follow you, as well. As sheep do.
You will be prime minister of this country. The foundation of civilization, it is yours.
And you think I have a question for you?
Did you not hear me? I am an Iraqi, and Iraqis are weak.
No, my friend, you are wrong.

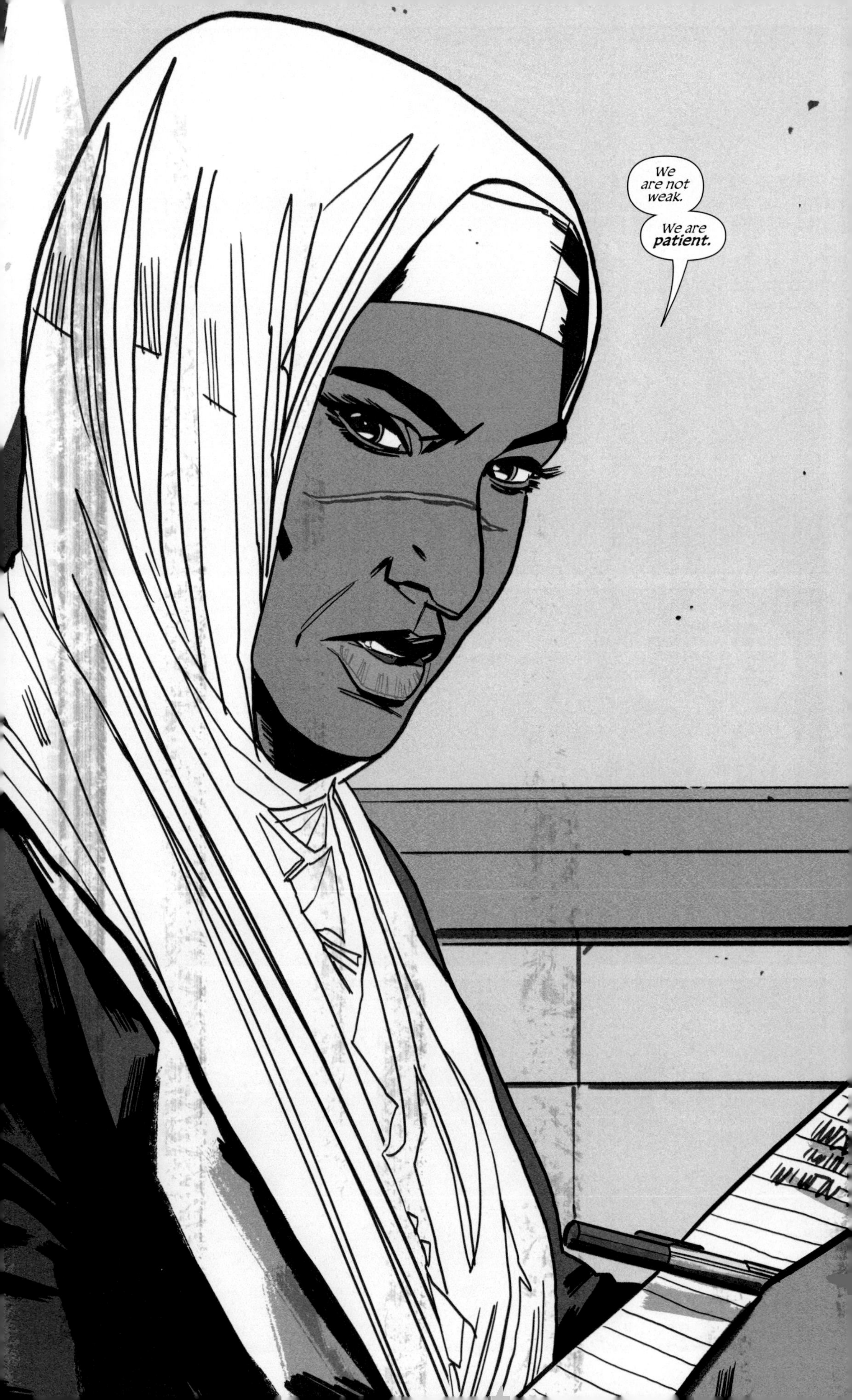
We are not weak.
We are *patient.*

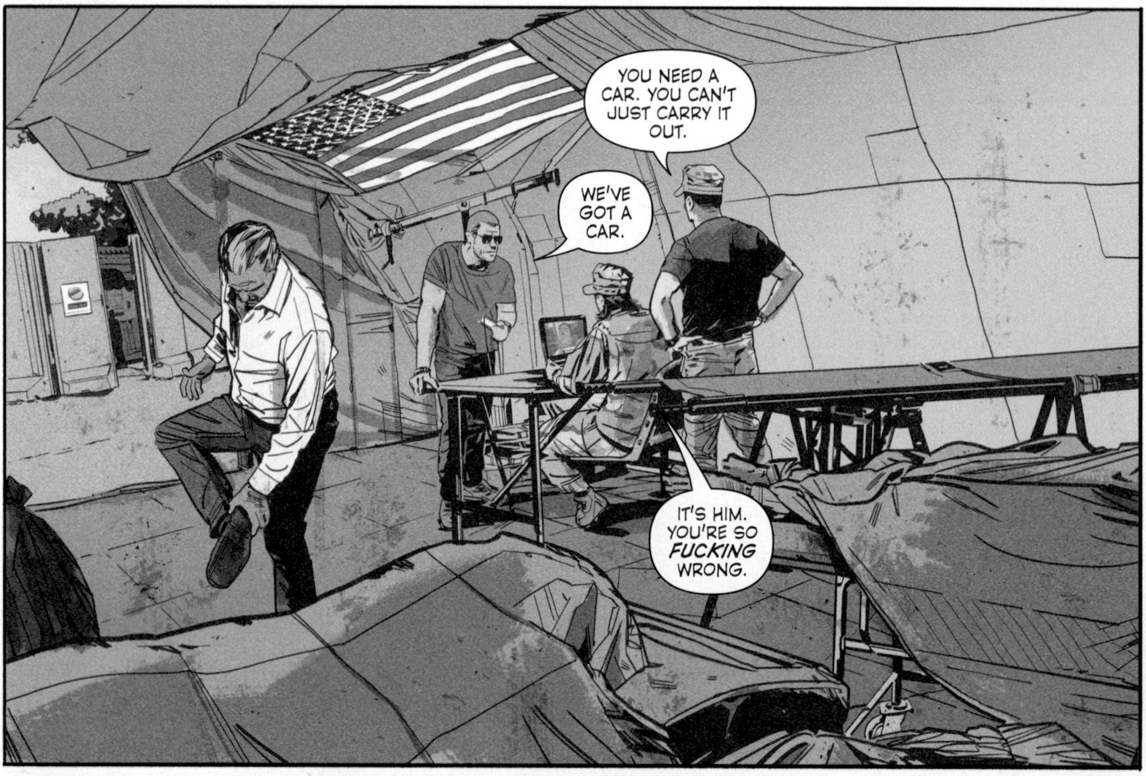
YOU NEED A CAR. YOU CAN'T JUST CARRY IT OUT.
WE'VE GOT A CAR.
IT'S HIM. YOU'RE SO *FUCKING* WRONG.

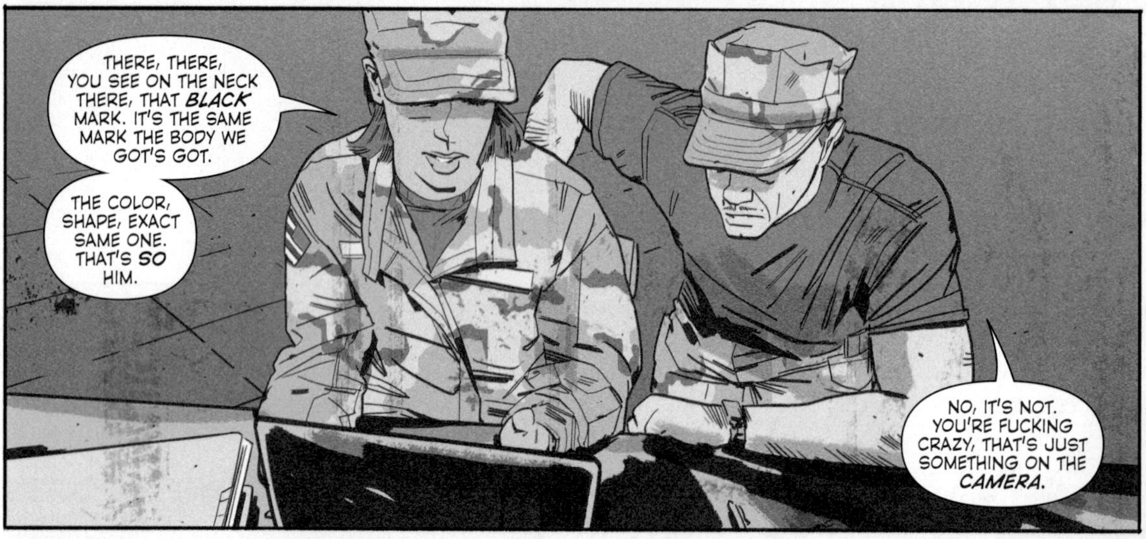
THERE, THERE, YOU SEE ON THE NECK THERE, THAT *BLACK* MARK. IT'S THE SAME MARK THE BODY WE GOT'S GOT.
THE COLOR, SHAPE, EXACT SAME ONE. THAT'S *SO* HIM.
NO, IT'S NOT. YOU'RE FUCKING CRAZY, THAT'S JUST SOMETHING ON THE *CAMERA*.

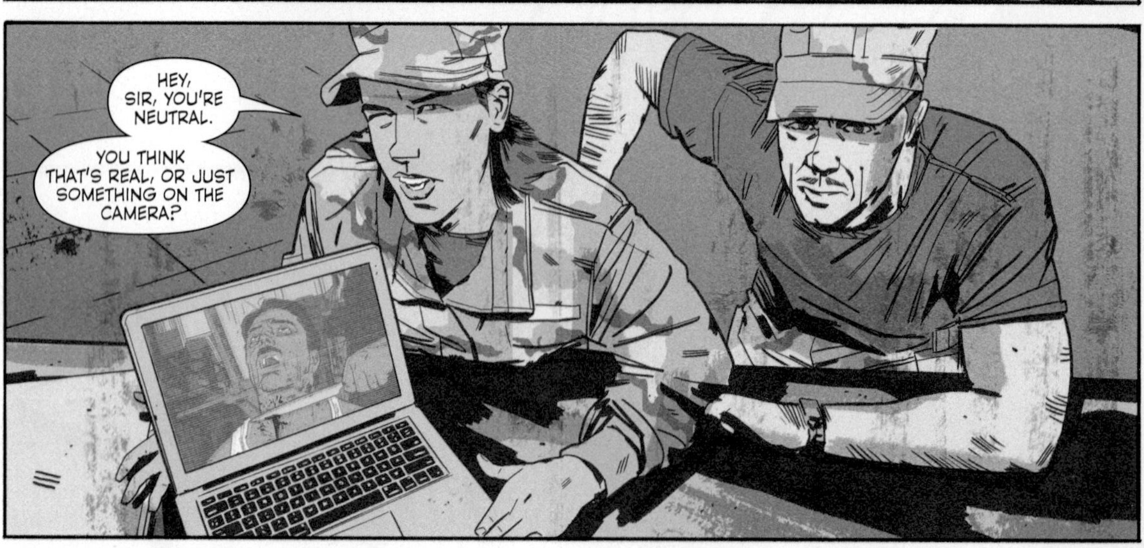
HEY, SIR, YOU'RE NEUTRAL.
YOU THINK THAT'S REAL, OR JUST SOMETHING ON THE CAMERA?

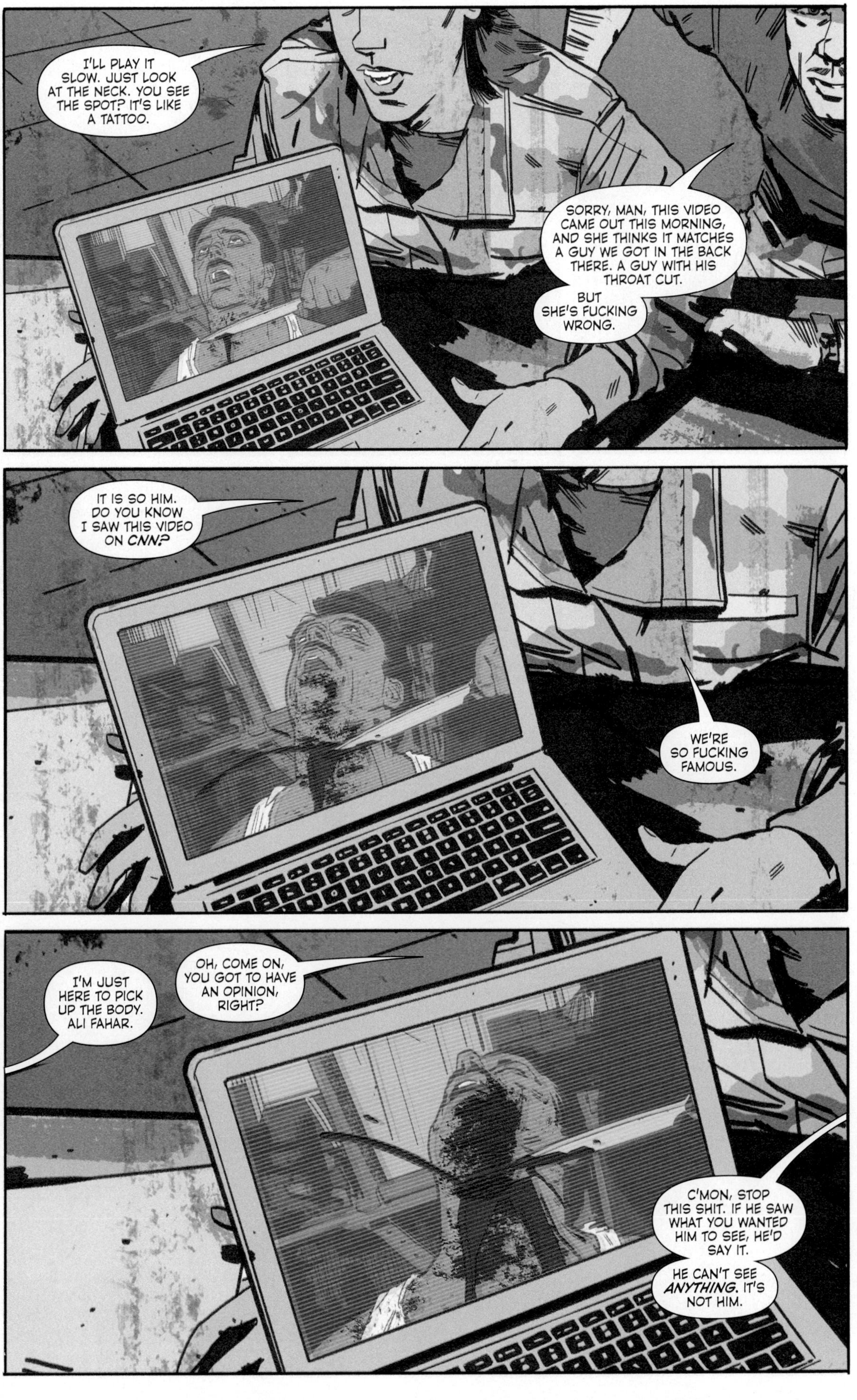
I'LL PLAY IT SLOW. JUST LOOK AT THE NECK. YOU SEE THE SPOT? IT'S LIKE A TATTOO.
SORRY, MAN, THIS VIDEO CAME OUT THIS MORNING, AND SHE THINKS IT MATCHES A GUY WE GOT IN THE BACK THERE. A GUY WITH HIS THROAT CUT.
BUT SHE'S FUCKING WRONG.
IT IS SO HIM. DO YOU KNOW I SAW THIS VIDEO ON *CNN?*
WE'RE SO FUCKING FAMOUS.
I'M JUST HERE TO PICK UP THE BODY. ALI FAHAR.
OH, COME ON, YOU GOT TO HAVE AN OPINION, RIGHT?
C'MON, STOP THIS SHIT. IF HE SAW WHAT YOU WANTED HIM TO SEE, HE'D SAY IT.
HE CAN'T SEE *ANYTHING*. IT'S NOT HIM.

WHICH BODY IS IT?

HEY, YOU CAN'T--WE'RE NOT SUPPOSED TO--

HE'S OKAY. HE'S WITH ME. HE'S IRAQ POLICE.

WHO ARE THE IRAQ POLICE?

THEY GOT TO HAVE POLICE, RIGHT? THIS IS POLICE.

SHOULD I RADIO COMMAND?

THIS IS HIM. THE *CUT*, YES?

YOU CAN'T TOUCH THEM! I DON'T CARE WHO YOU ARE. THERE'S THINGS--YOU'VE GOT TO GET *THINGS!*

I SEE THE BLACK SPOT ON THE CHIN. I THINK YOU ARE RIGHT. IT MATCHES THE BLACK SPOT ON THE VIDEO.

BUT THE PROBLEM HERE IS THAT THE CUT IS ON THE WRONG SIDE, NO?

THIS MAN HERE IS CUT LEFT TO RIGHT; THE MAN IN YOUR VIDEO IS RIGHT TO LEFT. SO I DO NOT THINK IT CAN BE THE SAME MAN.

WHAT?

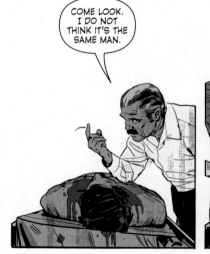

COME LOOK. I DO NOT THINK IT'S THE SAME MAN.

LOOK, LOOK HERE. YOU SEE, YES?

YOU MEAN THAT, THE WAY THE CUT IS THERE? LIKE THE KIND OF BUMPS, Y'KNOW?

YES, YES, WITH EDGES OF THE KNIFE IMPRINTED BY THE NECKLINE. YOU MUST SEE IT IS CUT LEFT TO RIGHT, YES?

HE'S RIGHT, HE'S TOTALLY RIGHT. LOOK AT THE CUT. EVEN WITH THE SPOT.

IT *CAN'T* BE HIM. NOT WITH THE CUT LIKE THAT.

WE'RE NOT FAMOUS. OBVIOUSLY.

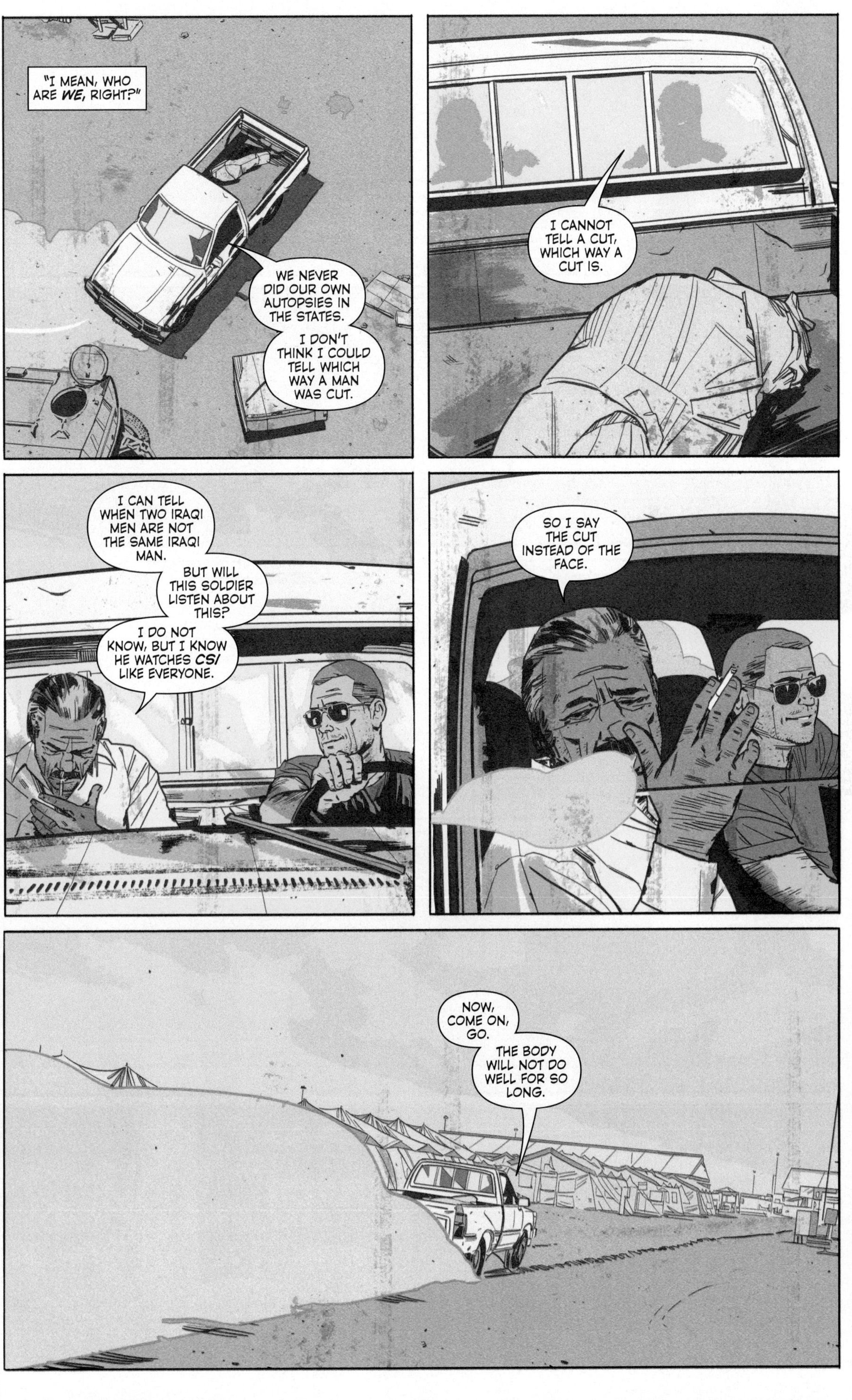
"I MEAN, WHO ARE *WE*, RIGHT?"
WE NEVER DID OUR OWN AUTOPSIES IN THE STATES.
I DON'T THINK I COULD TELL WHICH WAY A MAN WAS CUT.
I CANNOT TELL A CUT, WHICH WAY A CUT IS.
I CAN TELL WHEN TWO IRAQI MEN ARE NOT THE SAME IRAQI MAN.
BUT WILL THIS SOLDIER LISTEN ABOUT THIS?
I DO NOT KNOW, BUT I KNOW HE WATCHES *CSI* LIKE EVERYONE.
SO I SAY THE CUT INSTEAD OF THE FACE.
NOW, COME ON, GO.
THE BODY WILL NOT DO WELL FOR SO LONG.

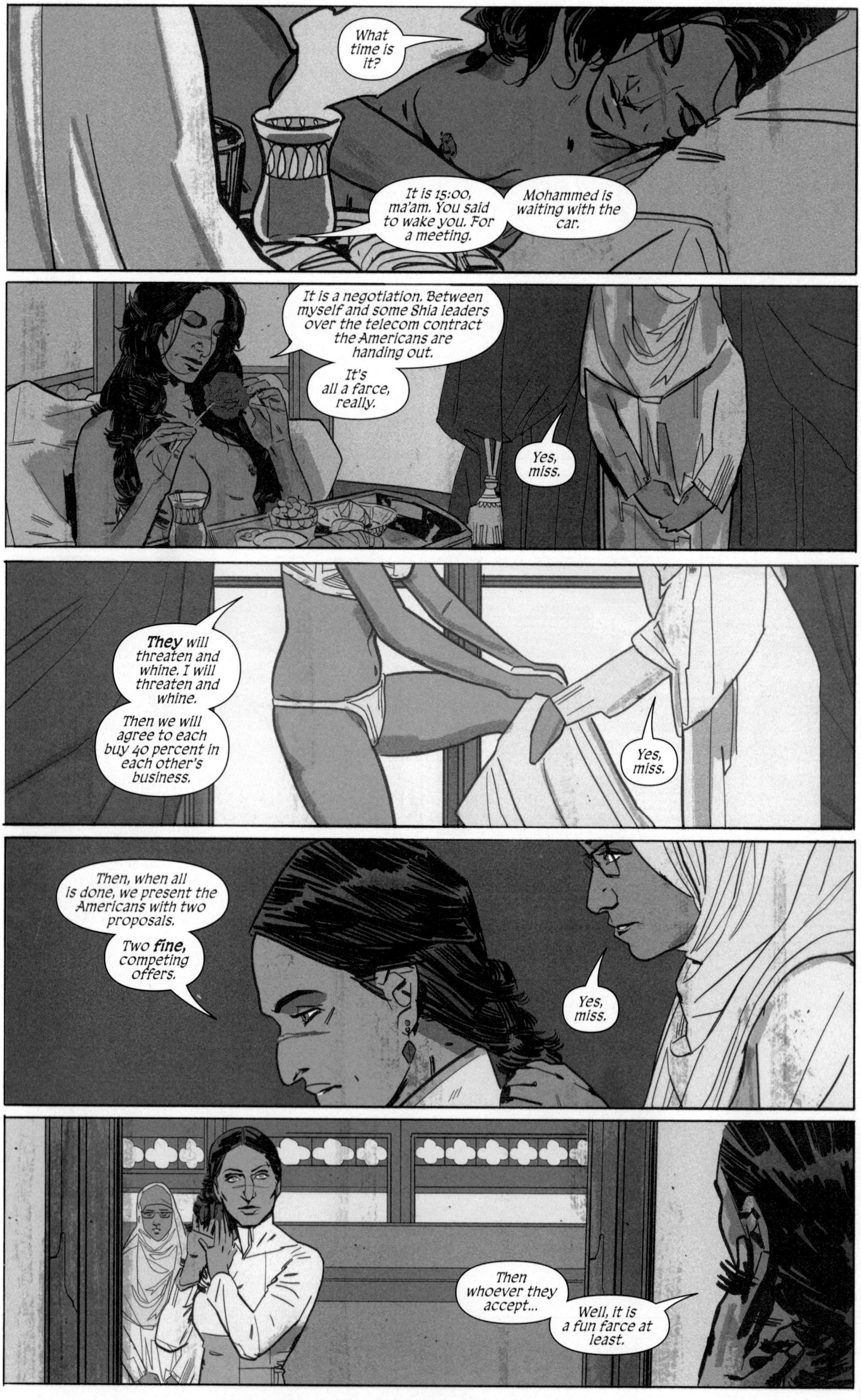
What time is it?
It is 15:00, ma'am. You said to wake you. For a meeting.
Mohammed is waiting with the car.
It is a negotiation. Between myself and some Shia leaders over the telecom contract the Americans are handing out.
It's all a farce, really.
Yes, miss.
They will threaten and whine. I will threaten and whine.
Then we will agree to each buy 40 percent in each other's business.
Yes, miss.
Then, when all is done, we present the Americans with two proposals.
Two fine, competing offers.
Yes, miss.
Then whoever they accept...
Well, it is a fun farce at least.

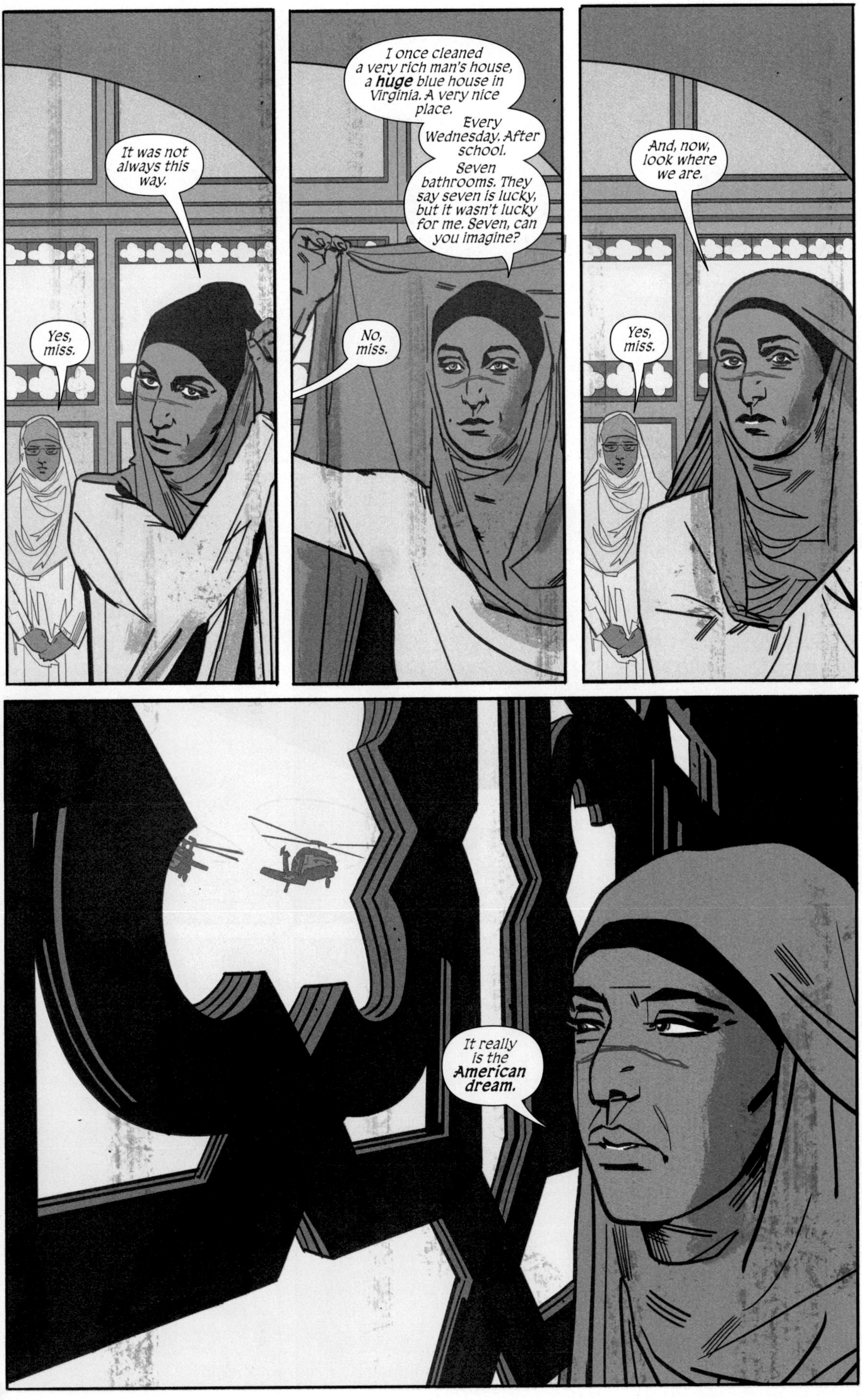
It was not always this way.
Yes, miss.
I once cleaned a very rich man's house, a **huge** blue house in Virginia. A very nice place.
Every Wednesday. After school.
Seven bathrooms. They say seven is lucky, but it wasn't lucky for me. Seven, can you imagine?
No, miss.
And, now, look where we are.
Yes, miss.
It really is the **American dream.**

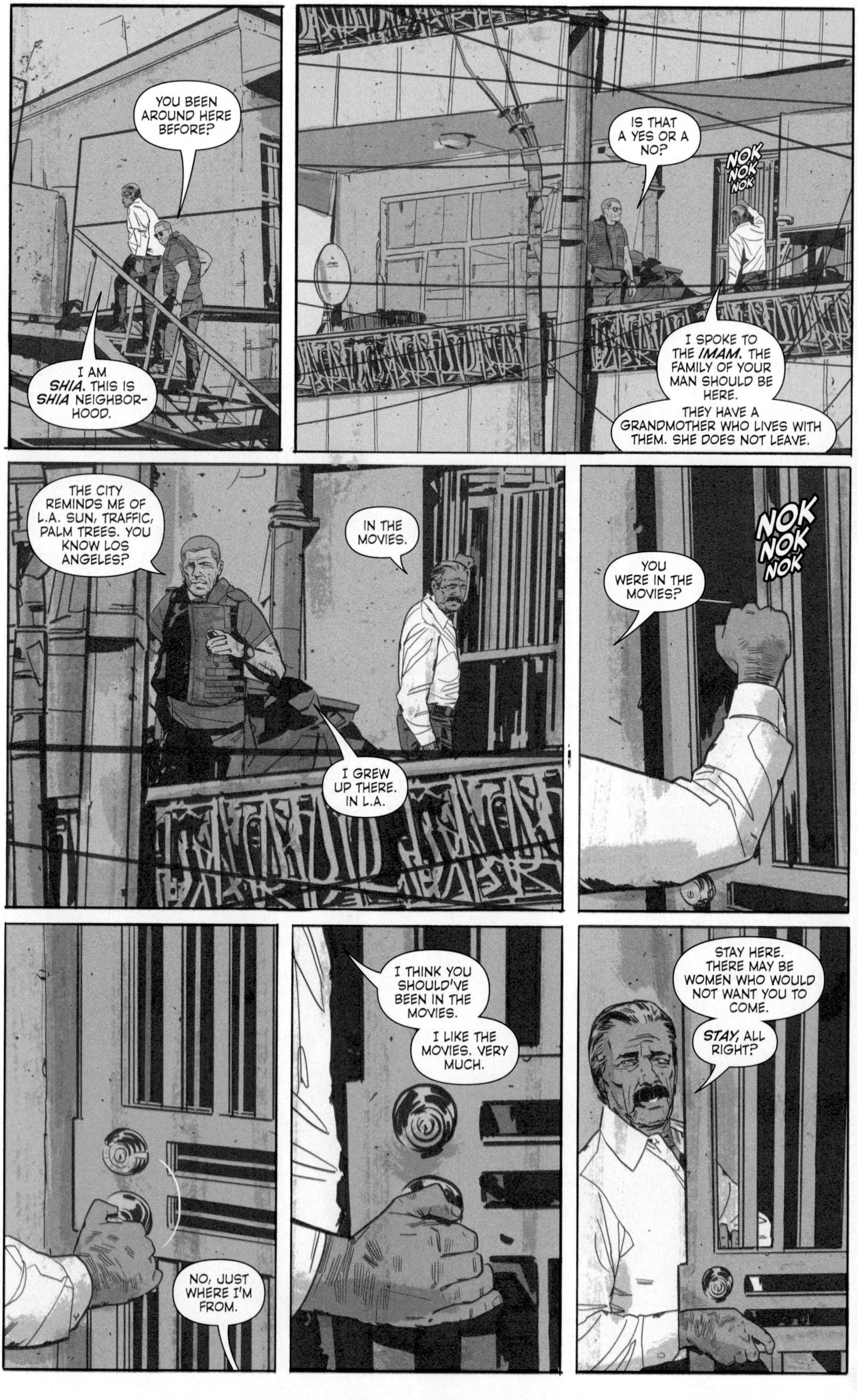
YOU BEEN AROUND HERE BEFORE?
I AM SHIA. THIS IS SHIA NEIGHBOR-HOOD.
IS THAT A YES OR A NO?
NOK NOK NOK
I SPOKE TO THE IMAM. THE FAMILY OF YOUR MAN SHOULD BE HERE.
THEY HAVE A GRANDMOTHER WHO LIVES WITH THEM. SHE DOES NOT LEAVE.
THE CITY REMINDS ME OF L.A. SUN, TRAFFIC, PALM TREES. YOU KNOW LOS ANGELES?
IN THE MOVIES.
I GREW UP THERE. IN L.A.
NOK NOK NOK
YOU WERE IN THE MOVIES?
NO, JUST WHERE I'M FROM.
I THINK YOU SHOULD'VE BEEN IN THE MOVIES.
I LIKE THE MOVIES. VERY MUCH.
STAY HERE. THERE MAY BE WOMEN WHO WOULD NOT WANT YOU TO COME.
STAY, ALL RIGHT?

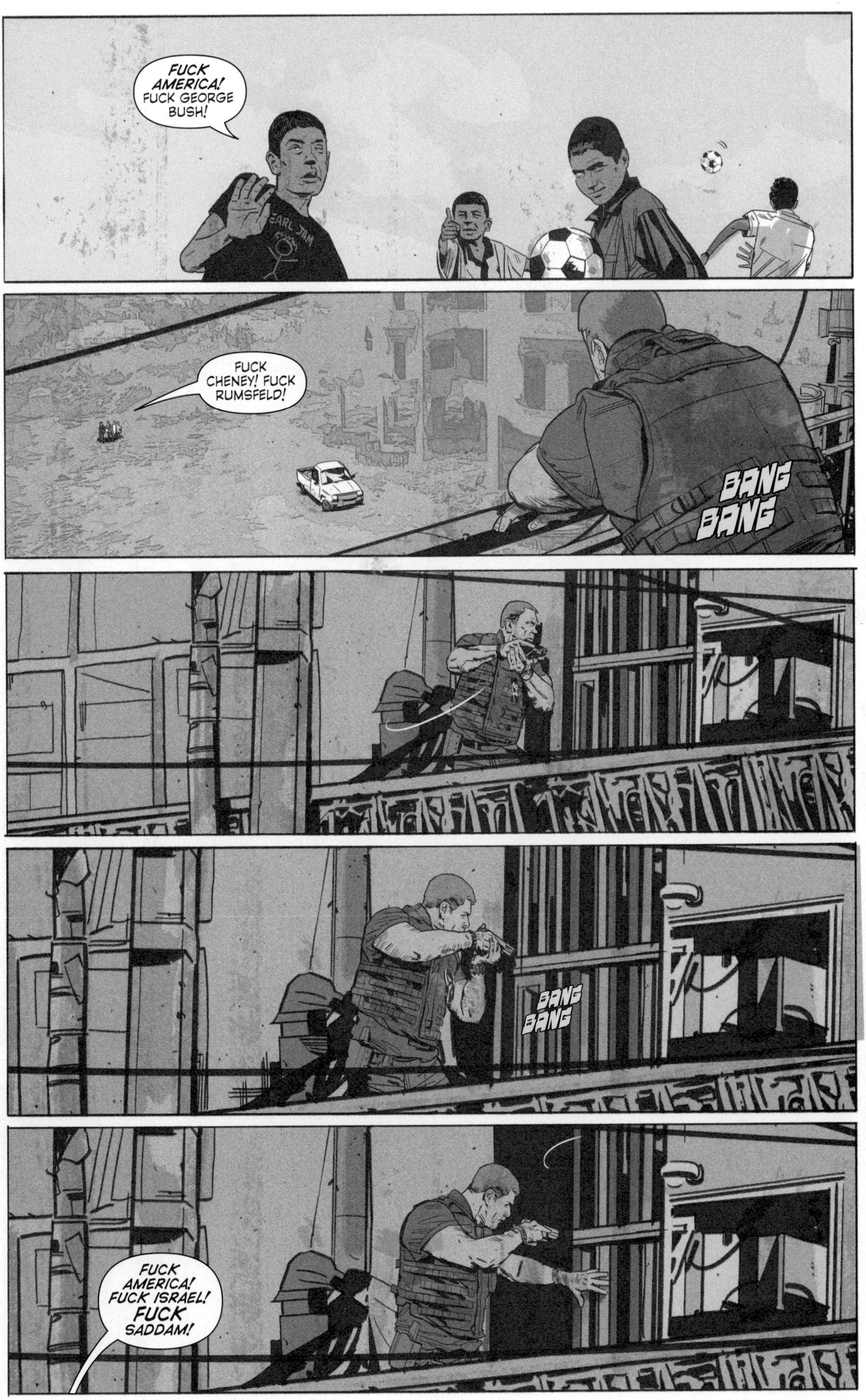
FUCK AMERICA! FUCK GEORGE BUSH!
EARL JAM
FUCK CHENEY! FUCK RUMSFELD!
BANG BANG
BANG BANG
FUCK AMERICA! FUCK ISRAEL! FUCK SADDAM!

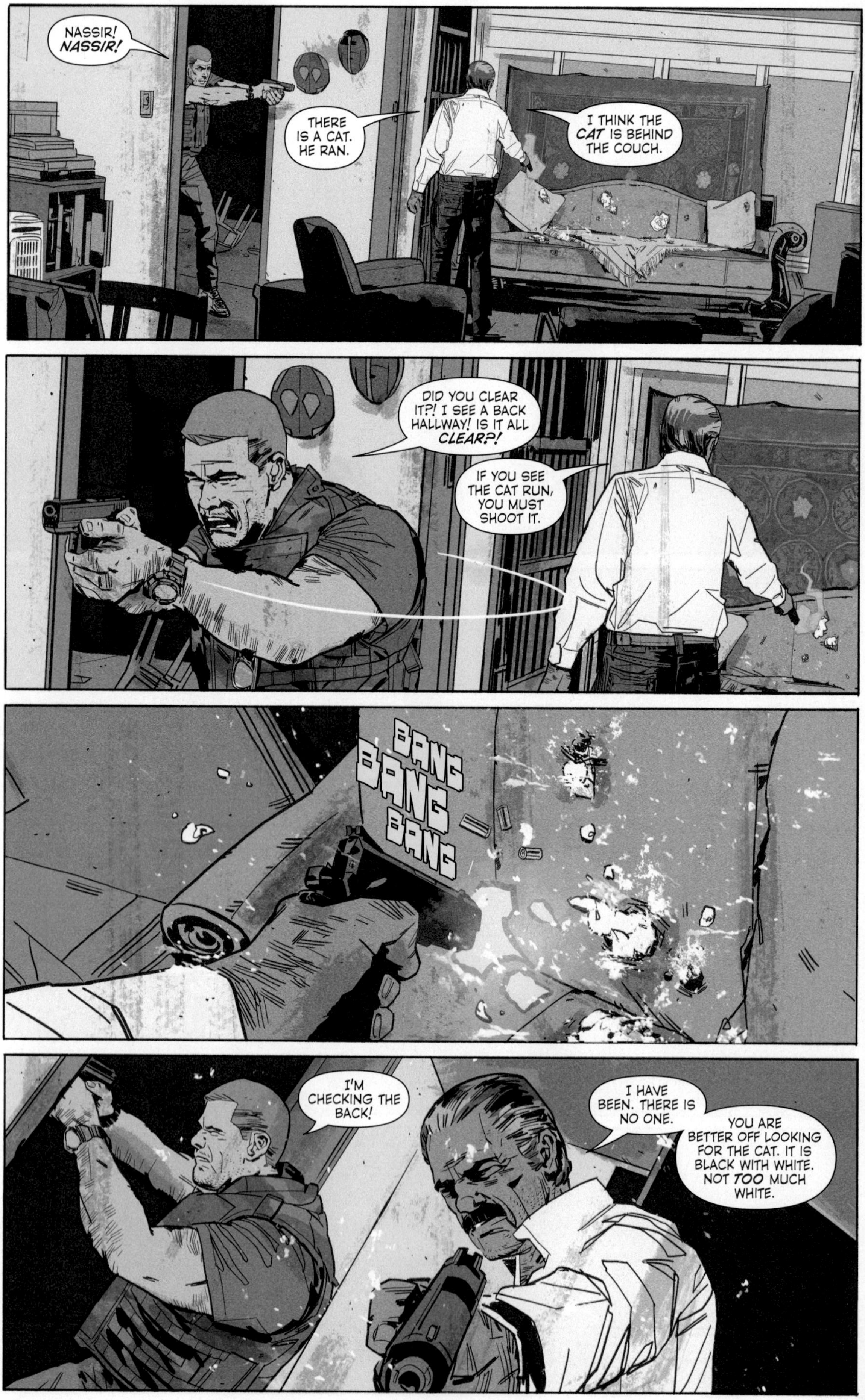
NASSIR! *NASSIR!*
THERE IS A CAT. HE RAN.
I THINK THE *CAT* IS BEHIND THE COUCH.
DID YOU CLEAR IT?! I SEE A BACK HALLWAY! IS IT ALL *CLEAR?!*
IF YOU SEE THE CAT RUN, YOU MUST SHOOT IT.
BANG
BANG
BANG
BANG
I'M CHECKING THE BACK!
I HAVE BEEN. THERE IS NO ONE.
YOU ARE BETTER OFF LOOKING FOR THE CAT. IT IS BLACK WITH WHITE. NOT *TOO* MUCH WHITE.

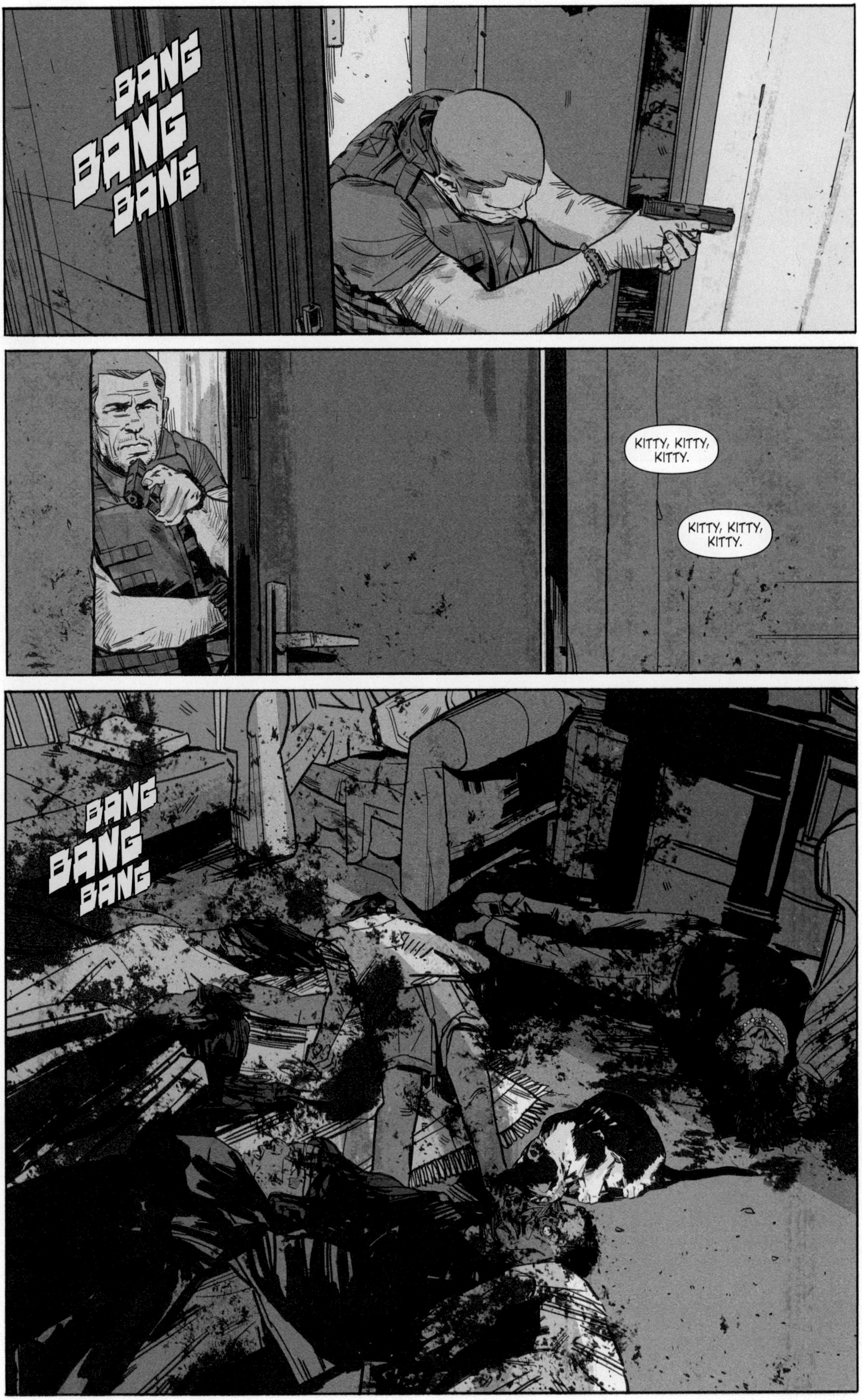
BANG
BANG
BANG
KITTY, KITTY, KITTY.
KITTY, KITTY, KITTY.
BANG
BANG
BANG

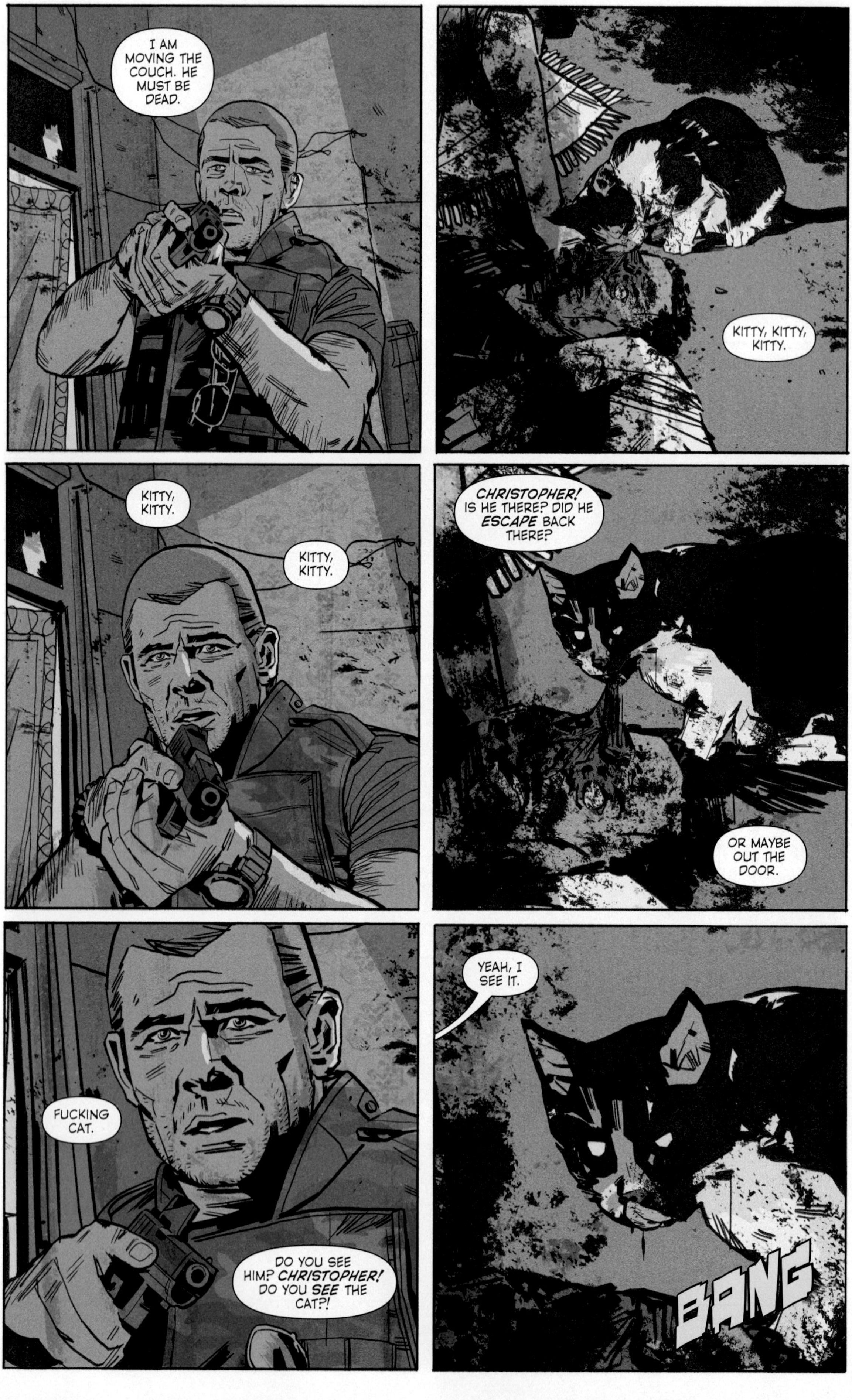
I AM MOVING THE COUCH. HE MUST BE DEAD.
KITTY, KITTY, KITTY.
KITTY, KITTY.
KITTY, KITTY.
CHRISTOPHER! IS HE THERE? DID HE ESCAPE BACK THERE?
OR MAYBE OUT THE DOOR.
FUCKING CAT.
DO YOU SEE HIM? CHRISTOPHER! DO YOU SEE THE CAT?!
YEAH, I SEE IT.
BANG

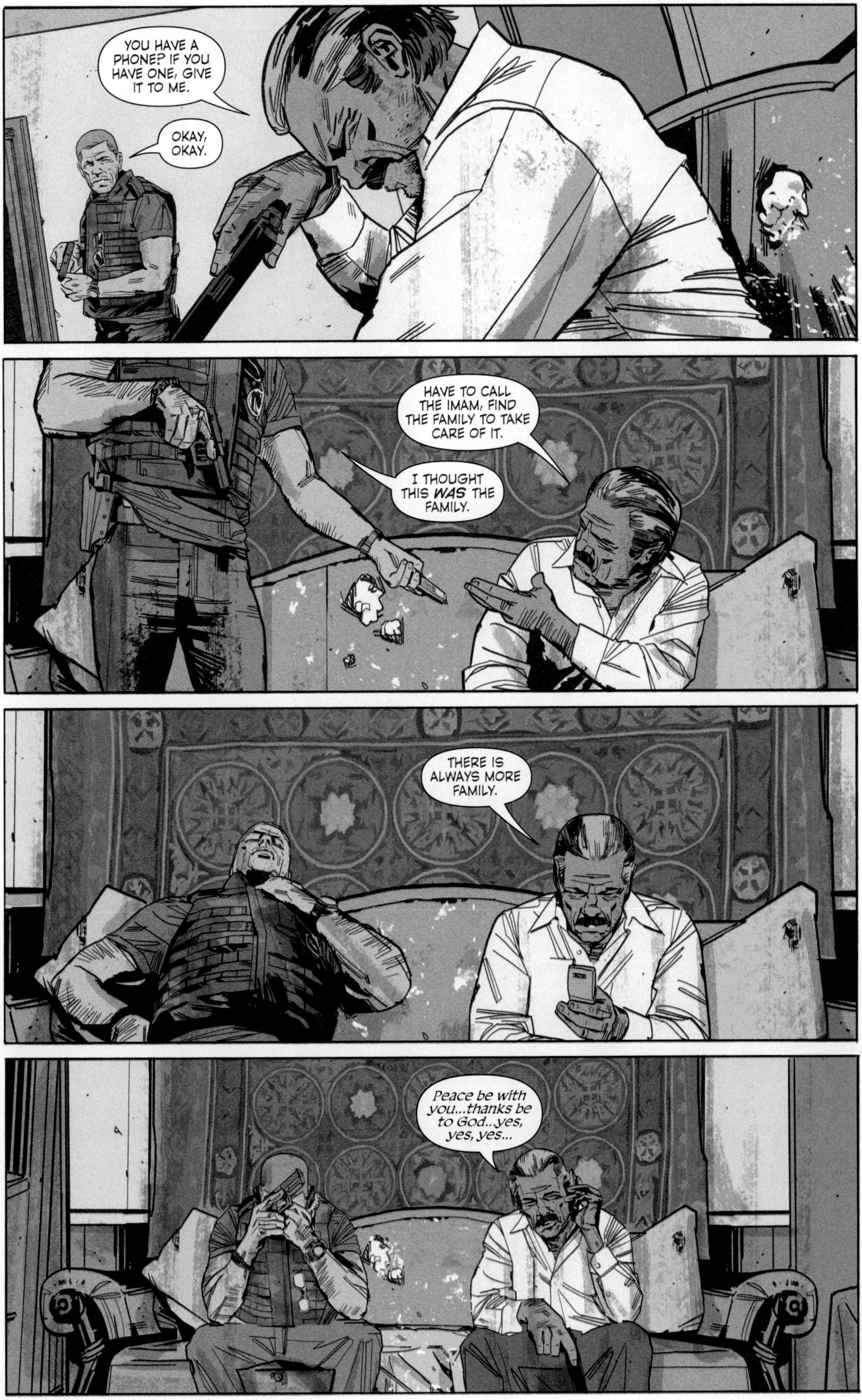
YOU HAVE A PHONE? IF YOU HAVE ONE, GIVE IT TO ME.
OKAY, OKAY.
HAVE TO CALL THE IMAM, FIND THE FAMILY TO TAKE CARE OF IT.
I THOUGHT THIS *WAS* THE FAMILY.
THERE IS ALWAYS MORE FAMILY.
Peace be with you...thanks be to God...yes, yes, yes...

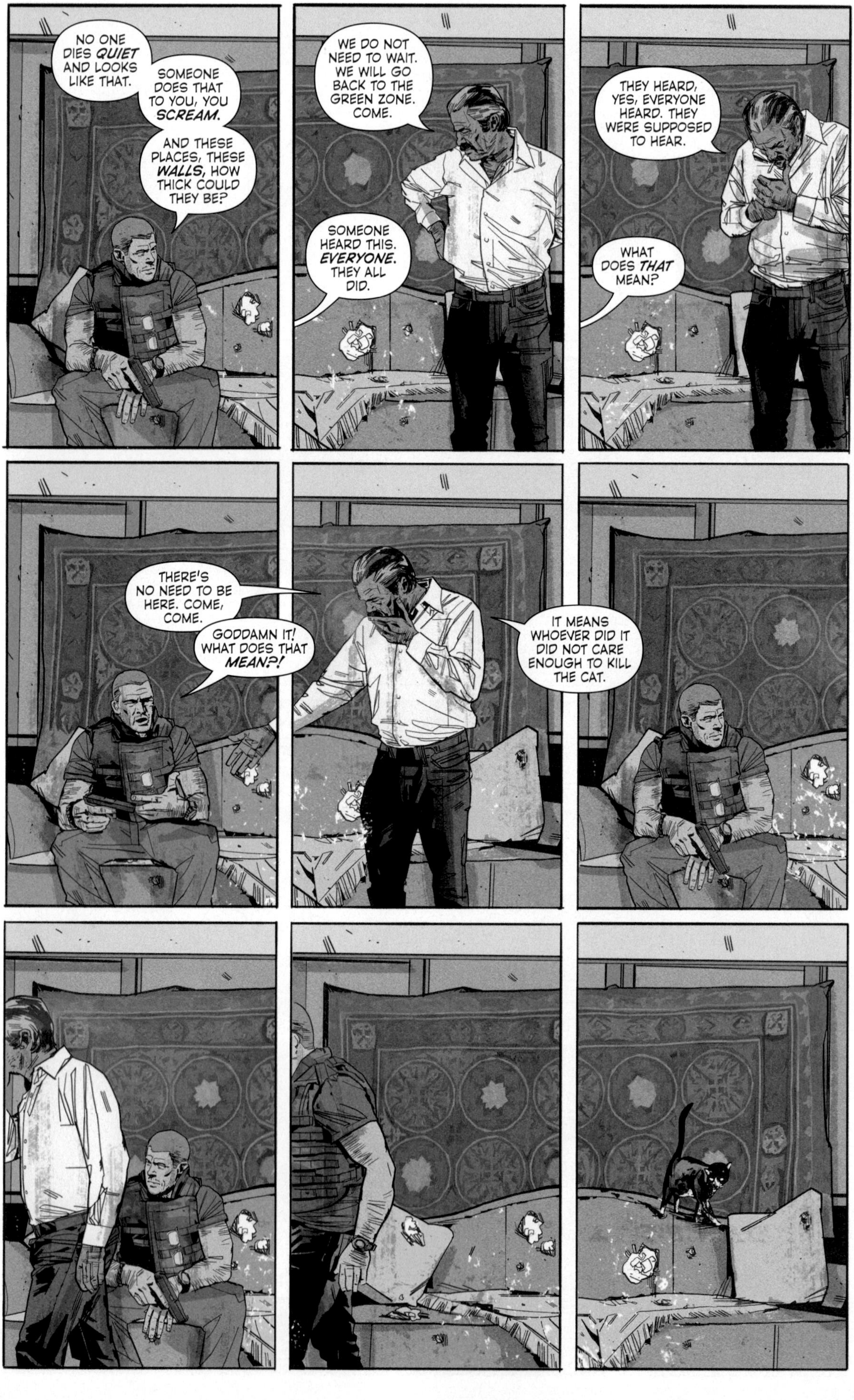

NO ONE DIES *QUIET* AND LOOKS LIKE THAT.
SOMEONE DOES THAT TO YOU, YOU ***SCREAM.***
AND THESE PLACES, THESE ***WALLS,*** HOW THICK COULD THEY BE?
WE DO NOT NEED TO WAIT. WE WILL GO BACK TO THE GREEN ZONE. COME.
SOMEONE HEARD THIS. ***EVERYONE.*** THEY ALL DID.
THEY HEARD, YES, EVERYONE HEARD. THEY WERE SUPPOSED TO HEAR.
WHAT DOES ***THAT*** MEAN?
THERE'S NO NEED TO BE HERE. COME, COME.
GODDAMN IT! WHAT DOES THAT ***MEAN?!***
IT MEANS WHOEVER DID IT DID NOT CARE ENOUGH TO KILL THE CAT.

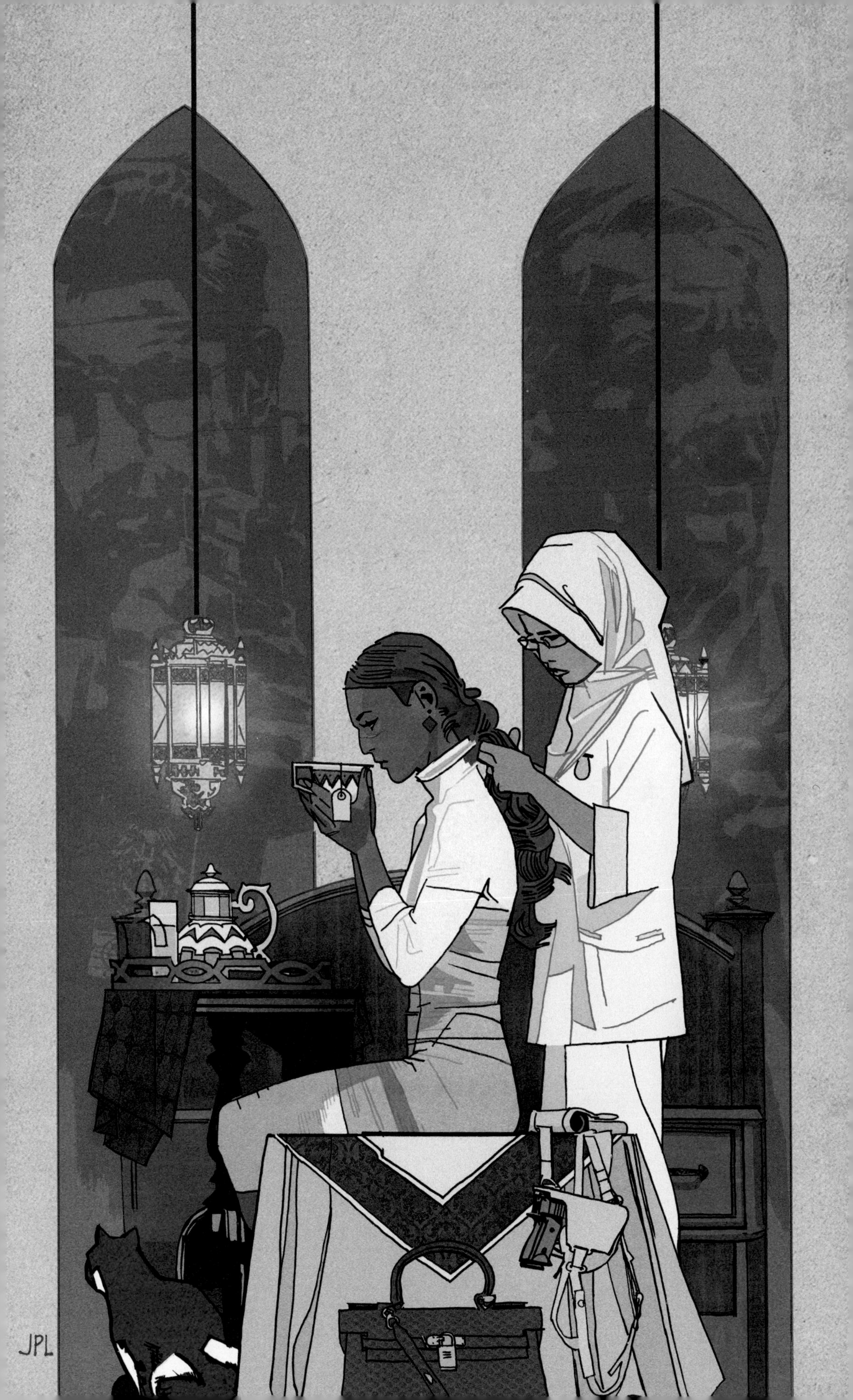
JPL

PART THREE

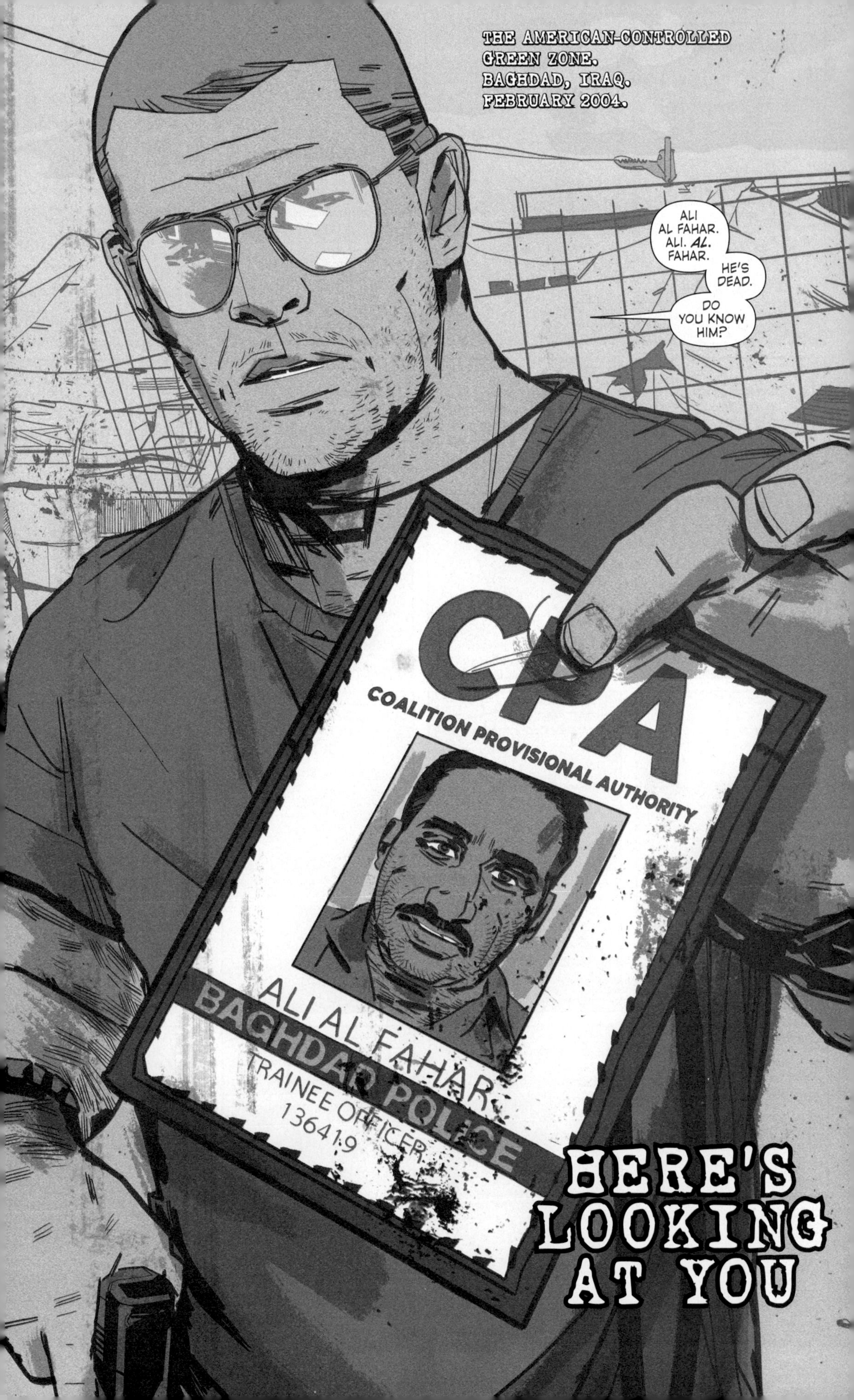
THE AMERICAN-CONTROLLED GREEN ZONE. BAGHDAD, IRAQ. FEBRUARY 2004.
ALI AL FAHAR. ALI. *AL.* FAHAR.
HE'S DEAD.
DO YOU KNOW HIM?
CPA
COALITION PROVISIONAL AUTHORITY
ALI AL FAHAR
BAGHDAD POLICE
TRAINEE OFFICER
136419
HERE'S LOOKING AT YOU

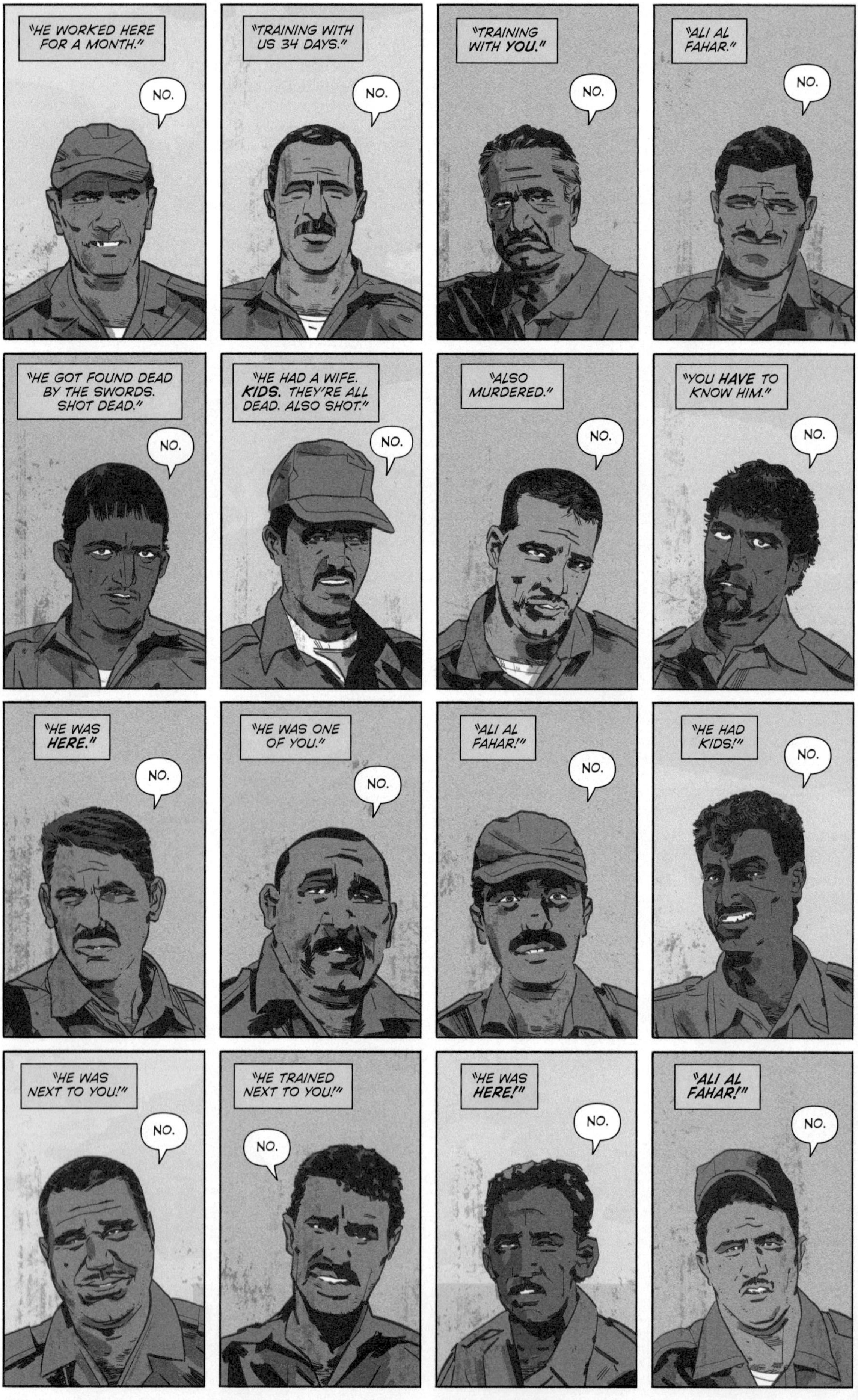
"HE WORKED HERE FOR A MONTH."
NO.
"TRAINING WITH US 34 DAYS."
NO.
"TRAINING WITH YOU."
NO.
"ALI AL FAHAR."
NO.
"HE GOT FOUND DEAD BY THE SWORDS. SHOT DEAD."
NO.
"HE HAD A WIFE. KIDS. THEY'RE ALL DEAD. ALSO SHOT."
NO.
"ALSO MURDERED."
NO.
"YOU HAVE TO KNOW HIM."
NO.
"HE WAS HERE."
NO.
"HE WAS ONE OF YOU."
NO.
"ALI AL FAHAR!"
NO.
"HE HAD KIDS!"
NO.
"HE WAS NEXT TO YOU!"
NO.
"HE TRAINED NEXT TO YOU!"
NO.
"HE WAS HERE!"
NO.
"ALI AL FAHAR!"
NO.

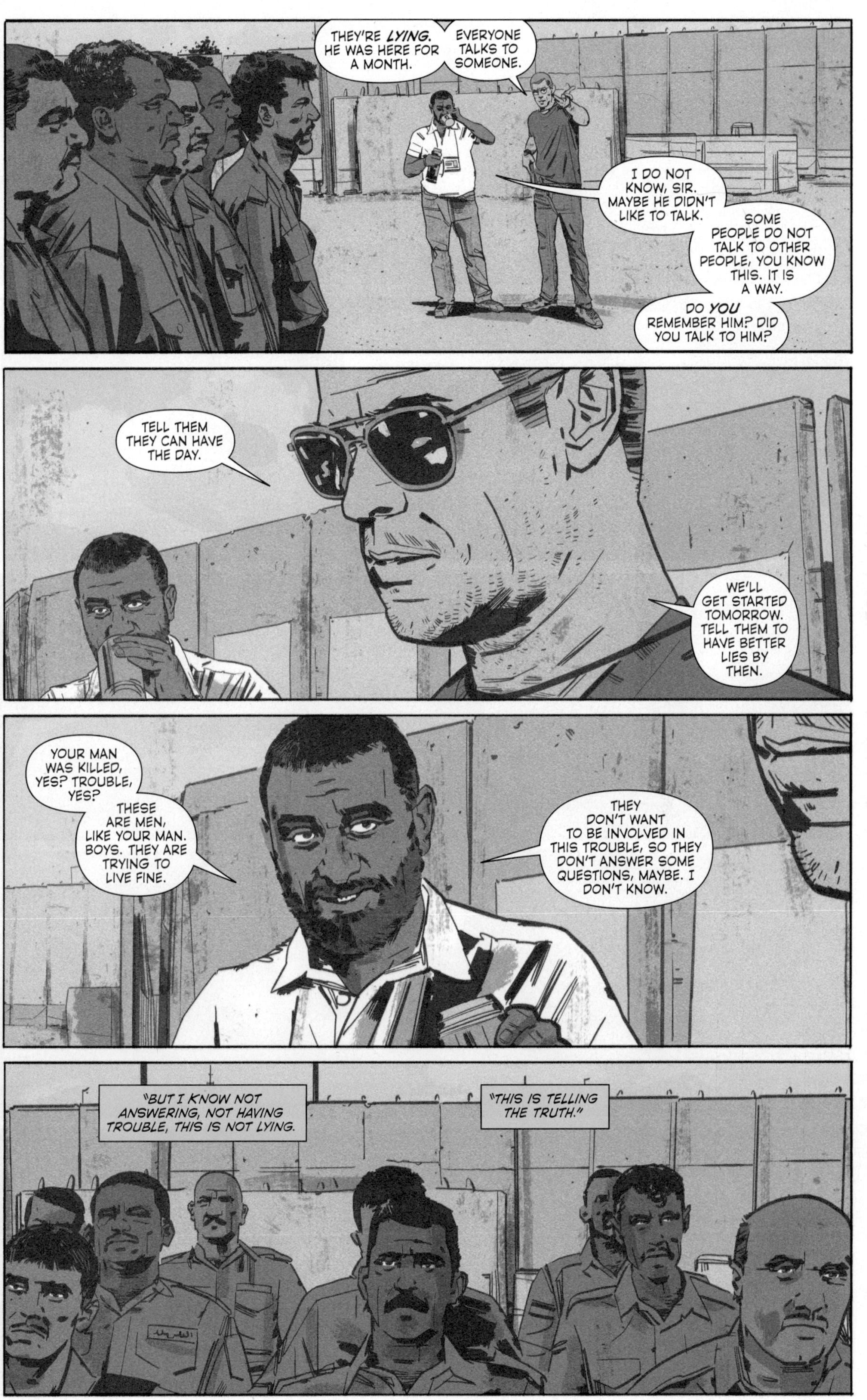
THEY'RE *LYING.* HE WAS HERE FOR A MONTH.
EVERYONE TALKS TO SOMEONE.
I DO NOT KNOW, SIR. MAYBE HE DIDN'T LIKE TO TALK.
SOME PEOPLE DO NOT TALK TO OTHER PEOPLE, YOU KNOW THIS. IT IS A WAY.
DO *YOU* REMEMBER HIM? DID YOU TALK TO HIM?
TELL THEM THEY CAN HAVE THE DAY.
WE'LL GET STARTED TOMORROW. TELL THEM TO HAVE BETTER LIES BY THEN.
YOUR MAN WAS KILLED, YES? TROUBLE, YES?
THESE ARE MEN, LIKE YOUR MAN. BOYS. THEY ARE TRYING TO LIVE FINE.
THEY DON'T WANT TO BE INVOLVED IN THIS TROUBLE, SO THEY DON'T ANSWER SOME QUESTIONS, MAYBE. I DON'T KNOW.
"BUT I KNOW NOT ANSWERING, NOT HAVING TROUBLE, THIS IS NOT LYING.
"THIS IS TELLING THE TRUTH."

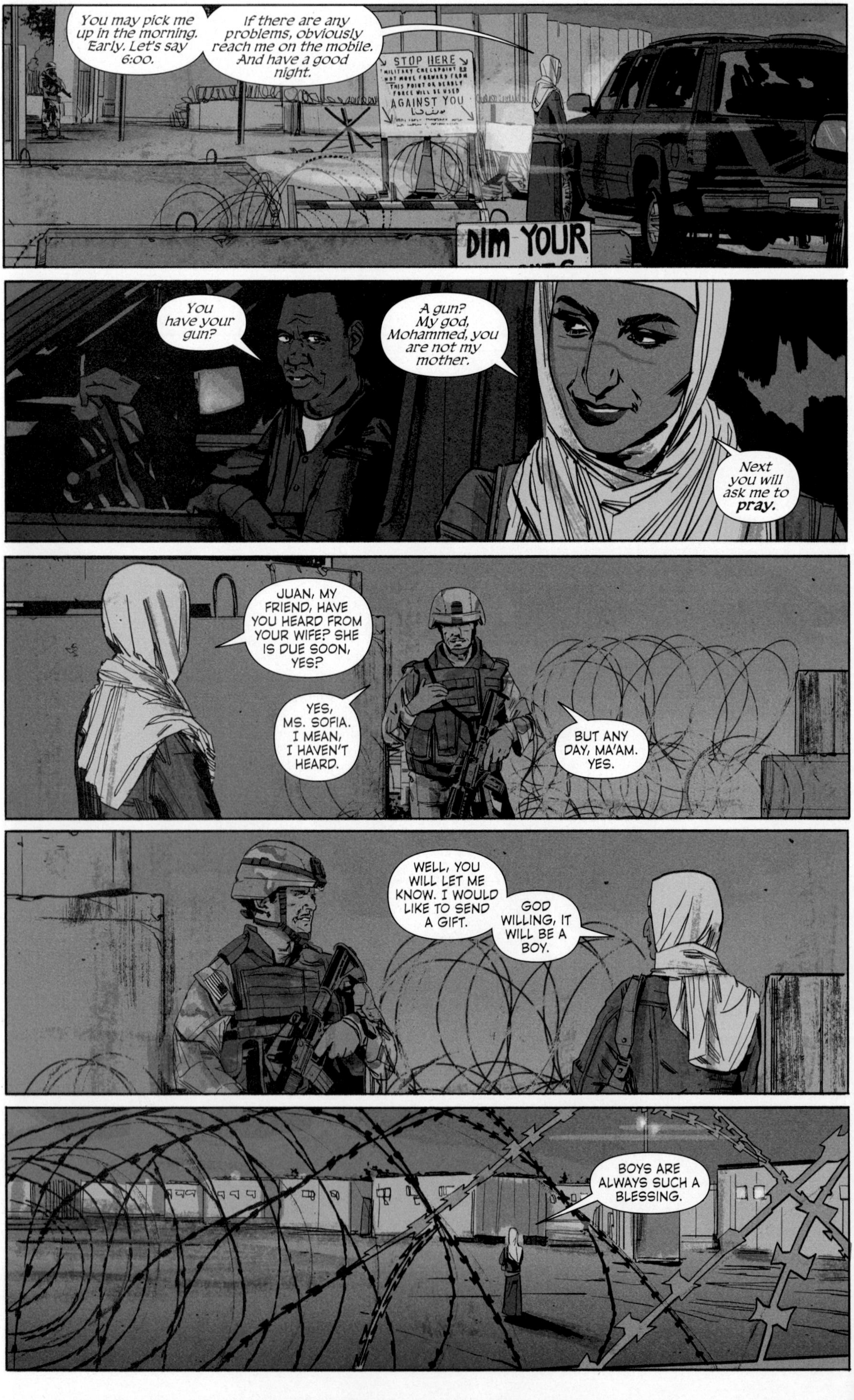
You may pick me up in the morning. Early. Let's say 6:00.
If there are any problems, obviously reach me on the mobile. And have a good night.
STOP HERE
AGAINST YOU
DIM YOUR
You have your gun?
A gun? My god, Mohammed, you are not my mother.
Next you will ask me to **pray.**
JUAN, MY FRIEND, HAVE YOU HEARD FROM YOUR WIFE? SHE IS DUE SOON, YES?
YES, MS. SOFIA. I MEAN, I HAVEN'T HEARD.
BUT ANY DAY, MA'AM. YES.
WELL, YOU WILL LET ME KNOW. I WOULD LIKE TO SEND A GIFT.
GOD WILLING, IT WILL BE A BOY.
BOYS ARE ALWAYS SUCH A BLESSING.

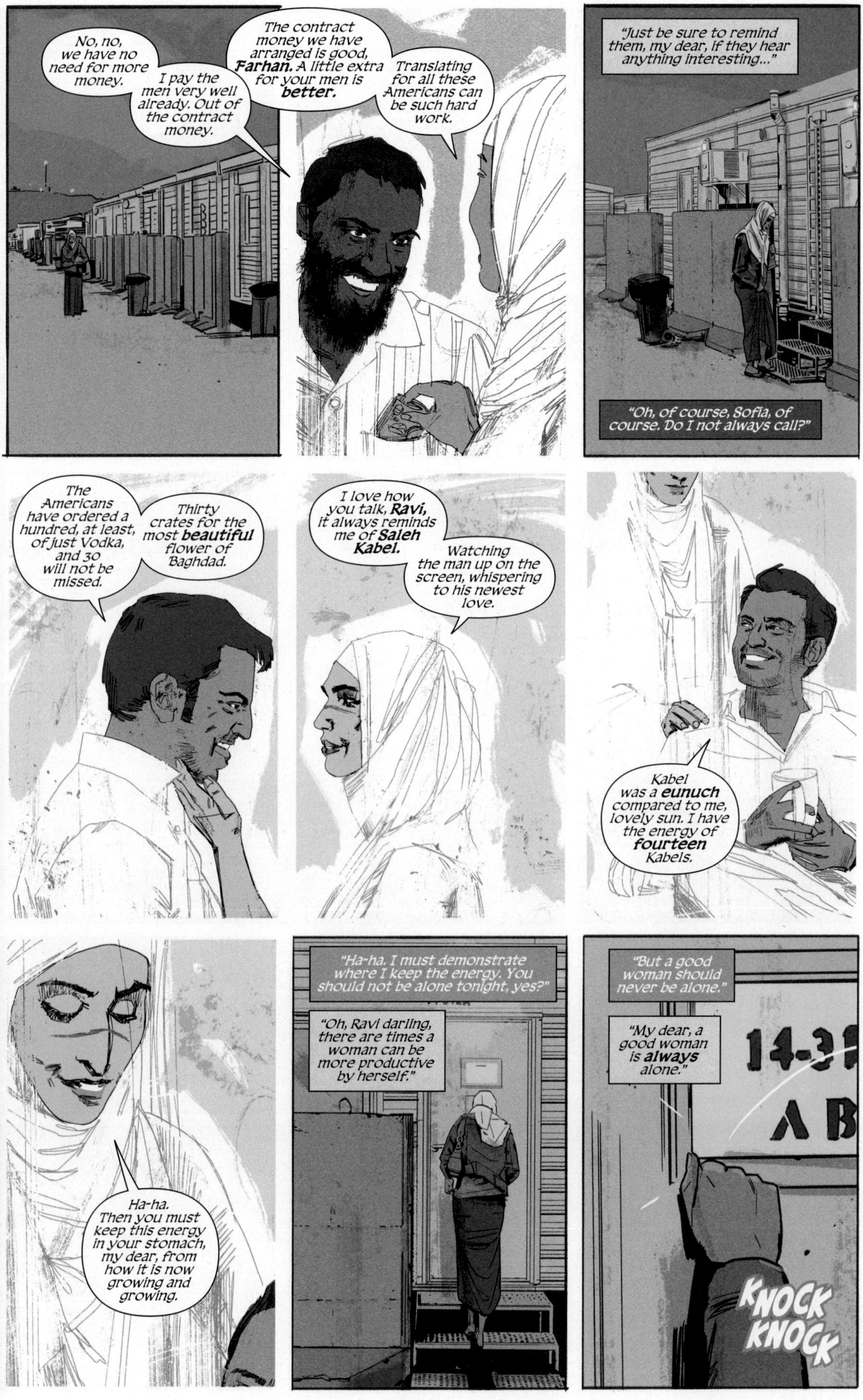
No, no, we have no need for more money.
I pay the men very well already. Out of the contract money.
The contract money we have arranged is good, Farhan. A little extra for your men is better.
Translating for all these Americans can be such hard work.
"Just be sure to remind them, my dear, if they hear anything interesting..."
"Oh, of course, Sofia, of course. Do I not always call?"
The Americans have ordered a hundred, at least, of just Vodka, and 30 will not be missed.
Thirty crates for the most beautiful flower of Baghdad.
I love how you talk, Ravi, it always reminds me of Saleh Kabel.
Watching the man up on the screen, whispering to his newest love.
Kabel was a eunuch compared to me, lovely sun. I have the energy of fourteen Kabels.
Ha-ha. Then you must keep this energy in your stomach, my dear, from how it is now growing and growing.
"Ha-ha. I must demonstrate where I keep the energy. You should not be alone tonight, yes?"
"Oh, Ravi darling, there are times a woman can be more productive by herself."
"But a good woman should never be alone."
"My dear, a good woman is always alone."
14-3
AB
KNOCK KNOCK

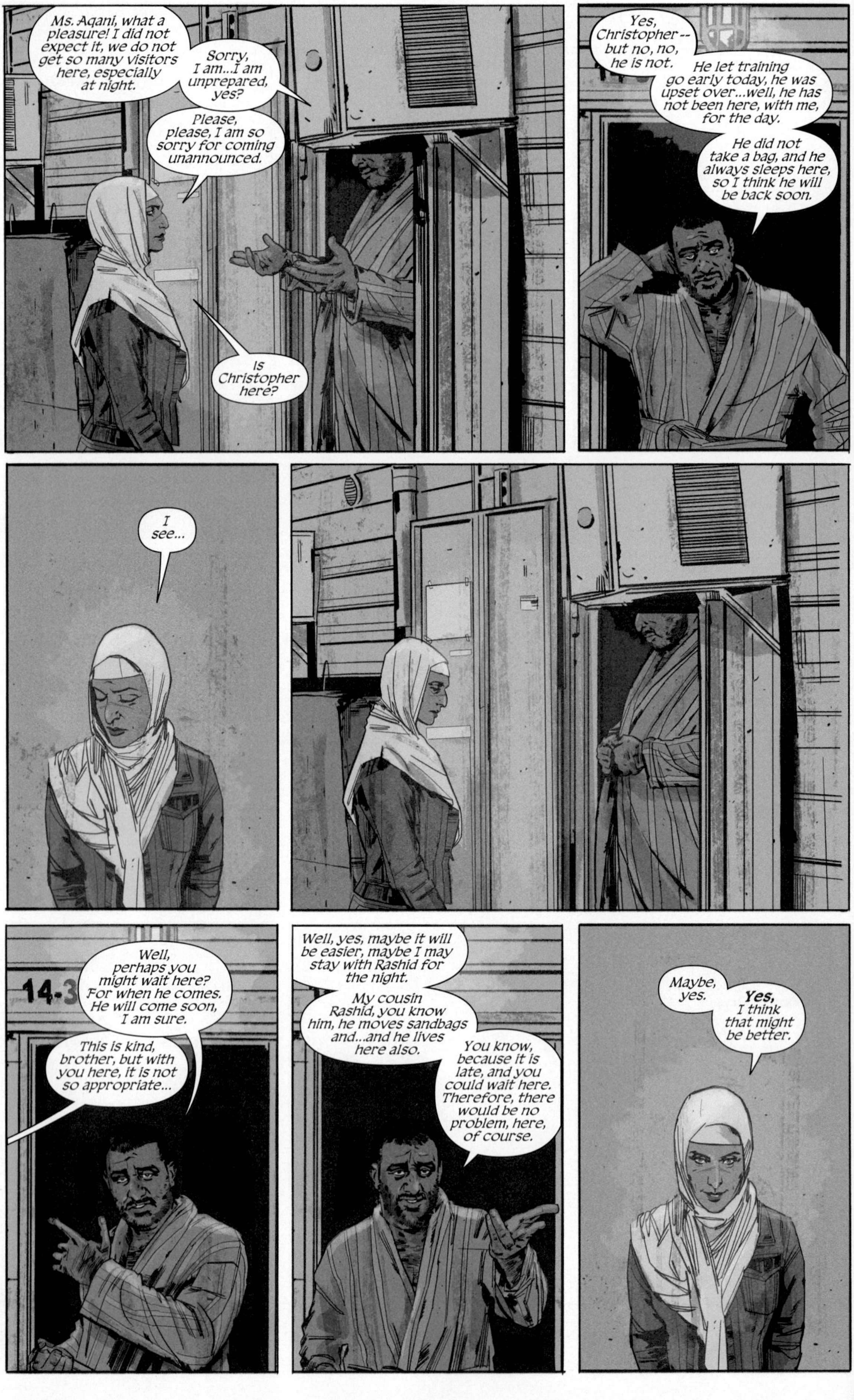
Ms. Aqani, what a pleasure! I did not expect it, we do not get so many visitors here, especially at night.
Sorry, I am...I am unprepared, yes?
Please, please, I am so sorry for coming unannounced.
Is Christopher here?
Yes, Christopher -- but no, no, he is not.
He let training go early today, he was upset over...well, he has not been here, with me, for the day.
He did not take a bag, and he always sleeps here, so I think he will be back soon.
I see...
14-3
Well, perhaps you might wait here? For when he comes. He will come soon, I am sure.
This is kind, brother, but with you here, it is not so appropriate...
Well, yes, maybe it will be easier, maybe I may stay with Rashid for the night.
My cousin Rashid, you know him, he moves sandbags and...and he lives here also.
You know, because it is late, and you could wait here. Therefore, there would be no problem, here, of course.
Maybe, yes.
Yes, I think that might be better.

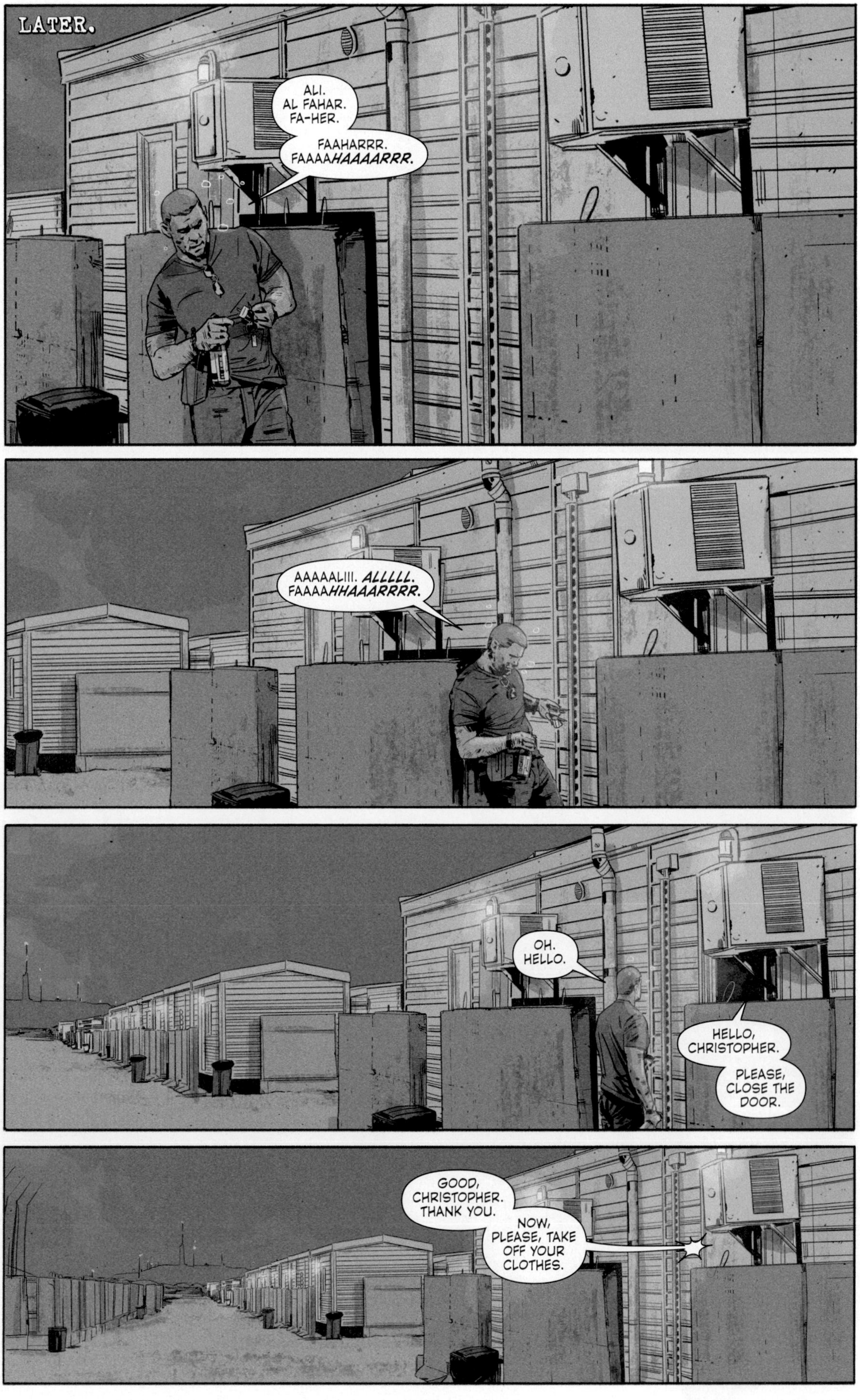
LATER.
ALI. AL FAHAR. FA-HER.
FAAHARRR. FAAAAHAAAARRR.
AAAAALIII. ALLLLL. FAAAAHHAAARRRR.
OH. HELLO.
HELLO, CHRISTOPHER.
PLEASE, CLOSE THE DOOR.
GOOD, CHRISTOPHER. THANK YOU.
NOW, PLEASE, TAKE OFF YOUR CLOTHES.

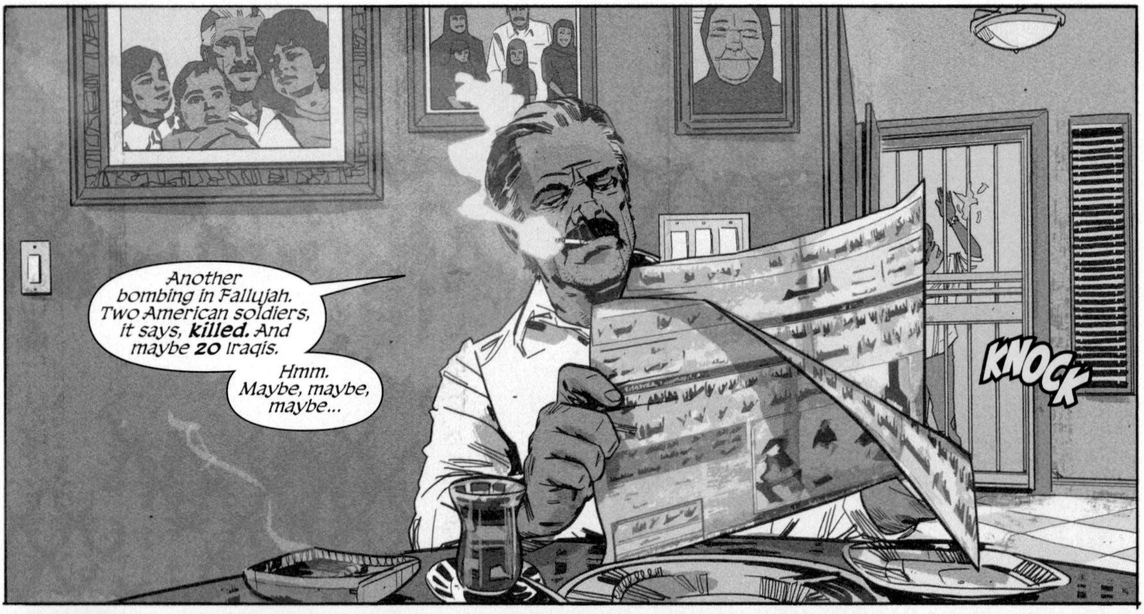
Another bombing in Fallujah. Two American soldiers, it says, **killed.** And maybe **20** Iraqis.
Hmm. Maybe, maybe, maybe...
KNOCK

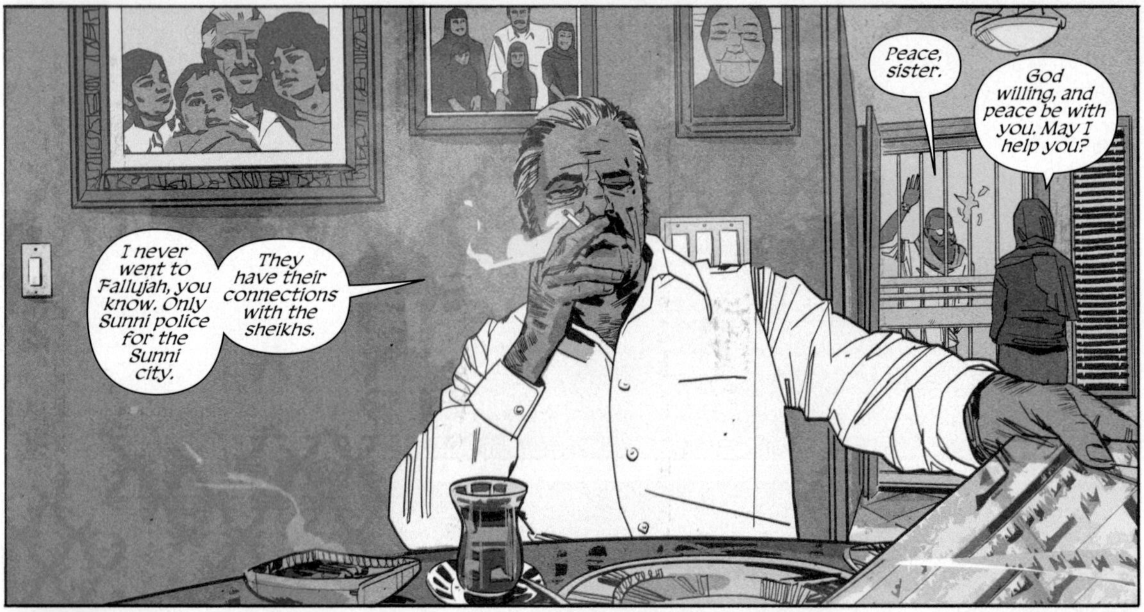
I never went to Fallujah, you know. Only Sunni police for the Sunni city.
They have their connections with the sheikhs.
Peace, sister.
God willing, and peace be with you. May I help you?

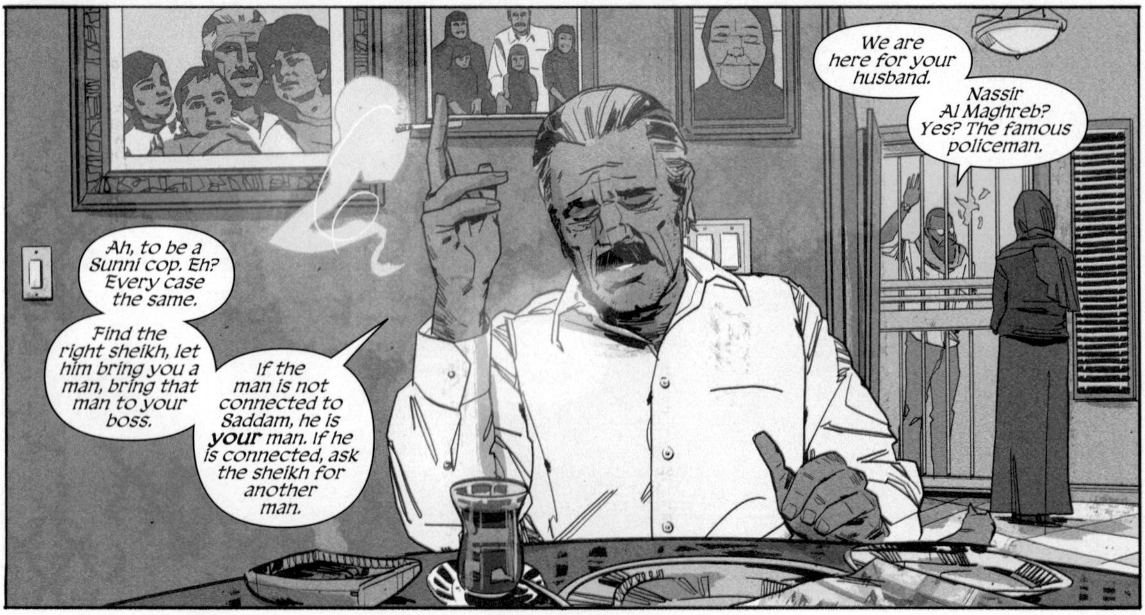
Ah, to be a Sunni cop. Eh? Every case the same.
Find the right sheikh, let him bring you a man, bring that man to your boss.
If the man is not connected to Saddam, he is **your** man. If he is connected, ask the sheikh for another man.
We are here for your husband.
Nassir Al Maghreb? Yes? The famous policeman.

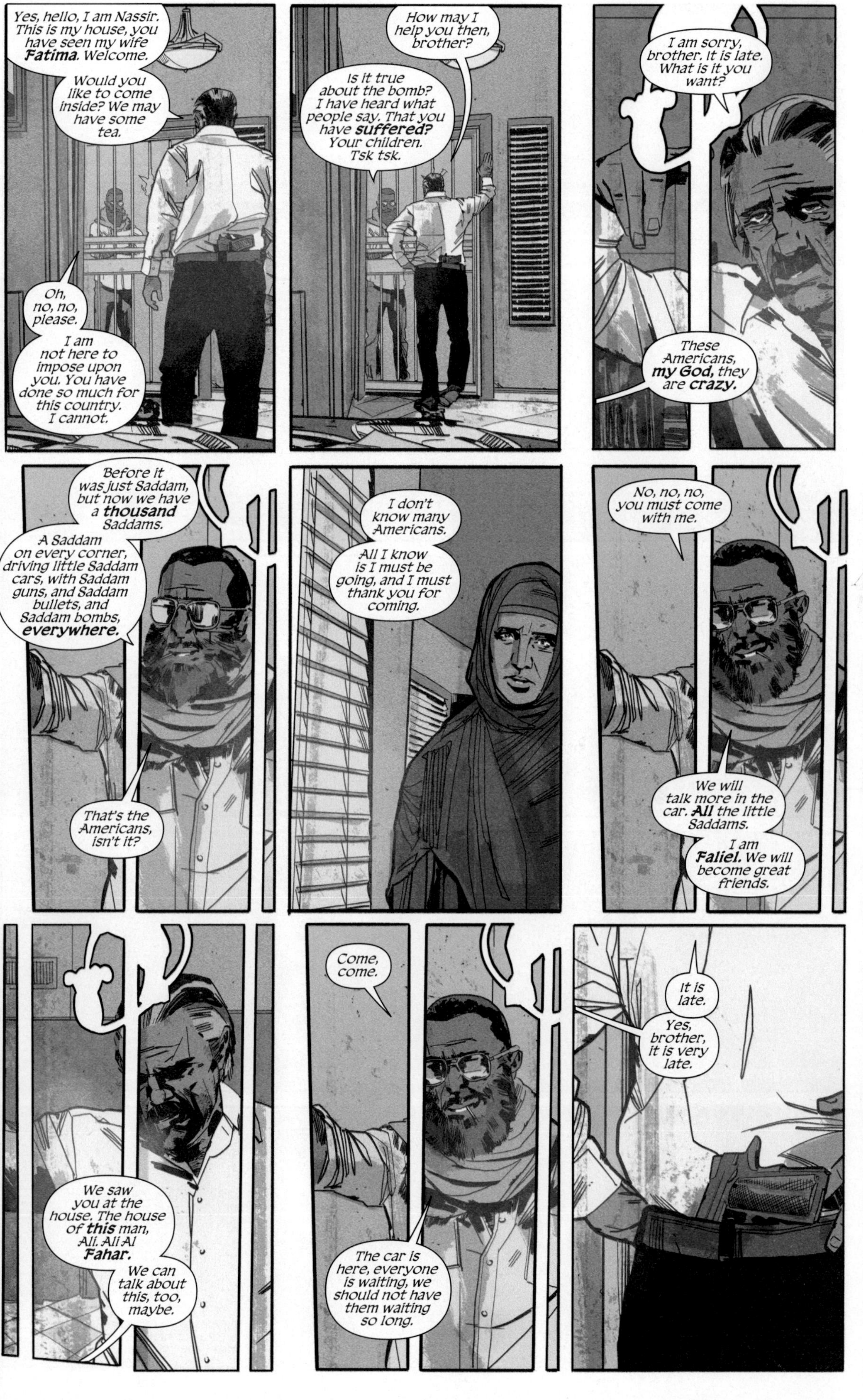

Yes, hello, I am Nassir. This is my house, you have seen my wife **Fatima**. Welcome.
Would you like to come inside? We may have some tea.
Oh, no, no, please.
I am not here to impose upon you. You have done so much for this country. I cannot.
How may I help you then, brother?
Is it true about the bomb? I have heard what people say. That you have **suffered?** Your children. Tsk tsk.
I am sorry, brother. It is late. What is it you want?
These Americans, **my God,** they are **crazy.**
Before it was just Saddam, but now we have a **thousand** Saddams.
A Saddam on every corner, driving little Saddam cars, with Saddam guns, and Saddam bullets, and Saddam bombs, **everywhere.**
That's the Americans, isn't it?
I don't know many Americans.
All I know is I must be going, and I must thank you for coming.
No, no, no, you must come with me.
We will talk more in the car. **All** the little Saddams.
I am **Faliel.** We will become great friends.
We saw you at the house. The house of **this** man, Ali. Ali Al **Fahar.**
We can talk about this, too, maybe.
Come, come.
The car is here, everyone is waiting, we should not have them waiting so long.
It is late.
Yes, brother, it is very late.

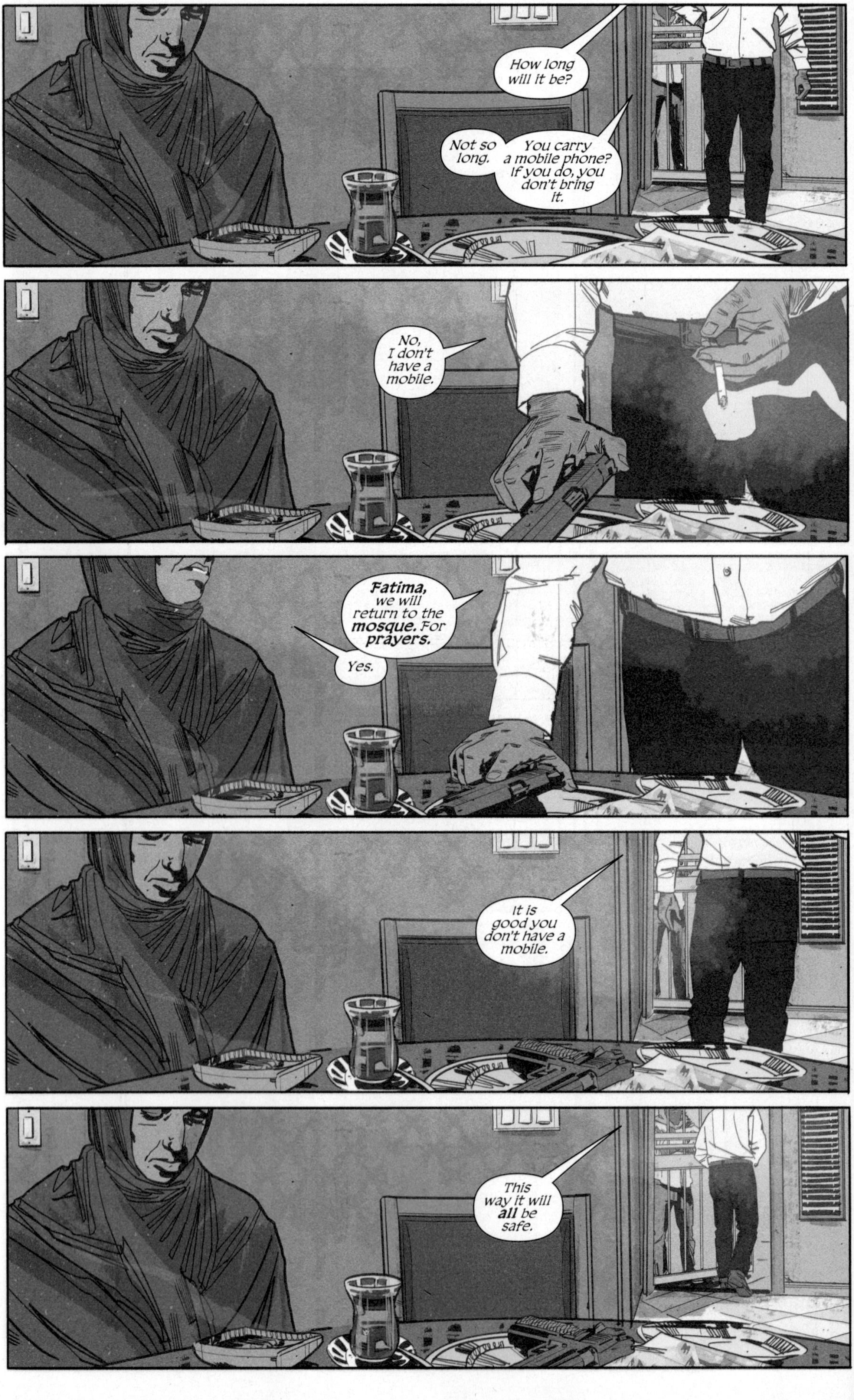
How long will it be?
Not so long.
You carry a mobile phone? If you do, you don't bring it.
No, I don't have a mobile.
Fatima, we will return to the mosque. For prayers.
Yes.
It is good you don't have a mobile.
This way it will all be safe.

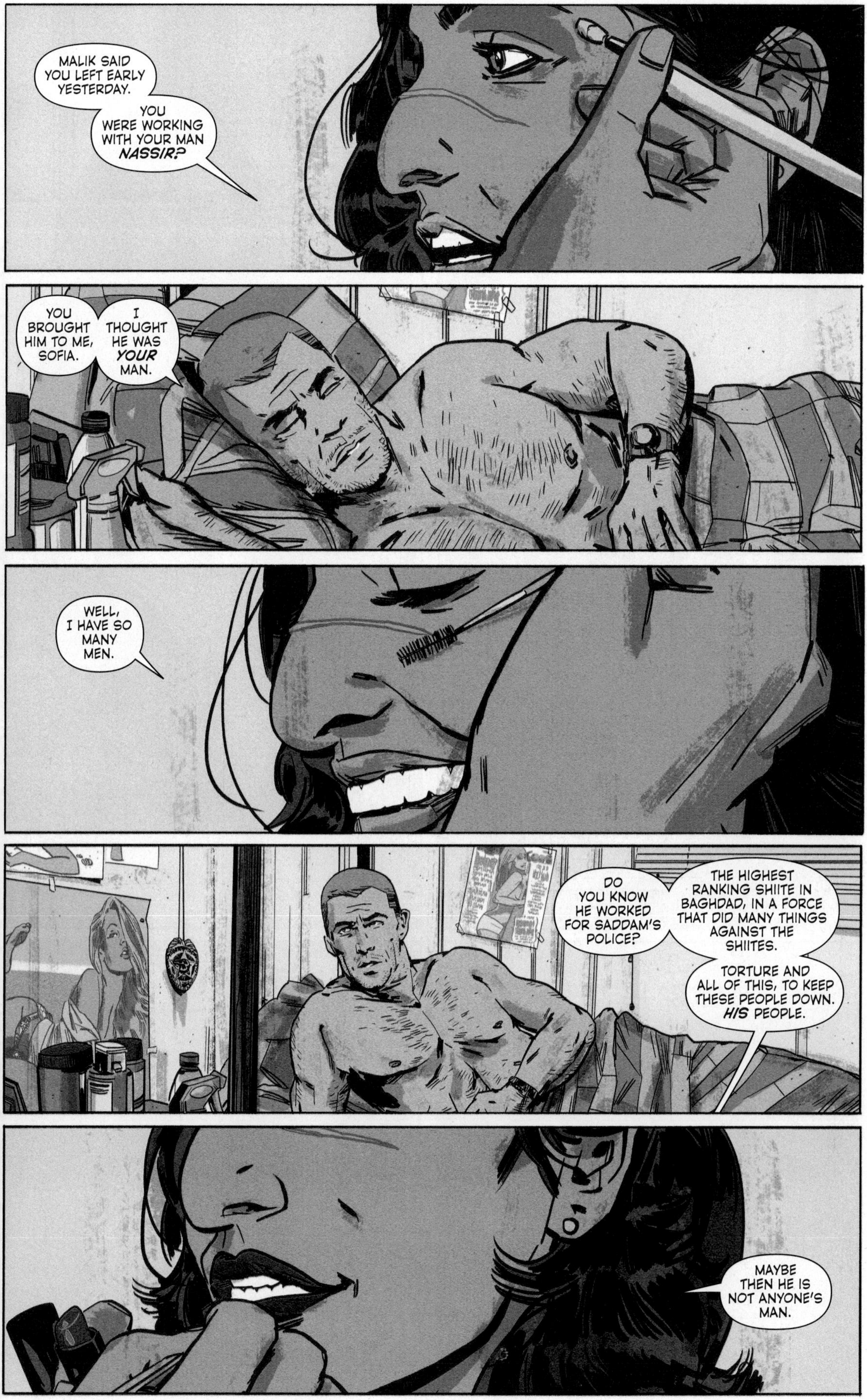
MALIK SAID YOU LEFT EARLY YESTERDAY.
YOU WERE WORKING WITH YOUR MAN *NASSIR?*
YOU BROUGHT HIM TO ME, SOFIA.
I THOUGHT HE WAS *YOUR* MAN.
WELL, I HAVE SO MANY MEN.
DO YOU KNOW HE WORKED FOR SADDAM'S POLICE?
THE HIGHEST RANKING SHIITE IN BAGHDAD, IN A FORCE THAT DID MANY THINGS AGAINST THE SHIITES.
TORTURE AND ALL OF THIS, TO KEEP THESE PEOPLE DOWN. *HIS* PEOPLE.
MAYBE THEN HE IS NOT ANYONE'S MAN.

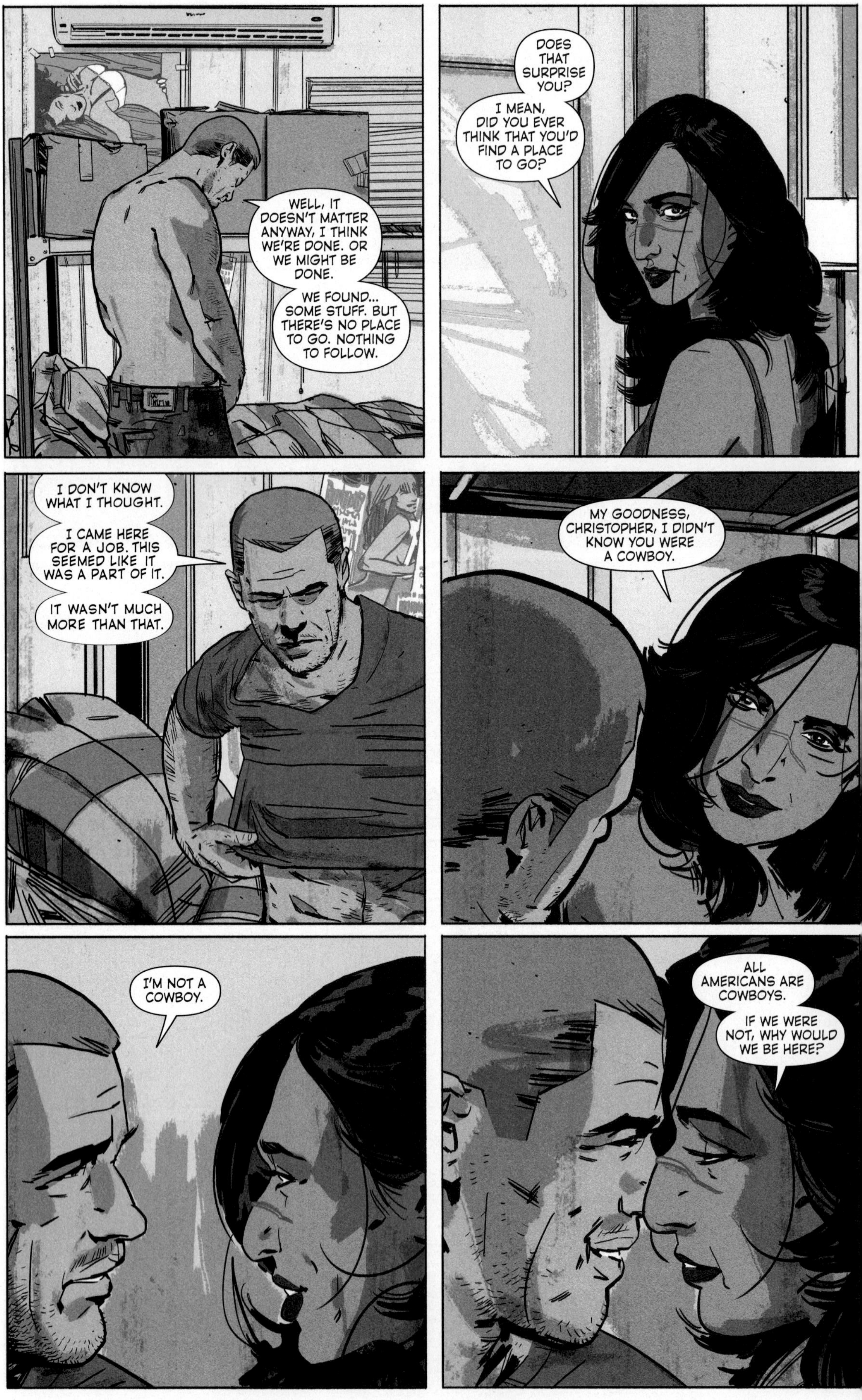
WELL, IT DOESN'T MATTER ANYWAY, I THINK WE'RE DONE. OR WE MIGHT BE DONE.
WE FOUND... SOME STUFF. BUT THERE'S NO PLACE TO GO. NOTHING TO FOLLOW.
DOES THAT SURPRISE YOU?
I MEAN, DID YOU EVER THINK THAT YOU'D FIND A PLACE TO GO?
I DON'T KNOW WHAT I THOUGHT.
I CAME HERE FOR A JOB. THIS SEEMED LIKE IT WAS A PART OF IT.
IT WASN'T MUCH MORE THAN THAT.
MY GOODNESS, CHRISTOPHER, I DIDN'T KNOW YOU WERE A COWBOY.
I'M NOT A COWBOY.
ALL AMERICANS ARE COWBOYS.
IF WE WERE NOT, WHY WOULD WE BE HERE?

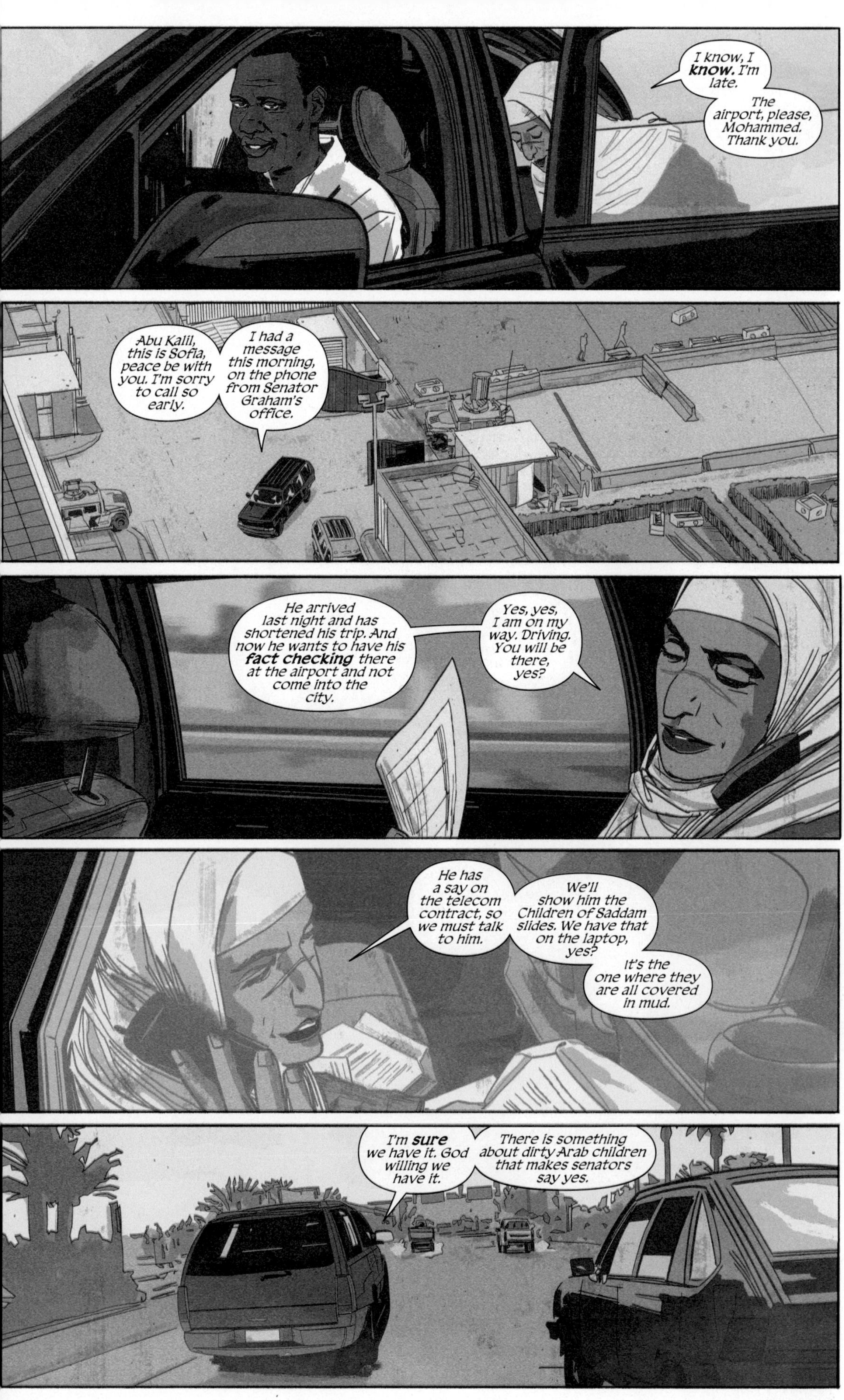
I know, I **know.** I'm late.
The airport, please, Mohammed. Thank you.
Abu Kalil, this is Sofia, peace be with you. I'm sorry to call so early.
I had a message this morning, on the phone from Senator Graham's office.
He arrived last night and has shortened his trip. And now he wants to have his **fact checking** there at the airport and not come into the city.
Yes, yes, I am on my way. Driving. You will be there, yes?
He has a say on the telecom contract, so we must talk to him.
We'll show him the Children of Saddam slides. We have that on the laptop, yes?
It's the one where they are all covered in mud.
I'm **sure** we have it. God willing we have it.
There is something about dirty Arab children that makes senators say yes.

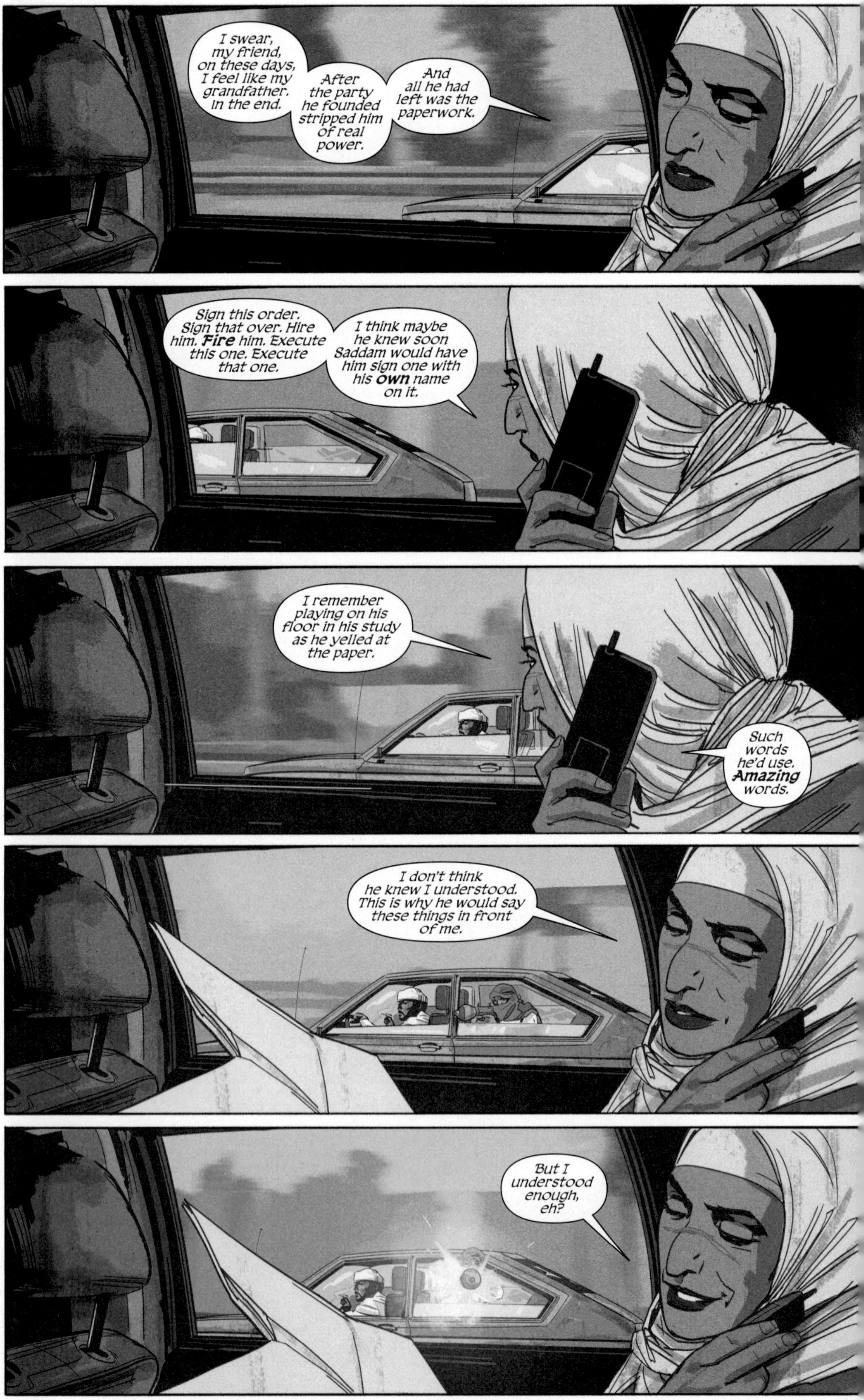

I swear, my friend, on these days, I feel like my grandfather. In the end.
After the party he founded stripped him of real power.
And all he had left was the paperwork.
Sign this order. Sign that over. Hire him. **Fire** him. Execute this one. Execute that one.
I think maybe he knew soon Saddam would have him sign one with his **own** name on it.
I remember playing on his floor in his study as he yelled at the paper.
Such words he'd use. **Amazing** words.
I don't think he knew I understood. This is why he would say these things in front of me.
But I understood enough, eh?

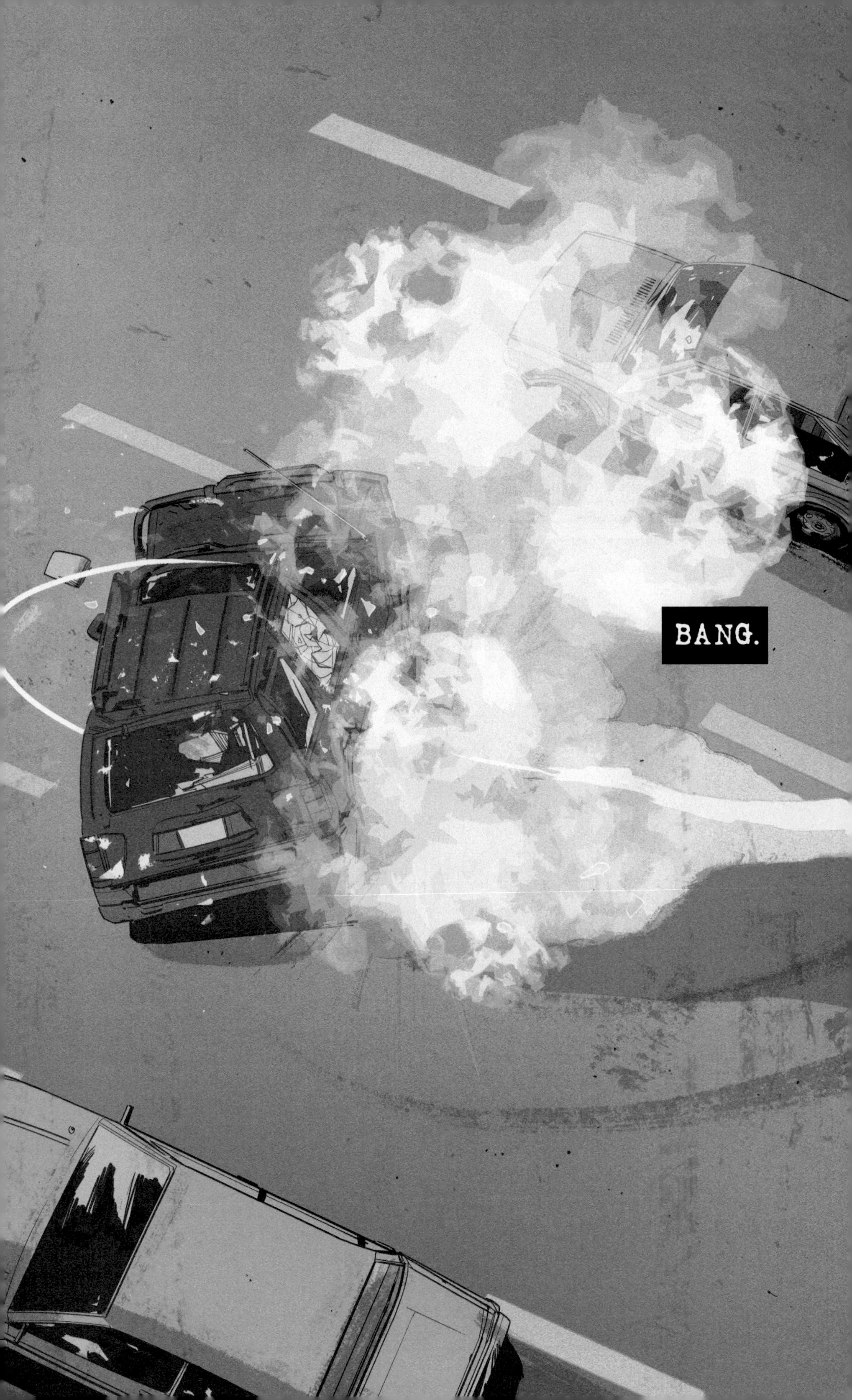
BANG.

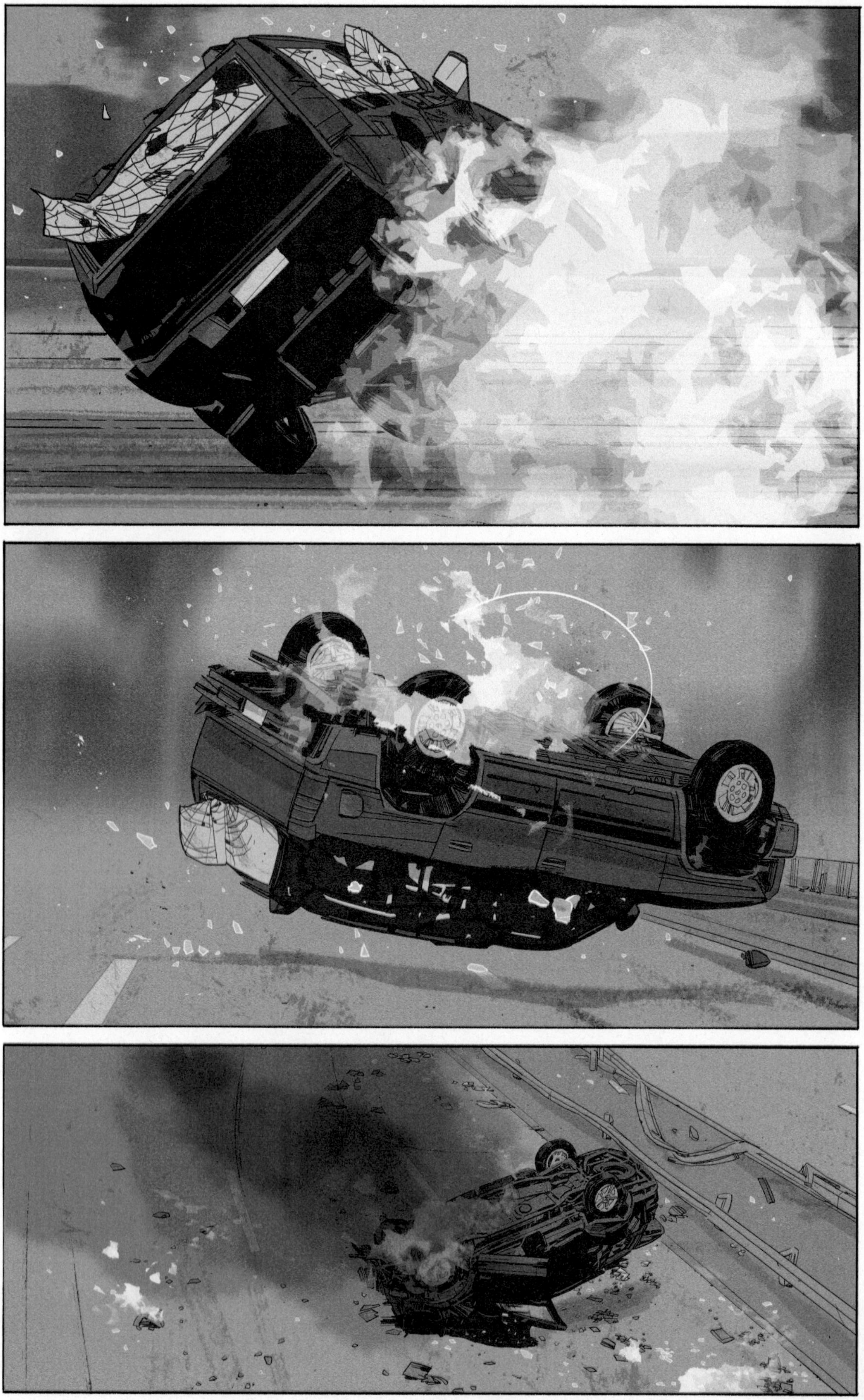

Do you know why you are here?

This is known only to God.

You are a religious man then?

I am a **Muslim**.

And all Muslims are the same?

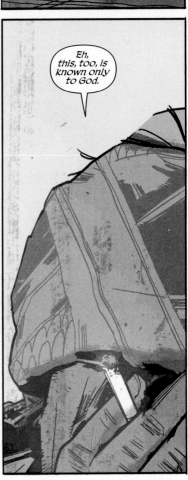

Eh, this, too, is known only to God.

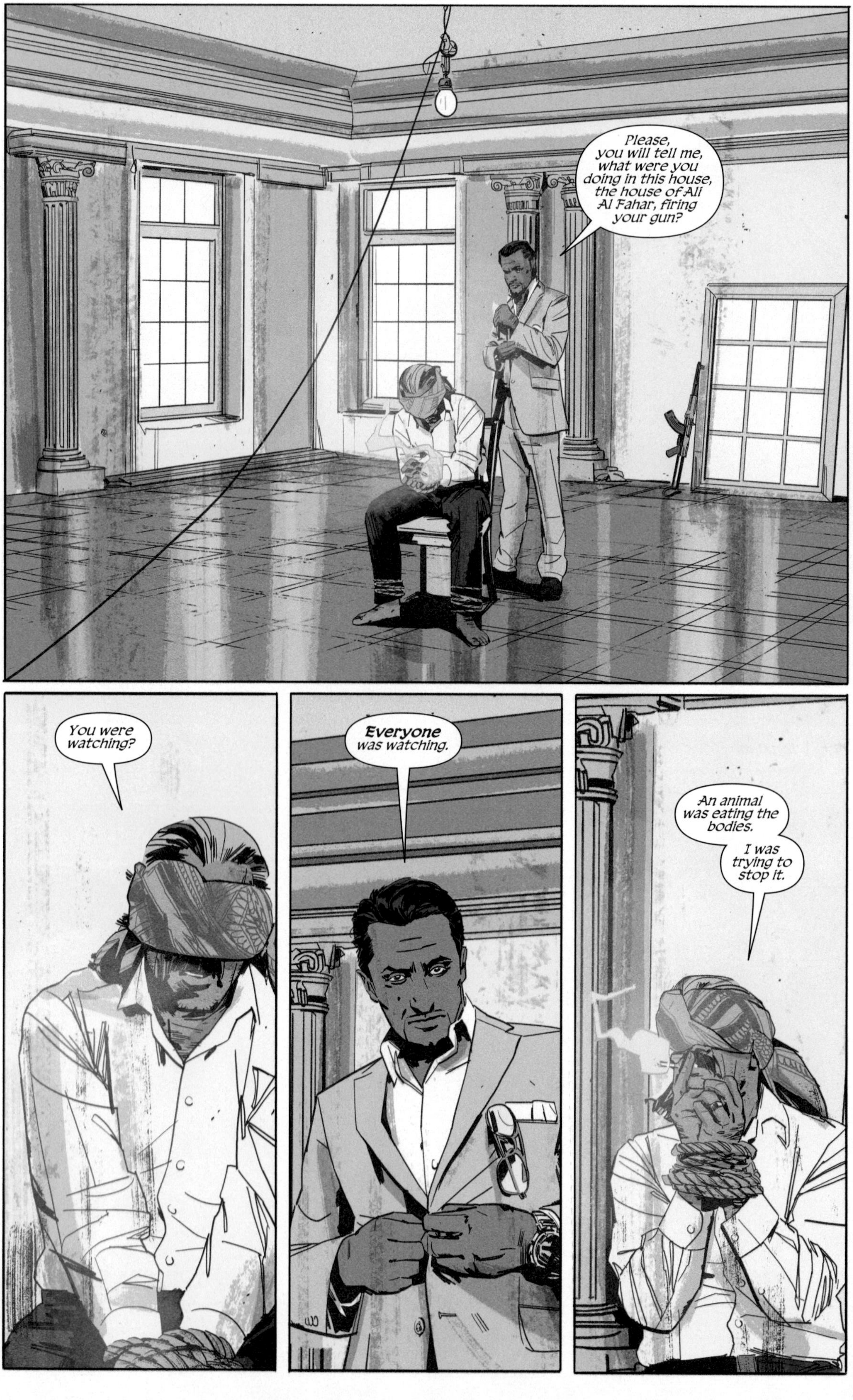
Please, you will tell me, what were you doing in this house, the house of Ali Al Fahar, firing your gun?
You were watching?
Everyone was watching.
An animal was eating the bodies.
I was trying to stop it.

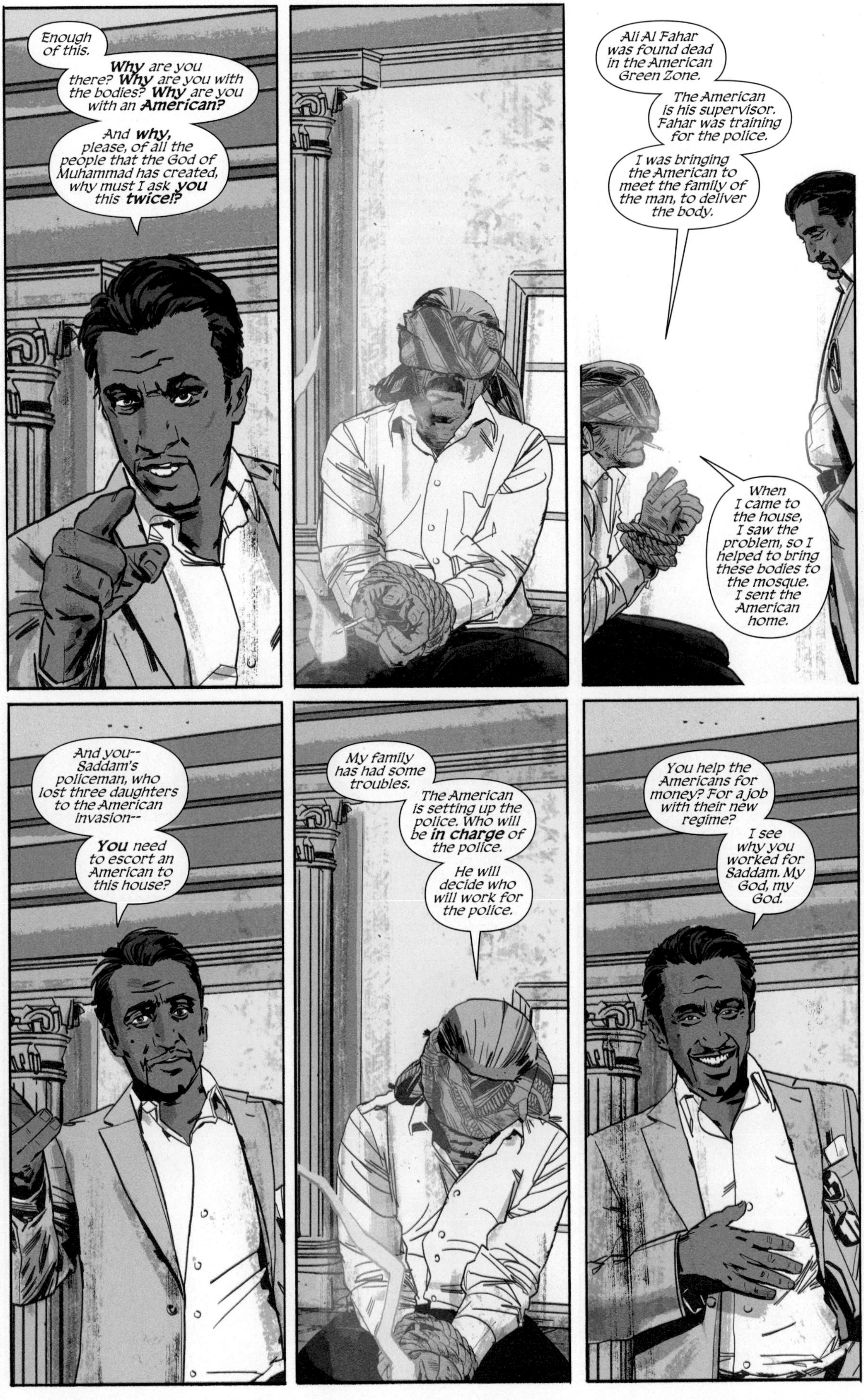
Enough of this.
Why are you there? Why are you with the bodies? Why are you with an American?
And why, please, of all the people that the God of Muhammad has created, why must I ask you this twice!?
Ali Al Fahar was found dead in the American Green Zone.
The American is his supervisor. Fahar was training for the police.
I was bringing the American to meet the family of the man, to deliver the body.
When I came to the house, I saw the problem, so I helped to bring these bodies to the mosque. I sent the American home.
And you-- Saddam's policeman, who lost three daughters to the American invasion--
You need to escort an American to this house?
My family has had some troubles.
The American is setting up the police. Who will be in charge of the police.
He will decide who will work for the police.
You help the Americans for money? For a job with their new regime?
I see why you worked for Saddam. My God, my God.

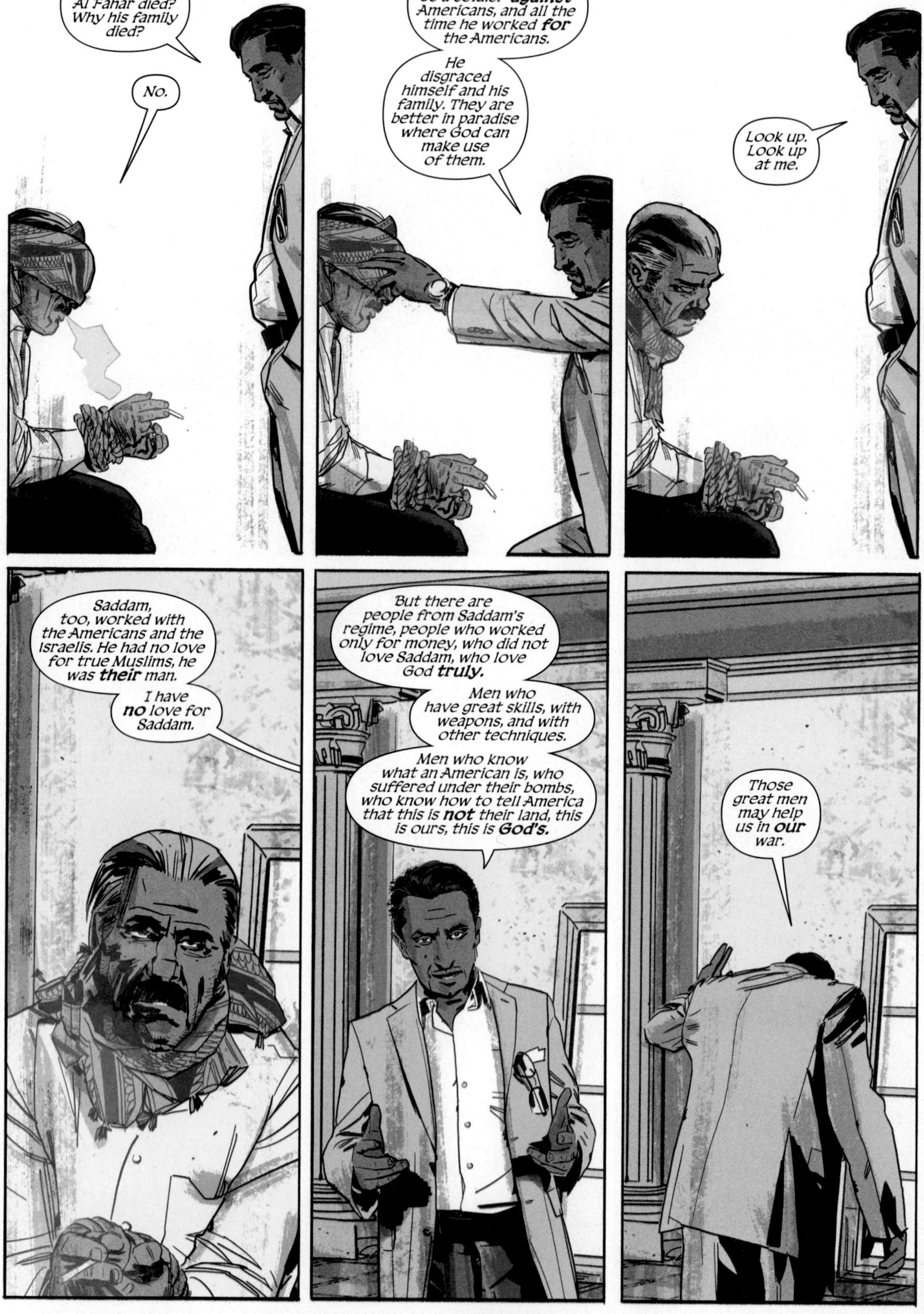

Do you know why Ali Al Fahar died? Why his family died?
No.
He was a traitor. He said he loved God, he prayed next to us, but in his heart, he hated God, hated all Muslims.
He said he was ready to be a soldier against Americans, and all the time he worked for the Americans.
He disgraced himself and his family. They are better in paradise where God can make use of them.
Look up. Look up at me.
Saddam, too, worked with the Americans and the Israelis. He had no love for true Muslims, he was their man.
I have no love for Saddam.
But there are people from Saddam's regime, people who worked only for money, who did not love Saddam, who love God truly.
Men who have great skills, with weapons, and with other techniques.
Men who know what an American is, who suffered under their bombs, who know how to tell America that this is not their land, this is ours, this is God's.
Those great men may help us in our war.

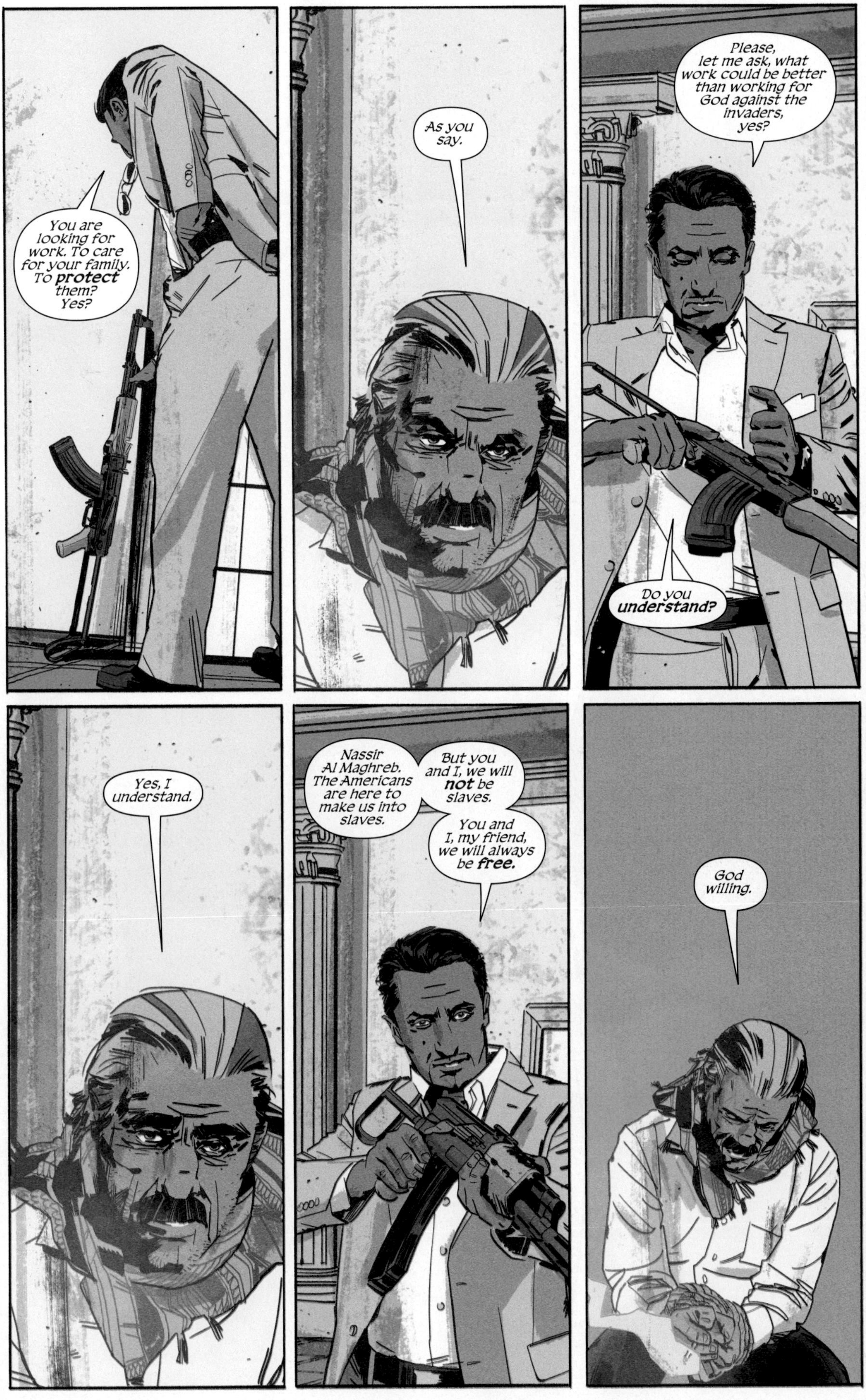
You are looking for work. To care for your family. To **protect** them? Yes?
As you say.
Please, let me ask, what work could be better than working for God against the invaders, yes?
Do you **understand?**
Yes, I understand.
Nassir Al Maghreb. The Americans are here to make us into slaves.
But you and I, we will **not** be slaves.
You and I, my friend, we will always be **free.**
God willing.

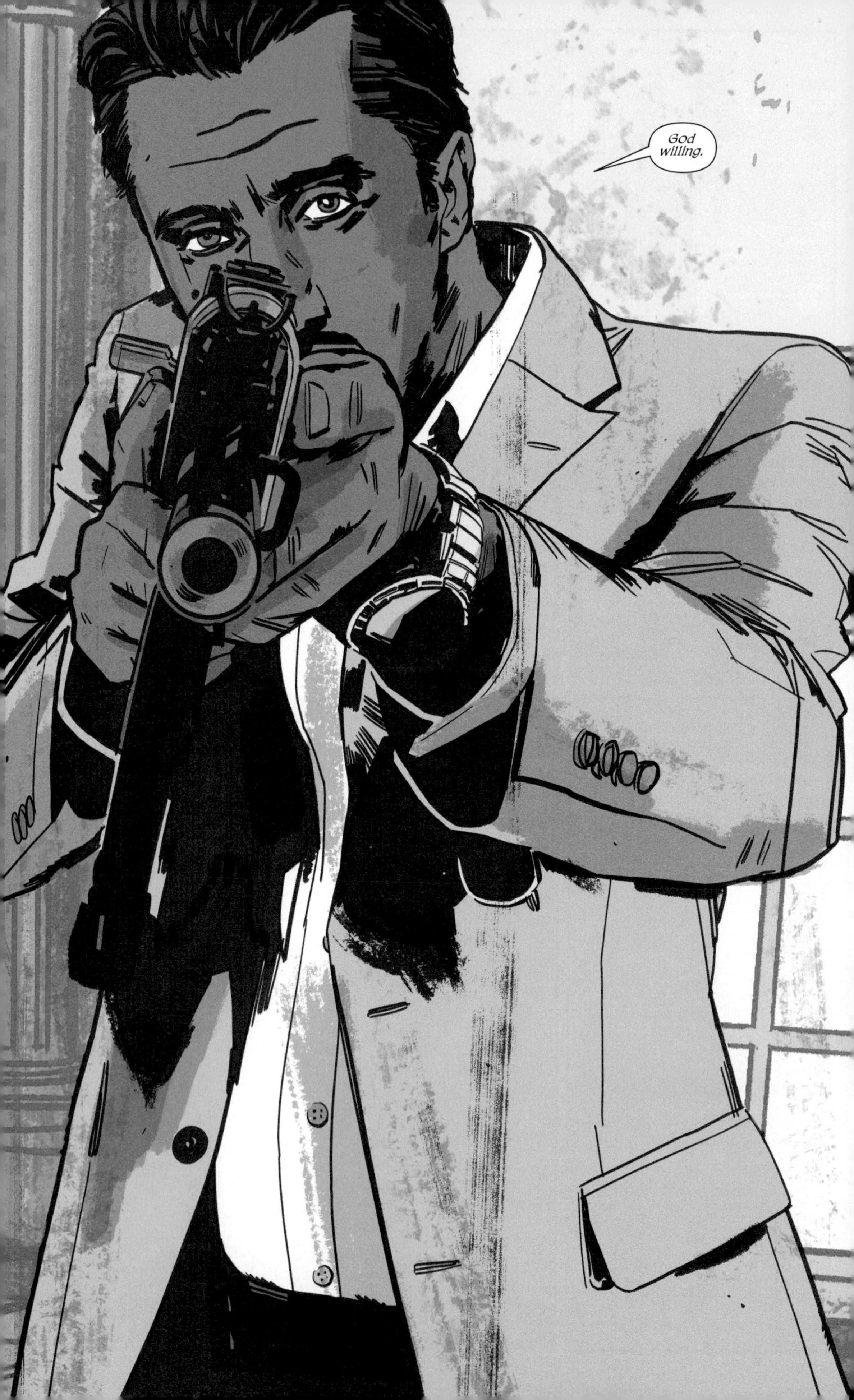
God willing.

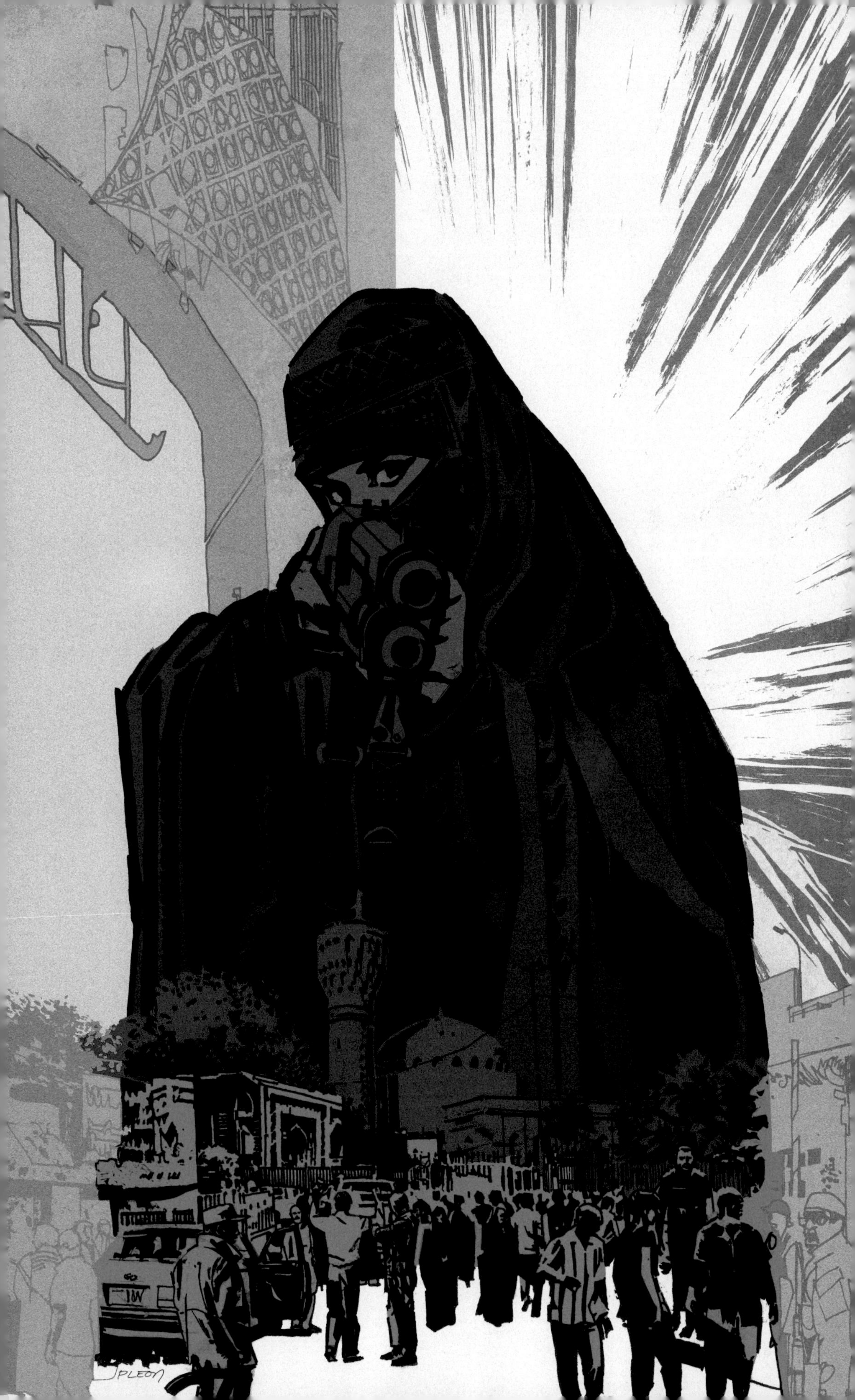
JPLEON

PART FOUR

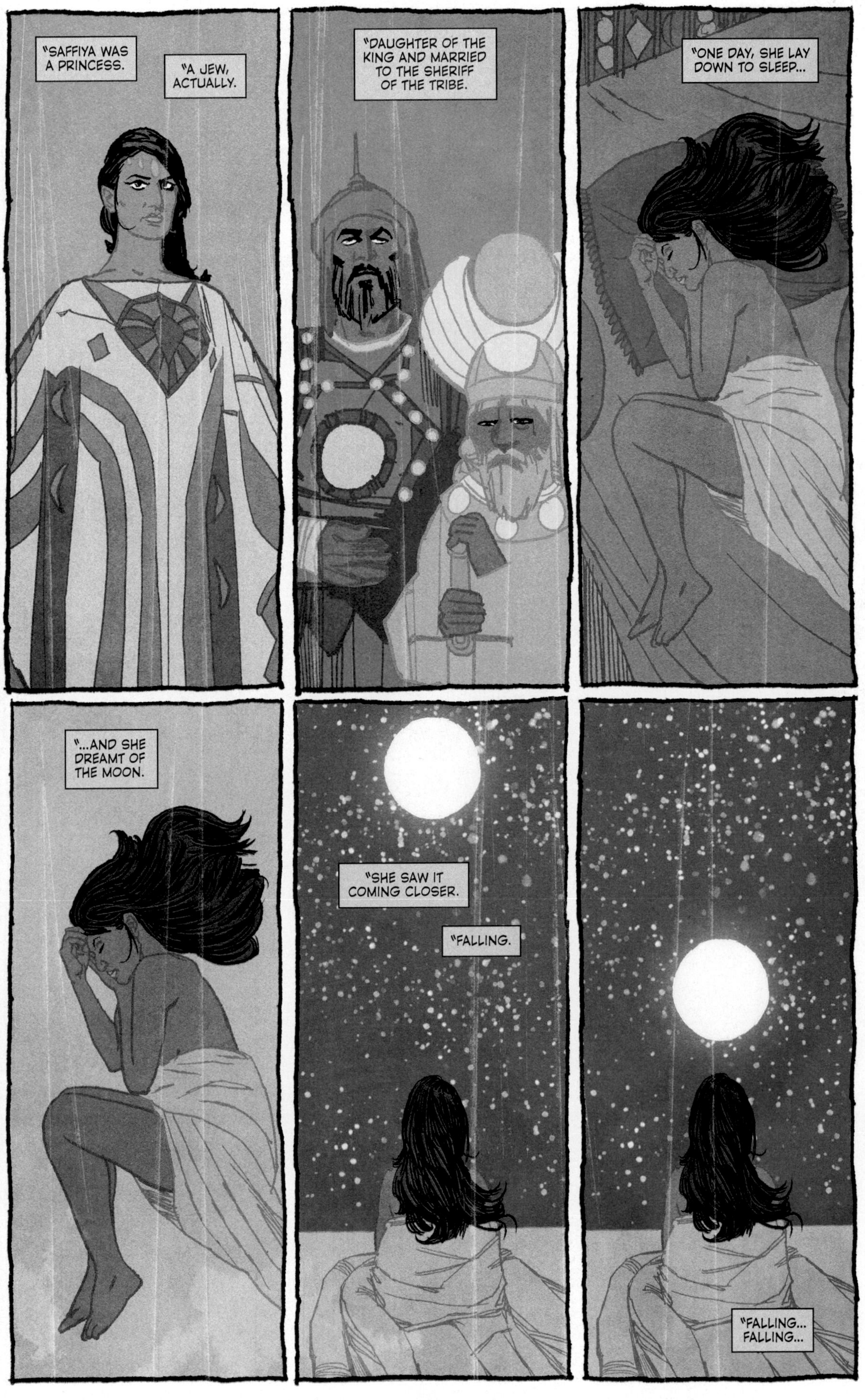
"SAFFIYA WAS A PRINCESS.
"A JEW, ACTUALLY.
"DAUGHTER OF THE KING AND MARRIED TO THE SHERIFF OF THE TRIBE.
"ONE DAY, SHE LAY DOWN TO SLEEP...
"...AND SHE DREAMT OF THE MOON.
"SHE SAW IT COMING CLOSER.
"FALLING.
"FALLING... FALLING...

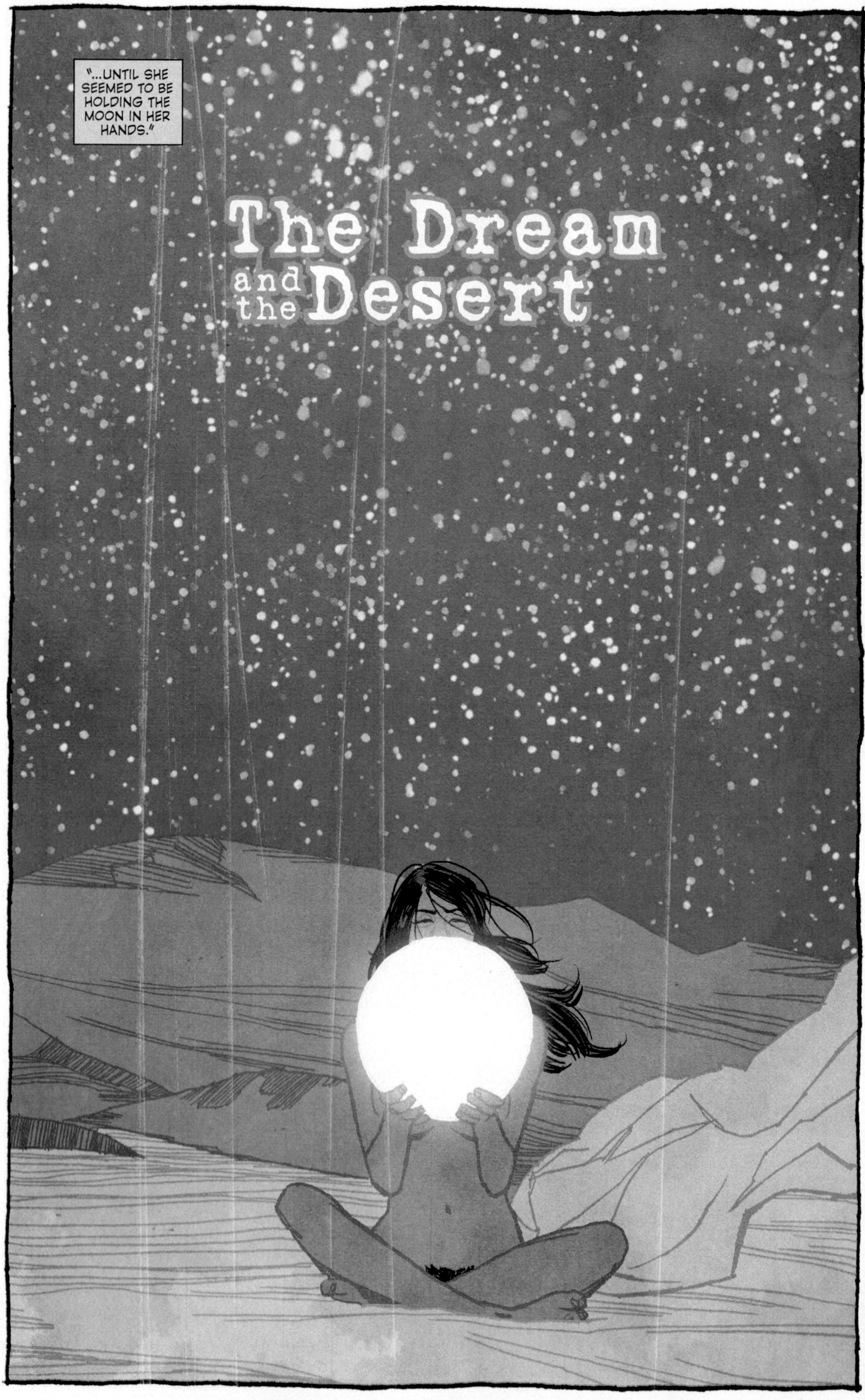
"...UNTIL SHE SEEMED TO BE HOLDING THE MOON IN HER HANDS."
The Dream and the Desert

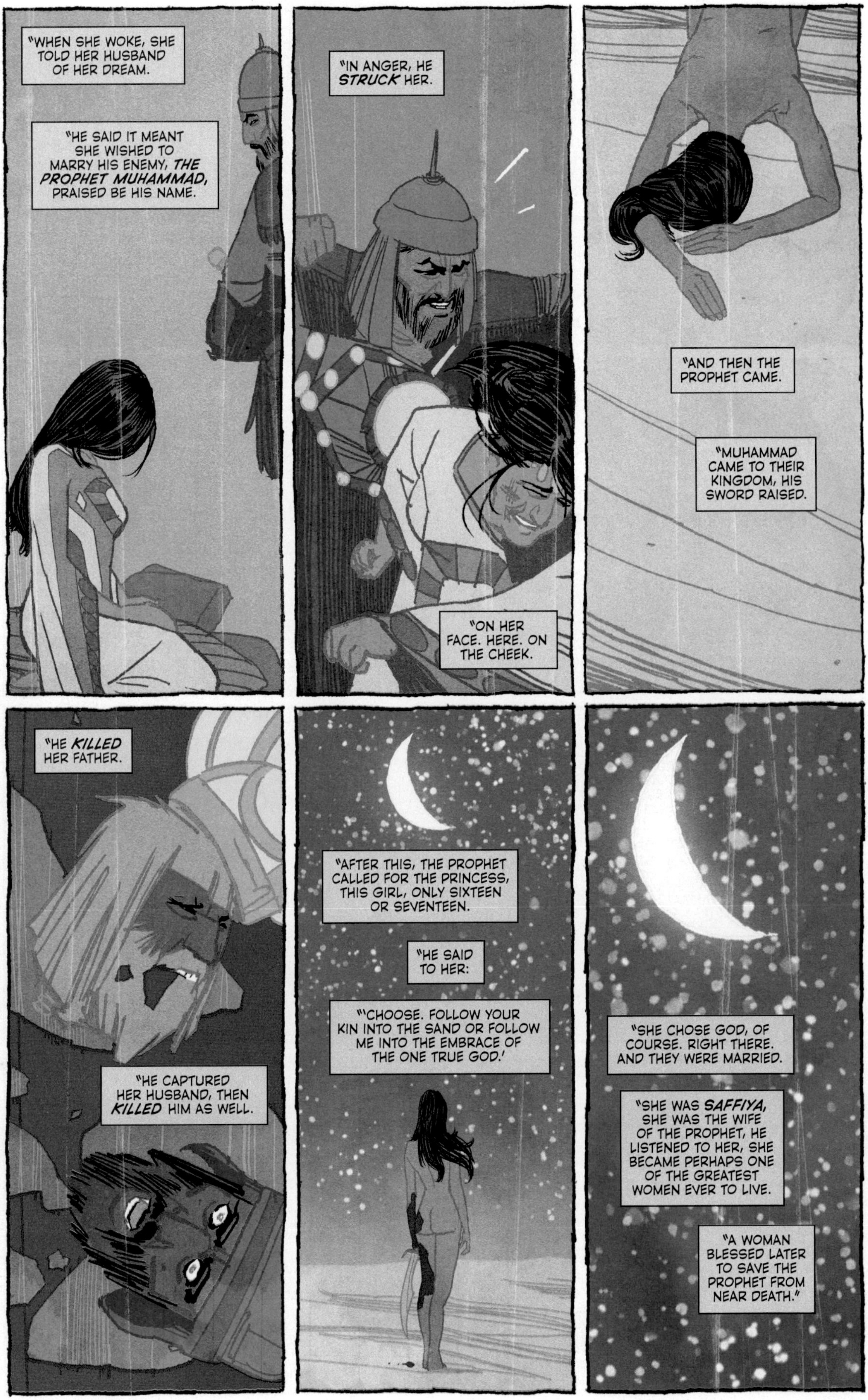
"WHEN SHE WOKE, SHE TOLD HER HUSBAND OF HER DREAM.
"HE SAID IT MEANT SHE WISHED TO MARRY HIS ENEMY, *THE PROPHET MUHAMMAD,* PRAISED BE HIS NAME.
"IN ANGER, HE *STRUCK* HER.
"ON HER FACE. HERE. ON THE CHEEK.
"AND THEN THE PROPHET CAME.
"MUHAMMAD CAME TO THEIR KINGDOM, HIS SWORD RAISED.
"HE *KILLED* HER FATHER.
"HE CAPTURED HER HUSBAND, THEN *KILLED* HIM AS WELL.
"AFTER THIS, THE PROPHET CALLED FOR THE PRINCESS, THIS GIRL, ONLY SIXTEEN OR SEVENTEEN.
"HE SAID TO HER:
"'CHOOSE. FOLLOW YOUR KIN INTO THE SAND OR FOLLOW ME INTO THE EMBRACE OF THE ONE TRUE GOD.'
"SHE CHOSE GOD, OF COURSE. RIGHT THERE. AND THEY WERE MARRIED.
"SHE WAS *SAFFIYA,* SHE WAS THE WIFE OF THE PROPHET, HE LISTENED TO HER, SHE BECAME PERHAPS ONE OF THE GREATEST WOMEN EVER TO LIVE.
"A WOMAN BLESSED LATER TO SAVE THE PROPHET FROM NEAR DEATH."

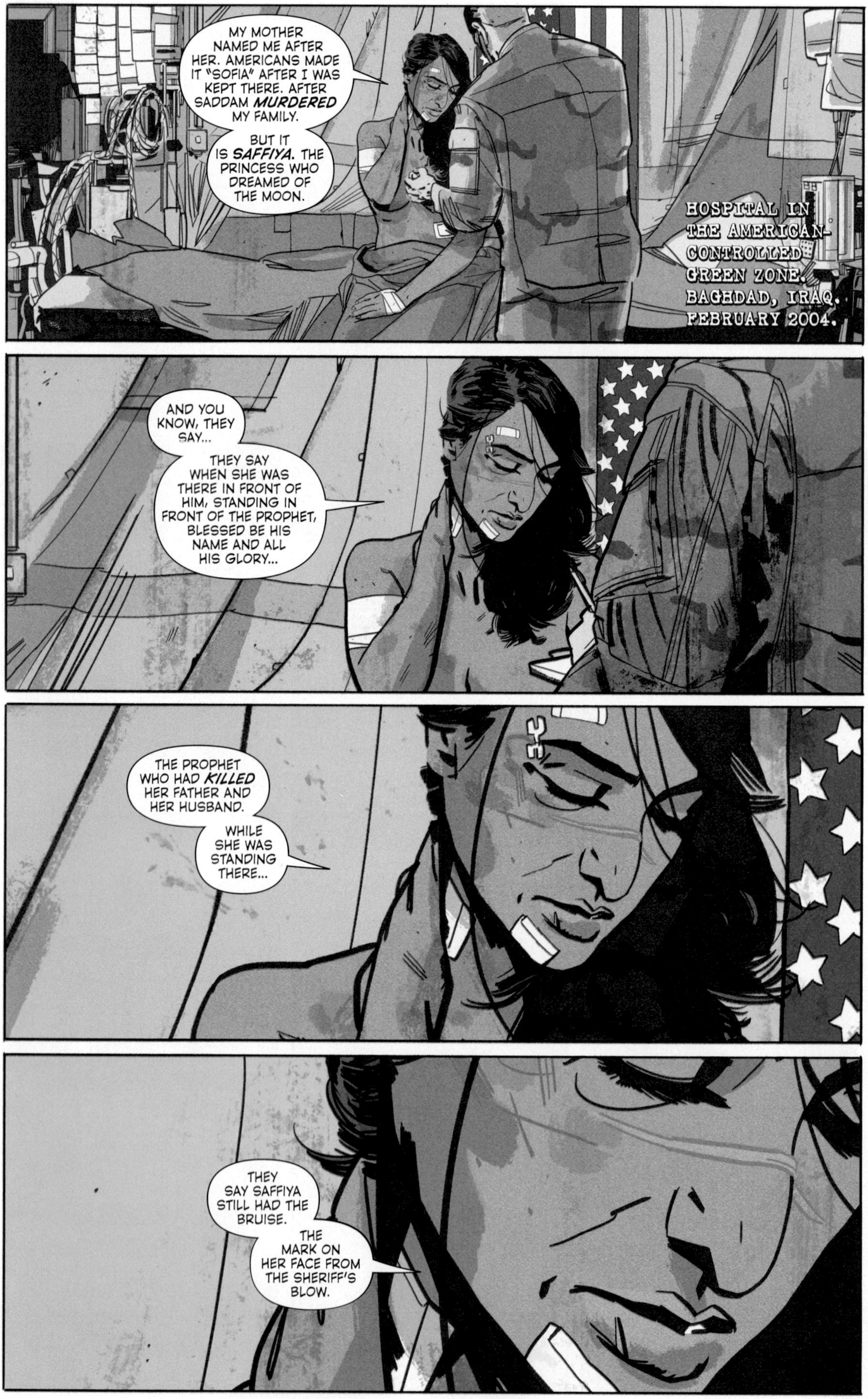
MY MOTHER NAMED ME AFTER HER. AMERICANS MADE IT "SOFIA" AFTER I WAS KEPT THERE. AFTER SADDAM MURDERED MY FAMILY.
BUT IT IS SAFFIYA. THE PRINCESS WHO DREAMED OF THE MOON.
HOSPITAL IN THE AMERICAN-CONTROLLED GREEN ZONE. BAGHDAD, IRAQ. FEBRUARY 2004.
AND YOU KNOW, THEY SAY...
THEY SAY WHEN SHE WAS THERE IN FRONT OF HIM, STANDING IN FRONT OF THE PROPHET, BLESSED BE HIS NAME AND ALL HIS GLORY...
THE PROPHET WHO HAD KILLED HER FATHER AND HER HUSBAND.
WHILE SHE WAS STANDING THERE...
THEY SAY SAFFIYA STILL HAD THE BRUISE.
THE MARK ON HER FACE FROM THE SHERIFF'S BLOW.

EVERYTHING PRETTY MUCH CHECKS OUT ALL RIGHT, I'M HAPPY TO REPORT.

NOT A LOT OF PEOPLE WHO HAVE BEEN HIT BY AN *RPG* CAN SAY THAT. IT'S A LITTLE MIRACLE.

MY VEHICLE WAS *LEVEL-SEVEN* ARMORED. IT IS NOT A MIRACLE.

IT IS PREPARATION.

HMMM. WELL, EITHER WAY, RIGHT?

ANY QUESTIONS BEFORE I GO?

YES, PLEASE, HOW LONG? I WOULD LIKE TO KNOW.

BEFORE IT... IT *PASSES,* I MEAN.

"PASSES" IS NOT THE RIGHT WORD. BUT YOU UNDERSTAND, YES?

RIGHT, YEAH, HARD TO SAY, HONESTLY. EVERY PREGNANCY NOT BROUGHT TO TERM IS DIFFERENT.

YOU SAY YOU WERE PROBABLY AT ABOUT SIX OR SEVEN WEEKS? IT SHOULDN'T BE TOO LONG.

THE FETUS SHOULD "PASS," AS *YOU* SAY, IN A FEW DAYS. MAYBE A WEEK OR SO.

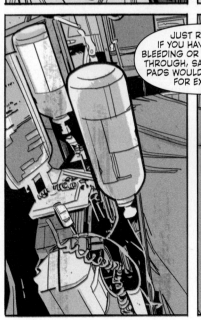

JUST REMEMBER, IF YOU HAVE EXCESSIVE BLEEDING OR PAIN--BLEEDING THROUGH, SAY, TWO NORMAL PADS WOULD BE EXCESSIVE, FOR EXAMPLE--

--THEN PLEASE CONTACT US *IMMEDIATELY.*

OR A LOCAL DOCTOR, IF YOU PREFER, OF COURSE.

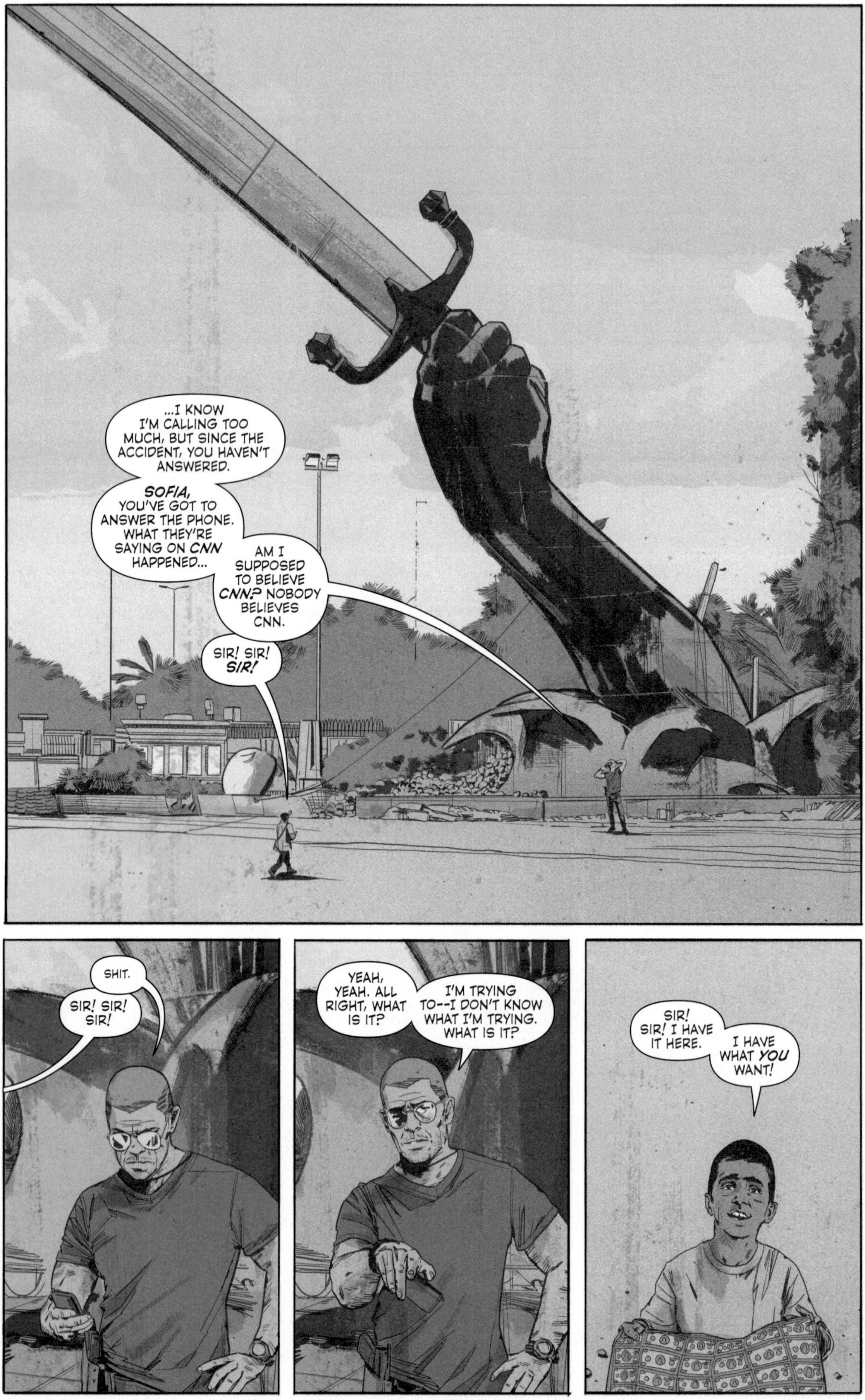
...I KNOW I'M CALLING TOO MUCH, BUT SINCE THE ACCIDENT, YOU HAVEN'T ANSWERED.
SOFIA, YOU'VE GOT TO ANSWER THE PHONE. WHAT THEY'RE SAYING ON *CNN* HAPPENED...
AM I SUPPOSED TO BELIEVE *CNN?* NOBODY BELIEVES CNN.
SIR! SIR! *SIR!*
SHIT.
SIR! SIR! SIR!
YEAH, YEAH. ALL RIGHT, WHAT IS IT?
I'M TRYING TO--I DON'T KNOW WHAT I'M TRYING. WHAT IS IT?
SIR! SIR! I HAVE IT HERE.
I HAVE WHAT *YOU* WANT!

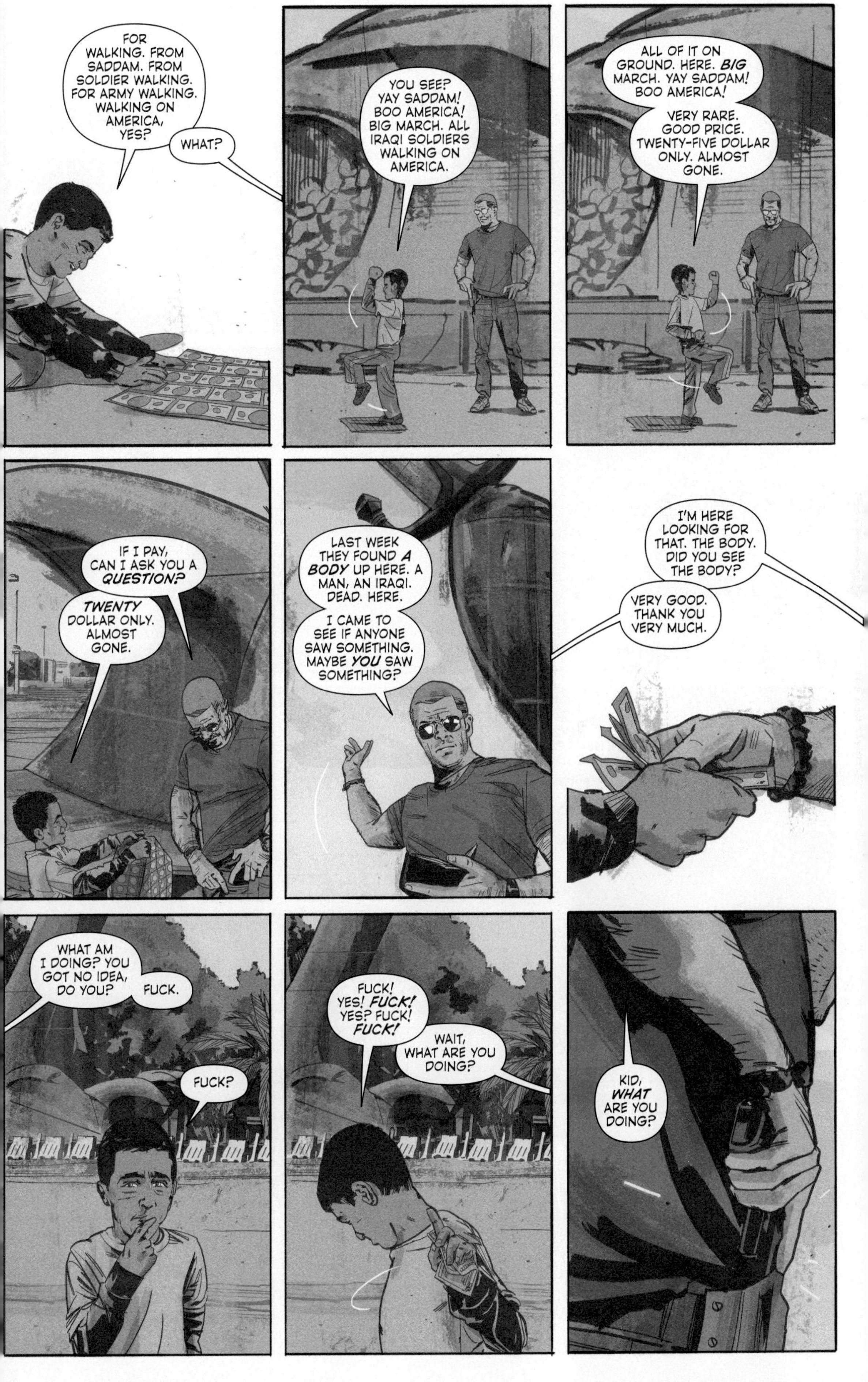
FOR WALKING. FROM SADDAM. FROM SOLDIER WALKING. FOR ARMY WALKING. WALKING ON AMERICA, YES?
WHAT?
YOU SEE? YAY SADDAM! BOO AMERICA! BIG MARCH. ALL IRAQI SOLDIERS WALKING ON AMERICA.
ALL OF IT ON GROUND. HERE. BIG MARCH. YAY SADDAM! BOO AMERICA!
VERY RARE. GOOD PRICE. TWENTY-FIVE DOLLAR ONLY. ALMOST GONE.
IF I PAY, CAN I ASK YOU A QUESTION?
TWENTY DOLLAR ONLY. ALMOST GONE.
LAST WEEK THEY FOUND A BODY UP HERE. A MAN, AN IRAQI. DEAD. HERE.
I CAME TO SEE IF ANYONE SAW SOMETHING. MAYBE YOU SAW SOMETHING?
I'M HERE LOOKING FOR THAT. THE BODY. DID YOU SEE THE BODY?
VERY GOOD. THANK YOU VERY MUCH.
WHAT AM I DOING? YOU GOT NO IDEA, DO YOU?
FUCK.
FUCK?
FUCK! YES! FUCK! YES? FUCK! FUCK!
WAIT, WHAT ARE YOU DOING?
KID, WHAT ARE YOU DOING?

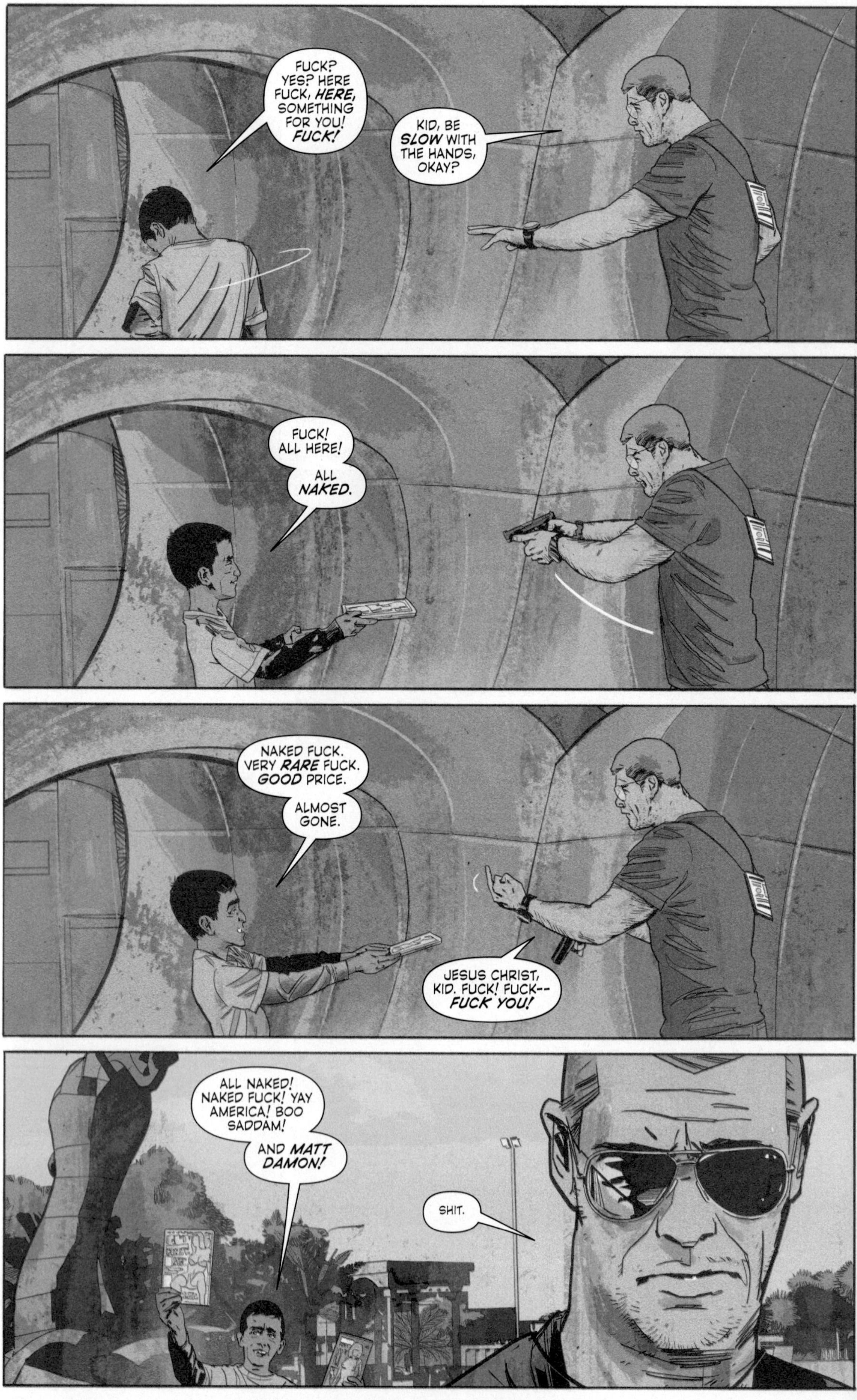
FUCK? YES? HERE FUCK, HERE, SOMETHING FOR YOU! FUCK!
KID, BE SLOW WITH THE HANDS, OKAY?
FUCK! ALL HERE!
ALL NAKED.
NAKED FUCK. VERY RARE FUCK. GOOD PRICE.
ALMOST GONE.
JESUS CHRIST, KID. FUCK! FUCK-- FUCK YOU!
ALL NAKED! NAKED FUCK! YAY AMERICA! BOO SADDAM!
AND MATT DAMON!
SHIT.

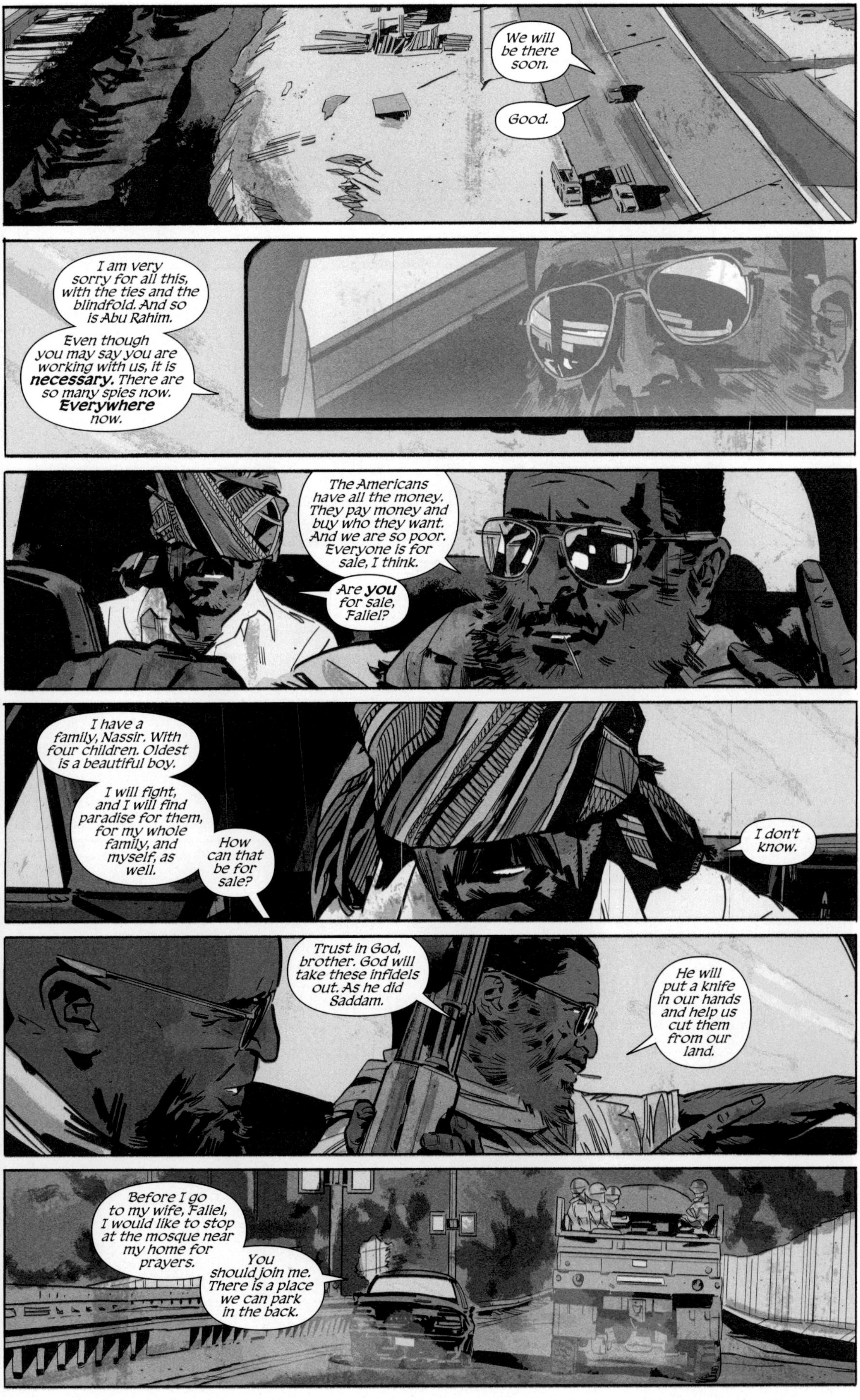
We will be there soon.
Good.
I am very sorry for all this, with the ties and the blindfold. And so is Abu Rahim.
Even though you may say you are working with us, it is **necessary.** There are so many spies now. **Everywhere** now.
The Americans have all the money. They pay money and buy who they want. And we are so poor. Everyone is for sale, I think.
Are **you** for sale, Faliel?
I have a family, Nassir. With four children. Oldest is a beautiful boy.
I will fight, and I will find paradise for them, for my whole family, and myself, as well.
How can that be for sale?
I don't know.
Trust in God, brother. God will take these infidels out. As he did Saddam.
He will put a knife in our hands and help us cut them from our land.
Before I go to my wife, Faliel, I would like to stop at the mosque near my home for prayers.
You should join me. There is a place we can park in the back.

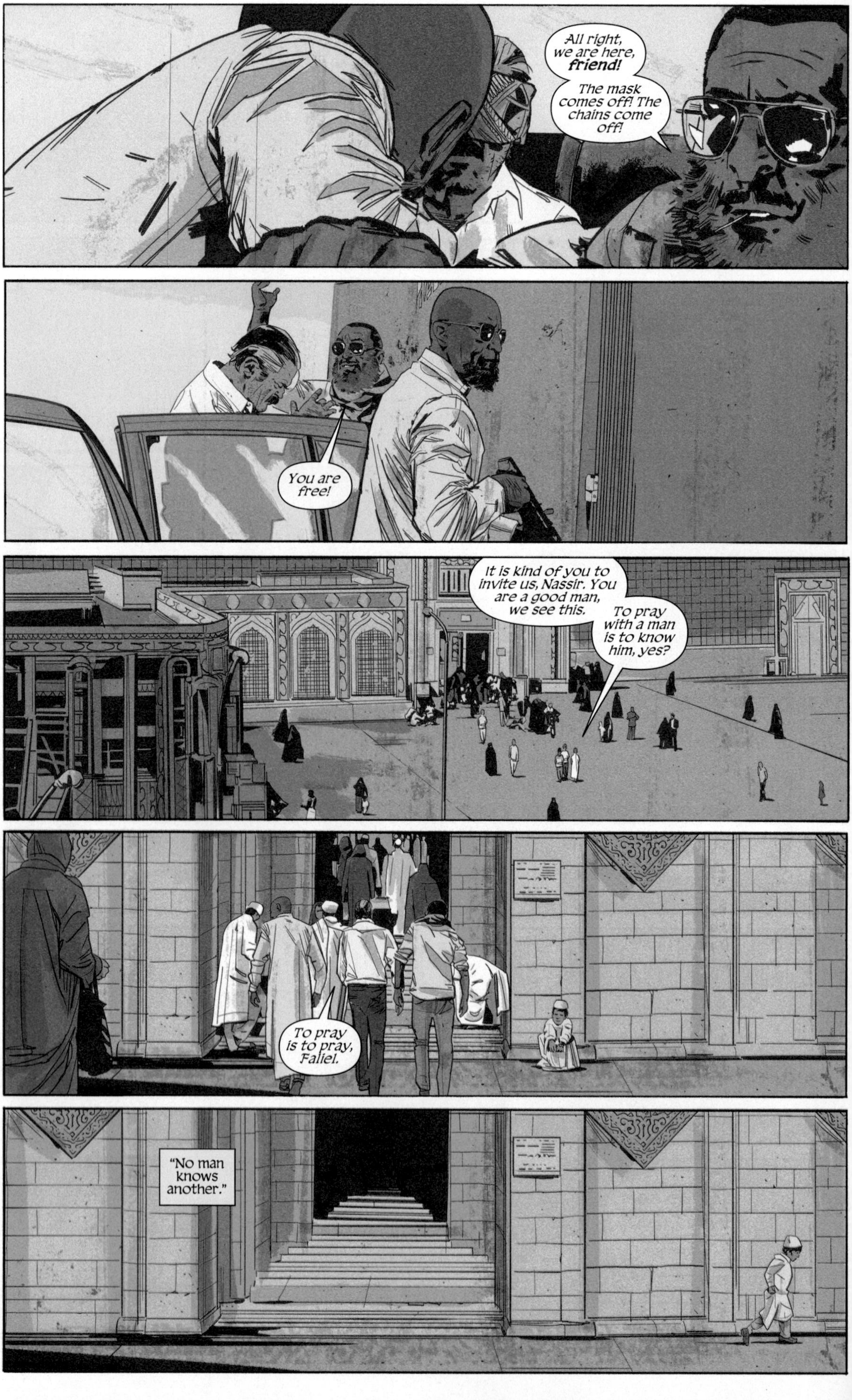
All right, we are here, **friend!**
The mask comes off! The chains come off!
You are free!
It is kind of you to invite us, Nassir. You are a good man, we see this.
To pray with a man is to know him, yes?
To pray is to pray, Faliel.
"No man knows another."

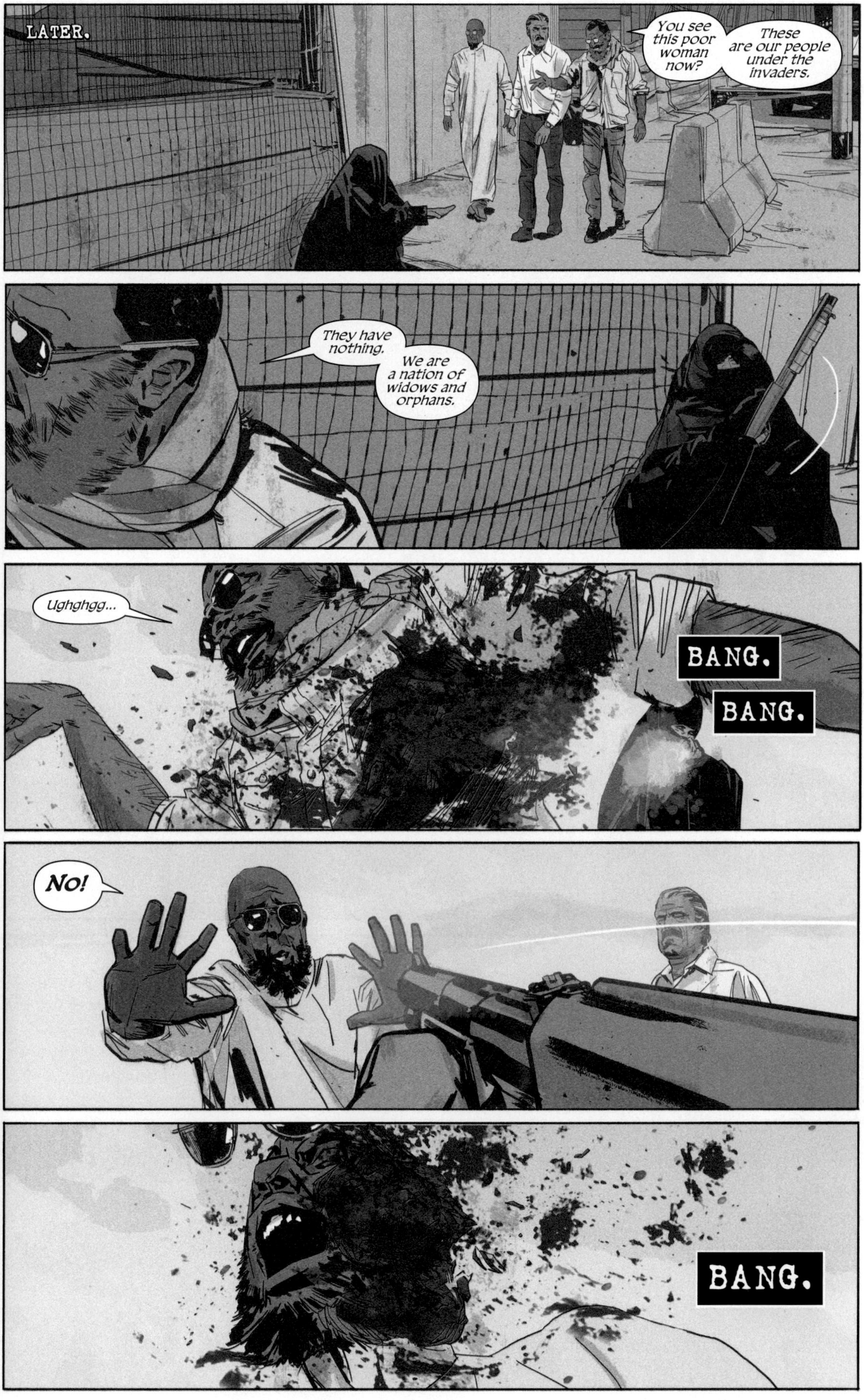
LATER.
You see this poor woman now?
These are our people under the invaders.
They have nothing.
We are a nation of widows and orphans.
Ughghgg...
BANG.
BANG.
No!
BANG.

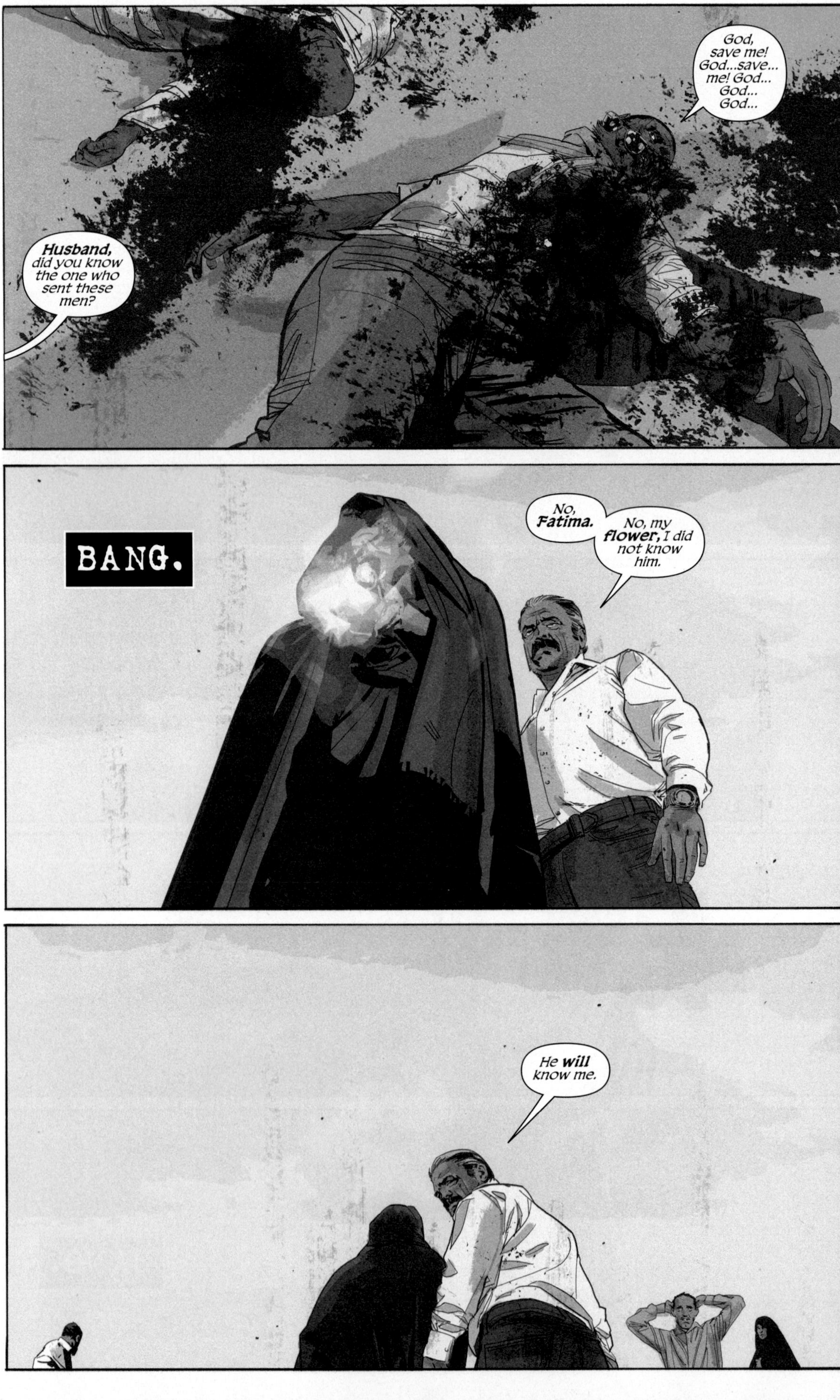
God, save me! God...save... me! God... God... God...
Husband, did you know the one who sent these men?
BANG.
No, Fatima.
No, my flower, I did not know him.
He will know me.

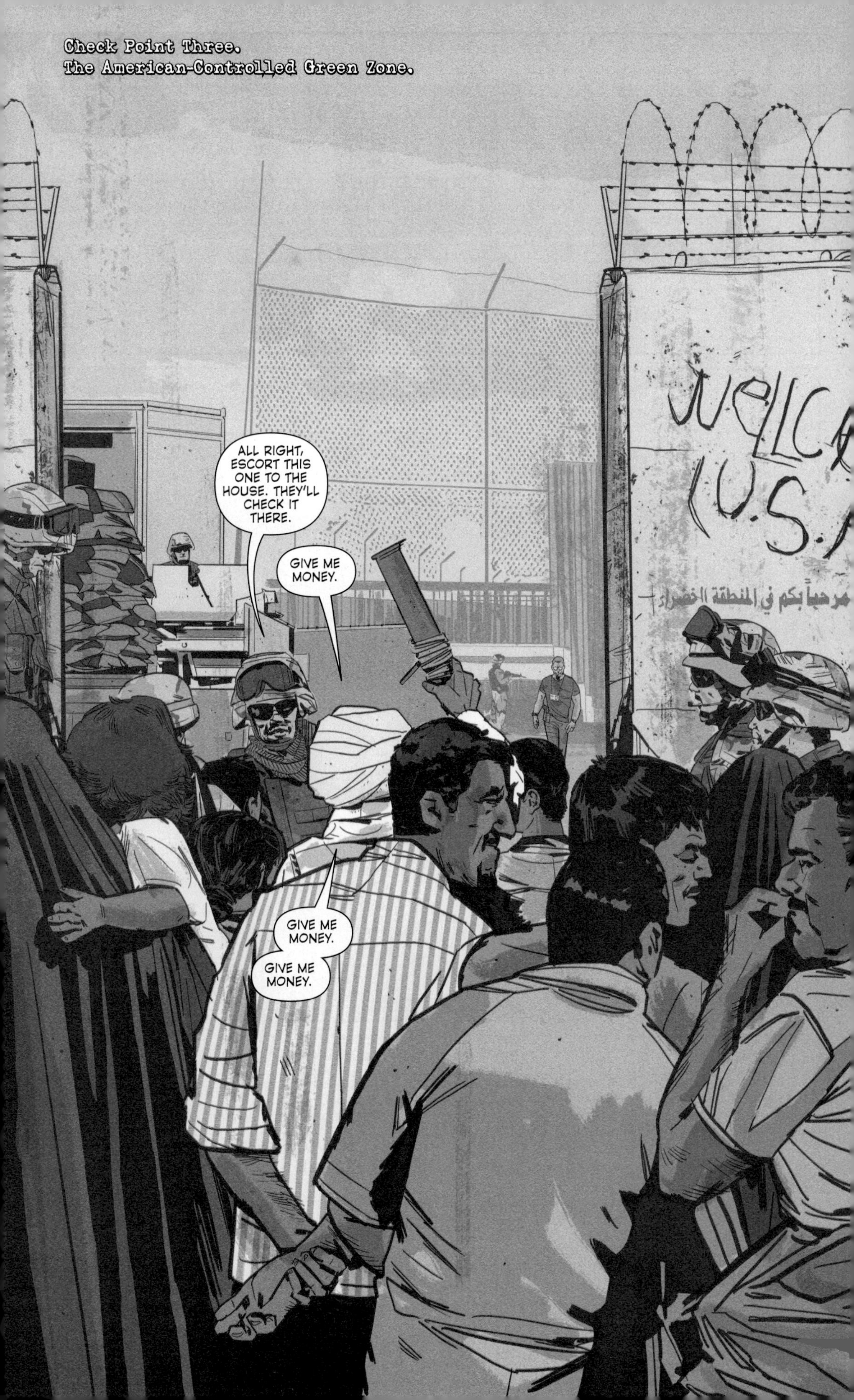
Check Point Three.
The American-Controlled Green Zone.
ALL RIGHT, ESCORT THIS ONE TO THE HOUSE. THEY'LL CHECK IT THERE.
GIVE ME MONEY.
مرحباً بكم في المنطقة الخضراء
GIVE ME MONEY.
GIVE ME MONEY.

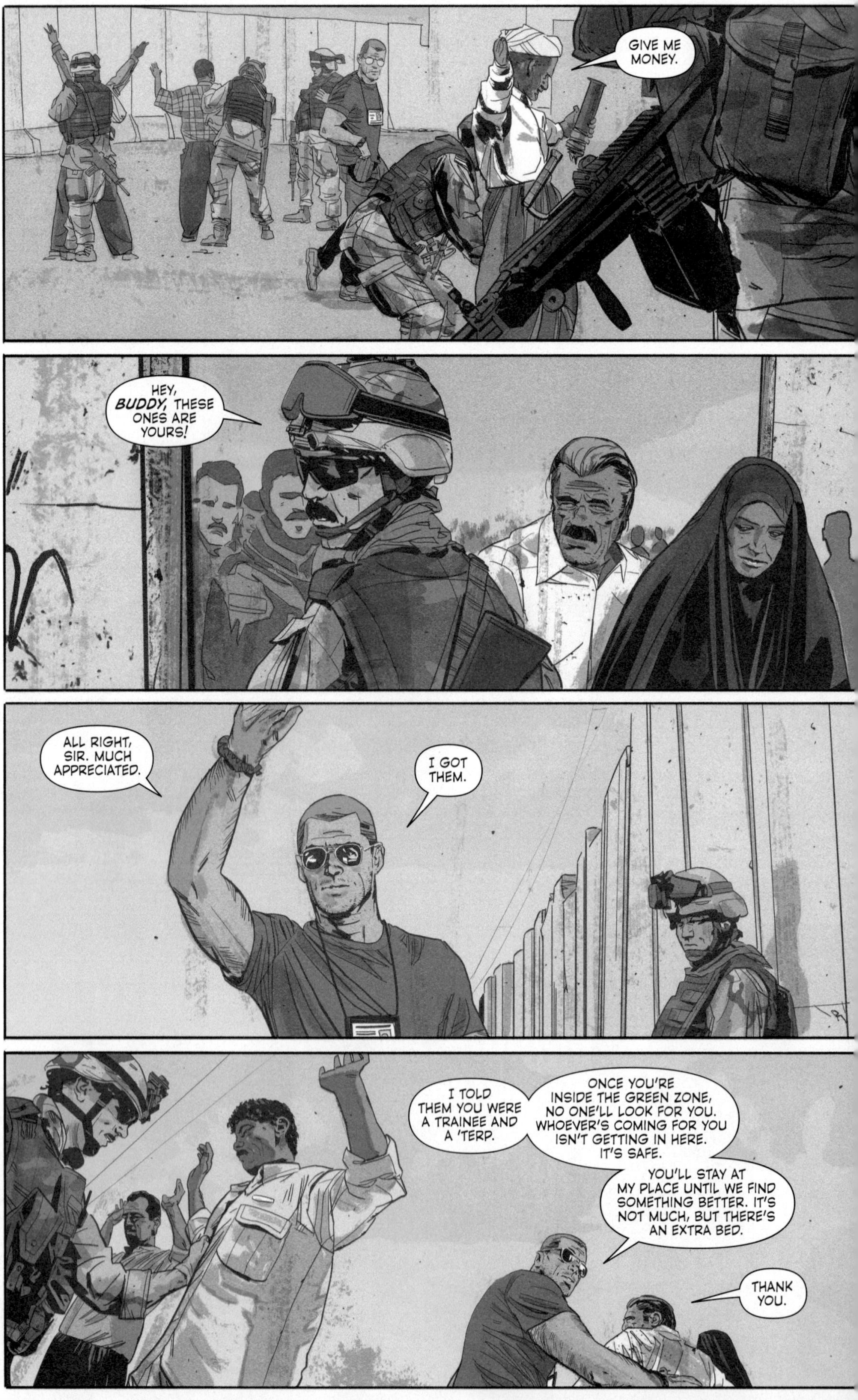
GIVE ME MONEY.
HEY, BUDDY, THESE ONES ARE YOURS!
ALL RIGHT, SIR. MUCH APPRECIATED.
I GOT THEM.
I TOLD THEM YOU WERE A TRAINEE AND A 'TERP.
ONCE YOU'RE INSIDE THE GREEN ZONE, NO ONE'LL LOOK FOR YOU. WHOEVER'S COMING FOR YOU ISN'T GETTING IN HERE. IT'S SAFE.
YOU'LL STAY AT MY PLACE UNTIL WE FIND SOMETHING BETTER. IT'S NOT MUCH, BUT THERE'S AN EXTRA BED.
THANK YOU.

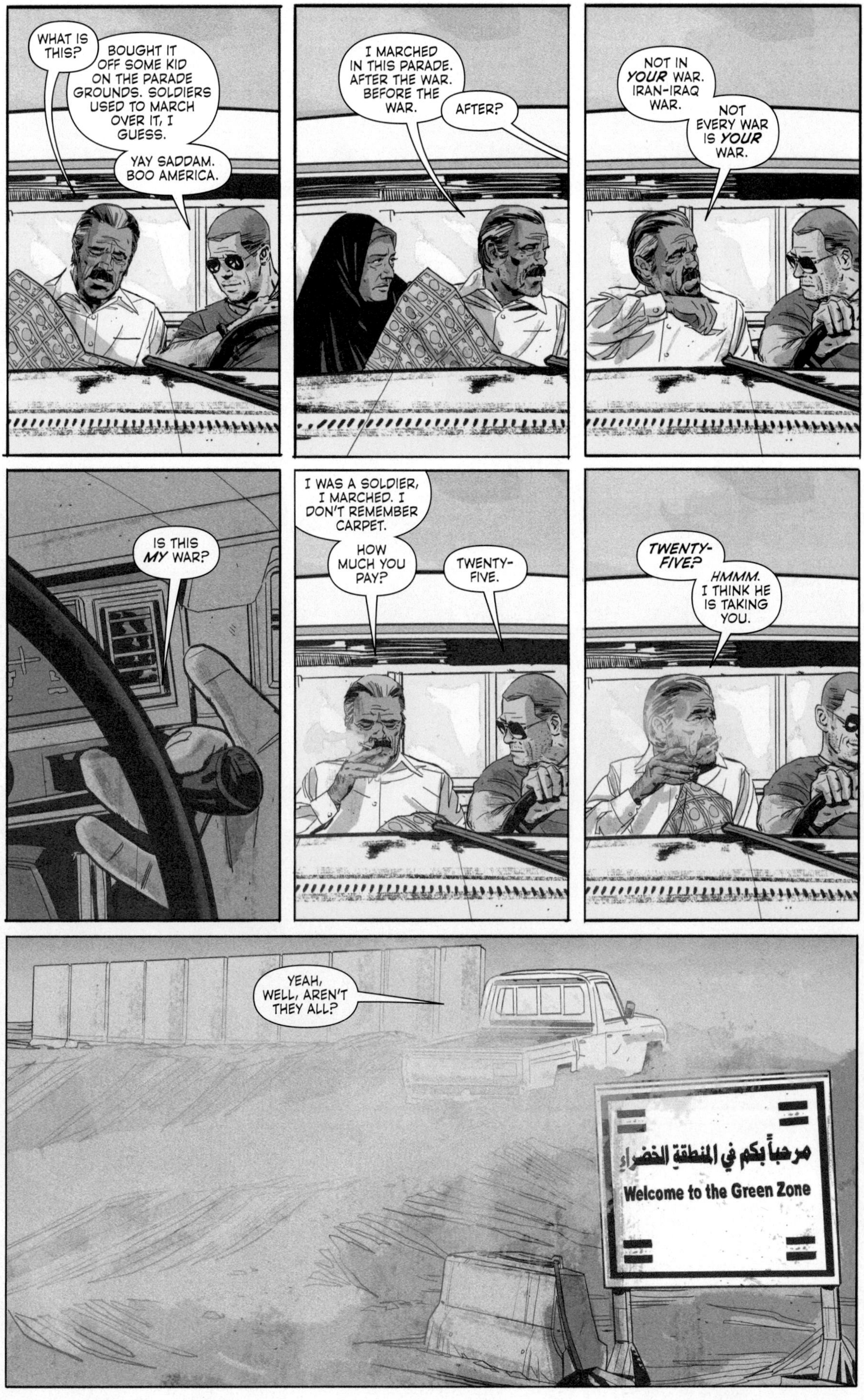
WHAT IS THIS?
BOUGHT IT OFF SOME KID ON THE PARADE GROUNDS. SOLDIERS USED TO MARCH OVER IT, I GUESS.
YAY SADDAM. BOO AMERICA.
I MARCHED IN THIS PARADE. AFTER THE WAR. BEFORE THE WAR.
AFTER?
NOT IN *YOUR* WAR. IRAN-IRAQ WAR.
NOT EVERY WAR IS *YOUR* WAR.
IS THIS *MY* WAR?
I WAS A SOLDIER, I MARCHED. I DON'T REMEMBER CARPET.
HOW MUCH YOU PAY?
TWENTY-FIVE.
TWENTY-FIVE?
HMMM. I THINK HE IS TAKING YOU.
YEAH, WELL, AREN'T THEY ALL?
مرحباً بكم في المنطقة الخضراء
Welcome to the Green Zone

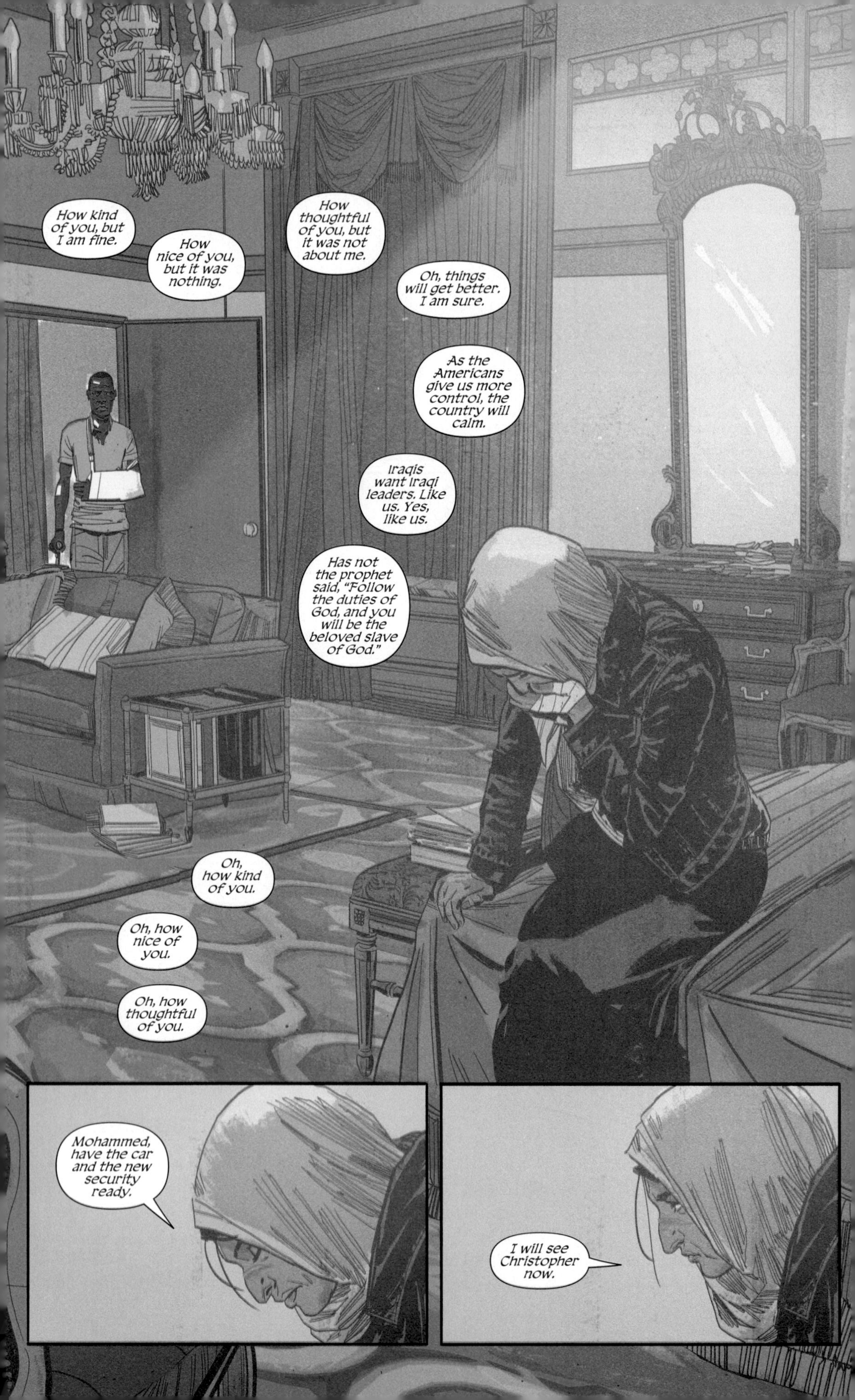
How kind of you, but I am fine.
How nice of you, but it was nothing.
How thoughtful of you, but it was not about me.
Oh, things will get better. I am sure.
As the Americans give us more control, the country will calm.
Iraqis want Iraqi leaders. Like us. Yes, like us.
Has not the prophet said, "Follow the duties of God, and you will be the beloved slave of God."
Oh, how kind of you.
Oh, how nice of you.
Oh, how thoughtful of you.
Mohammed, have the car and the new security ready.
I will see Christopher now.

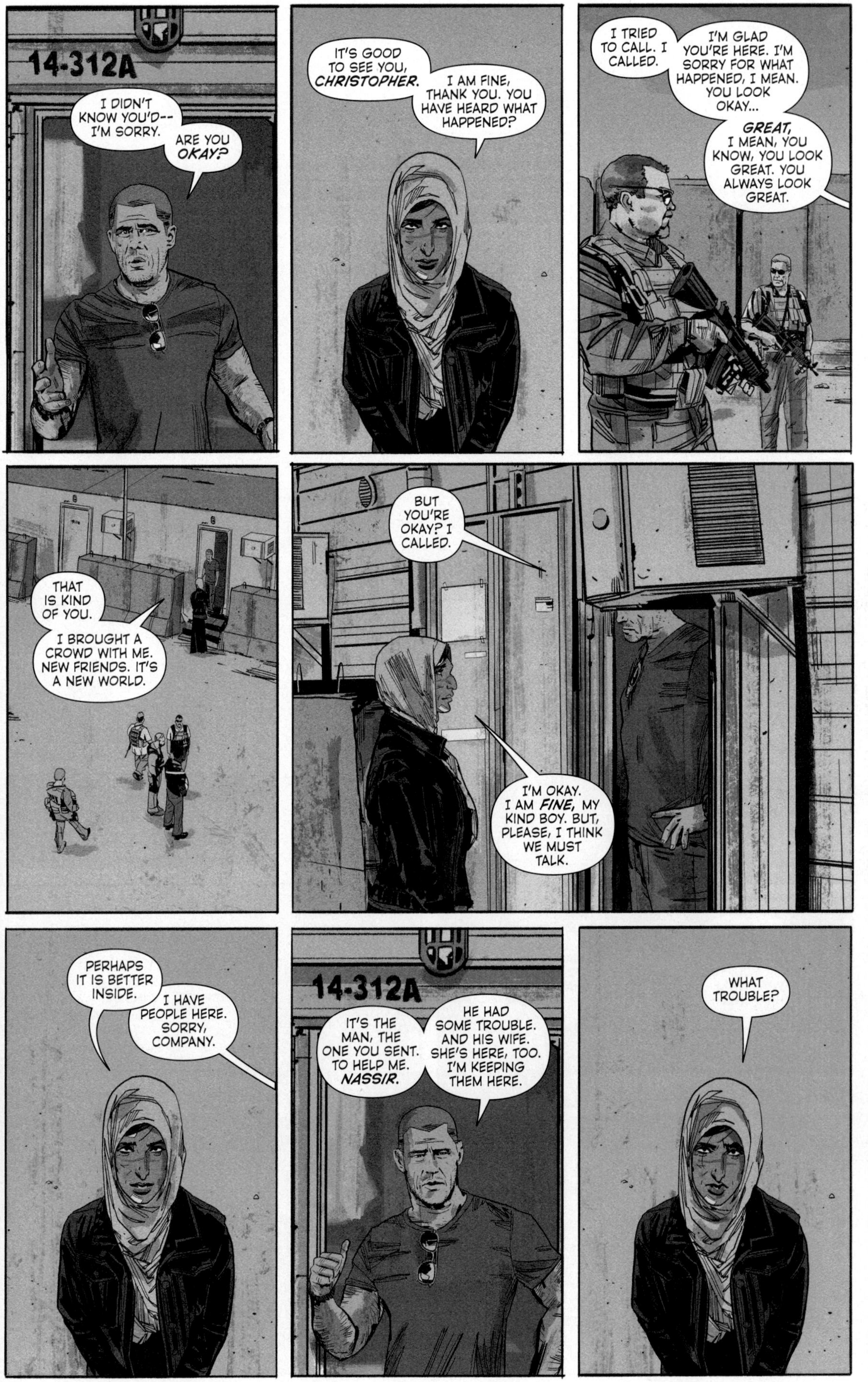
14-312A
I DIDN'T KNOW YOU'D-- I'M SORRY.
ARE YOU OKAY?
IT'S GOOD TO SEE YOU, CHRISTOPHER.
I AM FINE, THANK YOU. YOU HAVE HEARD WHAT HAPPENED?
I TRIED TO CALL. I CALLED.
I'M GLAD YOU'RE HERE. I'M SORRY FOR WHAT HAPPENED, I MEAN. YOU LOOK OKAY...
GREAT, I MEAN, YOU KNOW, YOU LOOK GREAT. YOU ALWAYS LOOK GREAT.
THAT IS KIND OF YOU.
I BROUGHT A CROWD WITH ME. NEW FRIENDS. IT'S A NEW WORLD.
BUT YOU'RE OKAY? I CALLED.
I'M OKAY. I AM FINE, MY KIND BOY. BUT, PLEASE, I THINK WE MUST TALK.
PERHAPS IT IS BETTER INSIDE.
I HAVE PEOPLE HERE. SORRY, COMPANY.
14-312A
IT'S THE MAN, THE ONE YOU SENT. TO HELP ME. NASSIR.
HE HAD SOME TROUBLE. AND HIS WIFE. SHE'S HERE, TOO. I'M KEEPING THEM HERE.
WHAT TROUBLE?

"THEY WENT AFTER HIM. AFTER HIM AND HIS FAMILY."

"WHO?"

"THE PEOPLE WHO KILLED MY TRAINEE. ALI.

"THEY SAW NASSIR AND ME AT ALI'S HOUSE, LOOKING FOR THE KILLERS, AND THEY FIGURED OUT WHO NASSIR WAS."

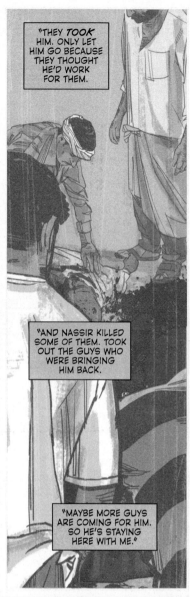

"THEY *TOOK* HIM. ONLY LET HIM GO BECAUSE THEY THOUGHT HE'D WORK FOR THEM.

"AND NASSIR KILLED SOME OF THEM. TOOK OUT THE GUYS WHO WERE BRINGING HIM BACK.

"MAYBE MORE GUYS ARE COMING FOR HIM. SO HE'S STAYING HERE WITH ME."

NASSIR SAYS THEY MIGHT HAVE COME AFTER YOU, TOO. WITH WHAT HAPPENED.

THE *TIMING*. IT MIGHT BE THE SAME PEOPLE. YOU DON'T KNOW.

I KNOW HE WANTS TO TALK TO YOU. ABOUT WHAT TO DO NEXT. HE HAS A *PLAN*.

PLEASE, CHRISTOPHER.

INVITE ME INSIDE.

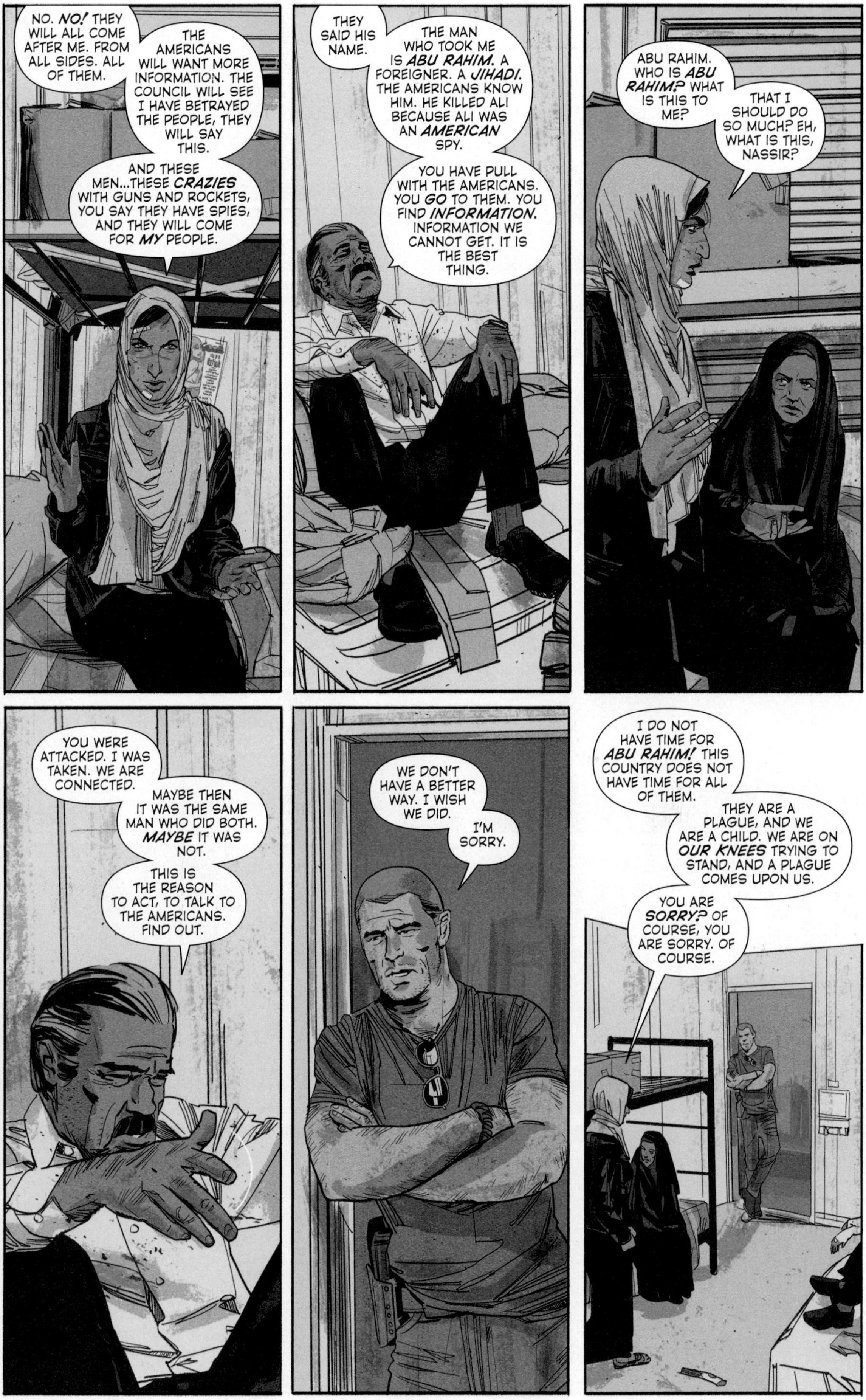
NO. NO! THEY WILL ALL COME AFTER ME. FROM ALL SIDES. ALL OF THEM.
THE AMERICANS WILL WANT MORE INFORMATION. THE COUNCIL WILL SEE I HAVE BETRAYED THE PEOPLE, THEY WILL SAY THIS.
AND THESE MEN...THESE CRAZIES WITH GUNS AND ROCKETS, YOU SAY THEY HAVE SPIES, AND THEY WILL COME FOR MY PEOPLE.
THEY SAID HIS NAME.
THE MAN WHO TOOK ME IS ABU RAHIM. A FOREIGNER. A JIHADI. THE AMERICANS KNOW HIM. HE KILLED ALI BECAUSE ALI WAS AN AMERICAN SPY.
YOU HAVE PULL WITH THE AMERICANS. YOU GO TO THEM. YOU FIND INFORMATION. INFORMATION WE CANNOT GET. IT IS THE BEST THING.
ABU RAHIM. WHO IS ABU RAHIM? WHAT IS THIS TO ME?
THAT I SHOULD DO SO MUCH? EH, WHAT IS THIS, NASSIR?
YOU WERE ATTACKED. I WAS TAKEN. WE ARE CONNECTED.
MAYBE THEN IT WAS THE SAME MAN WHO DID BOTH. MAYBE IT WAS NOT.
THIS IS THE REASON TO ACT, TO TALK TO THE AMERICANS. FIND OUT.
WE DON'T HAVE A BETTER WAY. I WISH WE DID.
I'M SORRY.
I DO NOT HAVE TIME FOR ABU RAHIM! THIS COUNTRY DOES NOT HAVE TIME FOR ALL OF THEM.
THEY ARE A PLAGUE, AND WE ARE A CHILD. WE ARE ON OUR KNEES TRYING TO STAND, AND A PLAGUE COMES UPON US.
YOU ARE SORRY? OF COURSE, YOU ARE SORRY. OF COURSE.

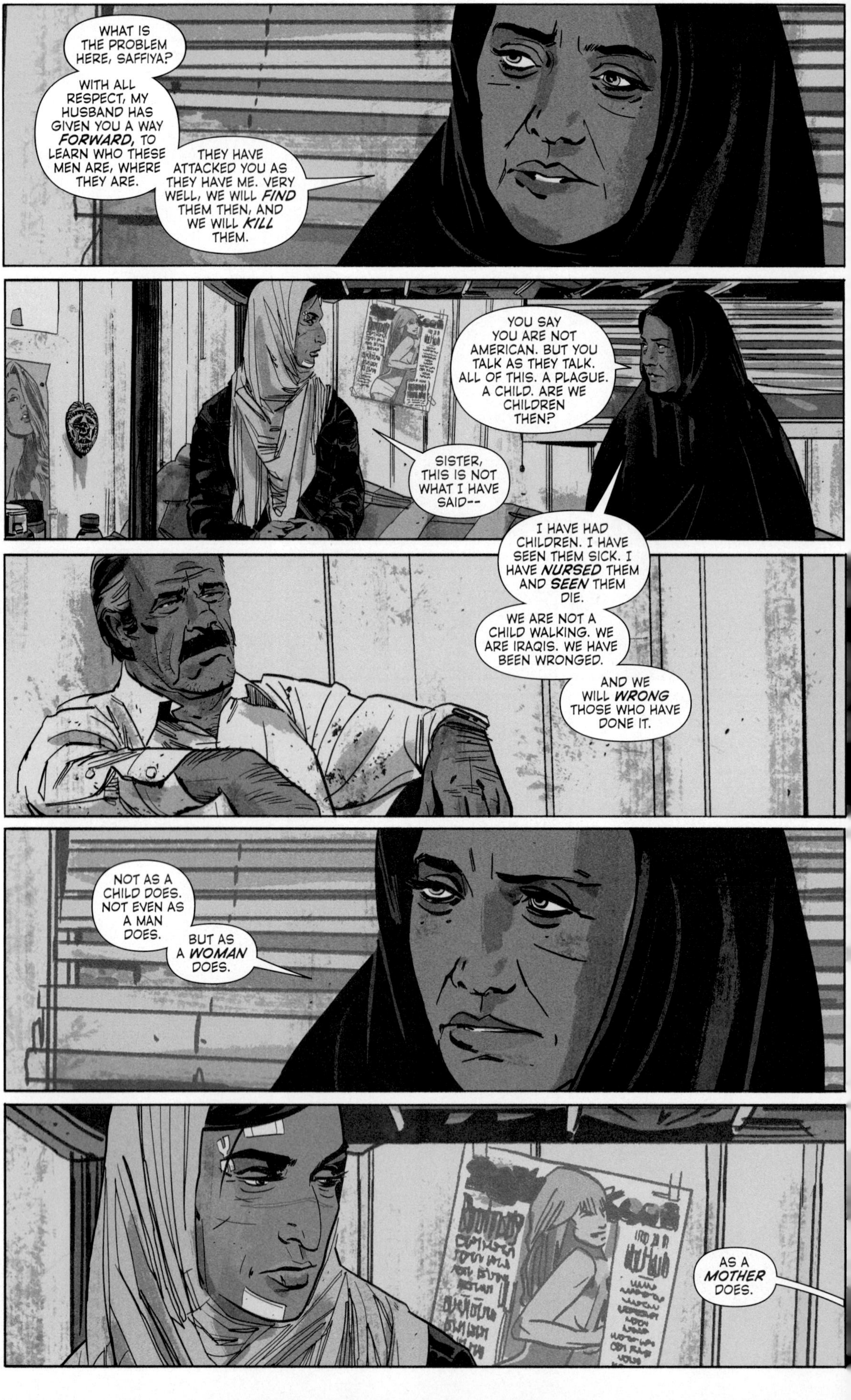
WHAT IS THE PROBLEM HERE, SAFFIYA?
WITH ALL RESPECT, MY HUSBAND HAS GIVEN YOU A WAY FORWARD, TO LEARN WHO THESE MEN ARE, WHERE THEY ARE.
THEY HAVE ATTACKED YOU AS THEY HAVE ME. VERY WELL, WE WILL FIND THEM THEN, AND WE WILL KILL THEM.
YOU SAY YOU ARE NOT AMERICAN. BUT YOU TALK AS THEY TALK. ALL OF THIS. A PLAGUE. A CHILD. ARE WE CHILDREN THEN?
SISTER, THIS IS NOT WHAT I HAVE SAID--
I HAVE HAD CHILDREN. I HAVE SEEN THEM SICK. I HAVE NURSED THEM AND SEEN THEM DIE.
WE ARE NOT A CHILD WALKING. WE ARE IRAQIS. WE HAVE BEEN WRONGED.
AND WE WILL WRONG THOSE WHO HAVE DONE IT.
NOT AS A CHILD DOES. NOT EVEN AS A MAN DOES.
BUT AS A WOMAN DOES.
AS A MOTHER DOES.

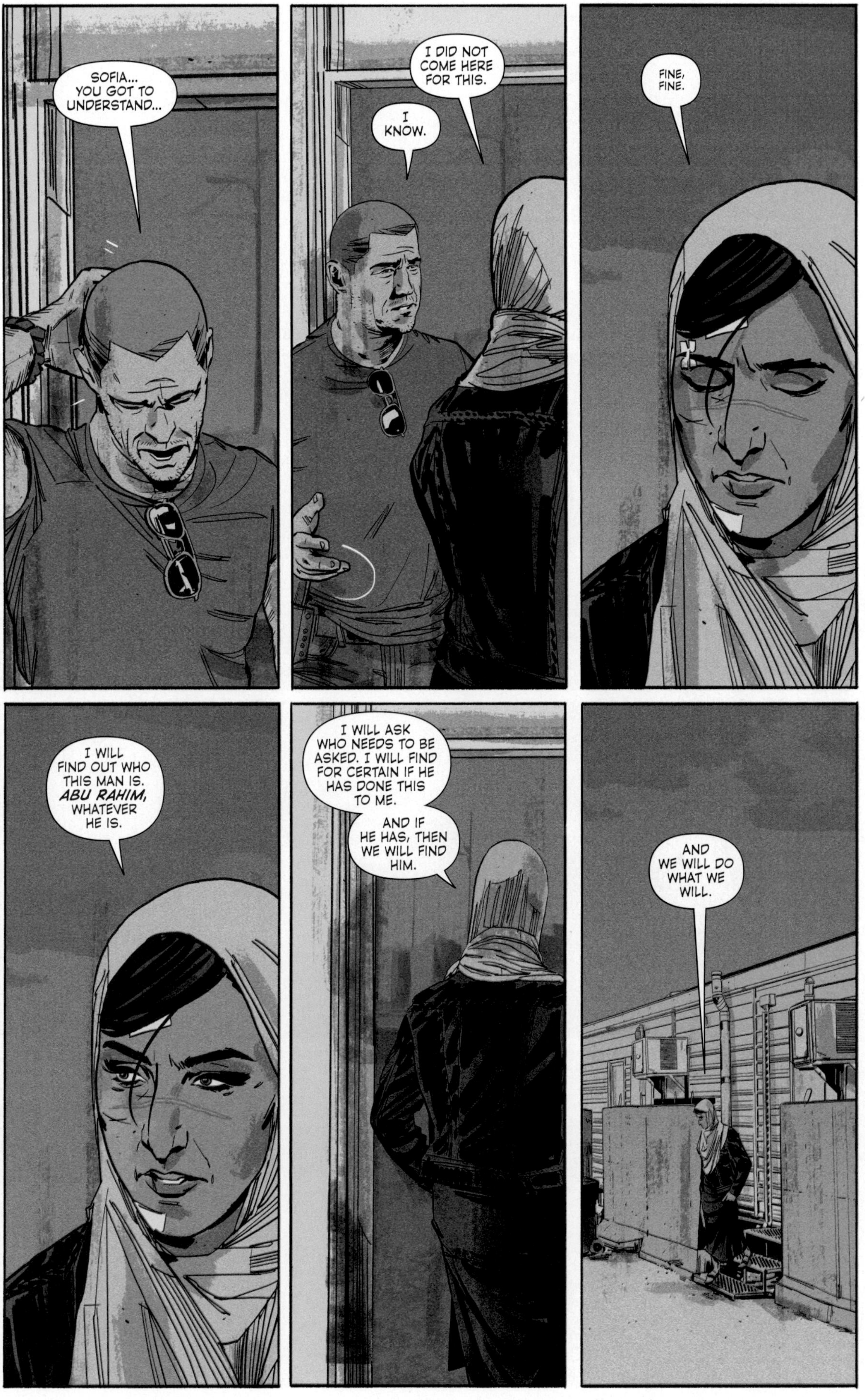
SOFIA... YOU GOT TO UNDERSTAND...
I DID NOT COME HERE FOR THIS.
I KNOW.
FINE, FINE.
I WILL FIND OUT WHO THIS MAN IS. ***ABU RAHIM,*** WHATEVER HE IS.
I WILL ASK WHO NEEDS TO BE ASKED. I WILL FIND FOR CERTAIN IF HE HAS DONE THIS TO ME.
AND IF HE HAS, THEN WE WILL FIND HIM.
AND WE WILL DO WHAT WE WILL.

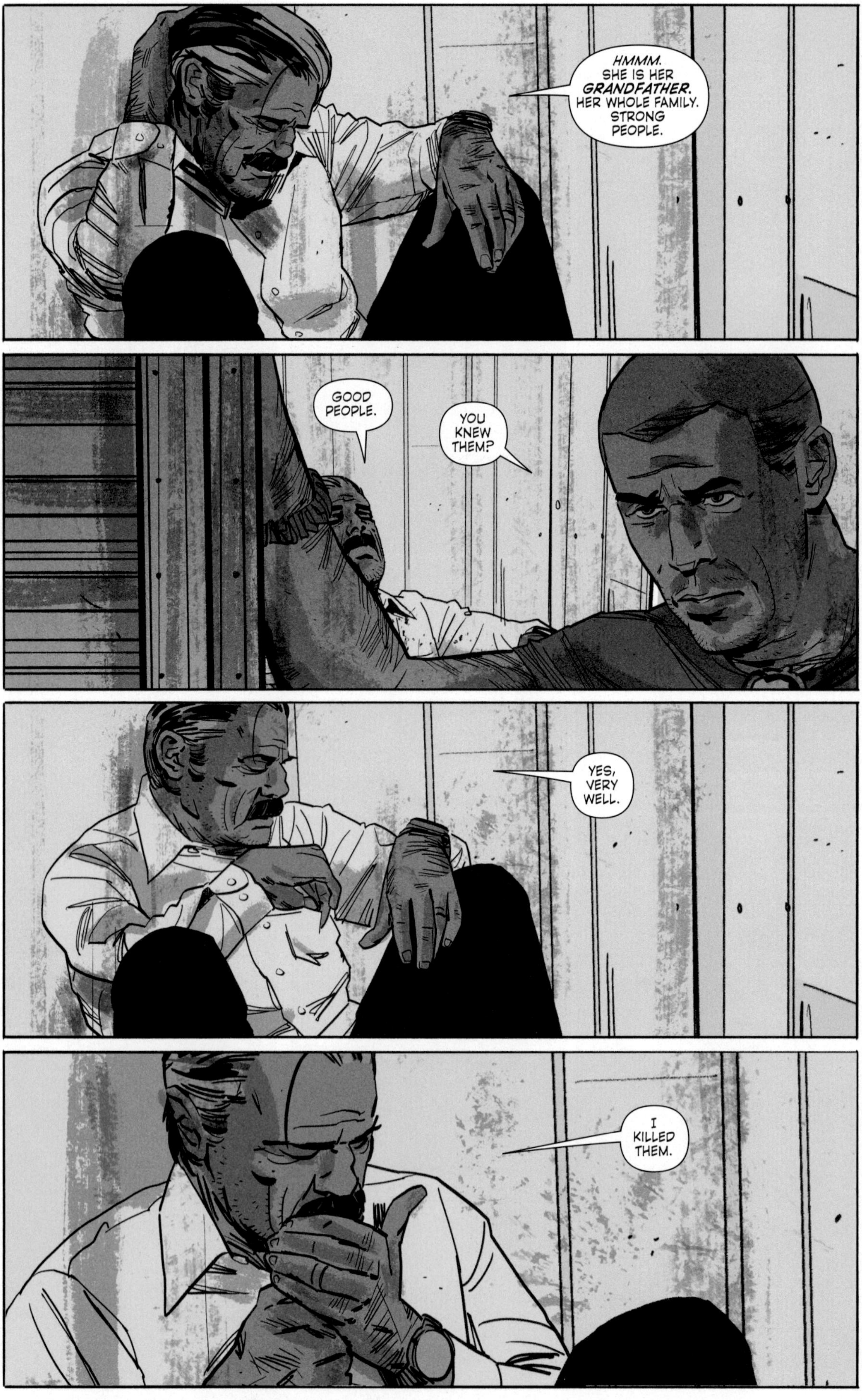
HMMM. SHE IS HER GRANDFATHER. HER WHOLE FAMILY. STRONG PEOPLE.
GOOD PEOPLE.
YOU KNEW THEM?
YES, VERY WELL.
I KILLED THEM.

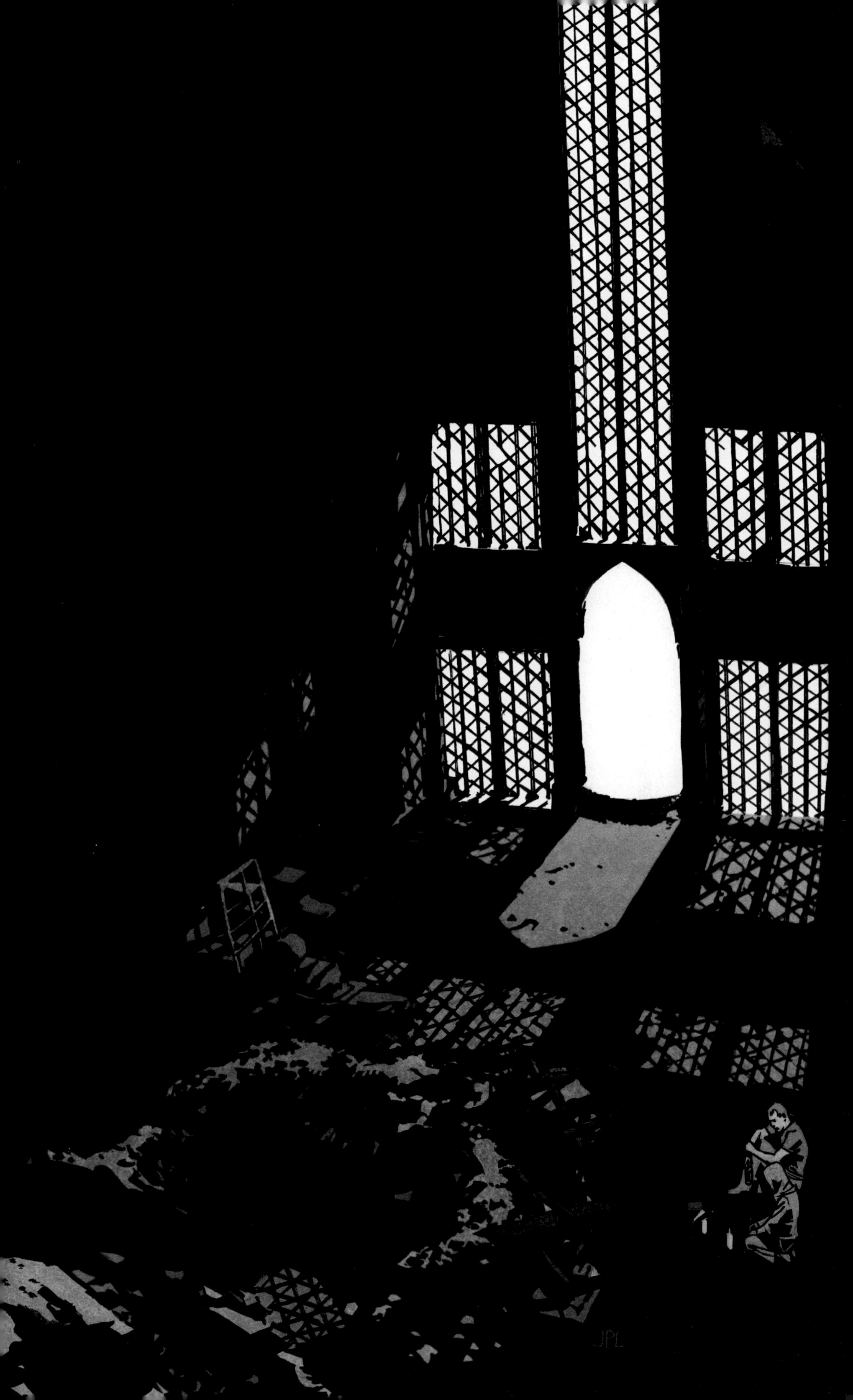
JPL

PART FIVE

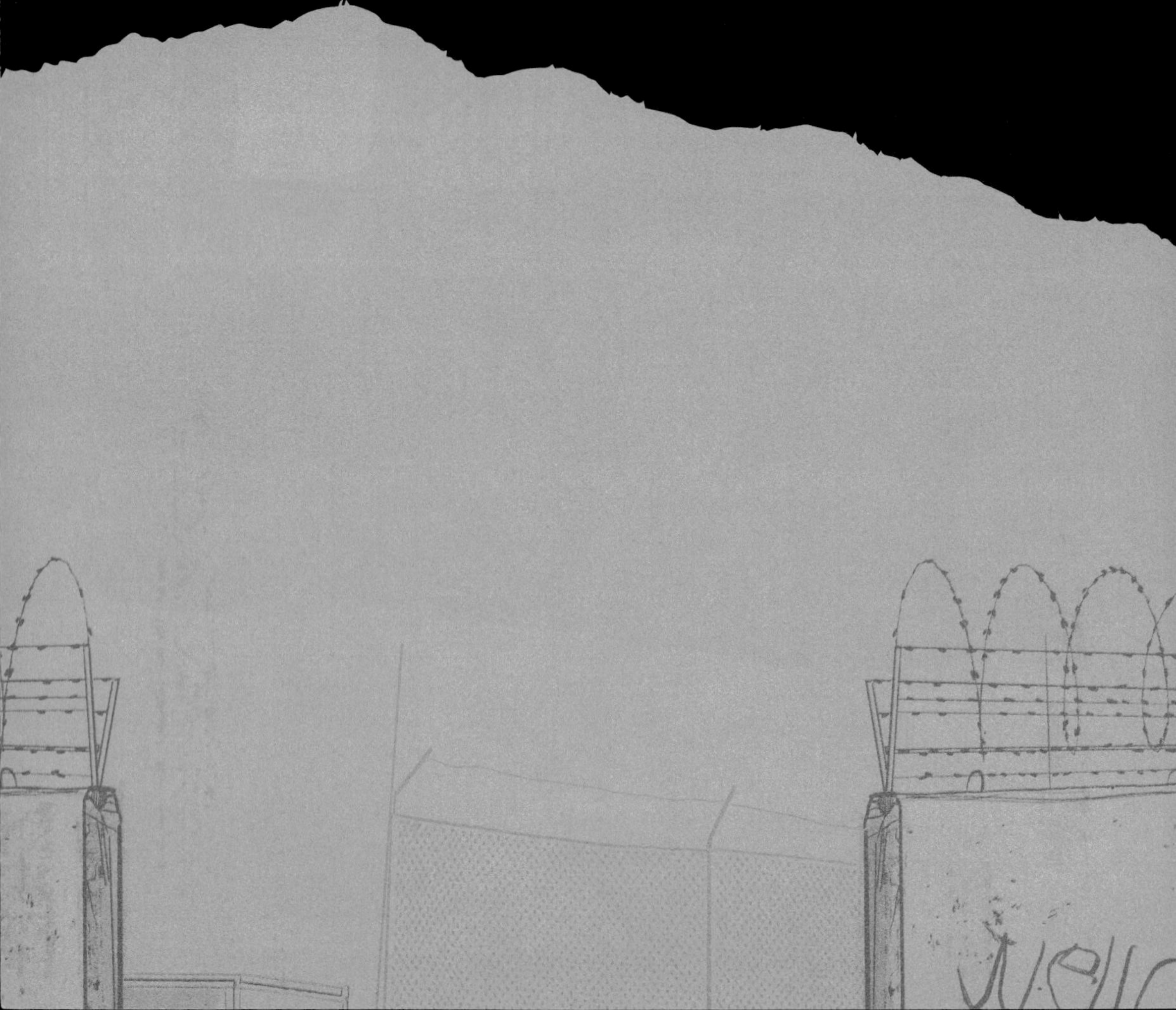

ZZZGRWCHHAXXZ

SZZZCCHHHHXXCK

GKCHXXRMNGHH...

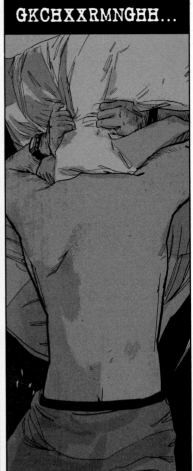

GKCHXXRMNGHH...

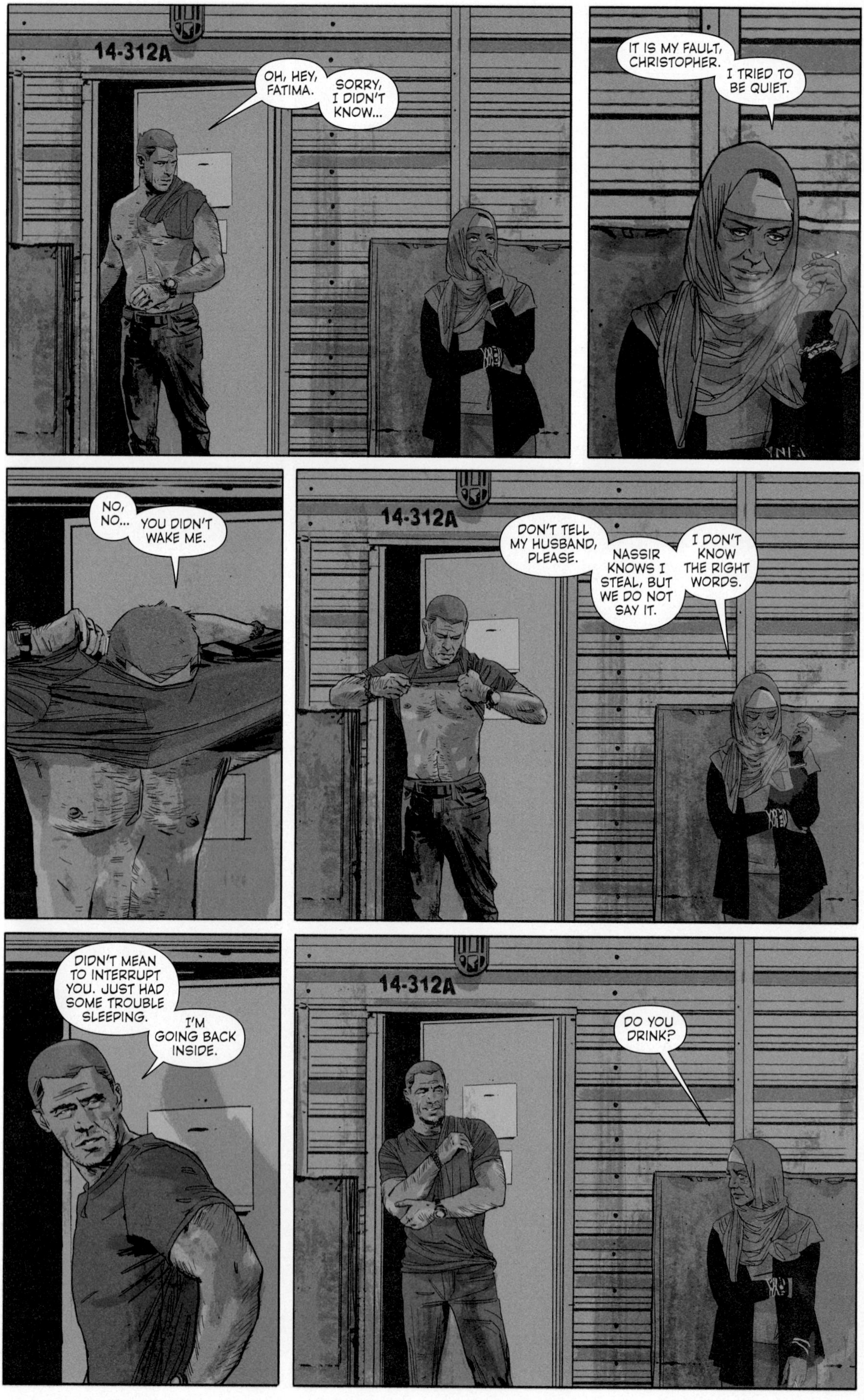
14-312A
OH, HEY, FATIMA.
SORRY, I DIDN'T KNOW...
IT IS MY FAULT, CHRISTOPHER.
I TRIED TO BE QUIET.
NO, NO...
YOU DIDN'T WAKE ME.
14-312A
DON'T TELL MY HUSBAND, PLEASE.
NASSIR KNOWS I STEAL, BUT WE DO NOT SAY IT.
I DON'T KNOW THE RIGHT WORDS.
DIDN'T MEAN TO INTERRUPT YOU. JUST HAD SOME TROUBLE SLEEPING.
I'M GOING BACK INSIDE.
14-312A
DO YOU DRINK?

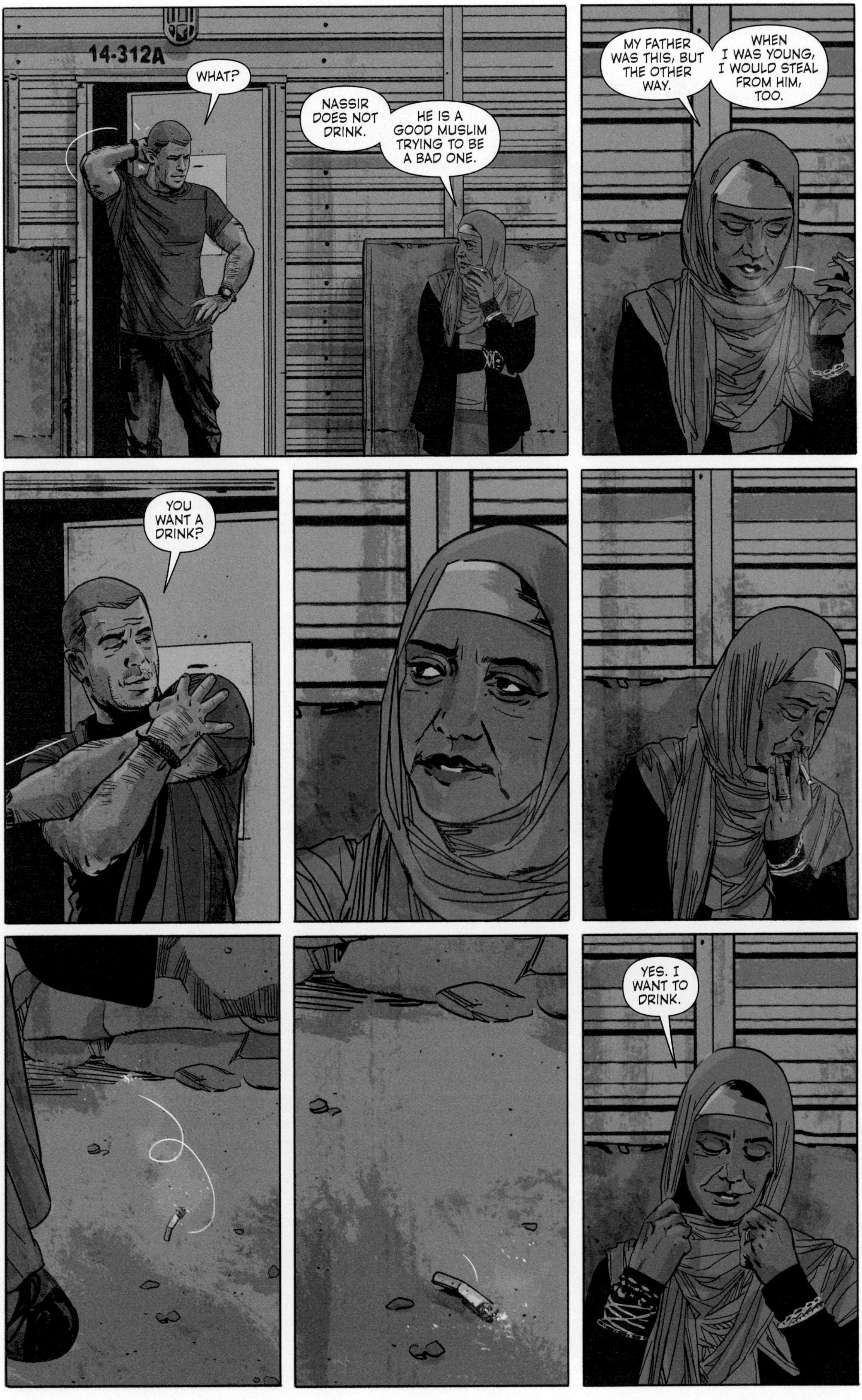
14-312A
WHAT?
NASSIR DOES NOT DRINK.
HE IS A GOOD MUSLIM TRYING TO BE A BAD ONE.
MY FATHER WAS THIS, BUT THE OTHER WAY.
WHEN I WAS YOUNG, I WOULD STEAL FROM HIM, TOO.
YOU WANT A DRINK?
YES. I WANT TO DRINK.

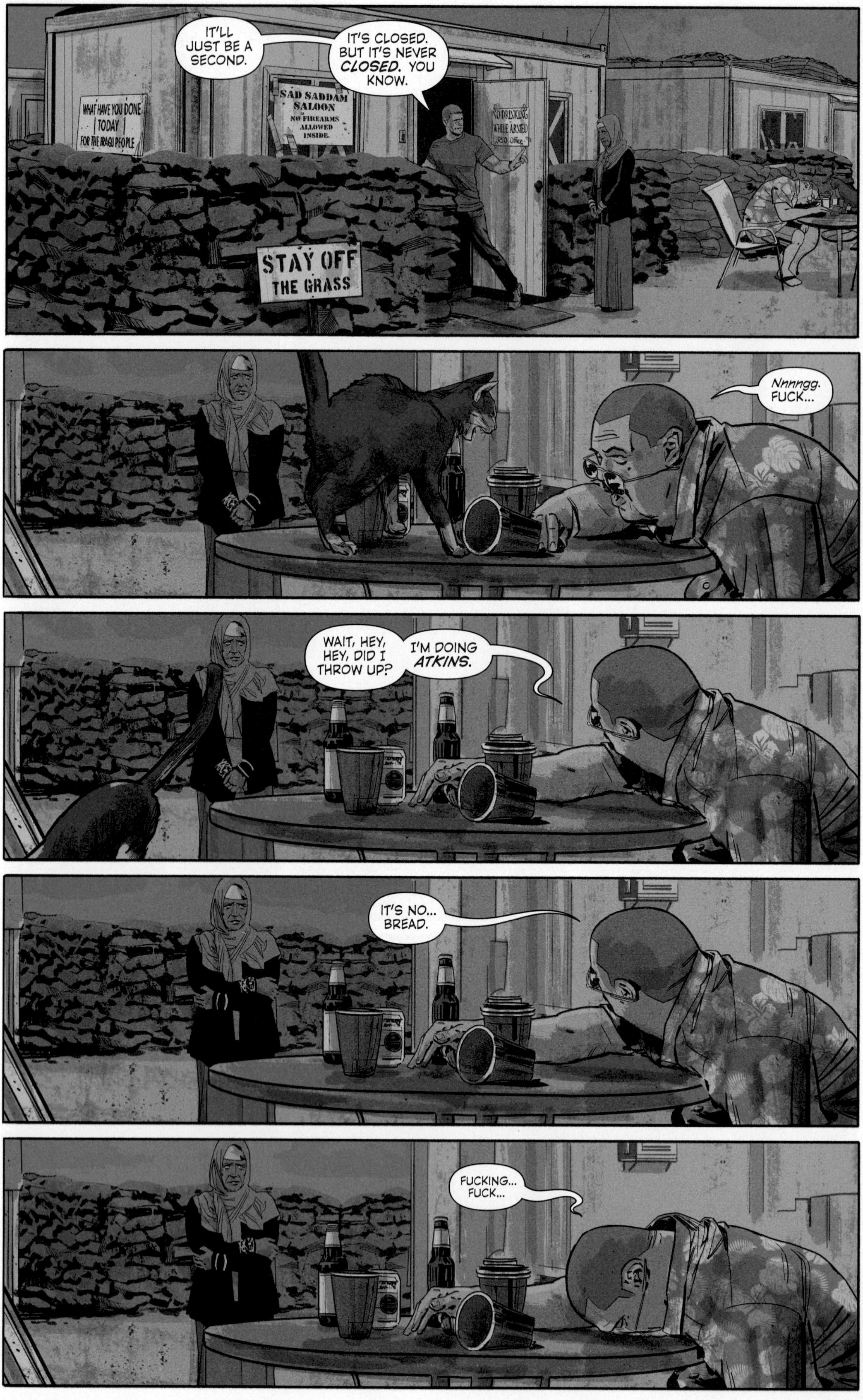

WHAT HAVE YOU DONE TODAY FOR THE IRAQI PEOPLE
SAD SADDAM SALOON NO FIREARMS ALLOWED INSIDE.
IT'LL JUST BE A SECOND.
IT'S CLOSED. BUT IT'S NEVER *CLOSED.* YOU KNOW.
NO DRINKING WHILE ARMED RSO Office
STAY OFF THE GRASS
Nnnngg. FUCK...
WAIT, HEY, HEY, DID I THROW UP?
I'M DOING *ATKINS.*
IT'S NO... BREAD.
FUCKING... FUCK...

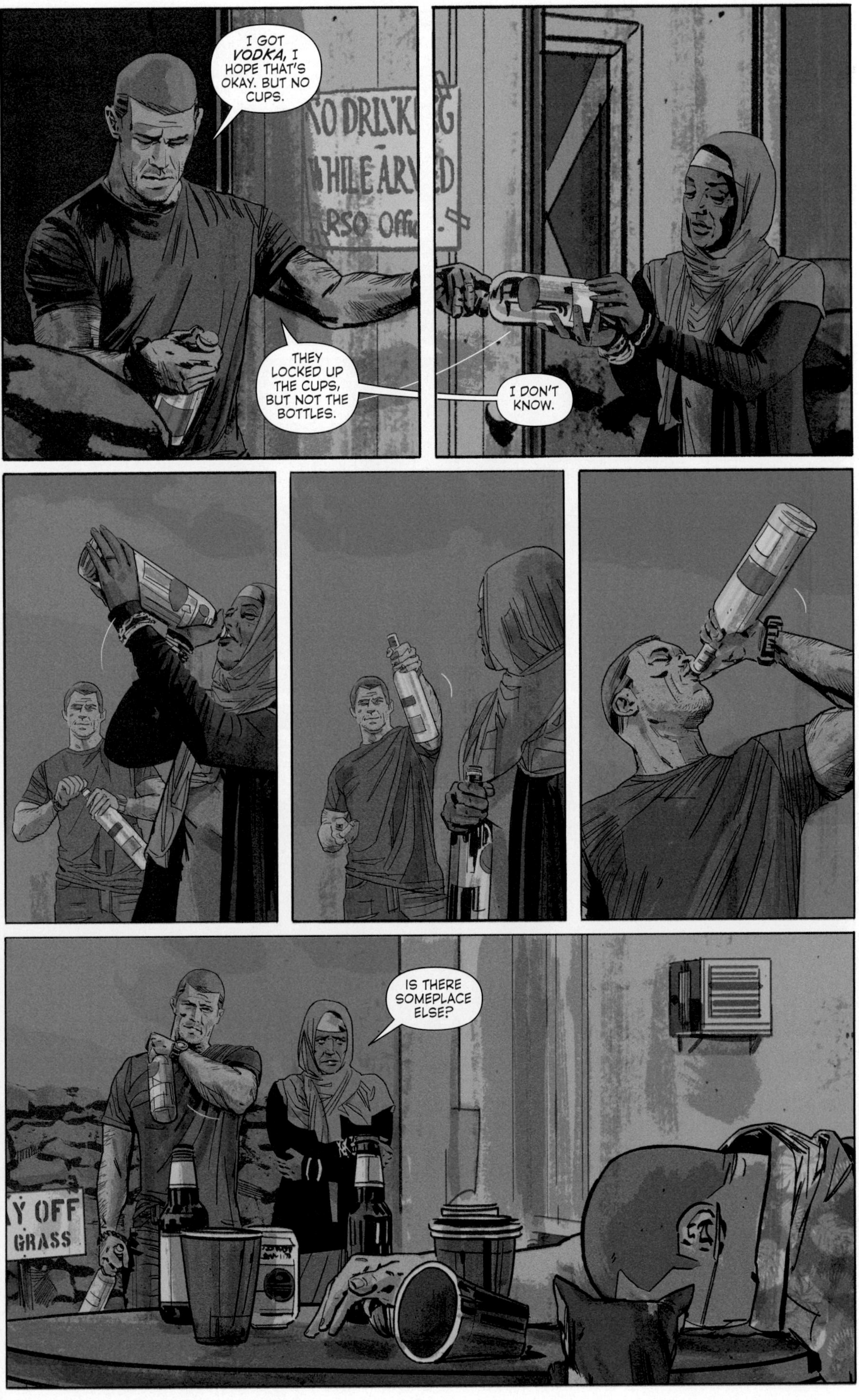
I GOT *VODKA,* I HOPE THAT'S OKAY. BUT NO CUPS.
THEY LOCKED UP THE CUPS, BUT NOT THE BOTTLES.
I DON'T KNOW.
IS THERE SOMEPLACE ELSE?
GRASS

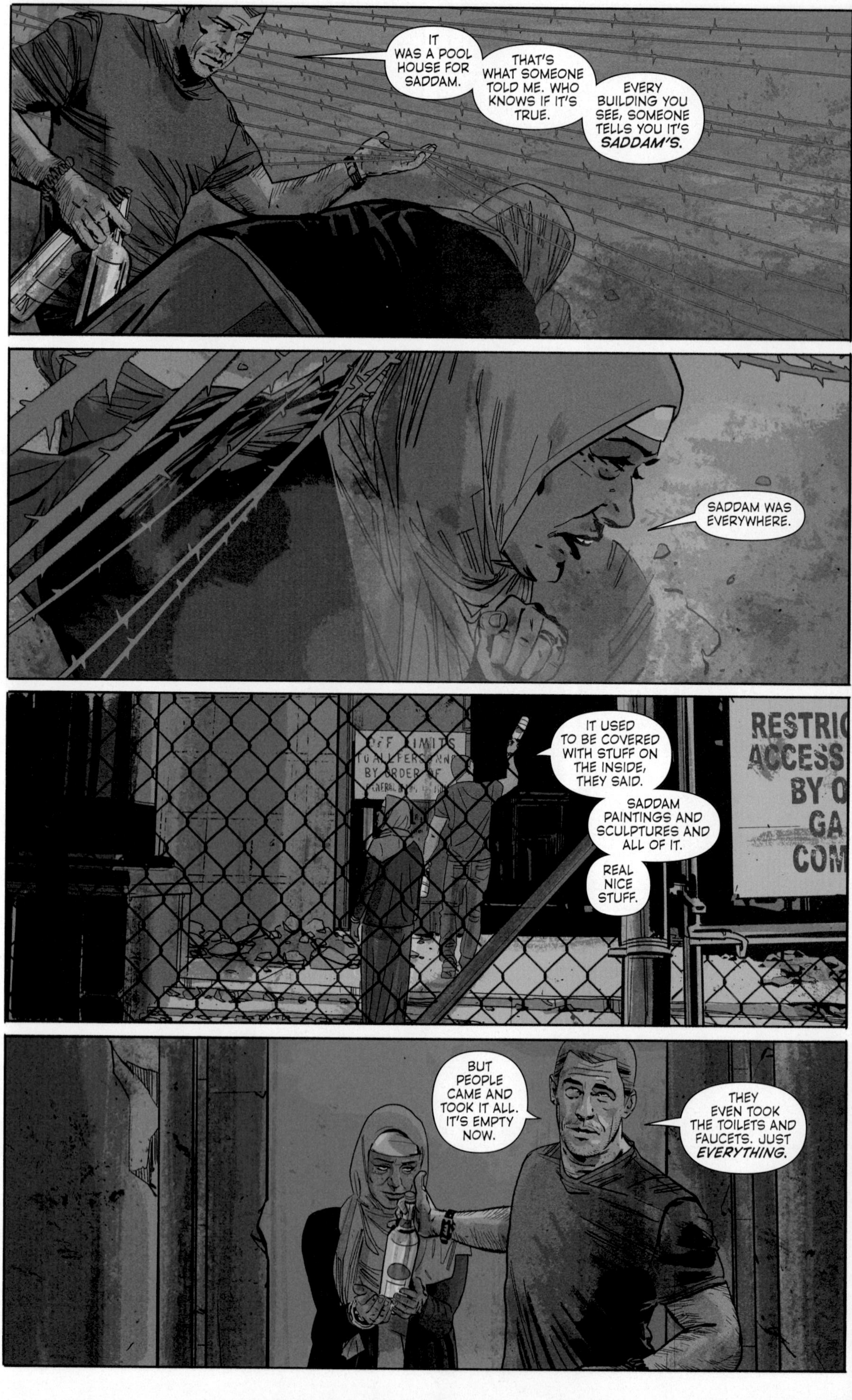
IT WAS A POOL HOUSE FOR SADDAM.
THAT'S WHAT SOMEONE TOLD ME. WHO KNOWS IF IT'S TRUE.
EVERY BUILDING YOU SEE, SOMEONE TELLS YOU IT'S *SADDAM'S*.
SADDAM WAS EVERYWHERE.
IT USED TO BE COVERED WITH STUFF ON THE INSIDE, THEY SAID.
SADDAM PAINTINGS AND SCULPTURES AND ALL OF IT.
REAL NICE STUFF.
BUT PEOPLE CAME AND TOOK IT ALL. IT'S EMPTY NOW.
THEY EVEN TOOK THE TOILETS AND FAUCETS. JUST *EVERYTHING*.

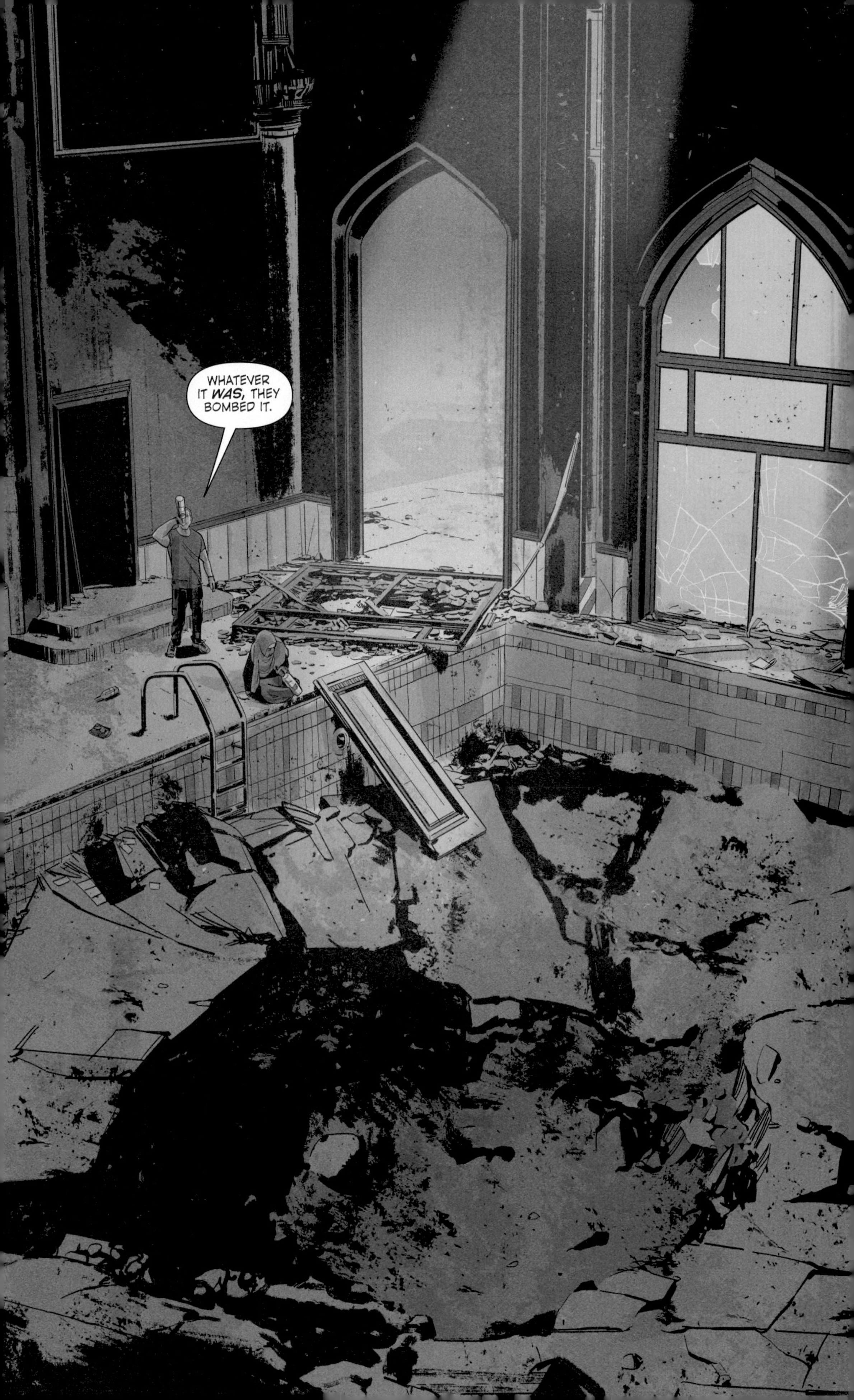
WHATEVER IT WAS, THEY BOMBED IT.

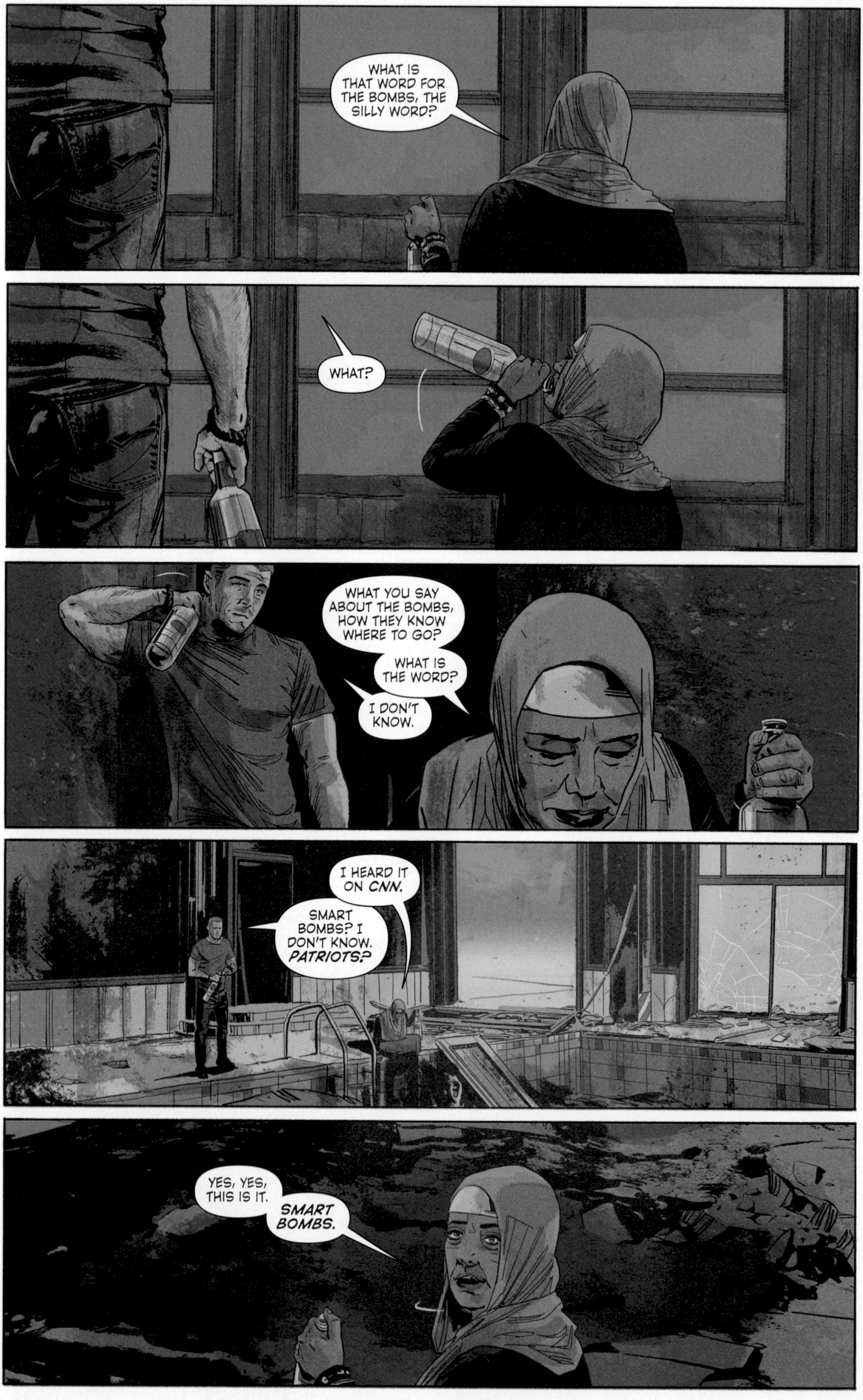
WHAT IS THAT WORD FOR THE BOMBS, THE SILLY WORD?
WHAT?
WHAT YOU SAY ABOUT THE BOMBS, HOW THEY KNOW WHERE TO GO?
WHAT IS THE WORD?
I DON'T KNOW.
SMART BOMBS? I DON'T KNOW. *PATRIOTS?*
I HEARD IT ON *CNN*.
YES, YES, THIS IS IT. *SMART BOMBS.*

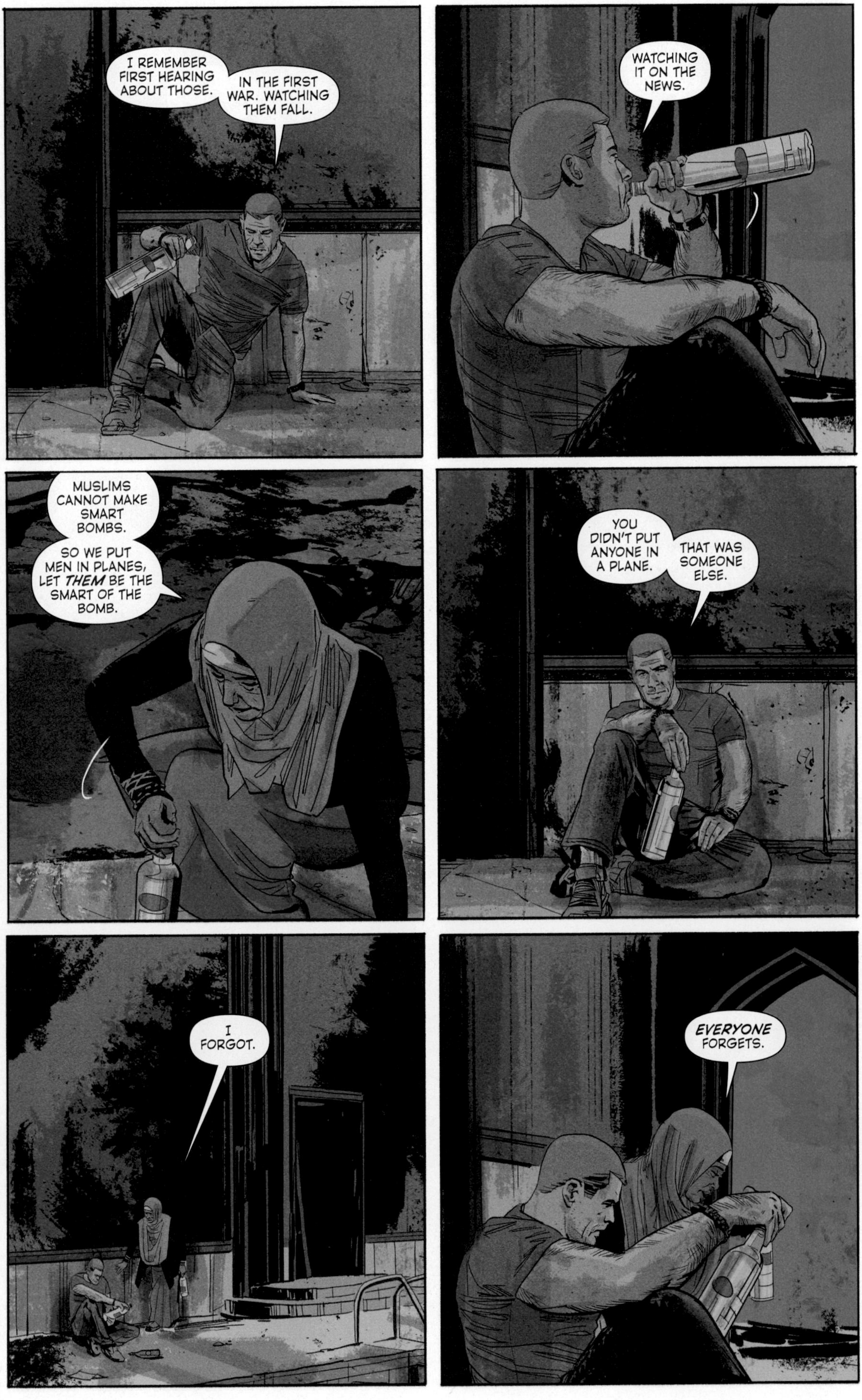
I REMEMBER FIRST HEARING ABOUT THOSE.
IN THE FIRST WAR. WATCHING THEM FALL.
WATCHING IT ON THE NEWS.
MUSLIMS CANNOT MAKE SMART BOMBS.
SO WE PUT MEN IN PLANES, LET *THEM* BE THE SMART OF THE BOMB.
YOU DIDN'T PUT ANYONE IN A PLANE.
THAT WAS SOMEONE ELSE.
I FORGOT.
EVERYONE FORGETS.

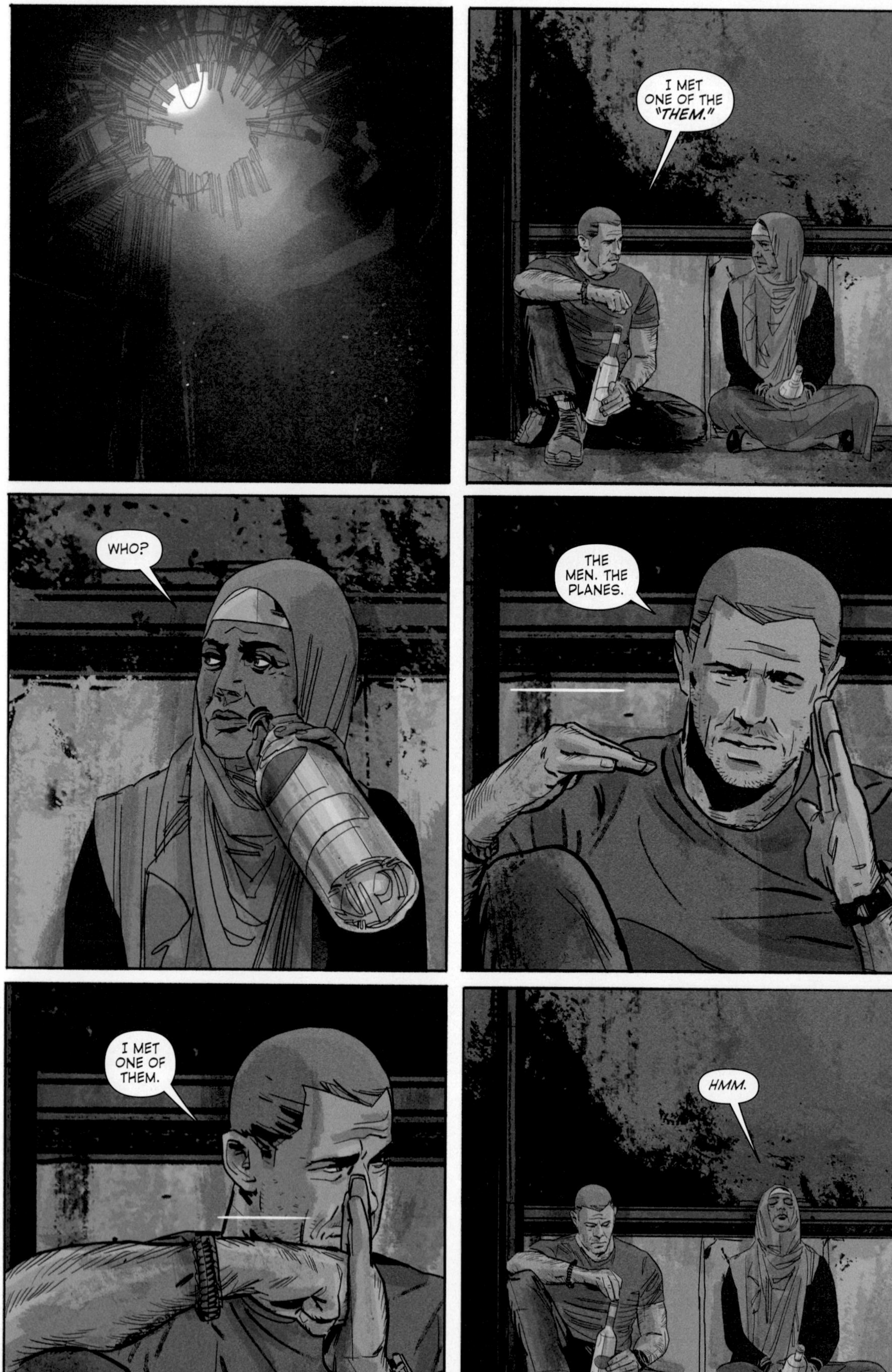
I MET ONE OF THE "*THEM.*"
WHO?
THE MEN. THE PLANES.
I MET ONE OF THEM.
HMM.

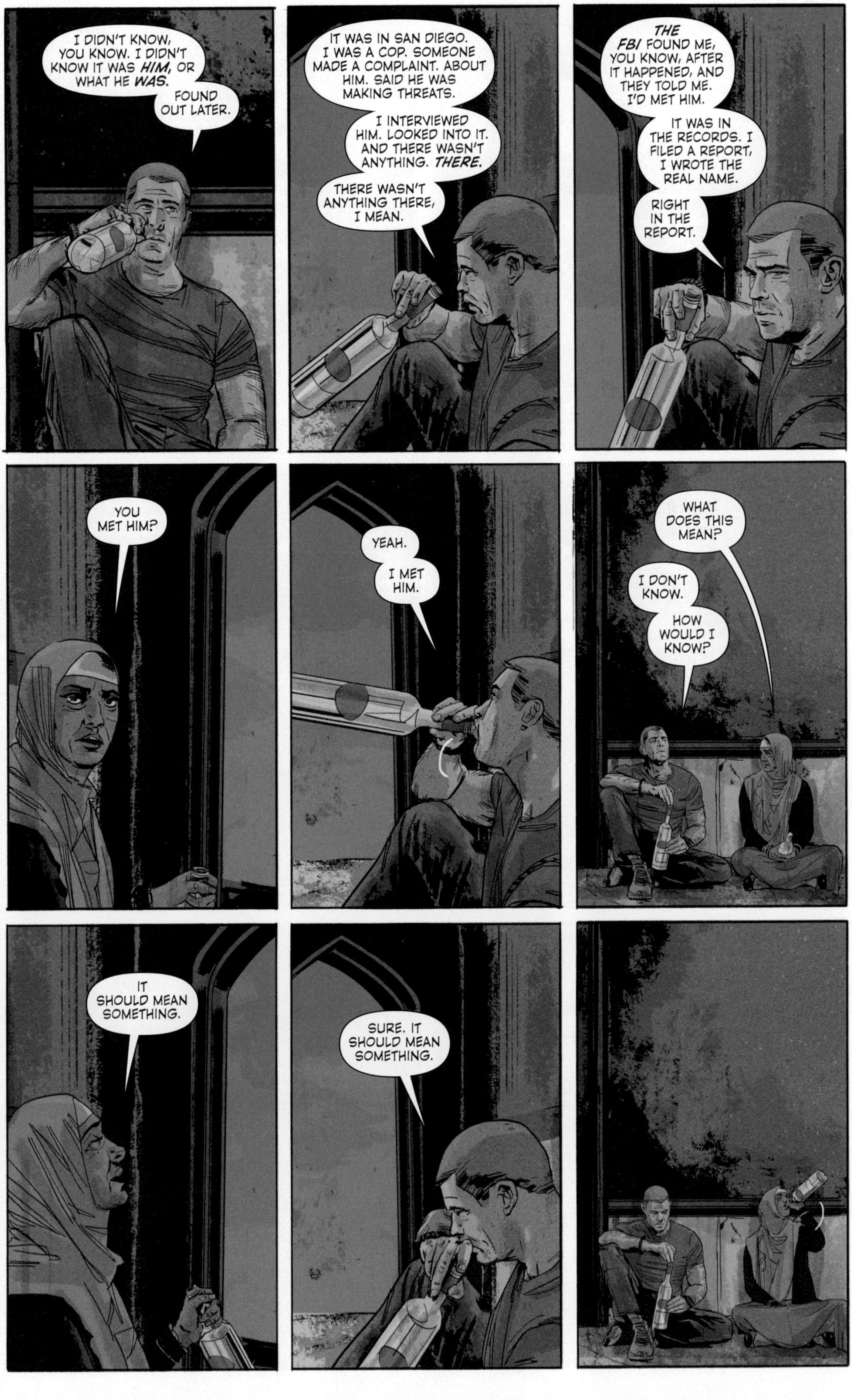
I DIDN'T KNOW, YOU KNOW. I DIDN'T KNOW IT WAS *HIM*, OR WHAT HE *WAS*.
FOUND OUT LATER.
IT WAS IN SAN DIEGO. I WAS A COP. SOMEONE MADE A COMPLAINT. ABOUT HIM. SAID HE WAS MAKING THREATS.
I INTERVIEWED HIM. LOOKED INTO IT. AND THERE WASN'T ANYTHING. *THERE*.
THERE WASN'T ANYTHING THERE, I MEAN.
THE FBI FOUND ME, YOU KNOW, AFTER IT HAPPENED, AND THEY TOLD ME. I'D MET HIM.
IT WAS IN THE RECORDS. I FILED A REPORT, I WROTE THE REAL NAME.
RIGHT IN THE REPORT.
YOU MET HIM?
YEAH.
I MET HIM.
WHAT DOES THIS MEAN?
I DON'T KNOW.
HOW WOULD I KNOW?
IT SHOULD MEAN SOMETHING.
SURE. IT SHOULD MEAN SOMETHING.

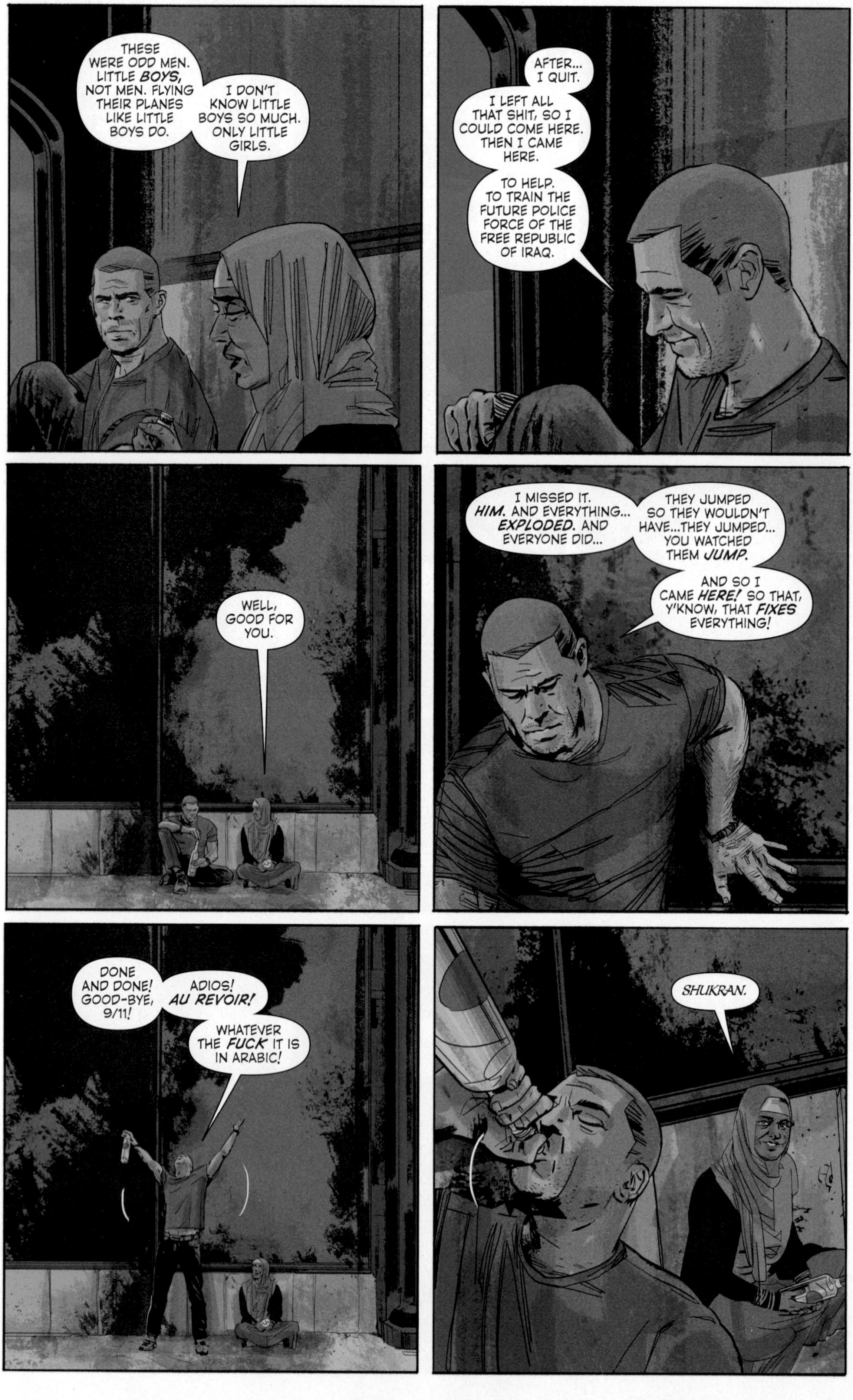
THESE WERE ODD MEN. LITTLE BOYS, NOT MEN. FLYING THEIR PLANES LIKE LITTLE BOYS DO.
I DON'T KNOW LITTLE BOYS SO MUCH. ONLY LITTLE GIRLS.
AFTER... I QUIT.
I LEFT ALL THAT SHIT, SO I COULD COME HERE. THEN I CAME HERE.
TO HELP. TO TRAIN THE FUTURE POLICE FORCE OF THE FREE REPUBLIC OF IRAQ.
WELL, GOOD FOR YOU.
I MISSED IT. HIM. AND EVERYTHING... EXPLODED. AND EVERYONE DID...
THEY JUMPED SO THEY WOULDN'T HAVE...THEY JUMPED... YOU WATCHED THEM JUMP.
AND SO I CAME HERE! SO THAT, Y'KNOW, THAT FIXES EVERYTHING!
DONE AND DONE! GOOD-BYE, 9/11!
ADIOS! AU REVOIR!
WHATEVER THE FUCK IT IS IN ARABIC!
SHUKRAN.

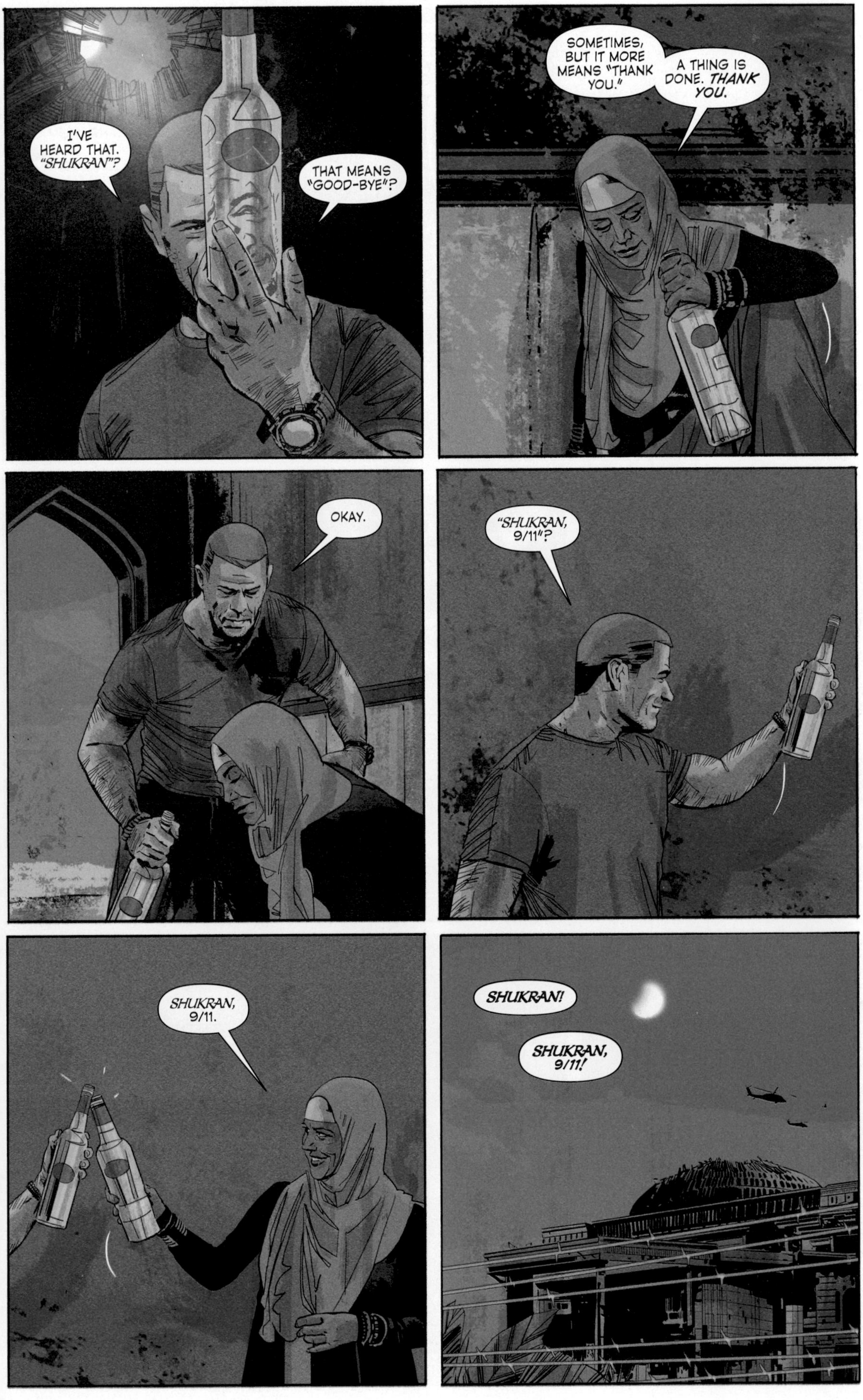

I'VE HEARD THAT. "SHUKRAN"?
THAT MEANS "GOOD-BYE"?
SOMETIMES, BUT IT MORE MEANS "THANK YOU."
A THING IS DONE. THANK YOU.
OKAY.
"SHUKRAN, 9/11"?
SHUKRAN, 9/11.
SHUKRAN!
SHUKRAN, 9/11!

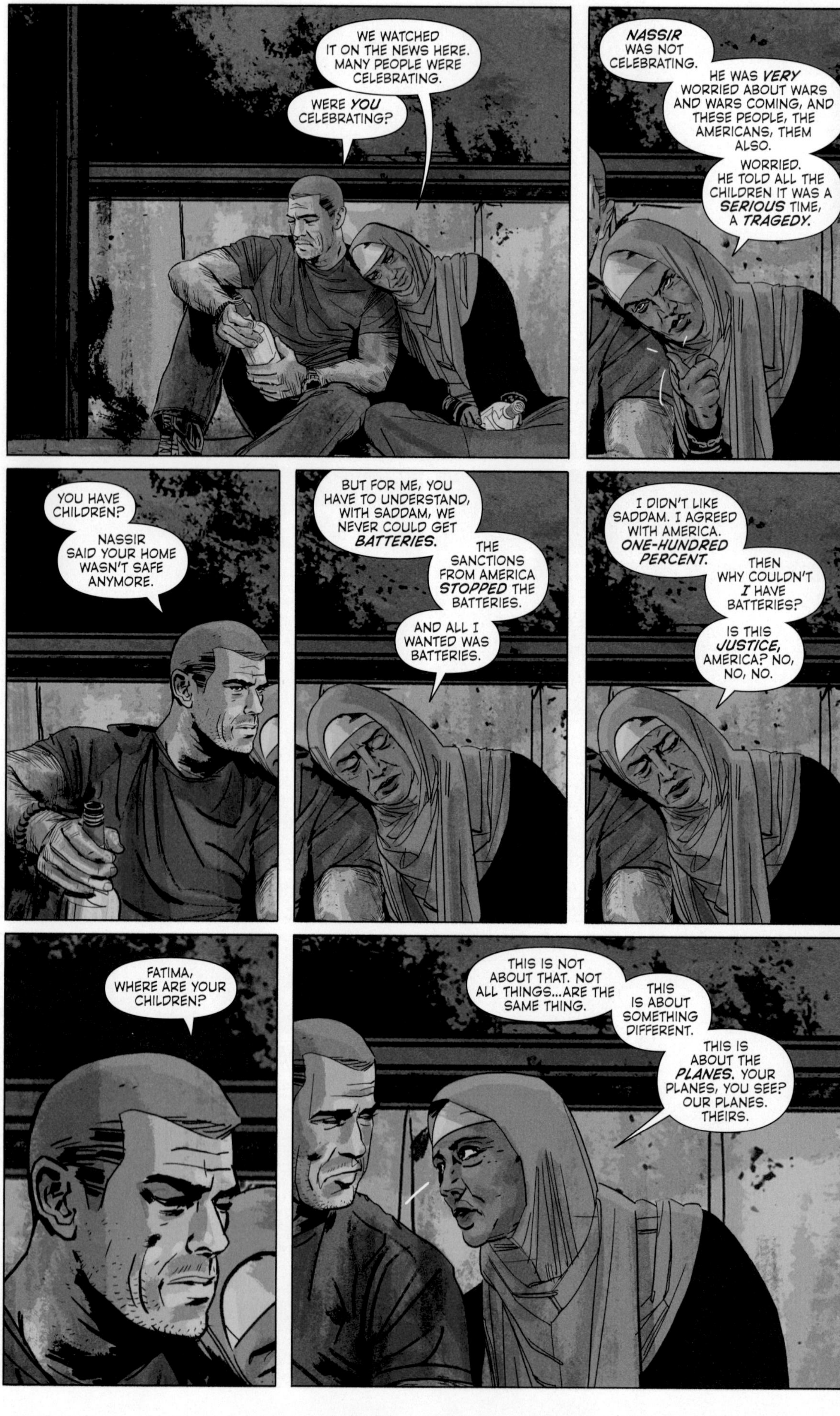
WE WATCHED IT ON THE NEWS HERE. MANY PEOPLE WERE CELEBRATING.
WERE *YOU* CELEBRATING?
NASSIR WAS NOT CELEBRATING.
HE WAS *VERY* WORRIED ABOUT WARS AND WARS COMING, AND THESE PEOPLE, THE AMERICANS, THEM ALSO.
WORRIED. HE TOLD ALL THE CHILDREN IT WAS A *SERIOUS* TIME, A *TRAGEDY.*
YOU HAVE CHILDREN?
NASSIR SAID YOUR HOME WASN'T SAFE ANYMORE.
BUT FOR ME, YOU HAVE TO UNDERSTAND, WITH SADDAM, WE NEVER COULD GET *BATTERIES.*
THE SANCTIONS FROM AMERICA *STOPPED* THE BATTERIES.
AND ALL I WANTED WAS BATTERIES.
I DIDN'T LIKE SADDAM. I AGREED WITH AMERICA. *ONE-HUNDRED PERCENT.*
THEN WHY COULDN'T *I* HAVE BATTERIES?
IS THIS *JUSTICE,* AMERICA? NO, NO, NO.
FATIMA, WHERE ARE YOUR CHILDREN?
THIS IS NOT ABOUT THAT. NOT ALL THINGS...ARE THE SAME THING.
THIS IS ABOUT SOMETHING DIFFERENT.
THIS IS ABOUT THE *PLANES.* YOUR PLANES, YOU SEE? OUR PLANES. THEIRS.

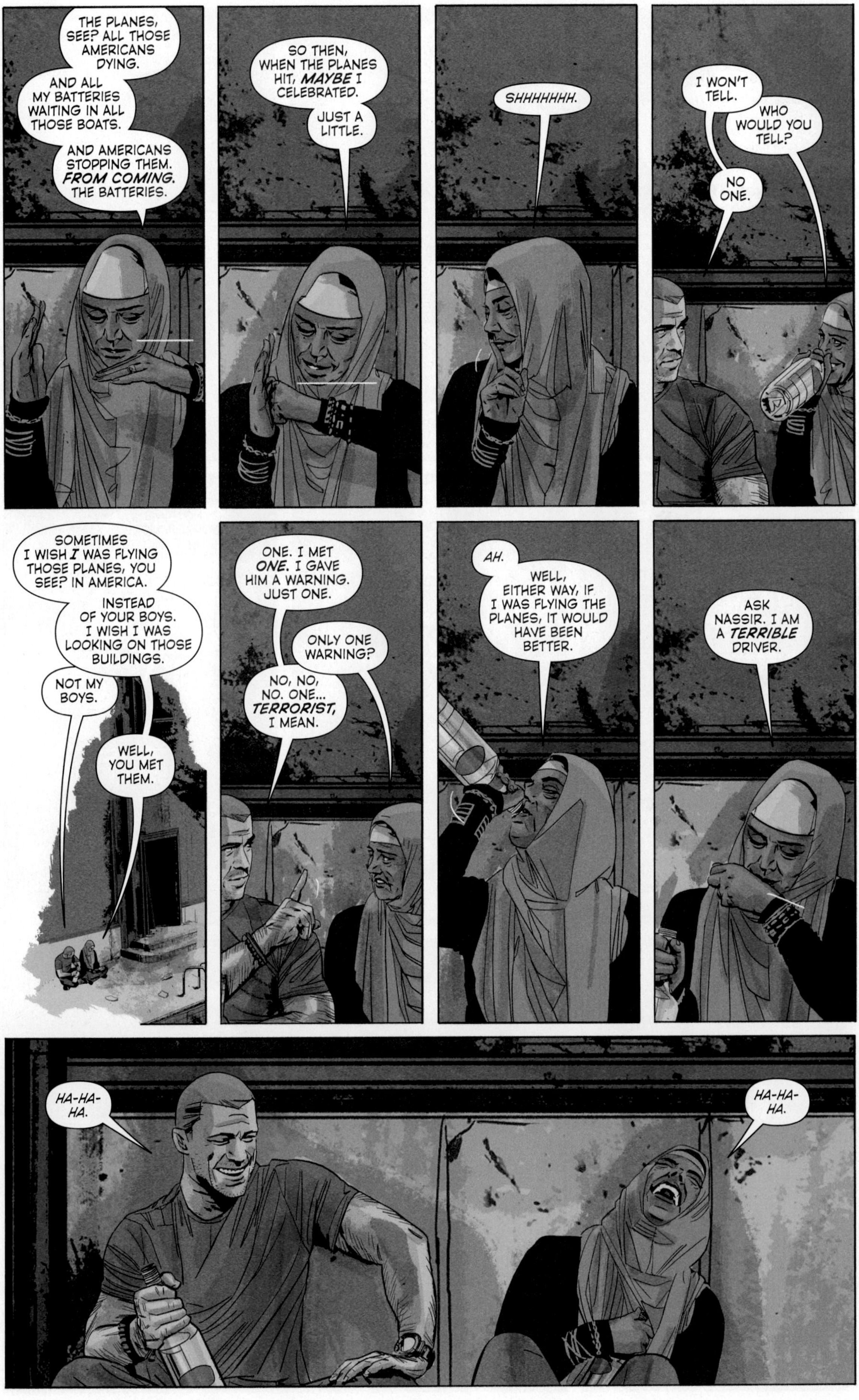
THE PLANES, SEE? ALL THOSE AMERICANS DYING.
AND ALL MY BATTERIES WAITING IN ALL THOSE BOATS.
AND AMERICANS STOPPING THEM. FROM COMING. THE BATTERIES.
SO THEN, WHEN THE PLANES HIT, MAYBE I CELEBRATED.
JUST A LITTLE.
SHHHHHHH.
I WON'T TELL.
WHO WOULD YOU TELL?
NO ONE.
SOMETIMES I WISH I WAS FLYING THOSE PLANES, YOU SEE? IN AMERICA.
INSTEAD OF YOUR BOYS. I WISH I WAS LOOKING ON THOSE BUILDINGS.
NOT MY BOYS.
WELL, YOU MET THEM.
ONE. I MET ONE. I GAVE HIM A WARNING. JUST ONE.
ONLY ONE WARNING?
NO, NO, NO. ONE... TERRORIST, I MEAN.
AH.
WELL, EITHER WAY, IF I WAS FLYING THE PLANES, IT WOULD HAVE BEEN BETTER.
ASK NASSIR. I AM A TERRIBLE DRIVER.
HA-HA-HA.
HA-HA-HA.

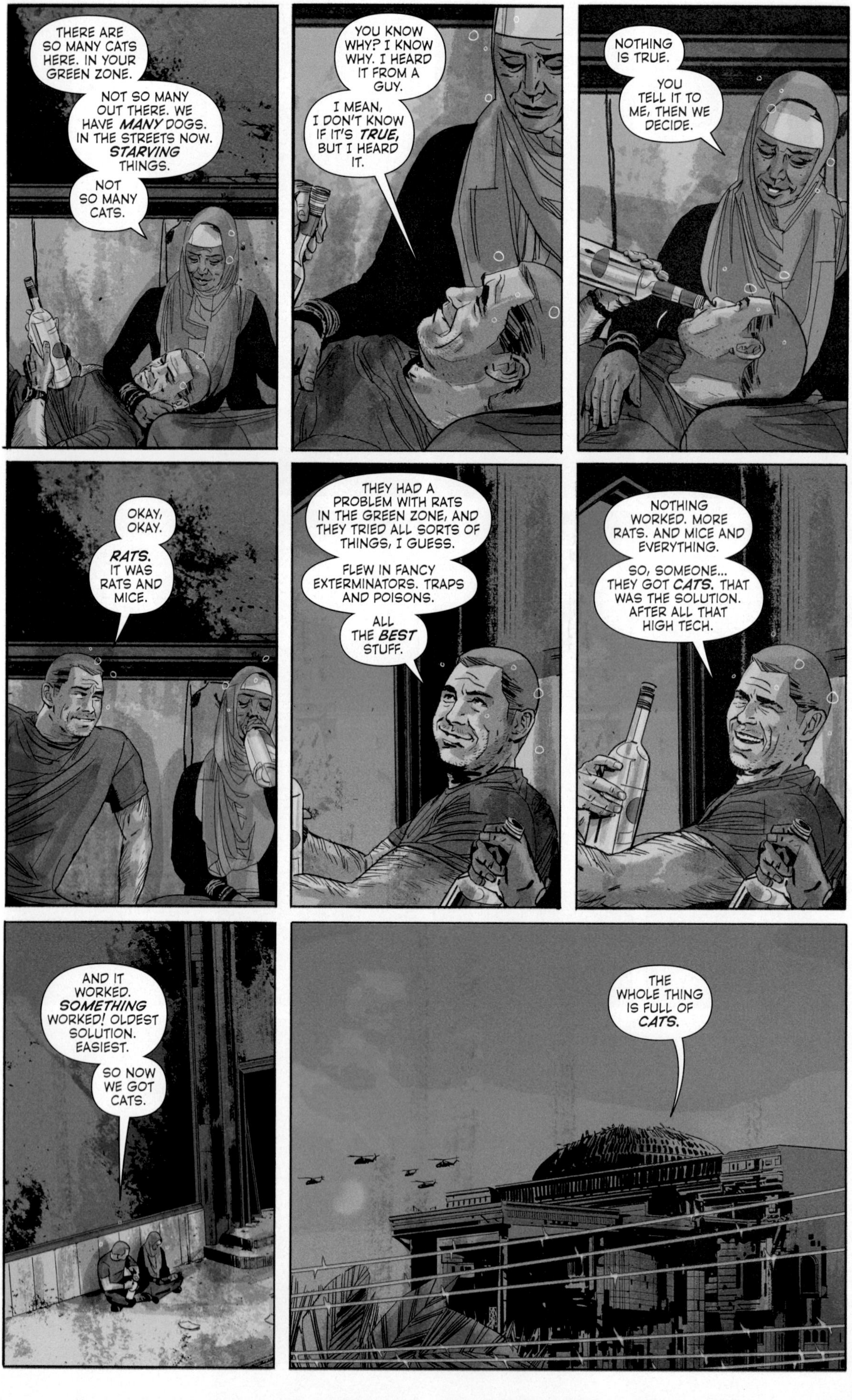
THERE ARE SO MANY CATS HERE. IN YOUR GREEN ZONE.
NOT SO MANY OUT THERE. WE HAVE *MANY* DOGS. IN THE STREETS NOW. *STARVING* THINGS.
NOT SO MANY CATS.
YOU KNOW WHY? I KNOW WHY. I HEARD IT FROM A GUY.
I MEAN, I DON'T KNOW IF IT'S *TRUE,* BUT I HEARD IT.
NOTHING IS TRUE.
YOU TELL IT TO ME, THEN WE DECIDE.
OKAY, OKAY.
RATS. IT WAS RATS AND MICE.
THEY HAD A PROBLEM WITH RATS IN THE GREEN ZONE, AND THEY TRIED ALL SORTS OF THINGS, I GUESS.
FLEW IN FANCY EXTERMINATORS. TRAPS AND POISONS.
ALL THE *BEST* STUFF.
NOTHING WORKED. MORE RATS. AND MICE AND EVERYTHING.
SO, SOMEONE... THEY GOT *CATS.* THAT WAS THE SOLUTION. AFTER ALL THAT HIGH TECH.
AND IT WORKED. *SOMETHING* WORKED! OLDEST SOLUTION. EASIEST.
SO NOW WE GOT CATS.
THE WHOLE THING IS FULL OF *CATS.*

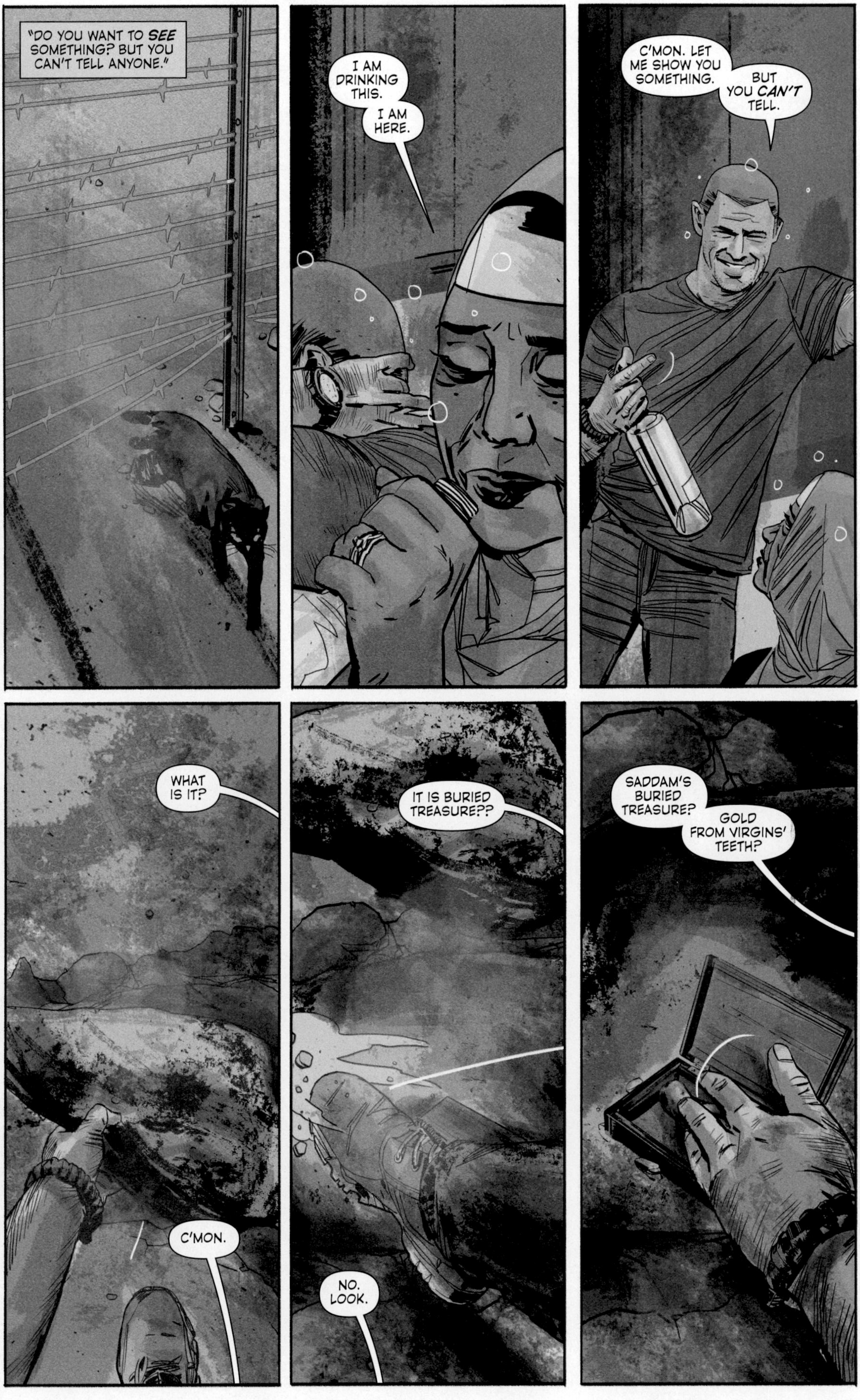
"DO YOU WANT TO *SEE* SOMETHING? BUT YOU CAN'T TELL ANYONE."
I AM DRINKING THIS.
I AM HERE.
C'MON. LET ME SHOW YOU SOMETHING.
BUT YOU *CAN'T* TELL.
WHAT IS IT?
C'MON.
IT IS BURIED TREASURE??
NO. LOOK.
SADDAM'S BURIED TREASURE?
GOLD FROM VIRGINS' TEETH?

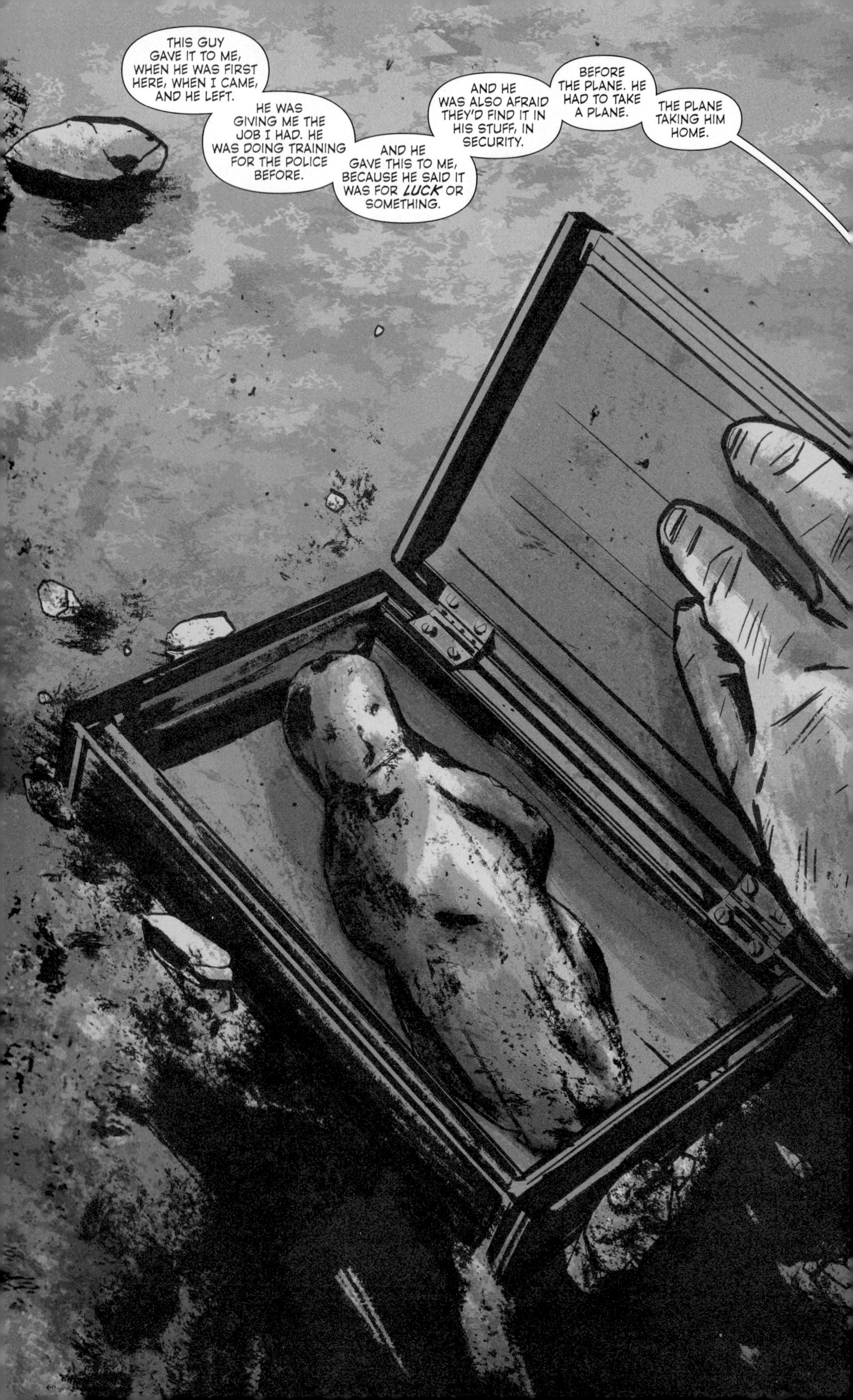
THIS GUY GAVE IT TO ME, WHEN HE WAS FIRST HERE, WHEN I CAME, AND HE LEFT.
HE WAS GIVING ME THE JOB I HAD. HE WAS DOING TRAINING FOR THE POLICE BEFORE.
AND HE GAVE THIS TO ME, BECAUSE HE SAID IT WAS FOR LUCK OR SOMETHING.
AND HE WAS ALSO AFRAID THEY'D FIND IT IN HIS STUFF, IN SECURITY.
BEFORE THE PLANE. HE HAD TO TAKE A PLANE.
THE PLANE TAKING HIM HOME.

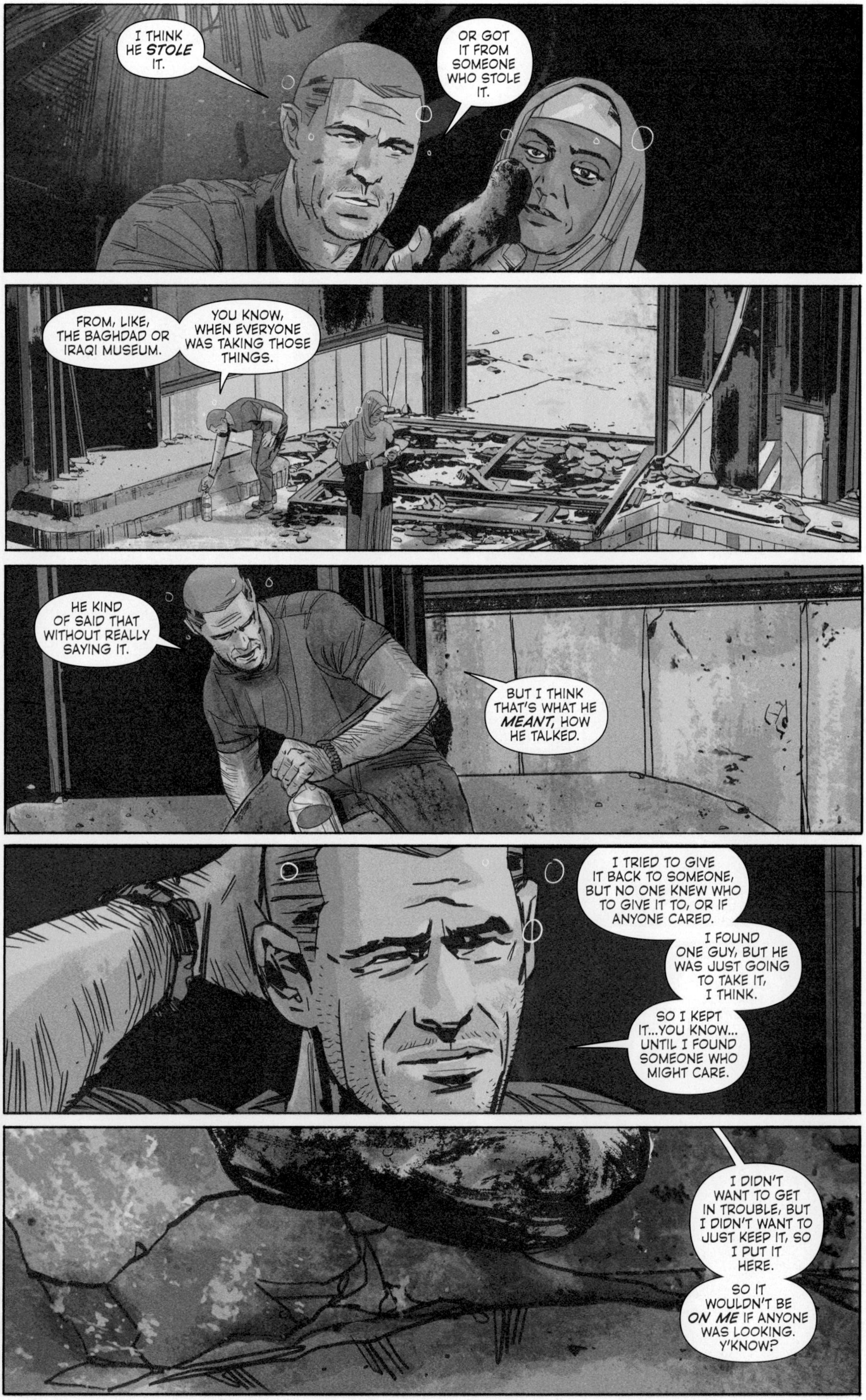
I THINK HE STOLE IT.
OR GOT IT FROM SOMEONE WHO STOLE IT.
FROM, LIKE, THE BAGHDAD OR IRAQI MUSEUM.
YOU KNOW, WHEN EVERYONE WAS TAKING THOSE THINGS.
HE KIND OF SAID THAT WITHOUT REALLY SAYING IT.
BUT I THINK THAT'S WHAT HE MEANT, HOW HE TALKED.
I TRIED TO GIVE IT BACK TO SOMEONE, BUT NO ONE KNEW WHO TO GIVE IT TO, OR IF ANYONE CARED.
I FOUND ONE GUY, BUT HE WAS JUST GOING TO TAKE IT, I THINK.
SO I KEPT IT...YOU KNOW... UNTIL I FOUND SOMEONE WHO MIGHT CARE.
I DIDN'T WANT TO GET IN TROUBLE, BUT I DIDN'T WANT TO JUST KEEP IT, SO I PUT IT HERE.
SO IT WOULDN'T BE ON ME IF ANYONE WAS LOOKING. Y'KNOW?

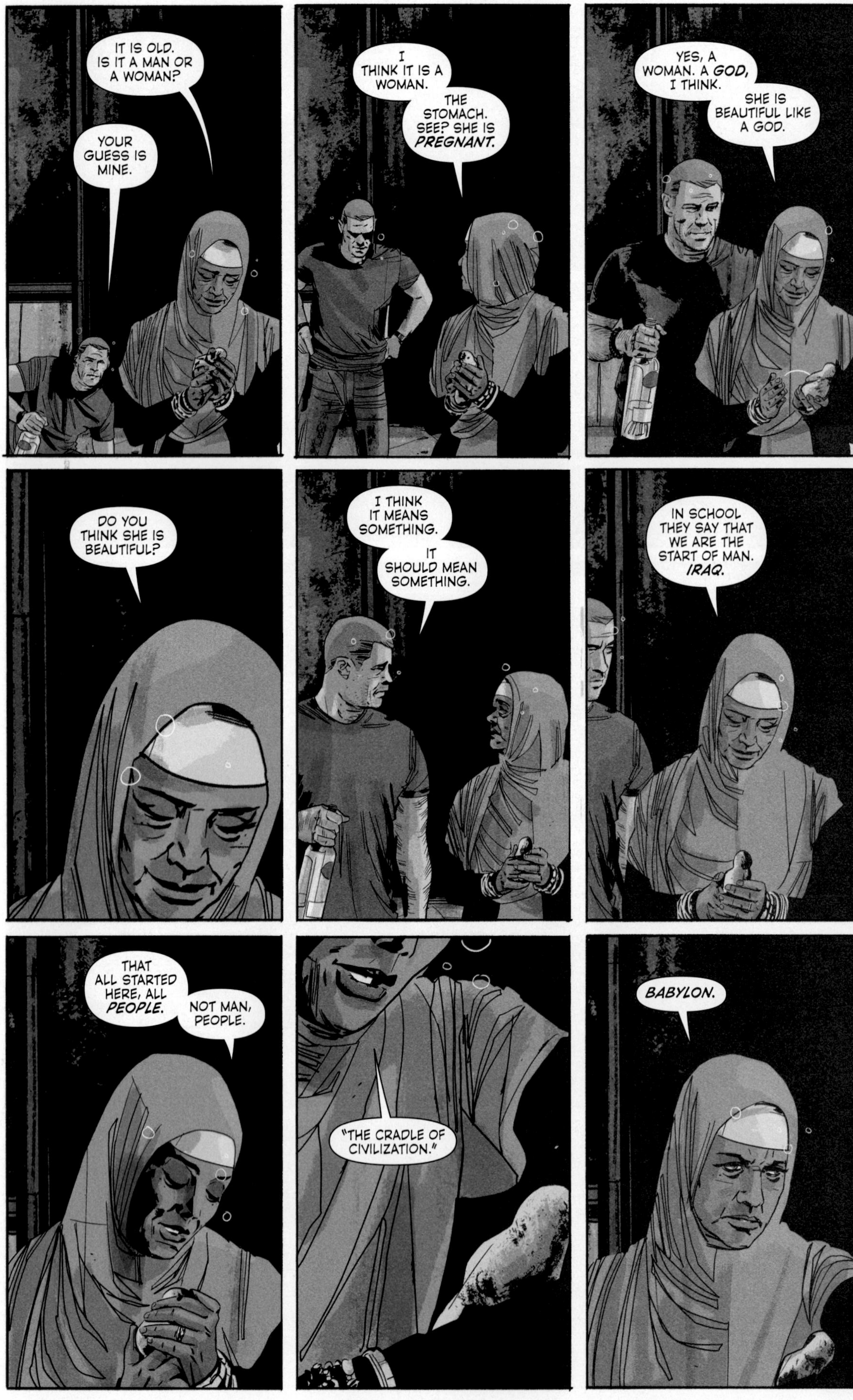
IT IS OLD. IS IT A MAN OR A WOMAN?
YOUR GUESS IS MINE.
I THINK IT IS A WOMAN.
THE STOMACH. SEE? SHE IS *PREGNANT.*
YES, A WOMAN. A *GOD,* I THINK.
SHE IS BEAUTIFUL LIKE A GOD.
DO YOU THINK SHE IS BEAUTIFUL?
I THINK IT MEANS SOMETHING.
IT SHOULD MEAN SOMETHING.
IN SCHOOL THEY SAY THAT WE ARE THE START OF MAN. *IRAQ.*
THAT ALL STARTED HERE, ALL *PEOPLE*.
NOT MAN, PEOPLE.
"THE CRADLE OF CIVILIZATION."
BABYLON.

MAYBE *THIS* IS FROM THE BEGINNING THEN?

FROM THE VERY TOP OF THINGS.

IT SHOULD ALL MEAN SOMETHING.

BUT STILL. YES? IN THE END.

NOT IN THE BEGINNING, MAYBE.

IN THE *END*.

THERE IS ONLY ONE GOD.

AND MUHAMMAD IS HIS PROPHET.

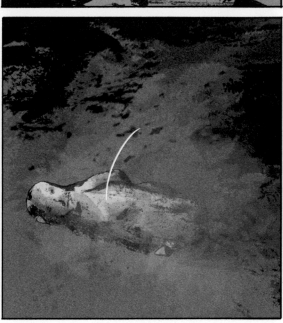

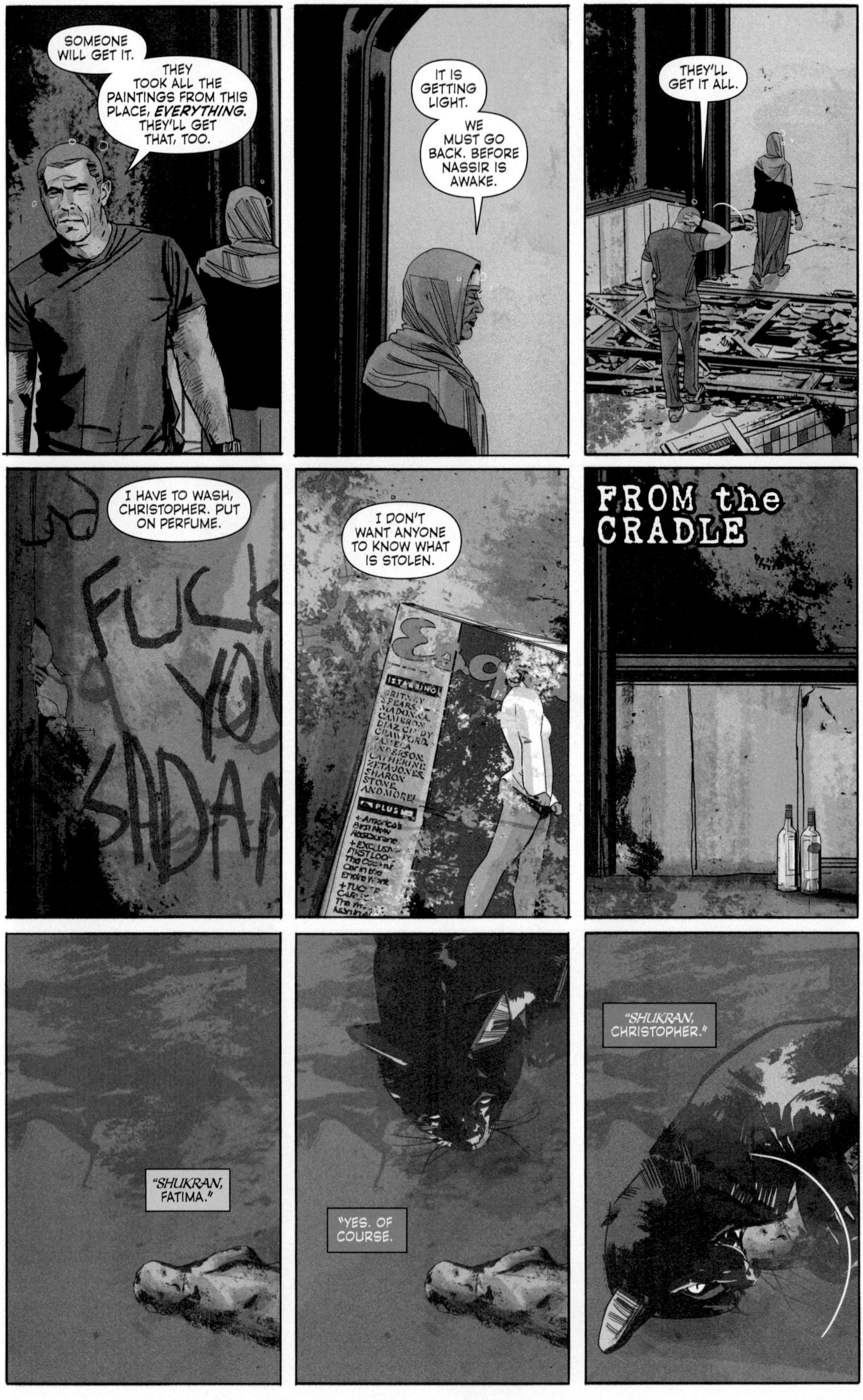
SOMEONE WILL GET IT.
THEY TOOK ALL THE PAINTINGS FROM THIS PLACE, ***EVERYTHING.*** THEY'LL GET THAT, TOO.
IT IS GETTING LIGHT.
WE MUST GO BACK. BEFORE NASSIR IS AWAKE.
THEY'LL GET IT ALL.
I HAVE TO WASH, CHRISTOPHER. PUT ON PERFUME.
I DON'T WANT ANYONE TO KNOW WHAT IS STOLEN.
FROM the CRADLE
"SHUKRAN, FATIMA."
"YES. OF COURSE.
"SHUKRAN, CHRISTOPHER."

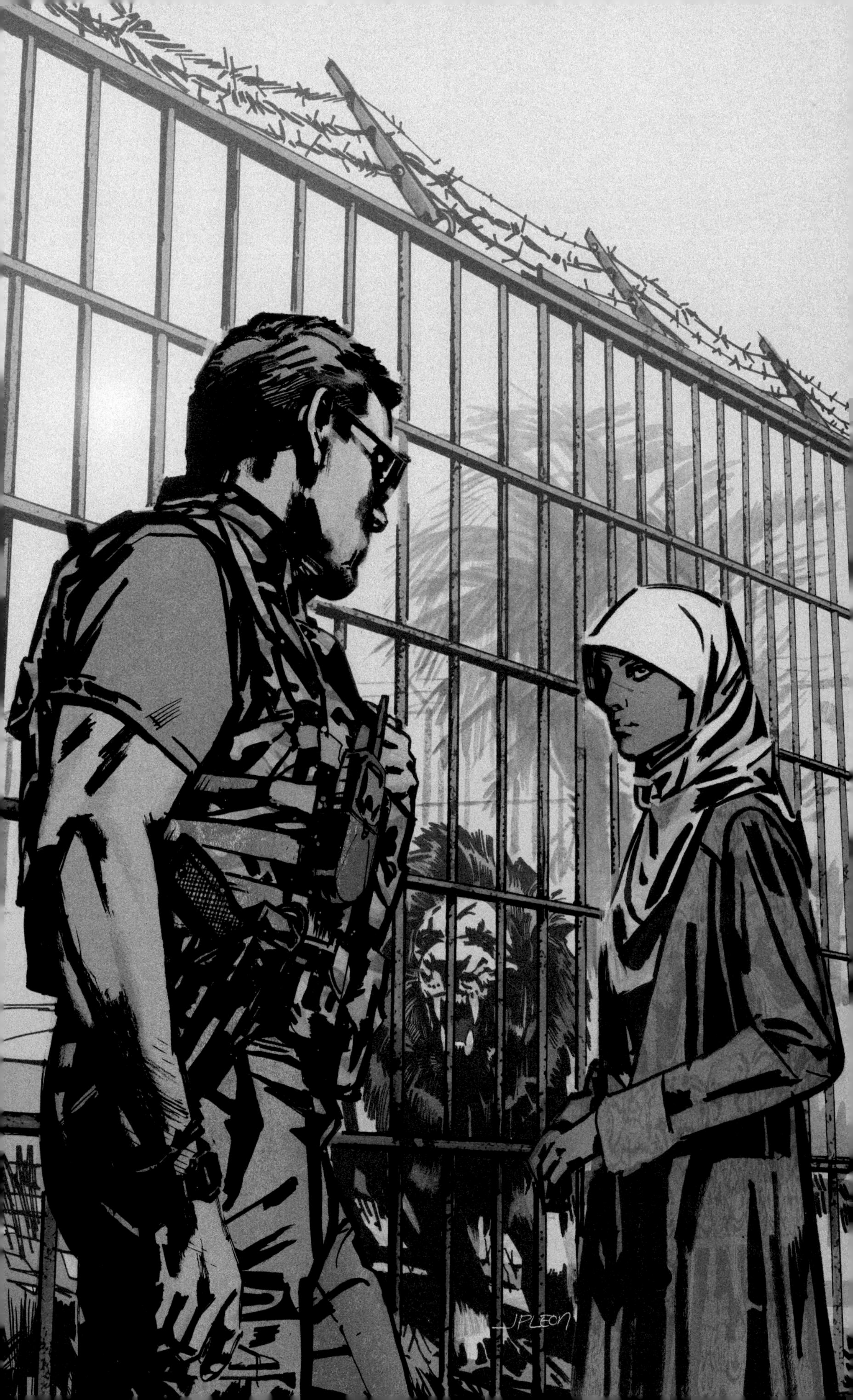
JPLEON

PART SIX

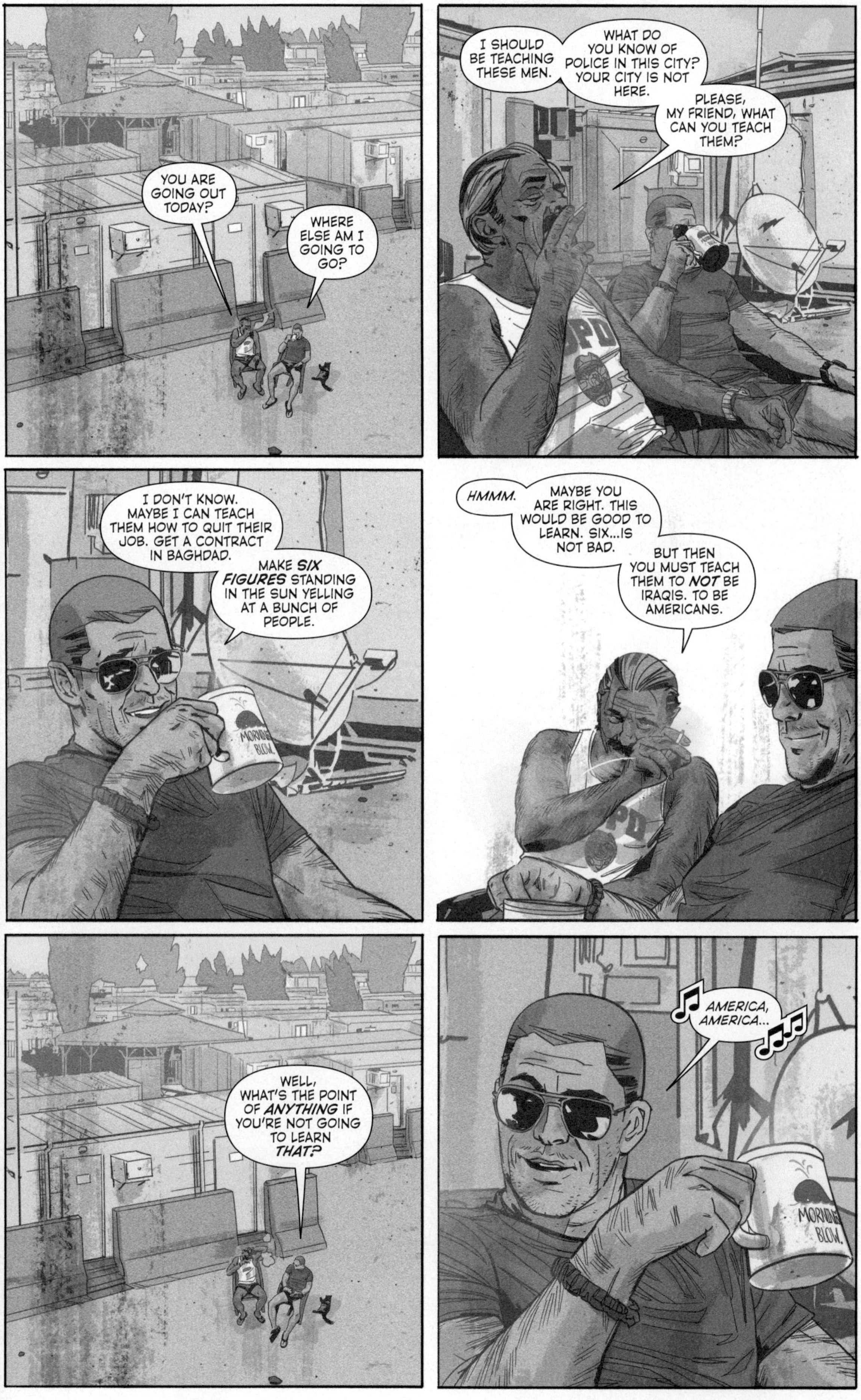
YOU ARE GOING OUT TODAY?
WHERE ELSE AM I GOING TO GO?
I SHOULD BE TEACHING THESE MEN.
WHAT DO YOU KNOW OF POLICE IN THIS CITY? YOUR CITY IS NOT HERE.
PLEASE, MY FRIEND, WHAT CAN YOU TEACH THEM?
I DON'T KNOW. MAYBE I CAN TEACH THEM HOW TO QUIT THEIR JOB. GET A CONTRACT IN BAGHDAD.
MAKE *SIX FIGURES* STANDING IN THE SUN YELLING AT A BUNCH OF PEOPLE.
MORNING BLOW.
HMMM.
MAYBE YOU ARE RIGHT. THIS WOULD BE GOOD TO LEARN. SIX...IS NOT BAD.
BUT THEN YOU MUST TEACH THEM TO *NOT* BE IRAQIS. TO BE AMERICANS.
WELL, WHAT'S THE POINT OF *ANYTHING* IF YOU'RE NOT GOING TO LEARN *THAT?*
AMERICA, AMERICA...
MORNING BLOW.

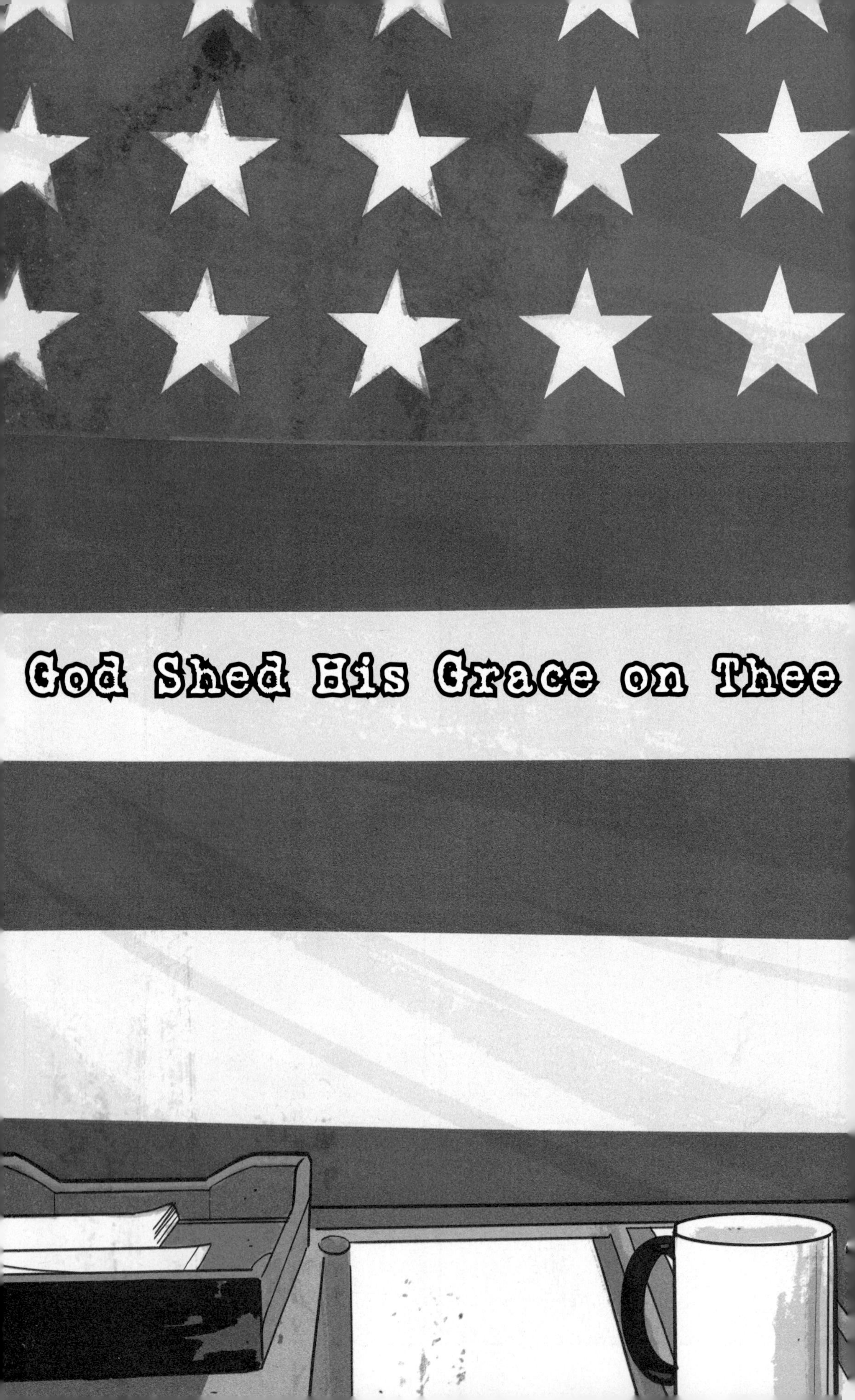
God Shed His Grace on Thee

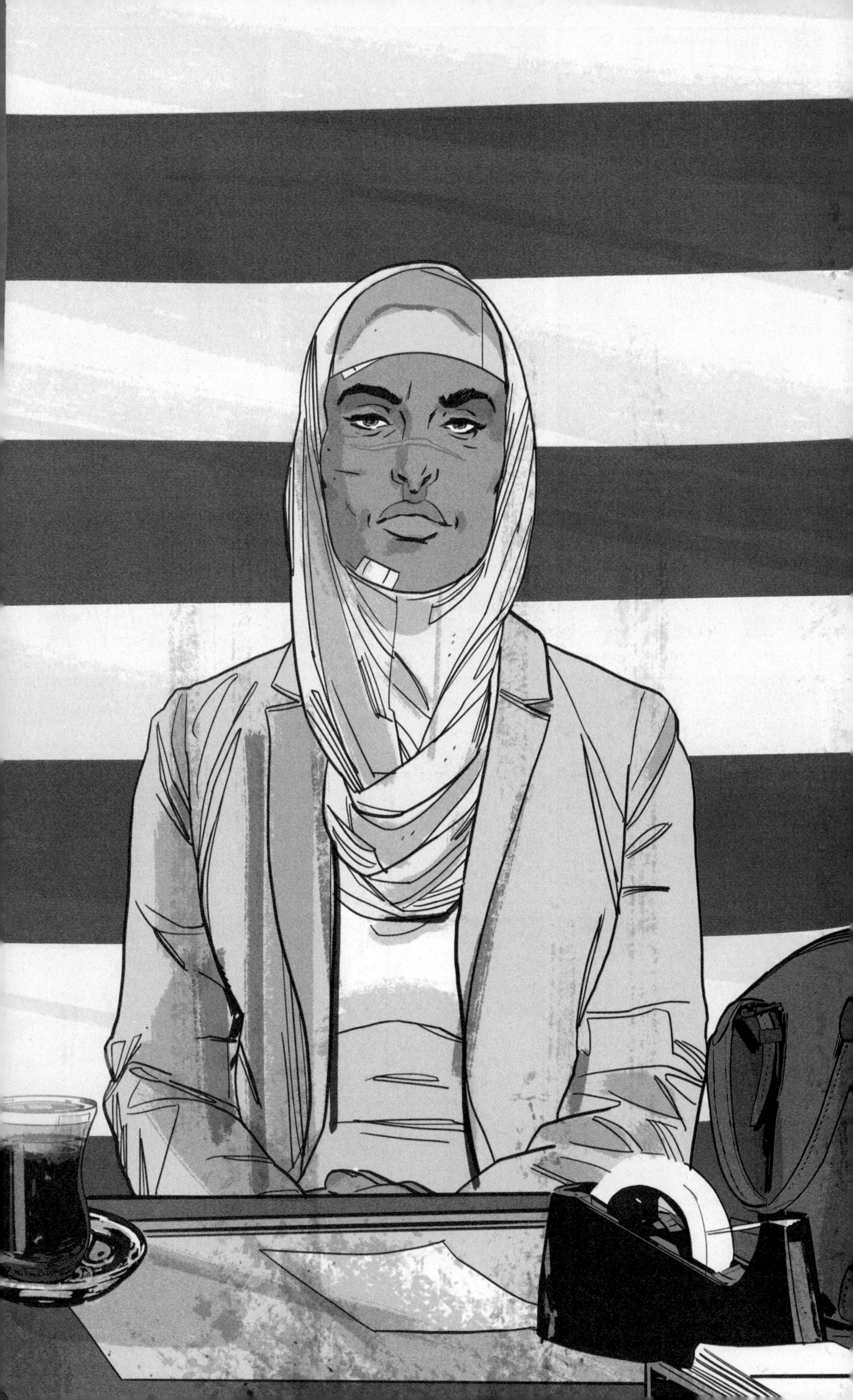

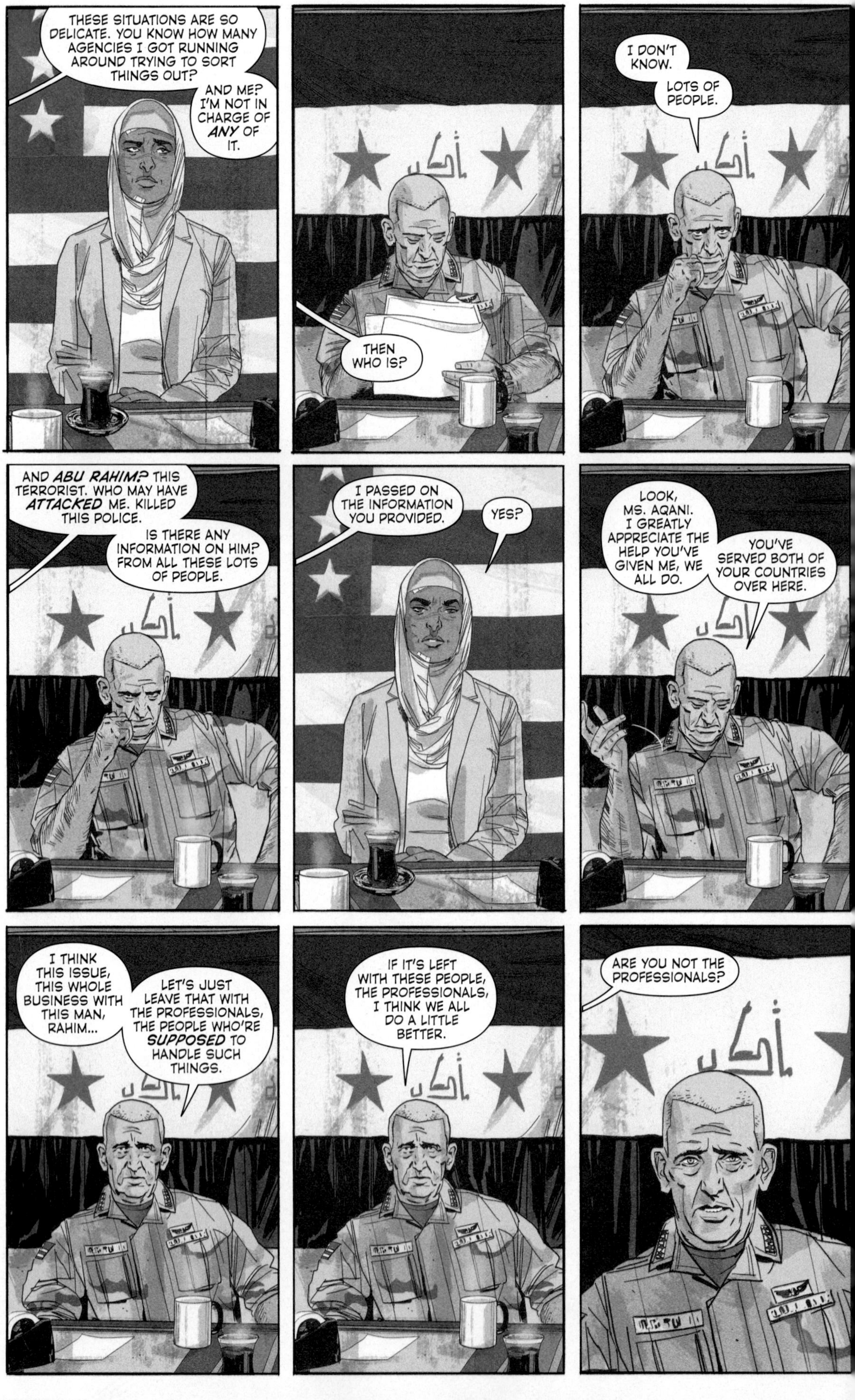
THESE SITUATIONS ARE SO DELICATE. YOU KNOW HOW MANY AGENCIES I GOT RUNNING AROUND TRYING TO SORT THINGS OUT?
AND ME? I'M NOT IN CHARGE OF ANY OF IT.
THEN WHO IS?
I DON'T KNOW.
LOTS OF PEOPLE.
AND ABU RAHIM? THIS TERRORIST. WHO MAY HAVE ATTACKED ME. KILLED THIS POLICE.
IS THERE ANY INFORMATION ON HIM? FROM ALL THESE LOTS OF PEOPLE.
I PASSED ON THE INFORMATION YOU PROVIDED.
YES?
LOOK, MS. AQANI. I GREATLY APPRECIATE THE HELP YOU'VE GIVEN ME, WE ALL DO.
YOU'VE SERVED BOTH OF YOUR COUNTRIES OVER HERE.
I THINK THIS ISSUE, THIS WHOLE BUSINESS WITH THIS MAN, RAHIM...
LET'S JUST LEAVE THAT WITH THE PROFESSIONALS, THE PEOPLE WHO'RE SUPPOSED TO HANDLE SUCH THINGS.
IF IT'S LEFT WITH THESE PEOPLE, THE PROFESSIONALS, I THINK WE ALL DO A LITTLE BETTER.
ARE YOU NOT THE PROFESSIONALS?

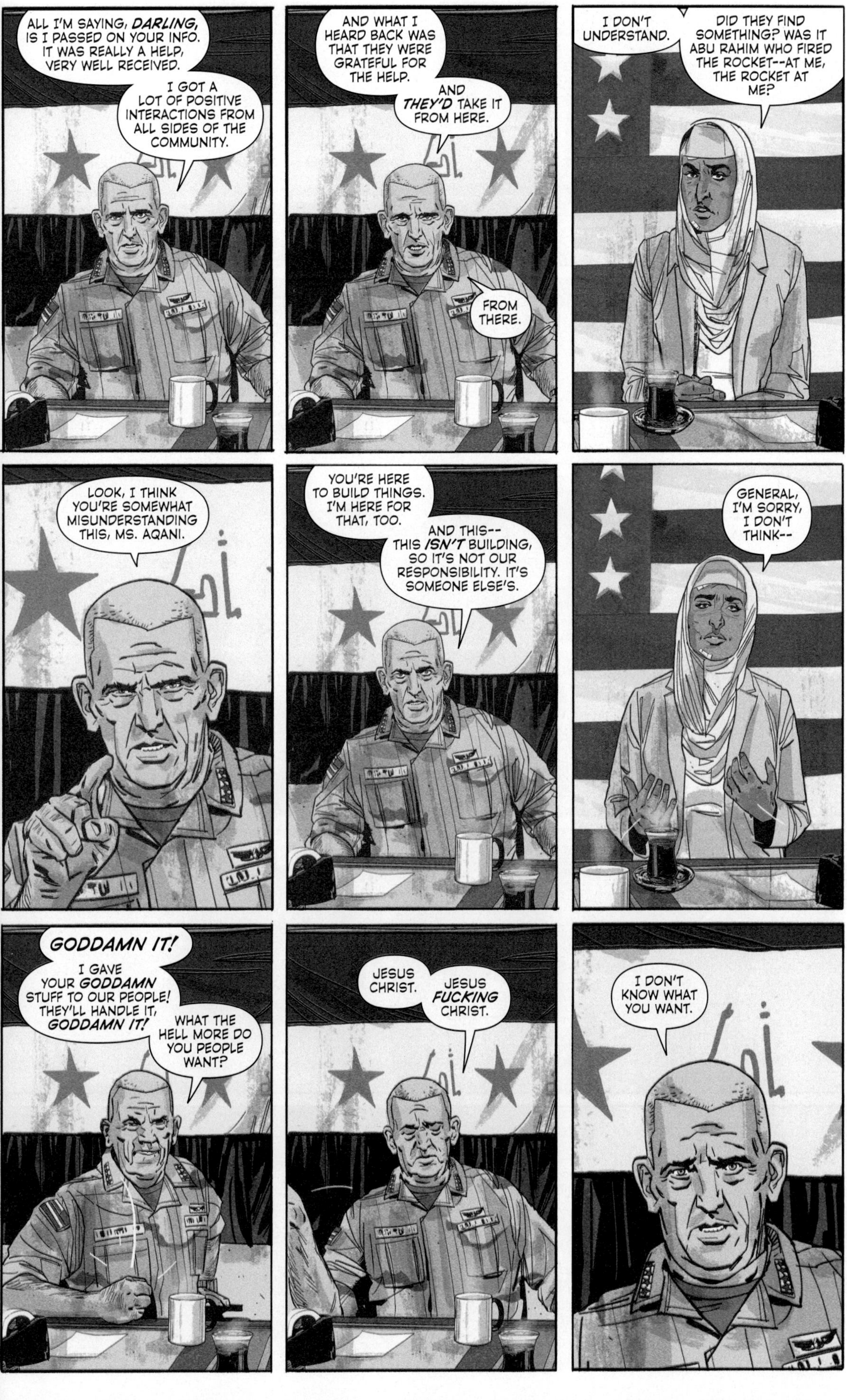
ALL I'M SAYING, *DARLING,* IS I PASSED ON YOUR INFO. IT WAS REALLY A HELP, VERY WELL RECEIVED.
I GOT A LOT OF POSITIVE INTERACTIONS FROM ALL SIDES OF THE COMMUNITY.
AND WHAT I HEARD BACK WAS THAT THEY WERE GRATEFUL FOR THE HELP.
AND *THEY'D* TAKE IT FROM HERE.
FROM THERE.
I DON'T UNDERSTAND.
DID THEY FIND SOMETHING? WAS IT ABU RAHIM WHO FIRED THE ROCKET--AT ME, THE ROCKET AT ME?
LOOK, I THINK YOU'RE SOMEWHAT MISUNDERSTANDING THIS, MS. AQANI.
YOU'RE HERE TO BUILD THINGS. I'M HERE FOR THAT, TOO.
AND THIS-- THIS *ISN'T* BUILDING, SO IT'S NOT OUR RESPONSIBILITY. IT'S SOMEONE ELSE'S.
GENERAL, I'M SORRY, I DON'T THINK--
GODDAMN IT!
I GAVE YOUR *GODDAMN* STUFF TO OUR PEOPLE! THEY'LL HANDLE IT, *GODDAMN IT!*
WHAT THE HELL MORE DO YOU PEOPLE WANT?
JESUS CHRIST.
JESUS *FUCKING* CHRIST.
I DON'T KNOW WHAT YOU WANT.

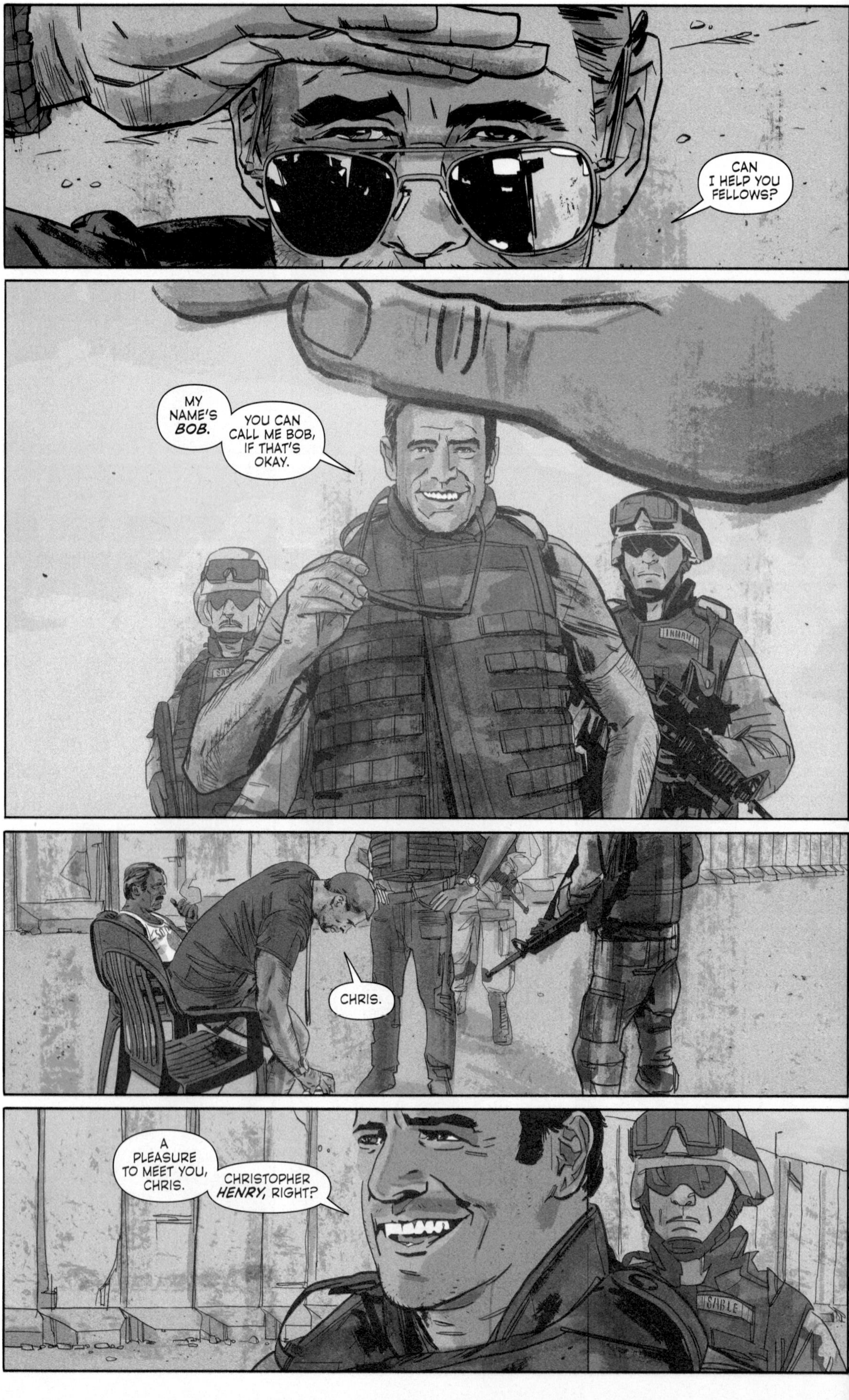
CAN I HELP YOU FELLOWS?
MY NAME'S *BOB*.
YOU CAN CALL ME BOB, IF THAT'S OKAY.
INMAN
CHRIS.
A PLEASURE TO MEET YOU, CHRIS.
CHRISTOPHER *HENRY,* RIGHT?
SABLE

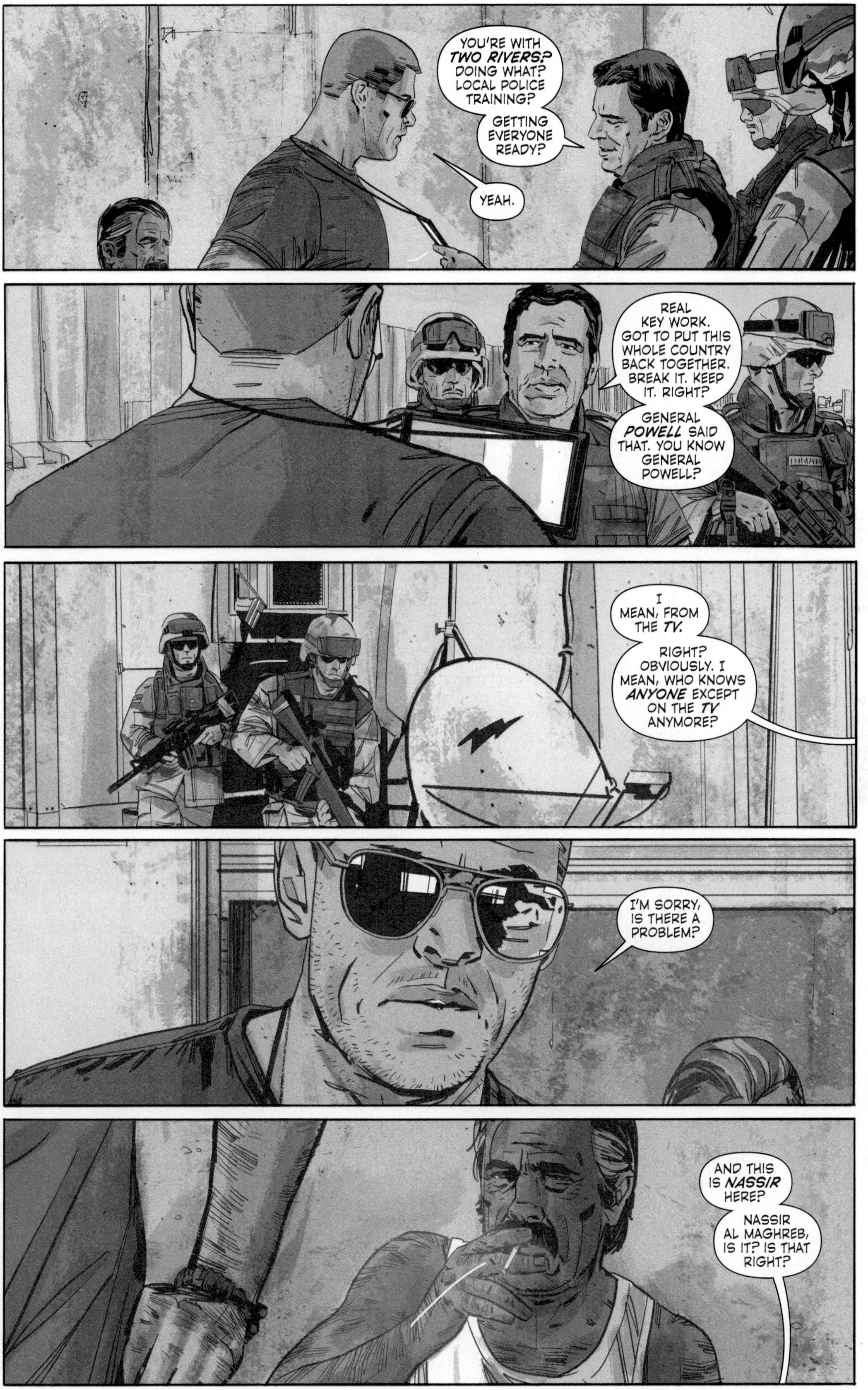
YOU'RE WITH *TWO RIVERS?* DOING WHAT? LOCAL POLICE TRAINING?
GETTING EVERYONE READY?
YEAH.
REAL KEY WORK. GOT TO PUT THIS WHOLE COUNTRY BACK TOGETHER. BREAK IT. KEEP IT. RIGHT?
GENERAL *POWELL* SAID THAT. YOU KNOW GENERAL POWELL?
INMAN
I MEAN, FROM THE *TV.*
RIGHT? OBVIOUSLY. I MEAN, ANYONE WHO KNOWS *ANYONE* EXCEPT ON THE *TV* ANYMORE?
I'M SORRY, IS THERE A PROBLEM?
AND THIS IS *NASSIR* HERE?
NASSIR AL MAGHREB, IS IT? IS THAT RIGHT?

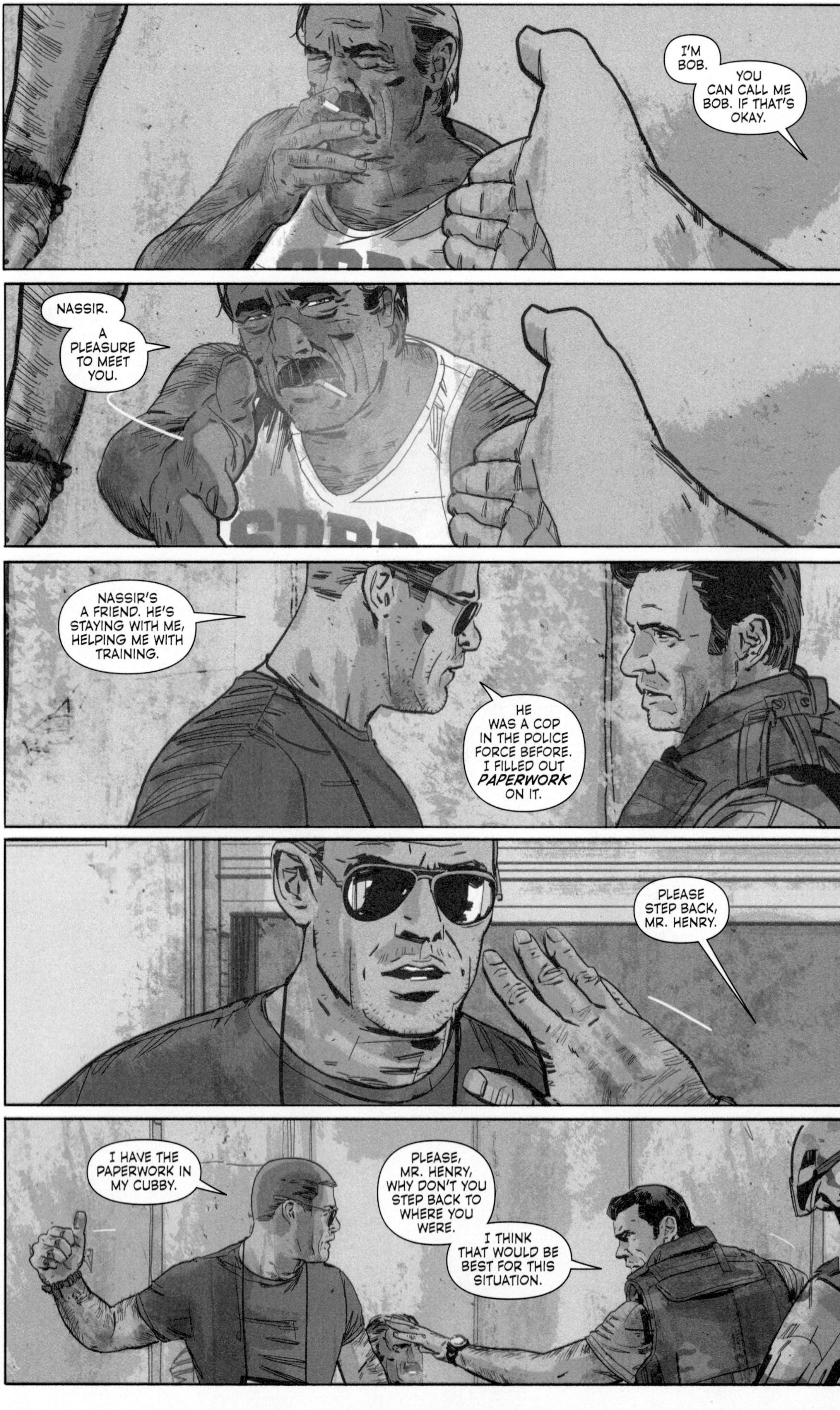
I'M BOB.
YOU CAN CALL ME BOB. IF THAT'S OKAY.
NASSIR.
A PLEASURE TO MEET YOU.
NASSIR'S A FRIEND. HE'S STAYING WITH ME, HELPING ME WITH TRAINING.
HE WAS A COP IN THE POLICE FORCE BEFORE. I FILLED OUT *PAPERWORK* ON IT.
PLEASE STEP BACK, MR. HENRY.
I HAVE THE PAPERWORK IN MY CUBBY.
PLEASE, MR. HENRY, WHY DON'T YOU STEP BACK TO WHERE YOU WERE.
I THINK THAT WOULD BE BEST FOR THIS SITUATION.

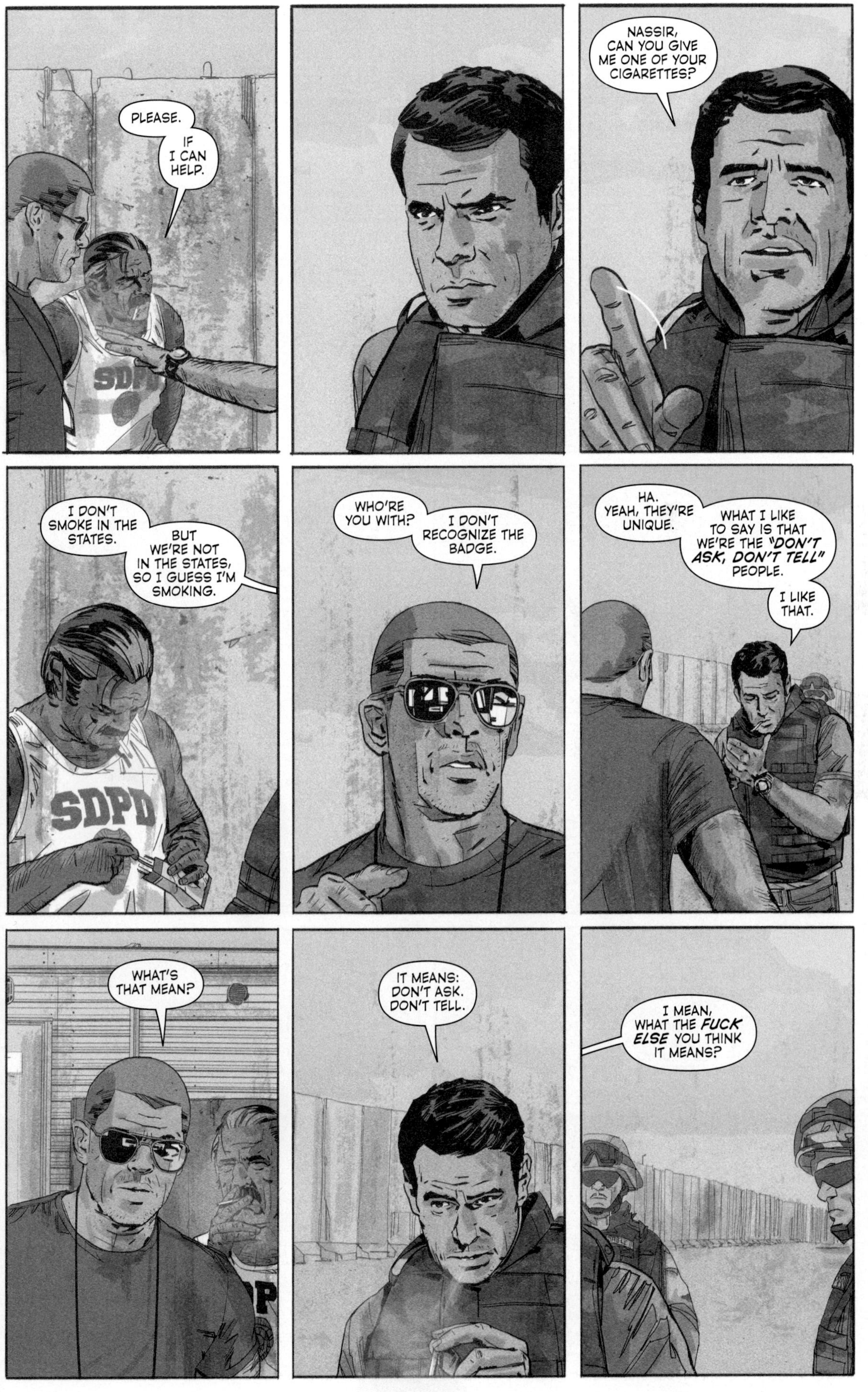
PLEASE.
IF I CAN HELP.
NASSIR, CAN YOU GIVE ME ONE OF YOUR CIGARETTES?
SDPD
I DON'T SMOKE IN THE STATES.
BUT WE'RE NOT IN THE STATES, SO I GUESS I'M SMOKING.
SDPD
WHO'RE YOU WITH?
I DON'T RECOGNIZE THE BADGE.
HA. YEAH, THEY'RE UNIQUE.
WHAT I LIKE TO SAY IS THAT WE'RE THE *"DON'T ASK, DON'T TELL"* PEOPLE.
I LIKE THAT.
WHAT'S THAT MEAN?
IT MEANS: DON'T ASK. DON'T TELL.
I MEAN, WHAT THE *FUCK ELSE* YOU THINK IT MEANS?

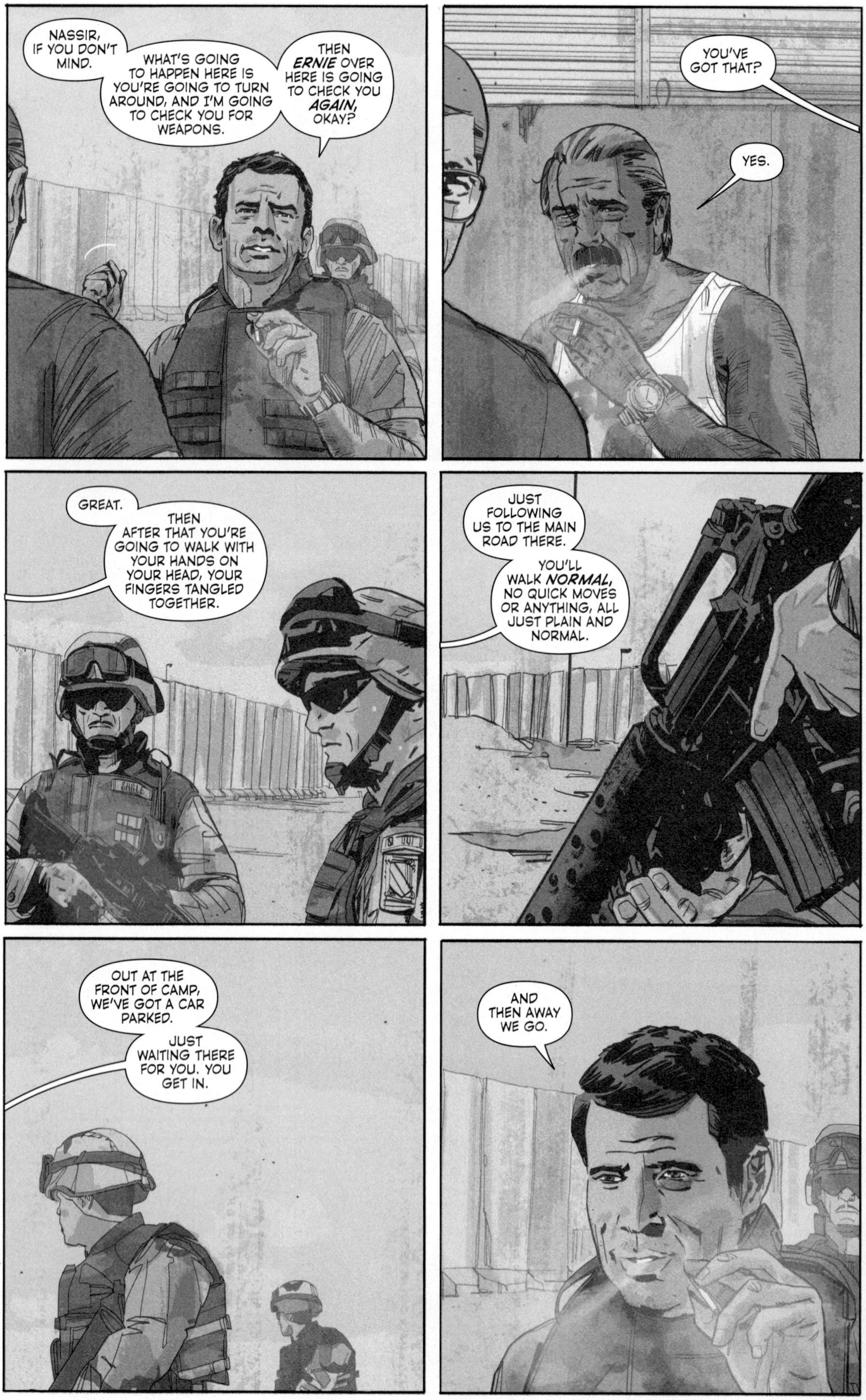
NASSIR, IF YOU DON'T MIND.
WHAT'S GOING TO HAPPEN HERE IS YOU'RE GOING TO TURN AROUND, AND I'M GOING TO CHECK YOU FOR WEAPONS.
THEN ERNIE OVER HERE IS GOING TO CHECK YOU AGAIN, OKAY?
YOU'VE GOT THAT?
YES.
GREAT.
THEN AFTER THAT YOU'RE GOING TO WALK WITH YOUR HANDS ON YOUR HEAD, YOUR FINGERS TANGLED TOGETHER.
JUST FOLLOWING US TO THE MAIN ROAD THERE.
YOU'LL WALK NORMAL, NO QUICK MOVES OR ANYTHING, ALL JUST PLAIN AND NORMAL.
OUT AT THE FRONT OF CAMP, WE'VE GOT A CAR PARKED.
JUST WAITING THERE FOR YOU. YOU GET IN.
AND THEN AWAY WE GO.

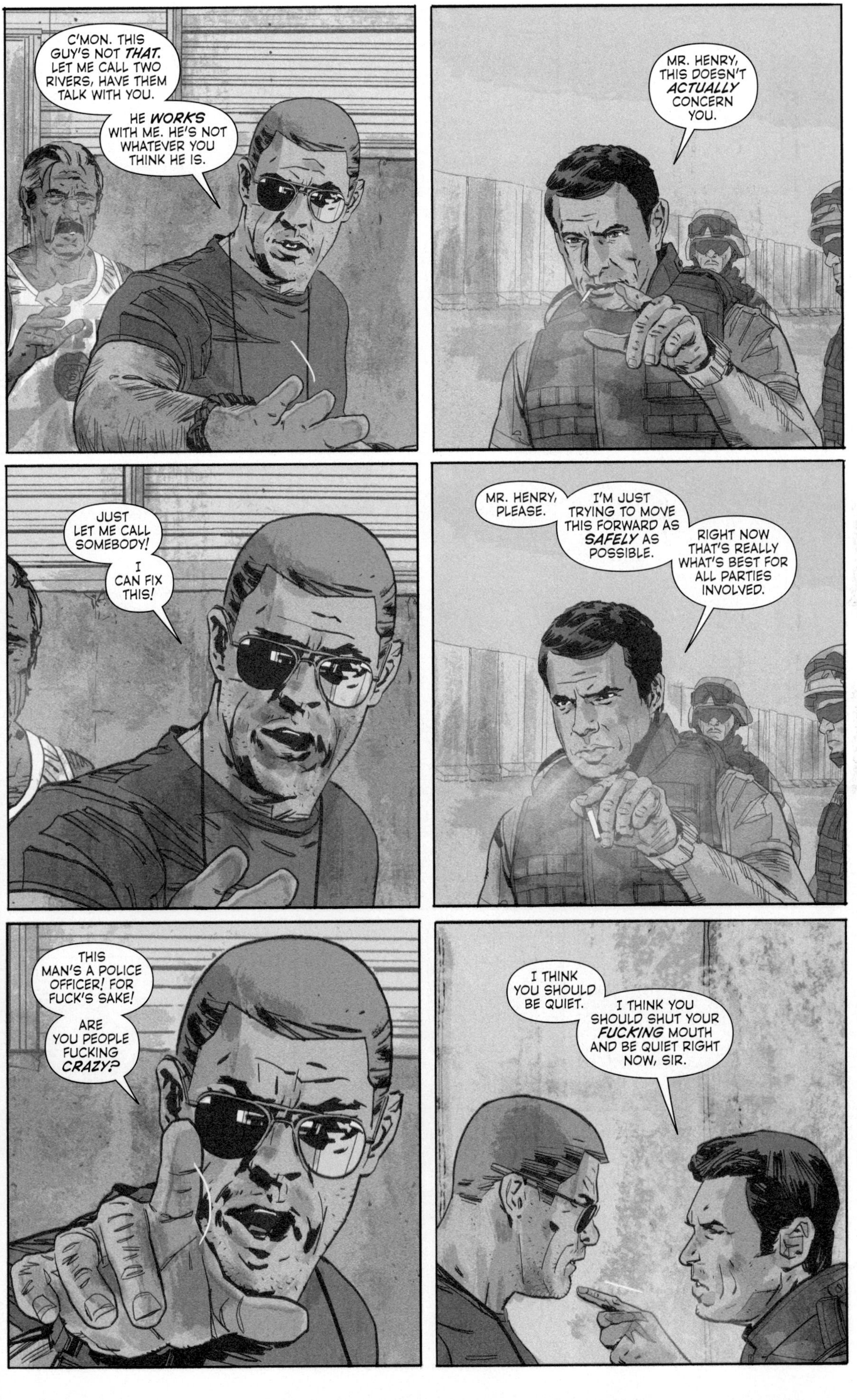
C'MON. THIS GUY'S NOT ***THAT.*** LET ME CALL TWO RIVERS, HAVE THEM TALK WITH YOU.
HE ***WORKS*** WITH ME. HE'S NOT WHATEVER YOU THINK HE IS.
MR. HENRY, THIS DOESN'T ***ACTUALLY*** CONCERN YOU.
JUST LET ME CALL SOMEBODY!
I CAN FIX THIS!
MR. HENRY, PLEASE.
I'M JUST TRYING TO MOVE THIS FORWARD AS ***SAFELY*** AS POSSIBLE.
RIGHT NOW THAT'S REALLY WHAT'S BEST FOR ALL PARTIES INVOLVED.
THIS MAN'S A POLICE OFFICER! FOR FUCK'S SAKE!
ARE YOU PEOPLE FUCKING ***CRAZY?***
I THINK YOU SHOULD BE QUIET.
I THINK YOU SHOULD SHUT YOUR ***FUCKING*** MOUTH AND BE QUIET RIGHT NOW, SIR.

FUCK YOU.

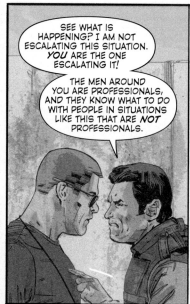

SEE WHAT IS HAPPENING? I AM NOT ESCALATING THIS SITUATION. *YOU* ARE THE ONE ESCALATING IT!

THE MEN AROUND YOU ARE PROFESSIONALS, AND THEY KNOW WHAT TO DO WITH PEOPLE IN SITUATIONS LIKE THIS THAT ARE *NOT* PROFESSIONALS.

I'M A POLICE OFFICER!

SIR, LOOK WHERE YOU ARE!

JUST LOOK WHERE YOU ARE AND HEAR YOUR VOICE AND *THINK* ABOUT YOUR VOICE!

OKAY? JUST *THINK!*

PLEASE! PLEASE, CHRISTOPHER. YOU *MUST* LISTEN. IT IS FINE. IT IS *ALL* FINE.

IT IS ALL FINE!

14-312A

What is this? What is this?

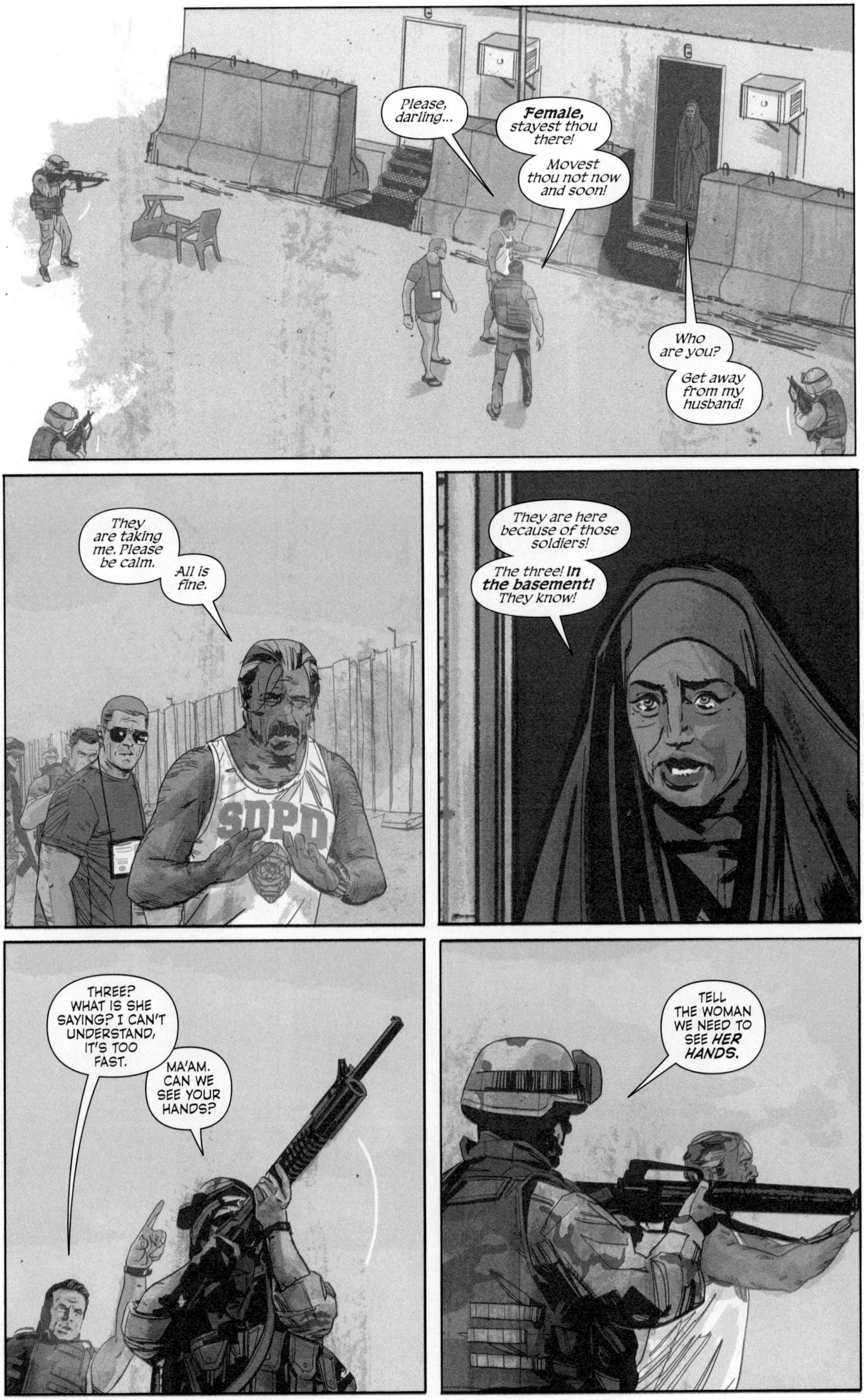
Please, darling...
Female, stayest thou there!
Movest thou not now and soon!
Who are you?
Get away from my husband!
They are taking me. Please be calm.
All is fine.
SDPD
They are here because of those soldiers!
The three! In the basement! They know!
THREE? WHAT IS SHE SAYING? I CAN'T UNDERSTAND, IT'S TOO FAST.
MA'AM. CAN WE SEE YOUR HANDS?
TELL THE WOMAN WE NEED TO SEE HER HANDS.

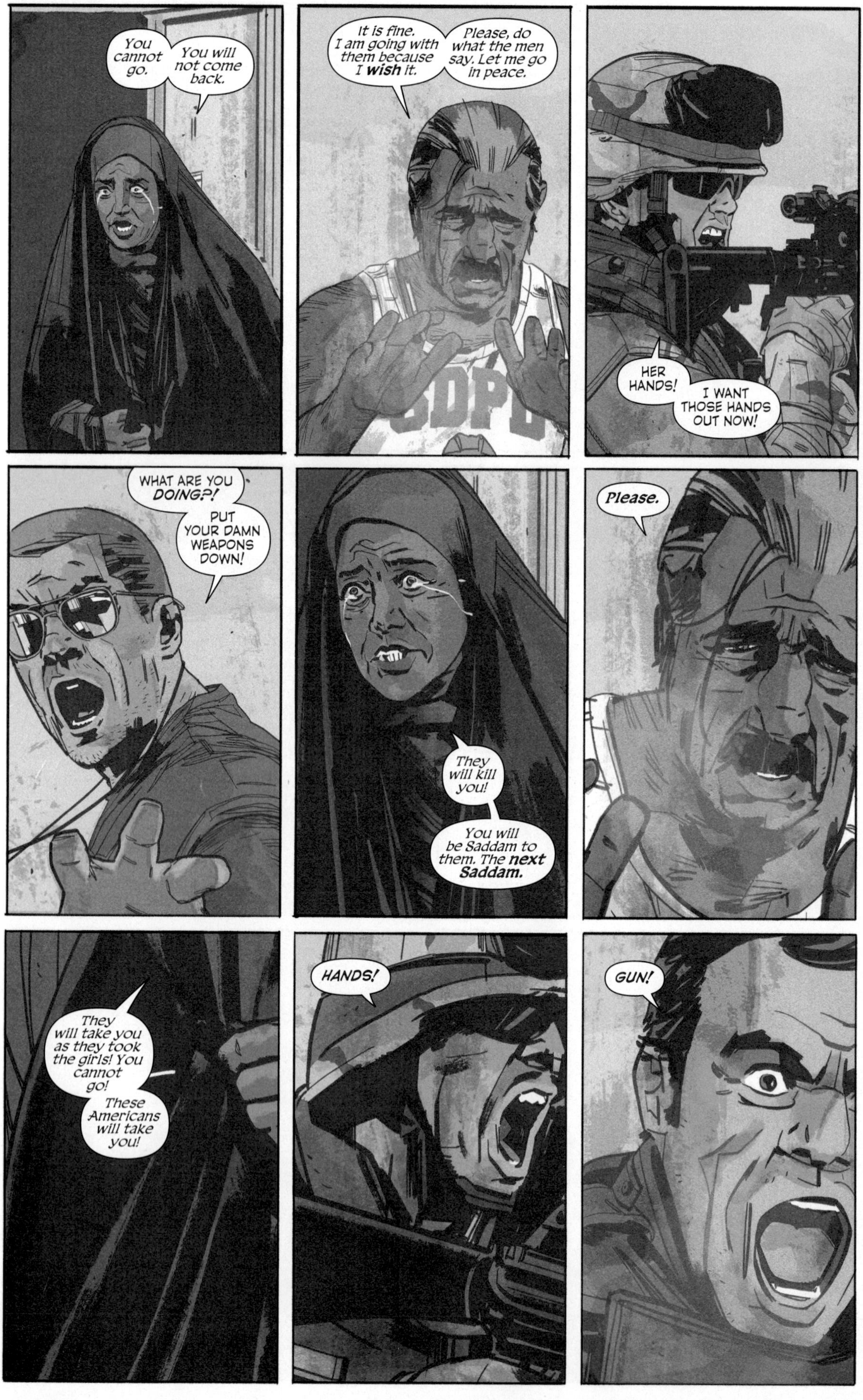

You cannot go.
You will not come back.
It is fine. I am going with them because I **wish** it.
Please, do what the men say. Let me go in peace.
HER HANDS!
I WANT THOSE HANDS OUT NOW!
WHAT ARE YOU ***DOING?!***
PUT YOUR DAMN WEAPONS DOWN!
They will kill you!
You will be Saddam to them. The **next Saddam.**
Please.
They will take you as they took the girls! You cannot go!
These Americans will take you!
HANDS!
GUN!

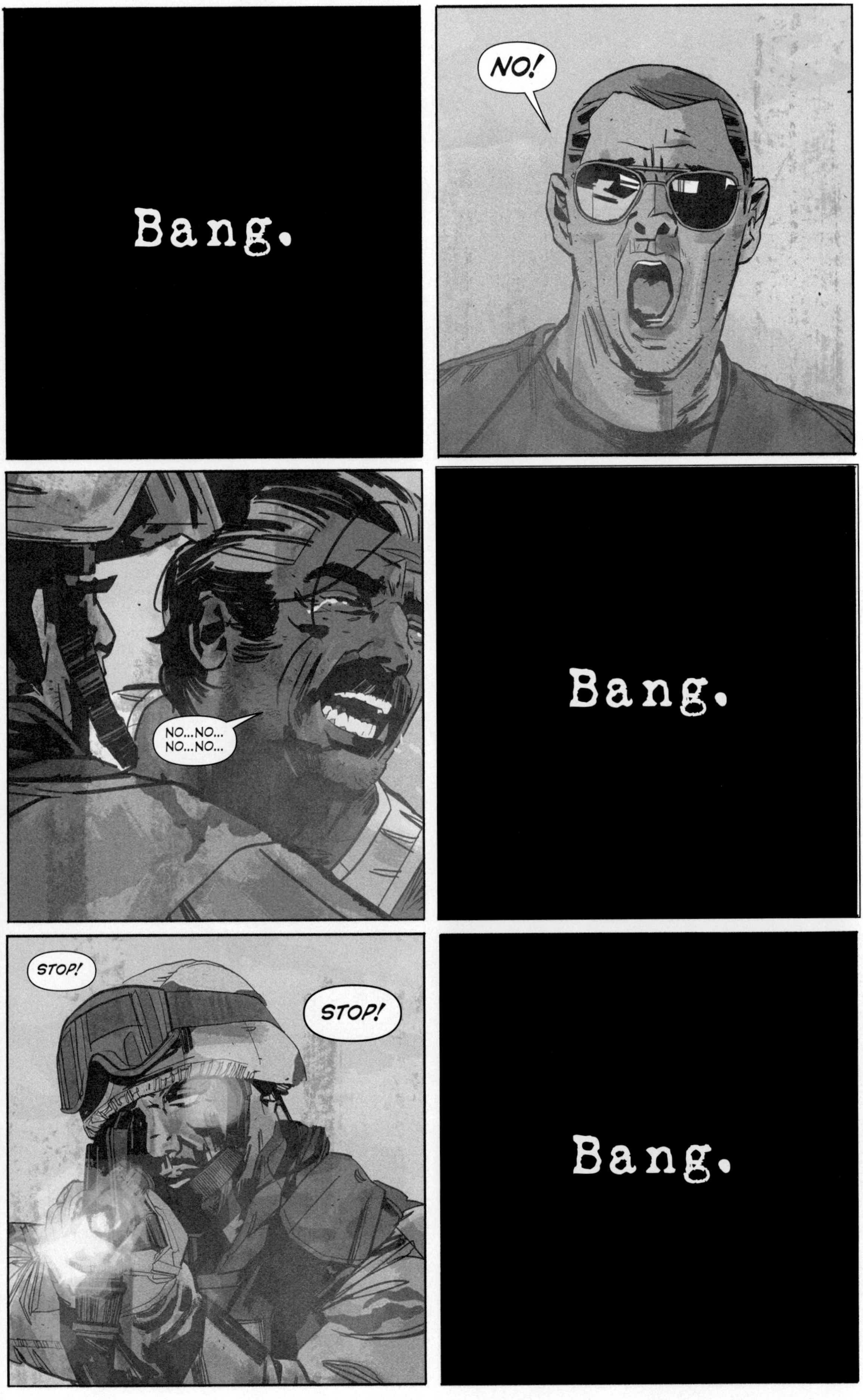
Bang.
NO!
NO...NO...
NO...NO...
Bang.
STOP!
STOP!
Bang.

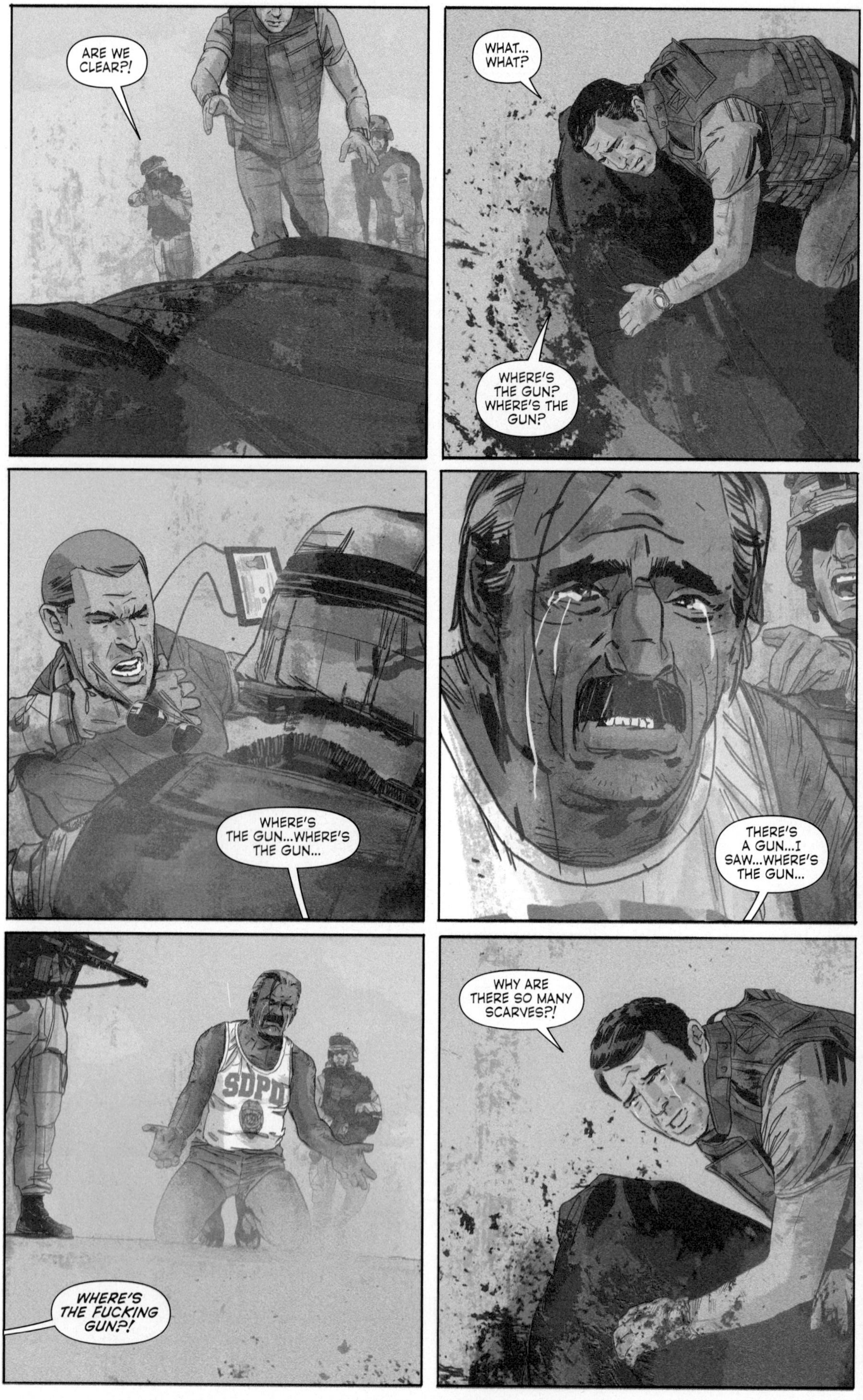
ARE WE CLEAR?!
WHAT... WHAT?
WHERE'S THE GUN? WHERE'S THE GUN?
WHERE'S THE GUN...WHERE'S THE GUN...
THERE'S A GUN...I SAW...WHERE'S THE GUN...
SDPD
WHERE'S THE FUCKING GUN?!
WHY ARE THERE SO MANY SCARVES?!

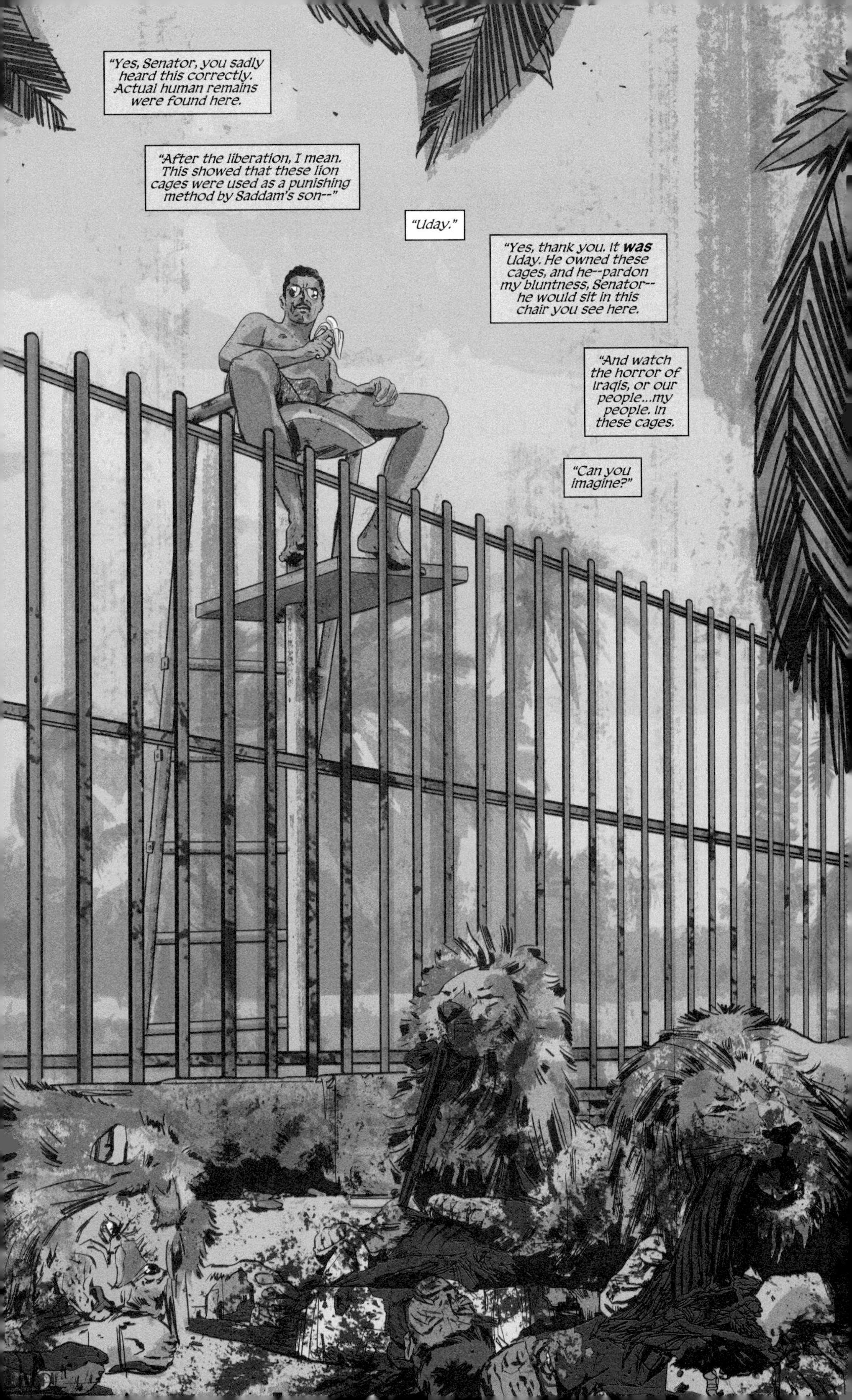
"Yes, Senator, you sadly heard this correctly. Actual human remains were found here.
"After the liberation, I mean. This showed that these lion cages were used as a punishing method by Saddam's son--"
"Uday."
"Yes, thank you. It **was** Uday. He owned these cages, and he--pardon my bluntness, Senator-- he would sit in this chair you see here.
"And watch the horror of Iraqis, or our people...my people. In these cages.
"Can you imagine?"

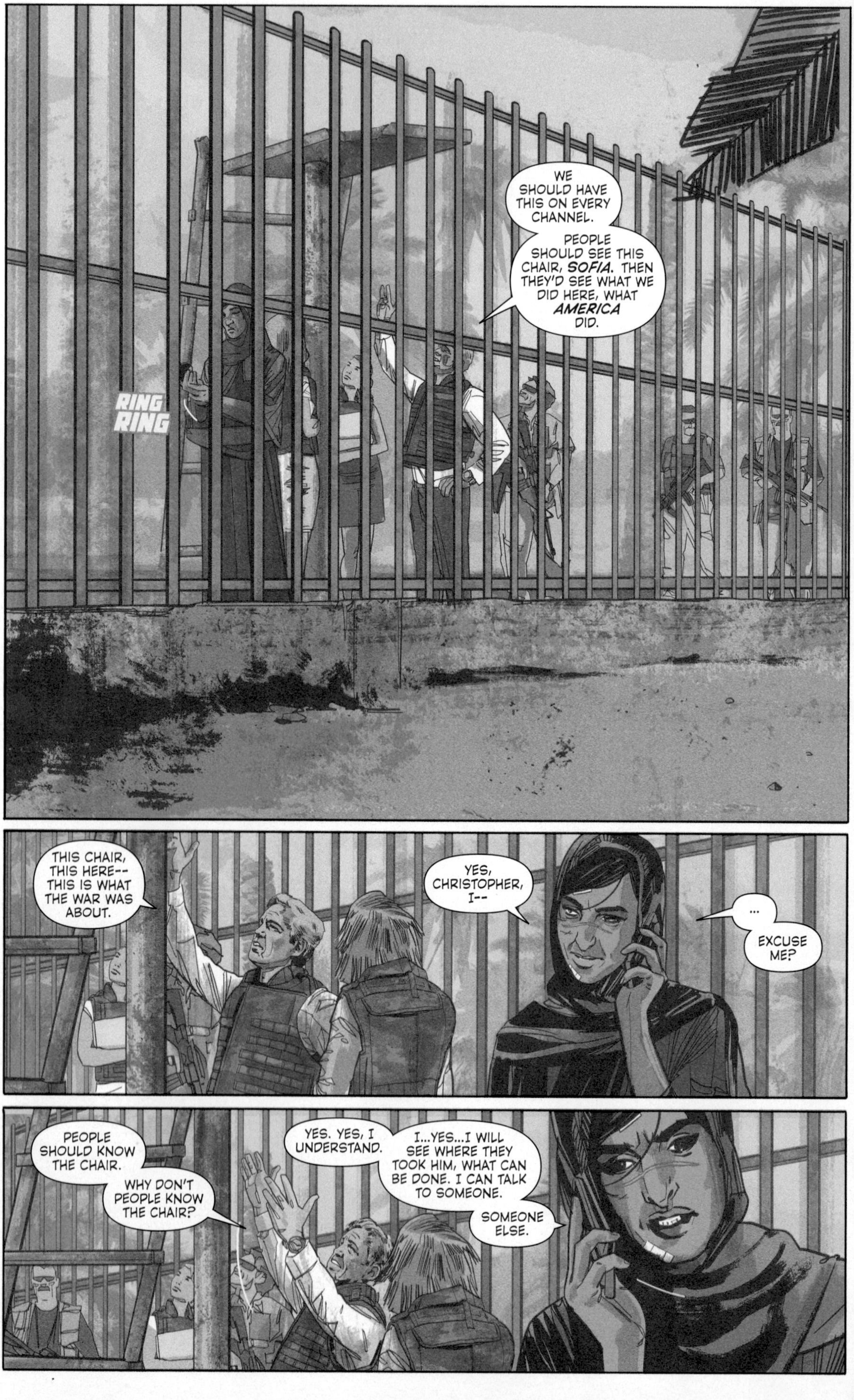
WE SHOULD HAVE THIS ON EVERY CHANNEL.
PEOPLE SHOULD SEE THIS CHAIR, SOFIA. THEN THEY'D SEE WHAT WE DID HERE, WHAT AMERICA DID.
RING RING
THIS CHAIR, THIS HERE-- THIS IS WHAT THE WAR WAS ABOUT.
YES, CHRISTOPHER, I--
...
EXCUSE ME?
PEOPLE SHOULD KNOW THE CHAIR.
WHY DON'T PEOPLE KNOW THE CHAIR?
YES. YES, I UNDERSTAND.
I...YES...I WILL SEE WHERE THEY TOOK HIM, WHAT CAN BE DONE. I CAN TALK TO SOMEONE.
SOMEONE ELSE.

I cannot thank you enough for your help, my brother.

Eh, **your** American general will not help you with your problems.

My American spy will. I will introduce you.

There is no need for thanks.

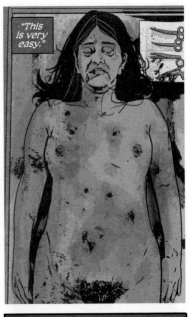

"This is very easy."

God willing.

"Sometimes I think America is the only God whose will we must care about."

With America, you can make the sky rain fire.

You can move a man who will not move, just by pointing a finger.

"The Americans have the most guns, Hassan."

"Having guns does not make you God."

I do not know, flower. What is and what is not God?

What is a son of a tea boy to say about such things?

Hassan, you are one of the **heirs** to the Kurdish empire.

Your father was no tea boy.

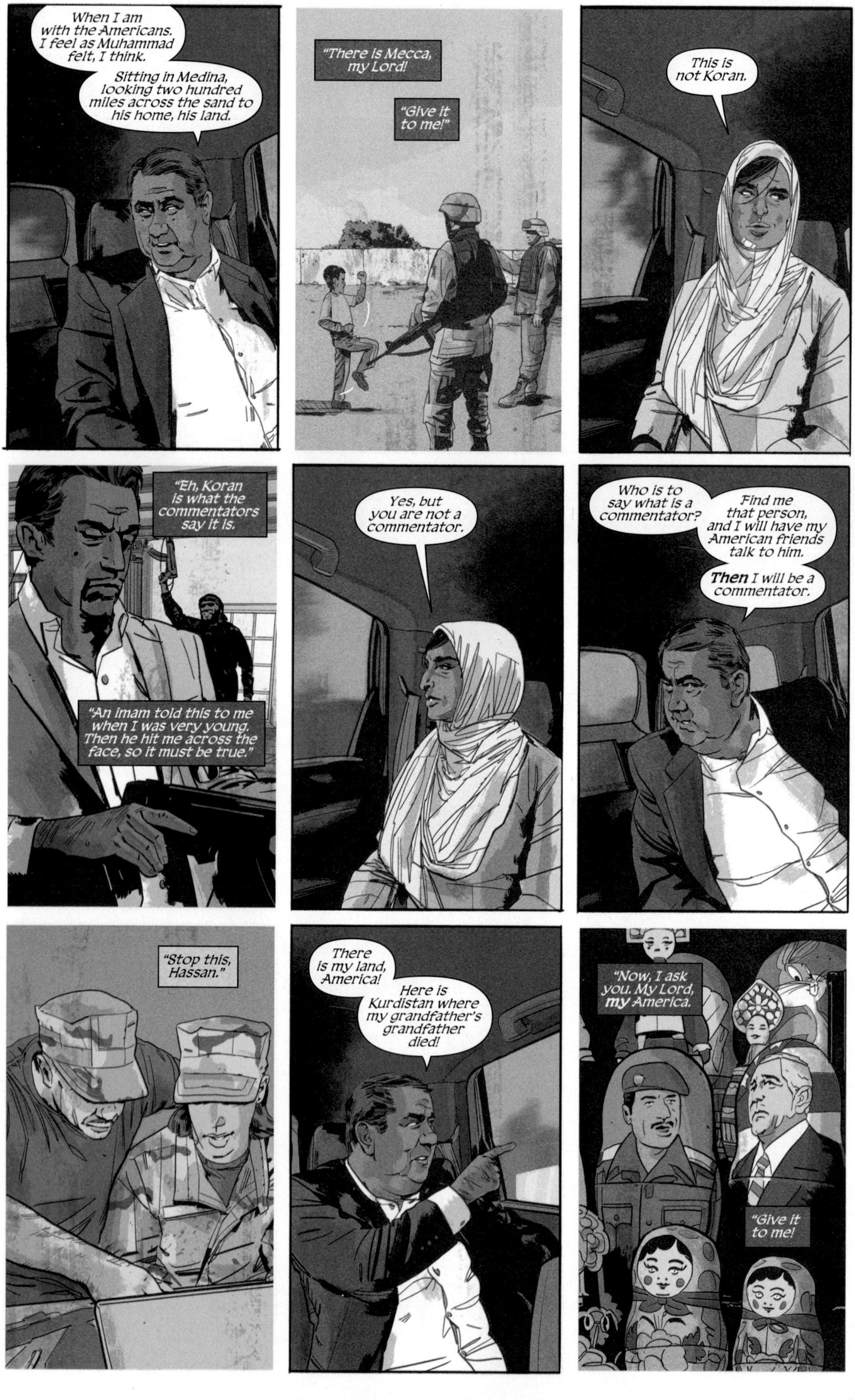
When I am with the Americans. I feel as Muhammad felt, I think.
Sitting in Medina, looking two hundred miles across the sand to his home, his land.
"There is Mecca, my Lord!
"Give it to me!"
This is not Koran.
"Eh, Koran is what the commentators say it is.
"An imam told this to me when I was very young. Then he hit me across the face, so it must be true."
Yes, but you are not a commentator.
Who is to say what is a commentator?
Find me that person, and I will have my American friends talk to him.
Then I will be a commentator.
"Stop this, Hassan."
There is my land, America!
Here is Kurdistan where my grandfather's grandfather died!
"Now, I ask you. My Lord, **my** America.
"Give it to me!

"Eh, but maybe you are right, my darling Saffiya."

"Maybe these Americans are not God."

Of course.

God is **one**, yes? I remember that, too, from the Imam.

He is unity. He is one. There is only Him. On and on like this. This is true Koran. Over and over. There is only one God.

"And Muhammad is His prophet."

But these Americans, these people here and there-- there is not one of them.

There are so many. One does this. The other **that**. You ask one for something, another for something else.

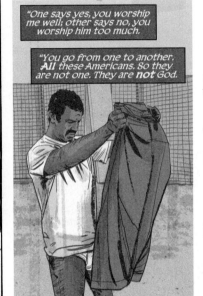

"One says yes, you worship me well; other says no, you worship him too much.

"You go from one to another. **All** these Americans. So they are not one. They are **not** God."

"That is **plain**, yes? But then, eh?"

What are they then?

Brother, you should listen to yourself.

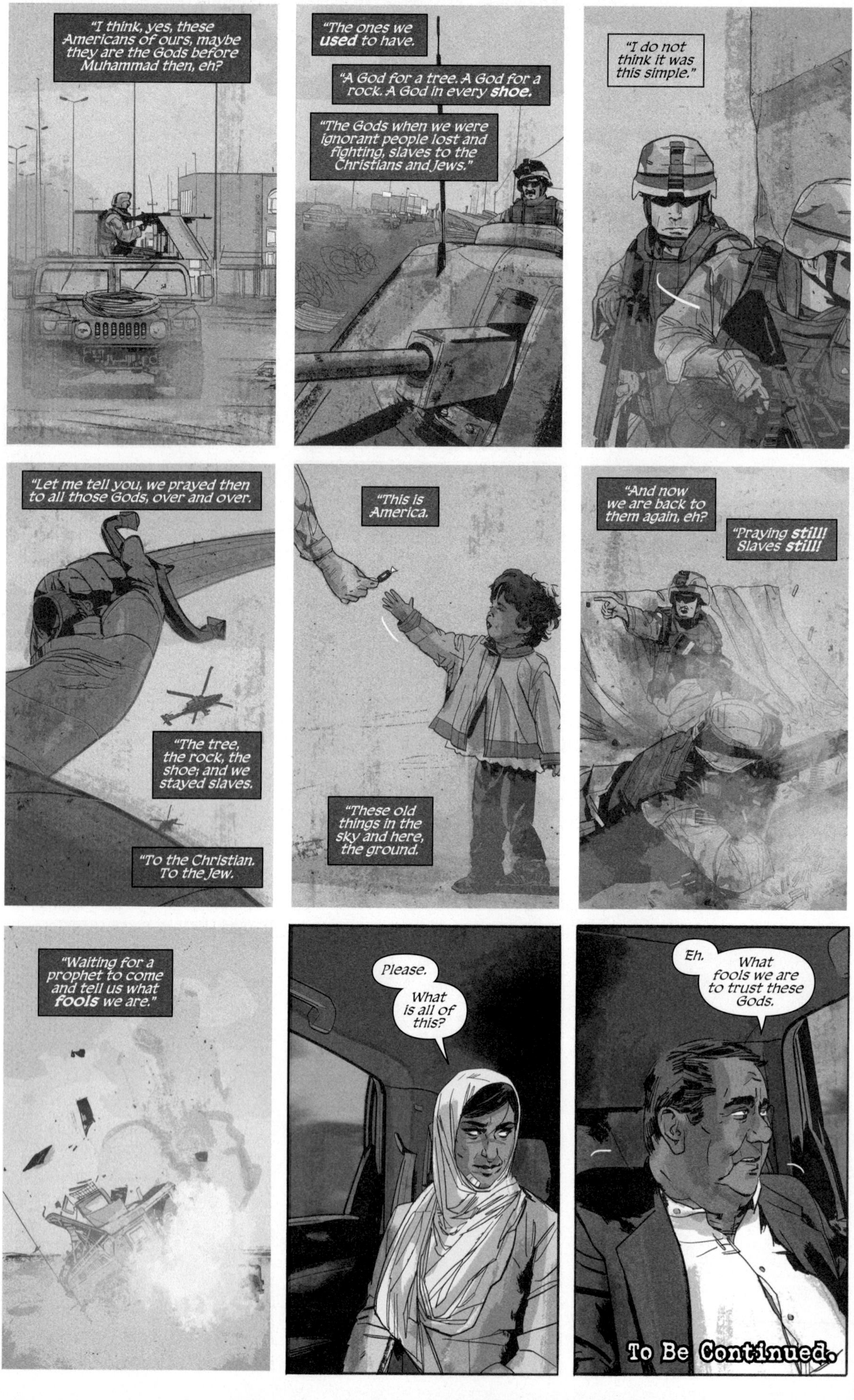
"I think, yes, these Americans of ours, maybe they are the Gods before Muhammad then, eh?
"The ones we used to have.
"A God for a tree. A God for a rock. A God in every shoe.
"The Gods when we were ignorant people lost and fighting, slaves to the Christians and Jews."
"I do not think it was this simple."
"Let me tell you, we prayed then to all those Gods, over and over.
"The tree, the rock, the shoe; and we stayed slaves.
"To the Christian. To the Jew.
"This is America.
"These old things in the sky and here, the ground.
"And now we are back to them again, eh?
"Praying still! Slaves still!
"Waiting for a prophet to come and tell us what fools we are."
Please.
What is all of this?
Eh.
What fools we are to trust these Gods.
To Be Continued.

CHARACTER DESIGNS FOR CHRIS

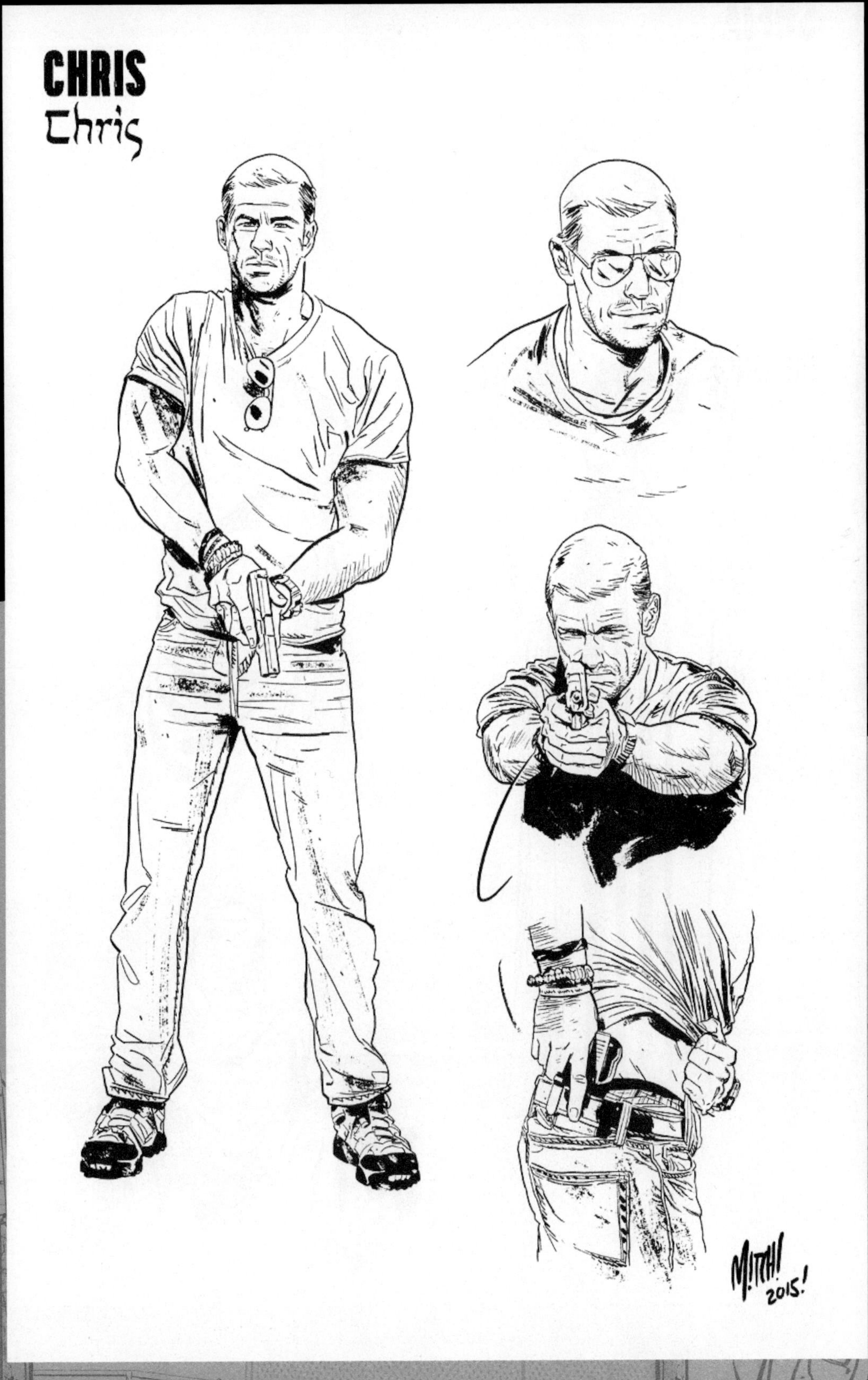
CHRIS
Chris
MITCH!
2015!

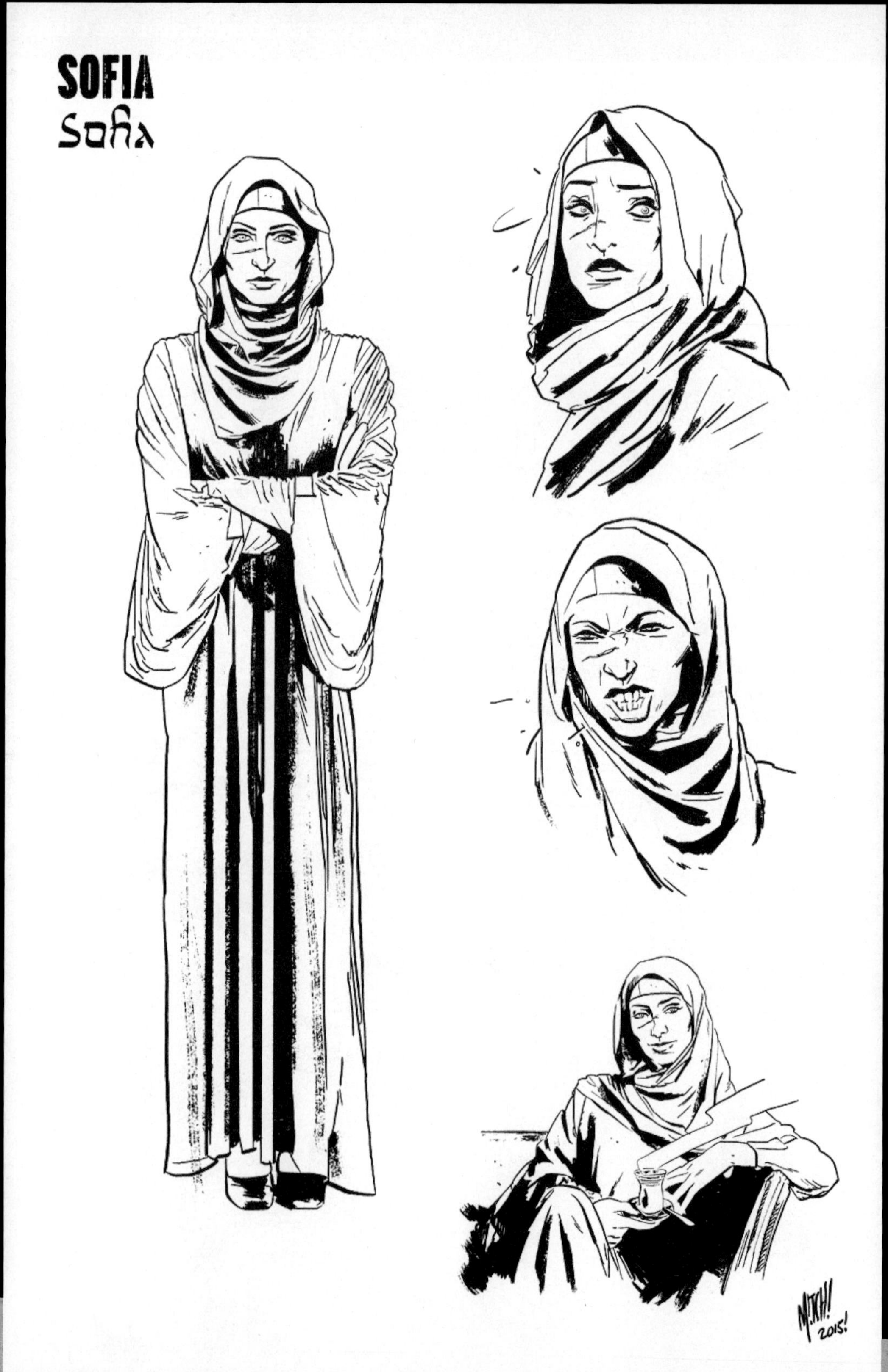
SOFIA
Sofia
MITCH! 2015!

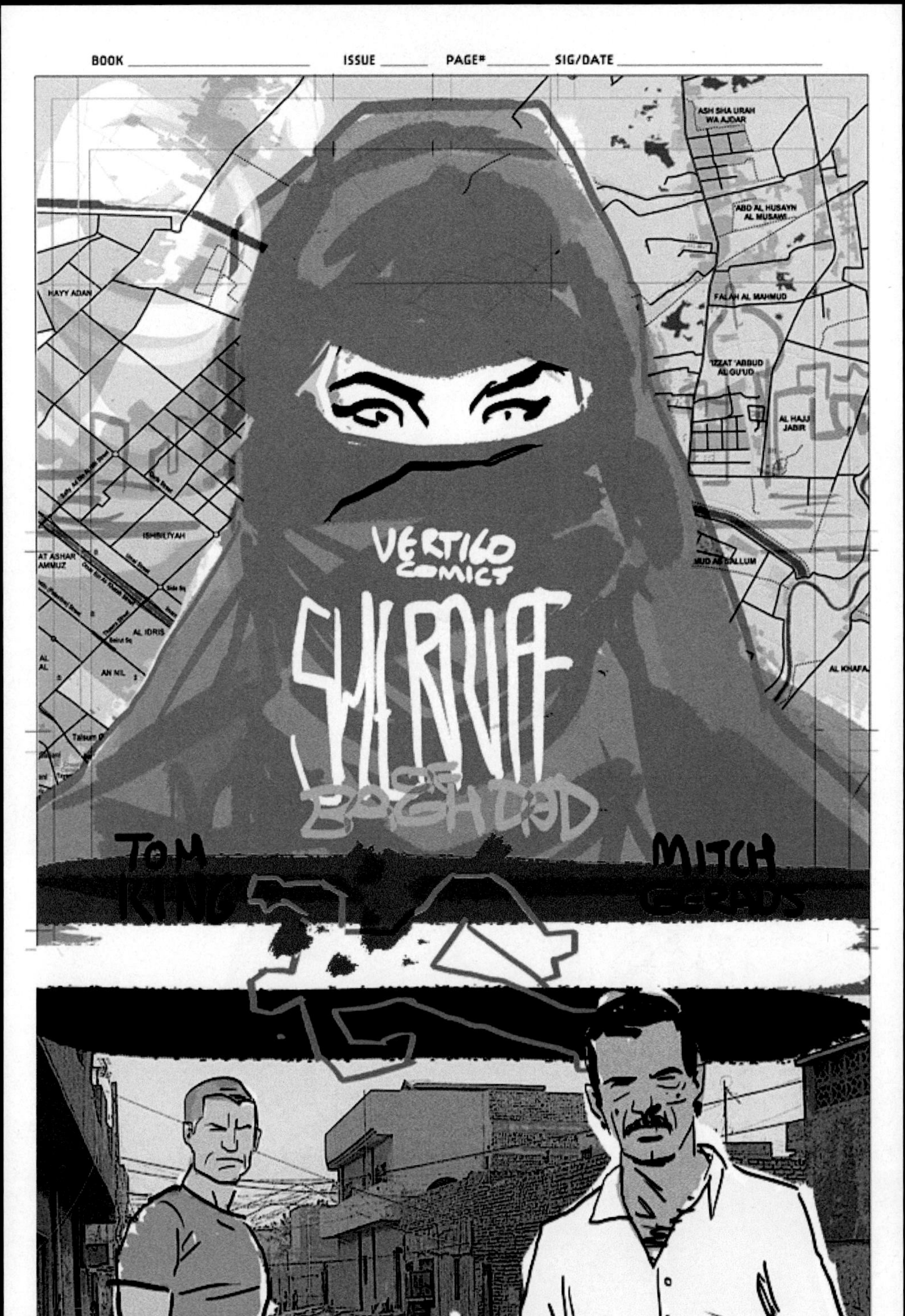
BOOK
ISSUE
PAGE#
SIG/DATE
ASH SHA URAH WA AJDAR
ABD AL HUSAYN AL MUSAWI
HAYY ADAN
FALAH AL MAHMUD
IZZAT 'ABBUD AL QU'UD
AL HAJJ JABIR
ISHBILIYAH
AL IDRIS
AL KHAFAJ
VERTIGO COMICS
SHERIFF
OF BAGHDAD
TOM KING
MITCH GERADS
NOV.

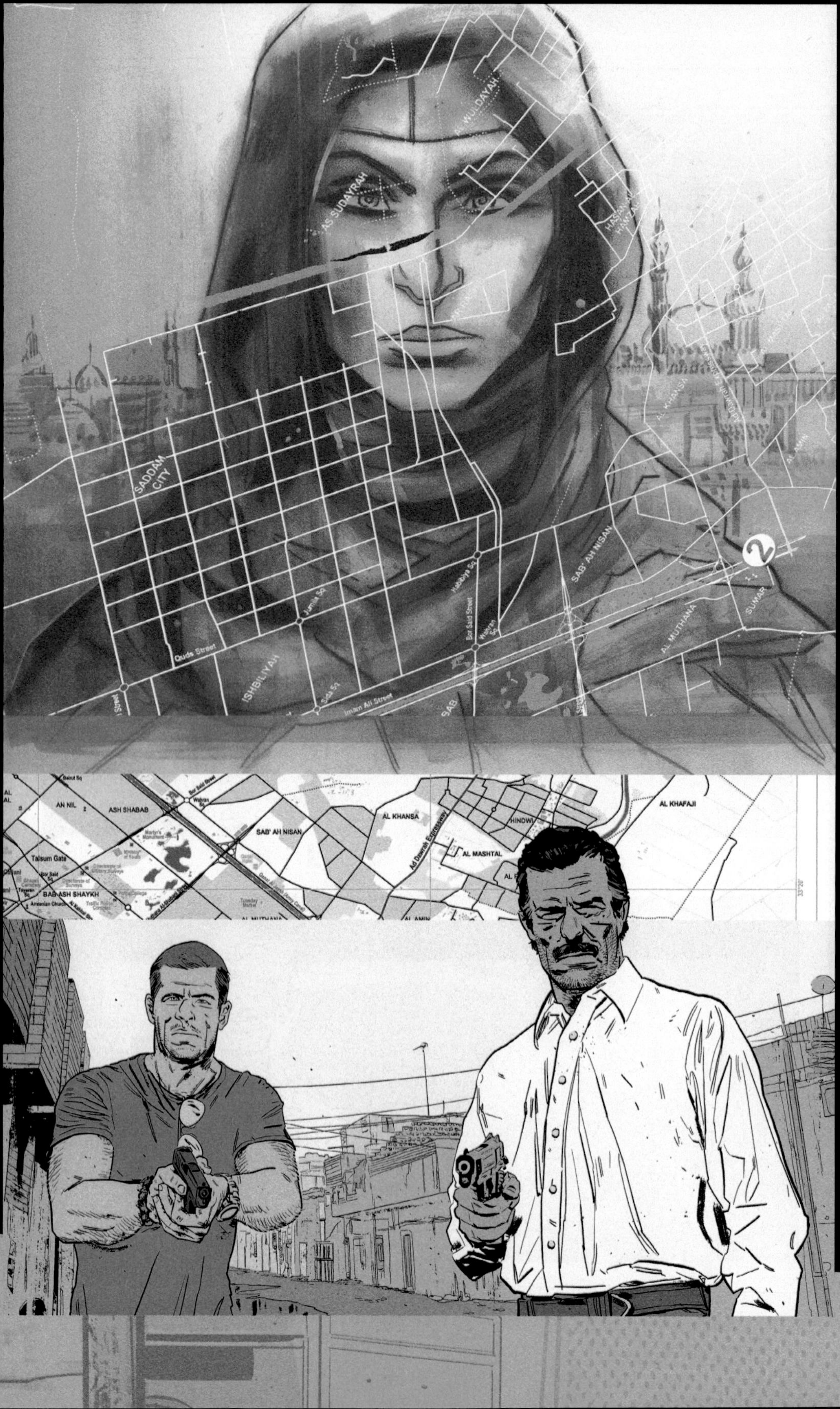
SADDAM CITY
AS SUDAYRAH
SAB' AH NISAN
AL MUTHANA
SUMAR
ISHBILIYAH
Quds Street
Imam Ali Street
AL KHANSA
AN NIL
ASH SHABAB
HINDWI
AL KHAFAJI
AL MASHTAL
BAB ASH SHAYKH
Ad Dawrah Expressway

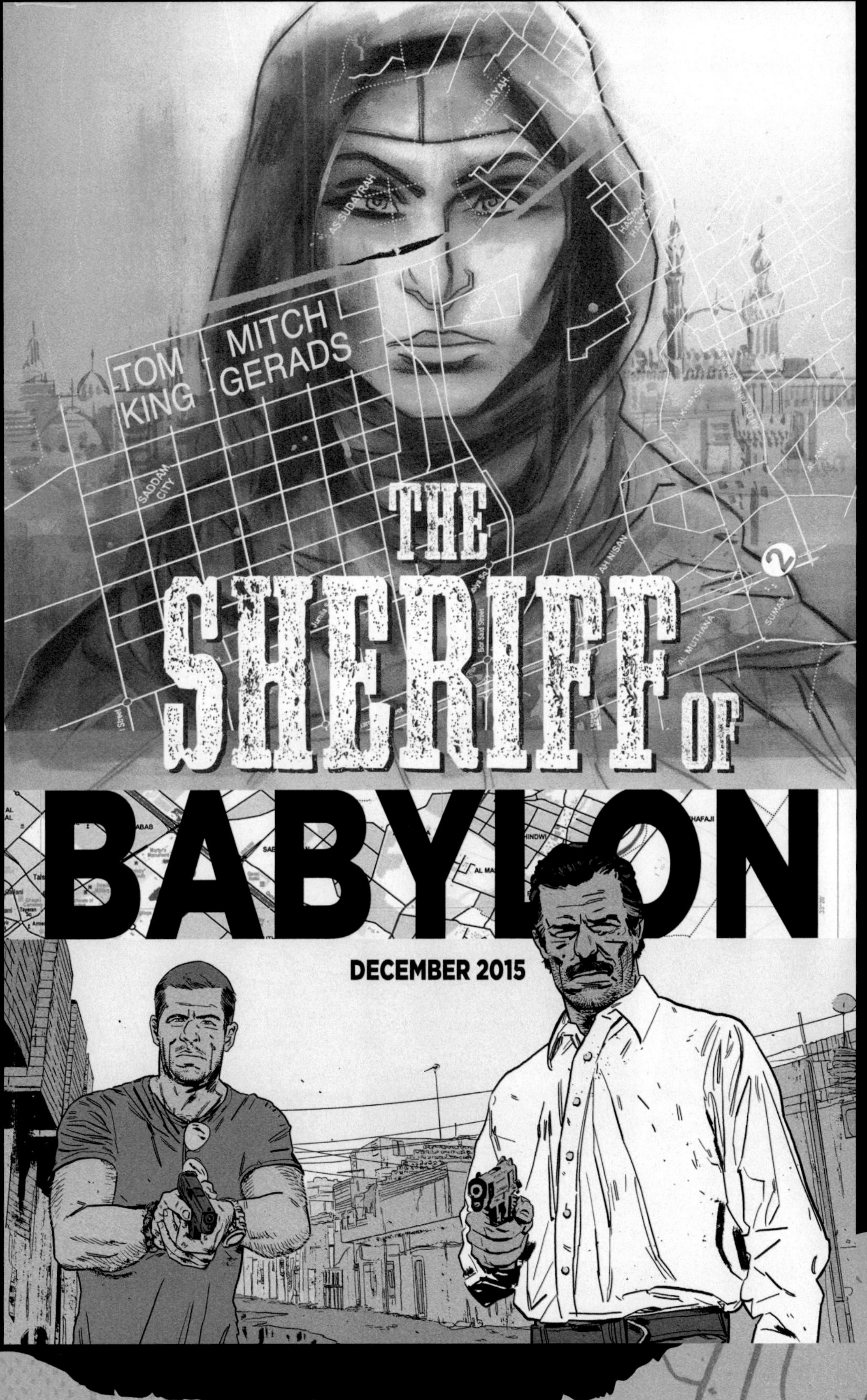
TOM KING
MITCH GERADS
THE SHERIFF OF BABYLON
DECEMBER 2015

DESKTOP

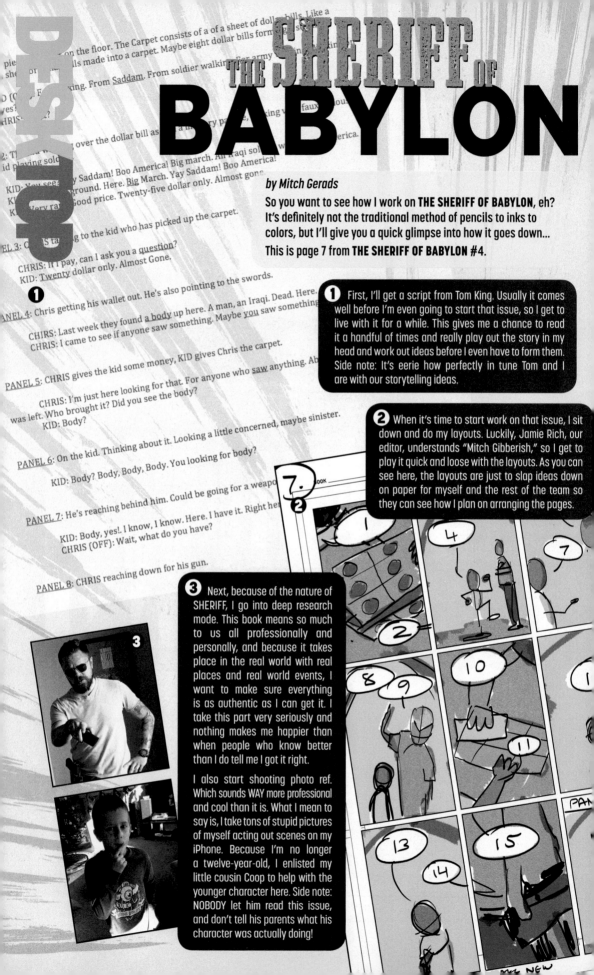

THE SHERIFF OF BABYLON

by Mitch Gerads

So you want to see how I work on THE SHERIFF OF BABYLON, eh? It's definitely not the traditional method of pencils to inks to colors, but I'll give you a quick glimpse into how it goes down...

This is page 7 from THE SHERIFF OF BABYLON #4.

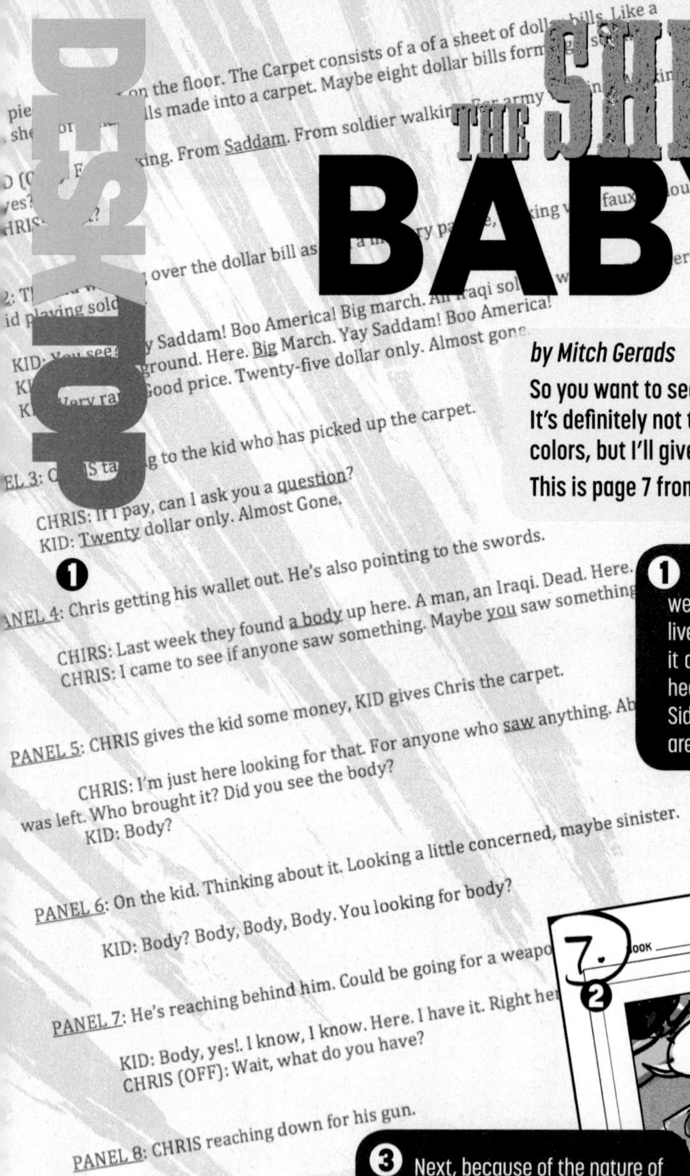

on the floor. The Carpet consists of a of a sheet of dollar bills. Like a
lls made into a carpet. Maybe eight dollar bills form
From soldier walkin
king. From Saddam. From soldier walking
over the dollar bill as
Saddam! Boo America! Big march. All Iraqi sol
ground. Here. Big March. Yay Saddam! Boo America!
Good price. Twenty-five dollar only. Almost gone.
g to the kid who has picked up the carpet.
CHRIS: If I pay, can I ask you a question?
KID: Twenty dollar only. Almost Gone.
1
PANEL 4: Chris getting his wallet out. He's also pointing to the swords.
CHIRS: Last week they found a body up here. A man, an Iraqi. Dead. Here.
CHRIS: I came to see if anyone saw something. Maybe you saw something
PANEL 5: CHRIS gives the kid some money, KID gives Chris the carpet.
CHRIS: I'm just here looking for that. For anyone who saw anything.
was left. Who brought it? Did you see the body?
KID: Body?
PANEL 6: On the kid. Thinking about it. Looking a little concerned, maybe sinister.
KID: Body? Body, Body, Body. You looking for body?
PANEL 7: He's reaching behind him. Could be going for a weapo
KID: Body, yes!. I know, I know. Here. I have it. Right he
CHRIS (OFF): Wait, what do you have?
PANEL 8: CHRIS reaching down for his gun.

① First, I'll get a script from Tom King. Usually it comes well before I'm even going to start that issue, so I get to live with it for a while. This gives me a chance to read it a handful of times and really play out the story in my head and work out ideas before I even have to form them. Side note: It's eerie how perfectly in tune Tom and I are with our storytelling ideas.

② When it's time to start work on that issue, I sit down and do my layouts. Luckily, Jamie Rich, our editor, understands "Mitch Gibberish," so I get to play it quick and loose with the layouts. As you can see here, the layouts are just to slap ideas down on paper for myself and the rest of the team so they can see how I plan on arranging the pages.

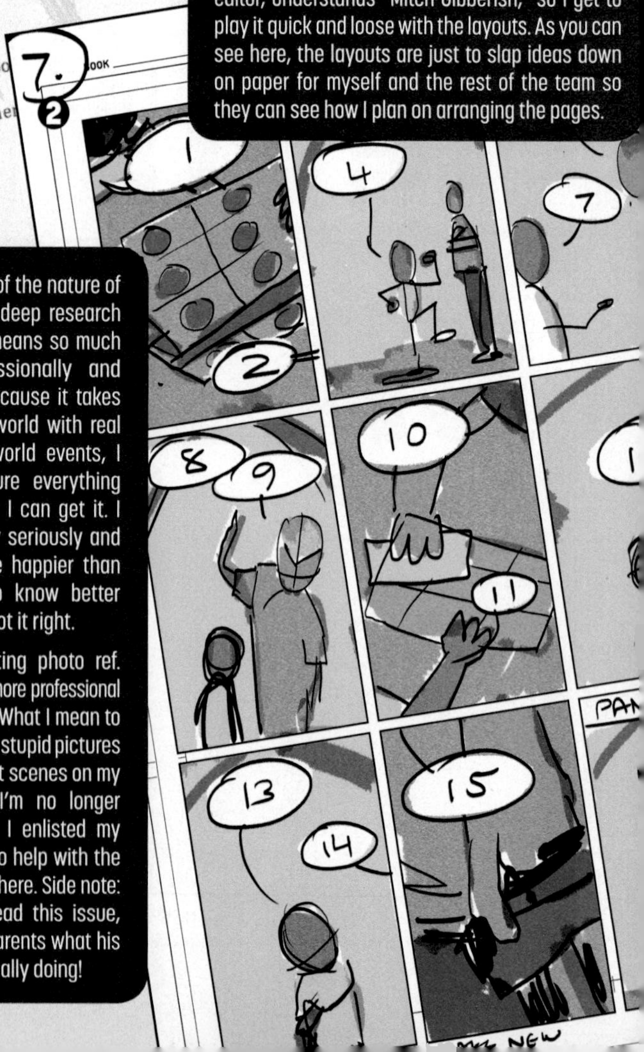

7.
BOOK
2
1
4
7
2
8
9
10
11
PAN
13
14
15

③ Next, because of the nature of SHERIFF, I go into deep research mode. This book means so much to us all professionally and personally, and because it takes place in the real world with real places and real world events, I want to make sure everything is as authentic as I can get it. I take this part very seriously and nothing makes me happier than when people who know better than I do tell me I got it right.

I also start shooting photo ref. Which sounds WAY more professional and cool than it is. What I mean to say is, I take tons of stupid pictures of myself acting out scenes on my iPhone. Because I'm no longer a twelve-year-old, I enlisted my little cousin Coop to help with the younger character here. Side note: NOBODY let him read this issue, and don't tell his parents what his character was actually doing!

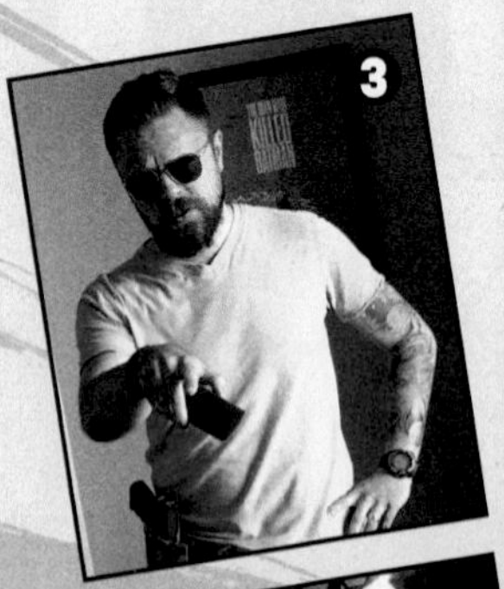

3

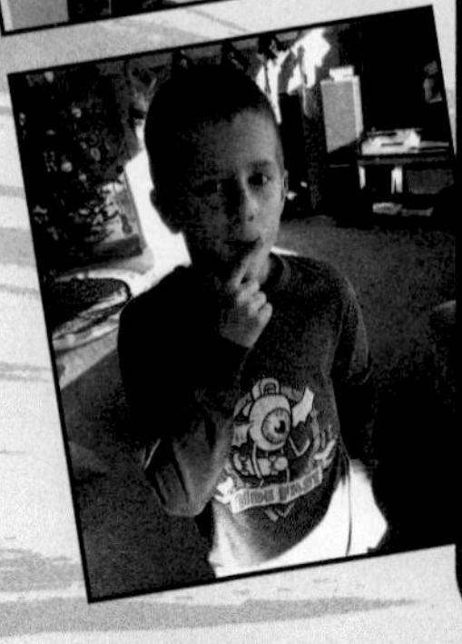

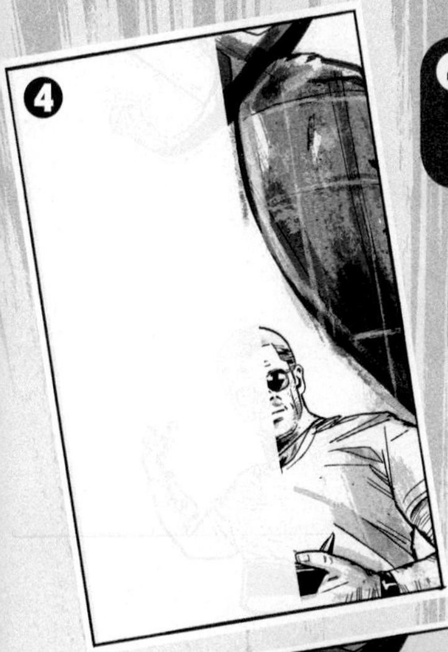
4

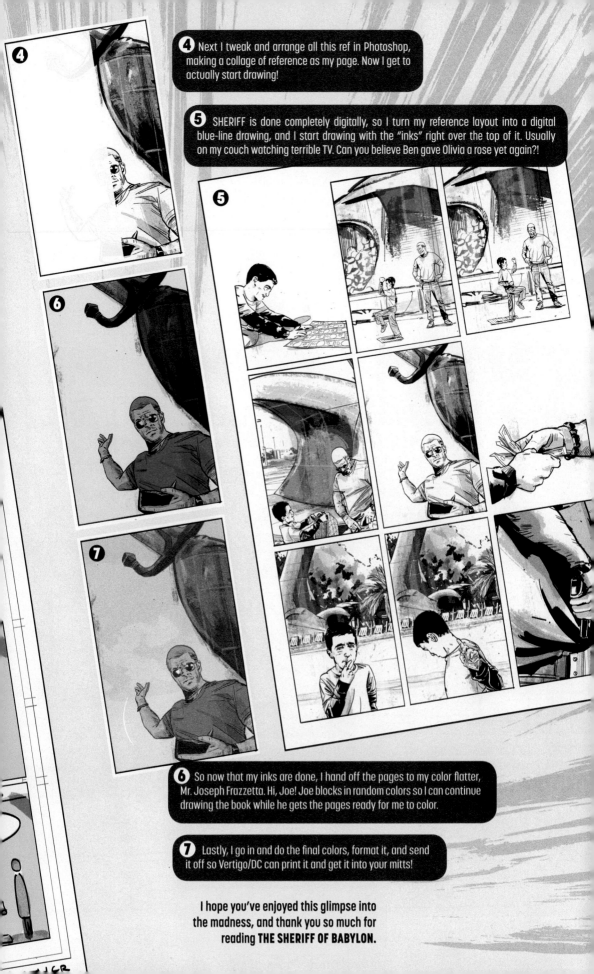

4 Next I tweak and arrange all this ref in Photoshop, making a collage of reference as my page. Now I get to actually start drawing!

5 SHERIFF is done completely digitally, so I turn my reference layout into a digital blue-line drawing, and I start drawing with the "inks" right over the top of it. Usually on my couch watching terrible TV. Can you believe Ben gave Olivia a rose yet again?!

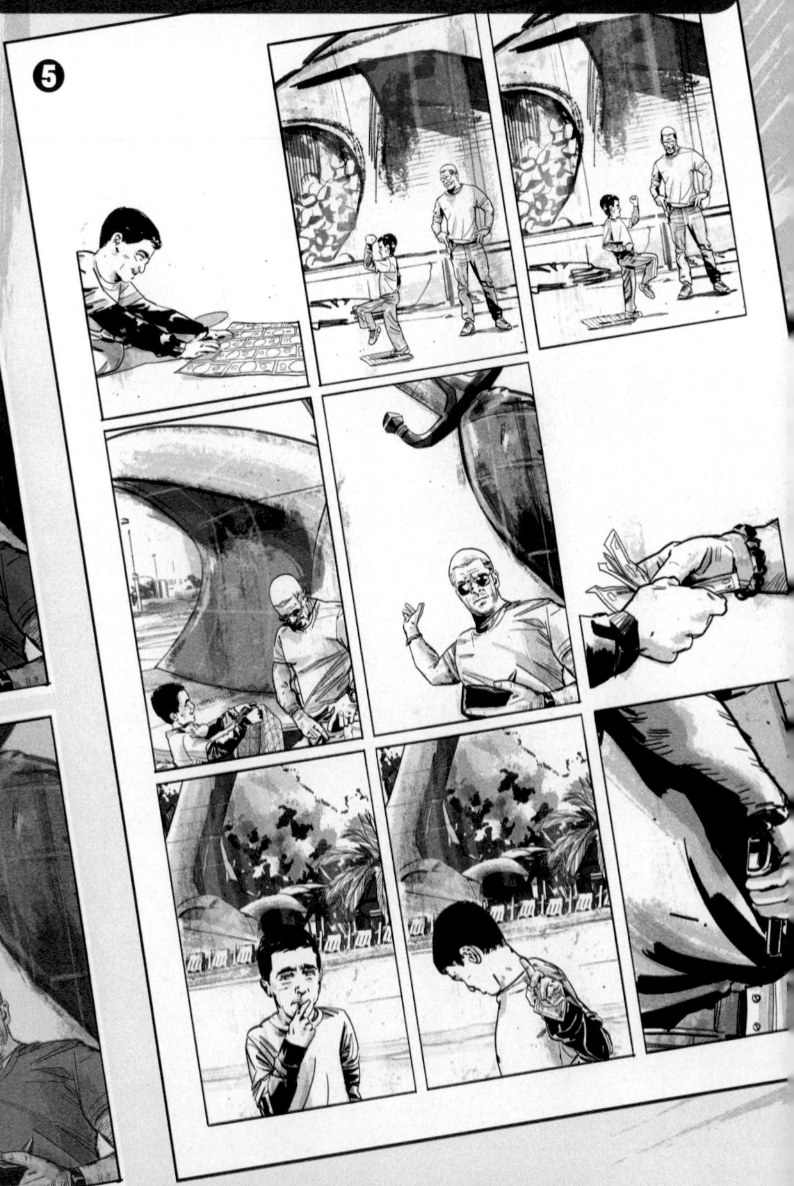
5

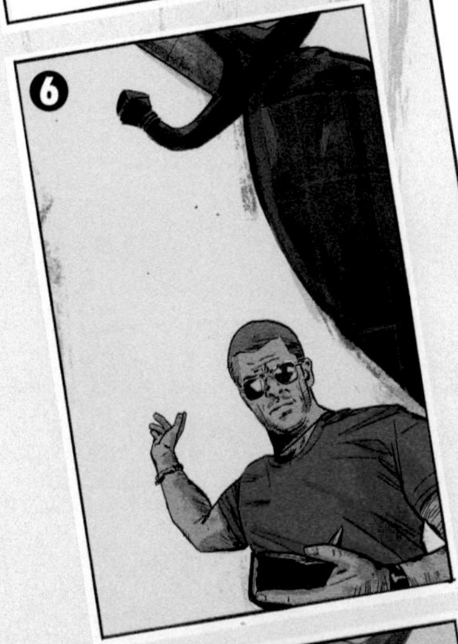
6

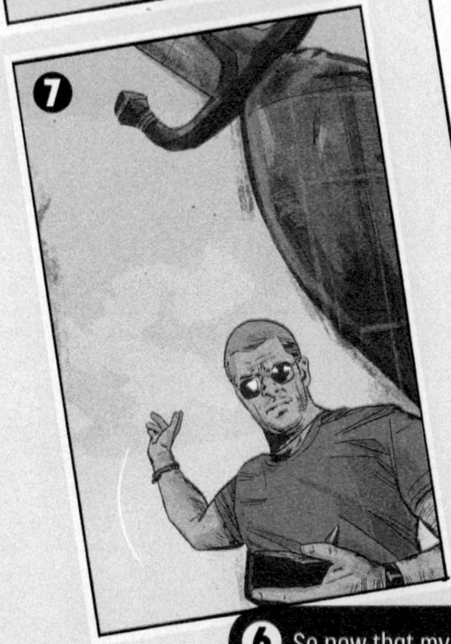
7

6 So now that my inks are done, I hand off the pages to my color flatter, Mr. Joseph Frazzetta. Hi, Joe! Joe blocks in random colors so I can continue drawing the book while he gets the pages ready for me to color.

7 Lastly, I go in and do the final colors, format it, and send it off so Vertigo/DC can print it and get it into your mitts!

I hope you've enjoyed this glimpse into the madness, and thank you so much for reading THE SHERIFF OF BABYLON.

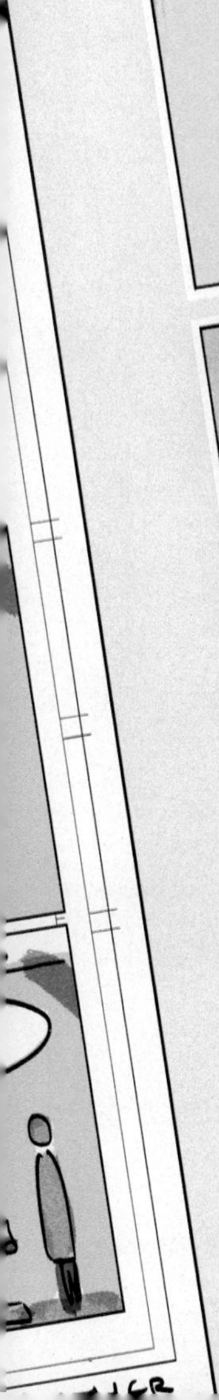

COVER LAYOUT FOR ISSUE #1

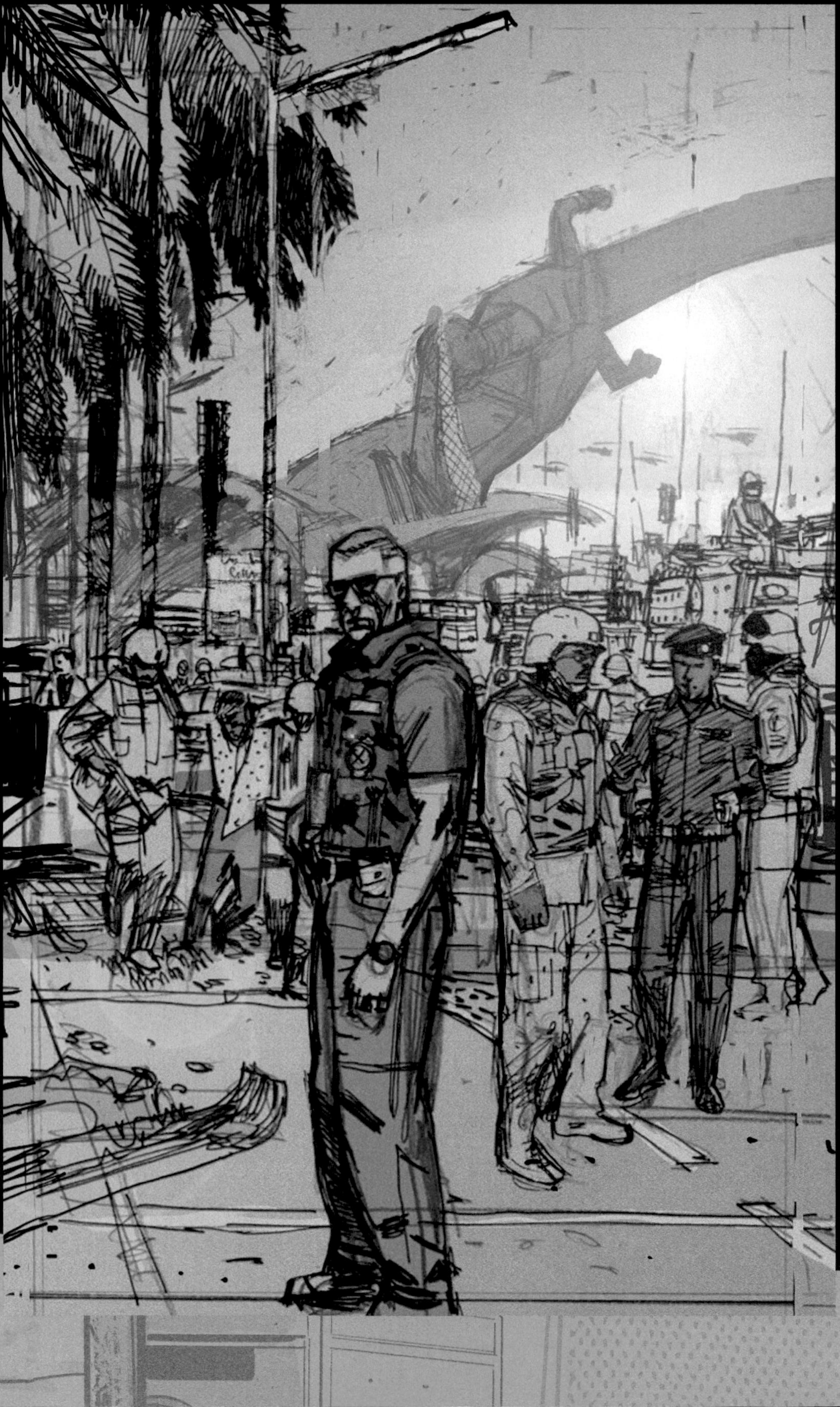

COVER SKETCHES FOR ISSUES #2 AND #3

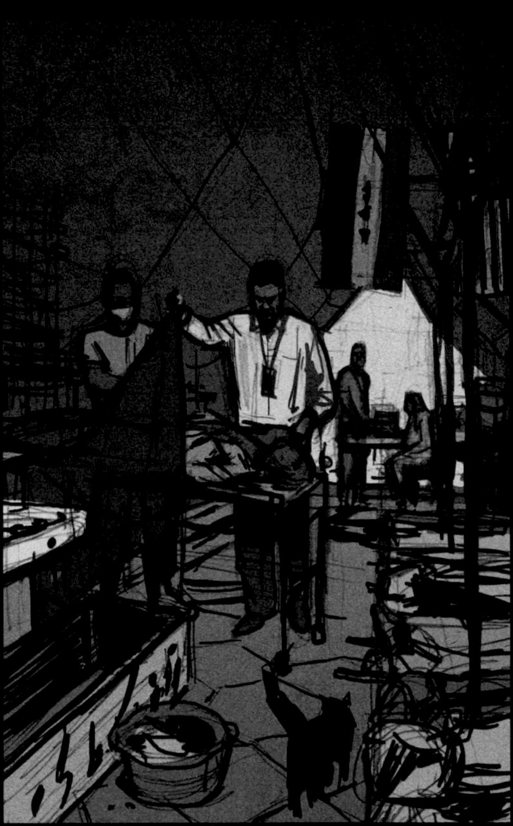

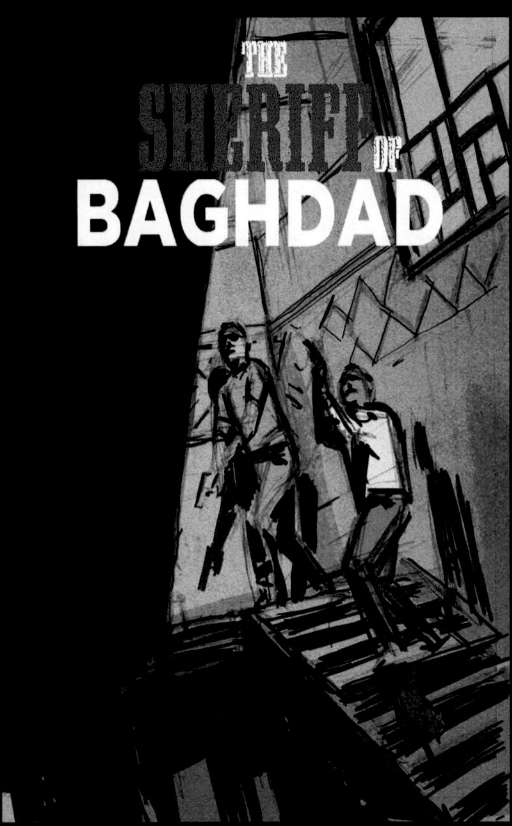
THE SHERIFF OF
BAGHDAD

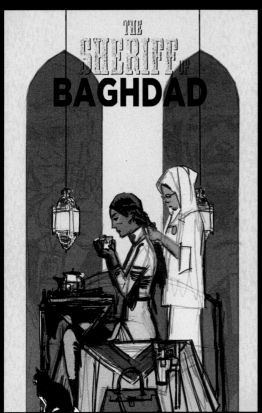

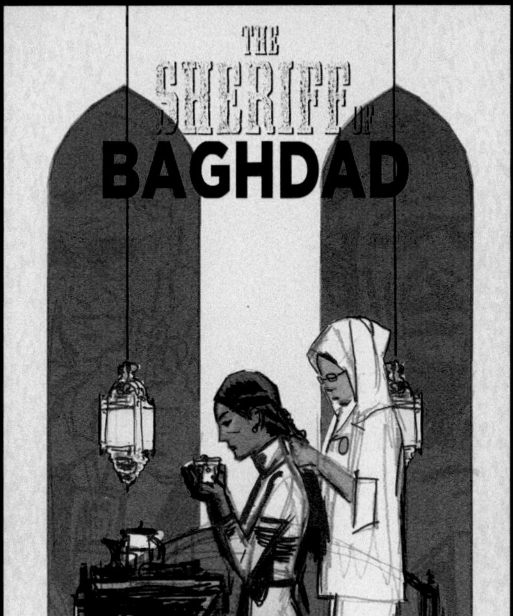
THE SHERIFF OF
BAGHDAD

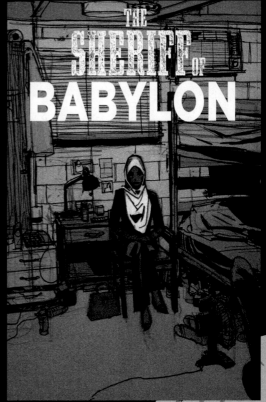

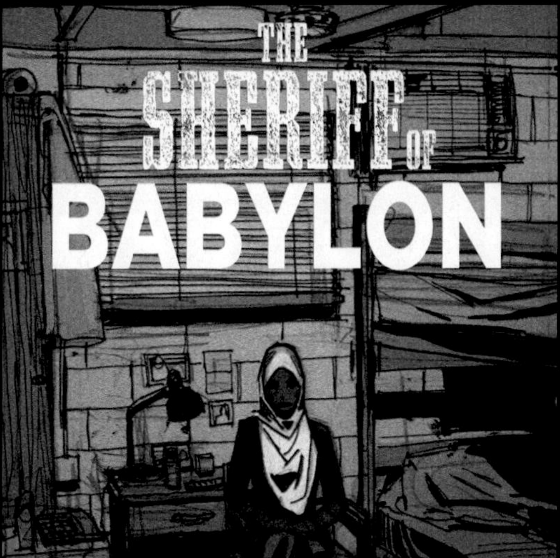
THE SHERIFF OF
BABYLON

COVER SKETCHES FOR ISSUES #5 AND #6

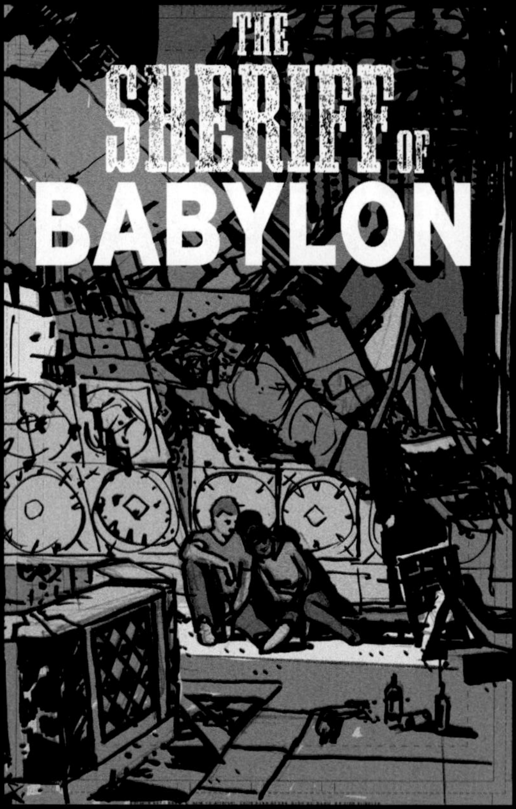
THE SHERIFF OF BABYLON

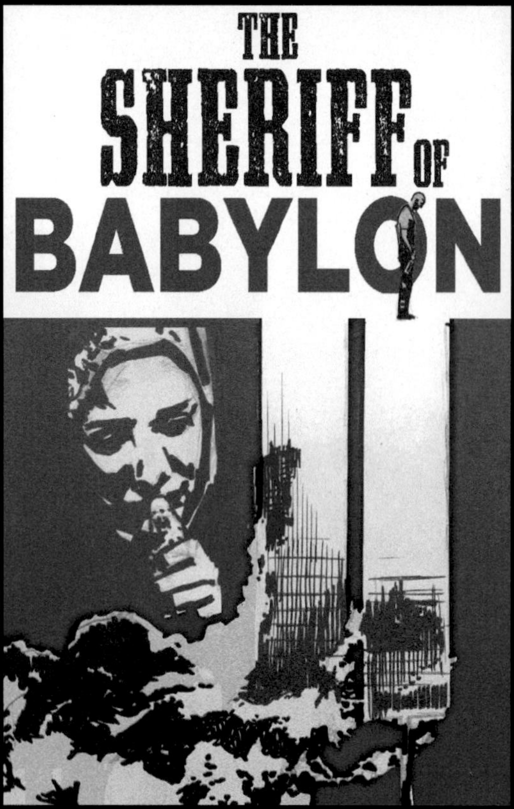
THE SHERIFF OF BABYLON

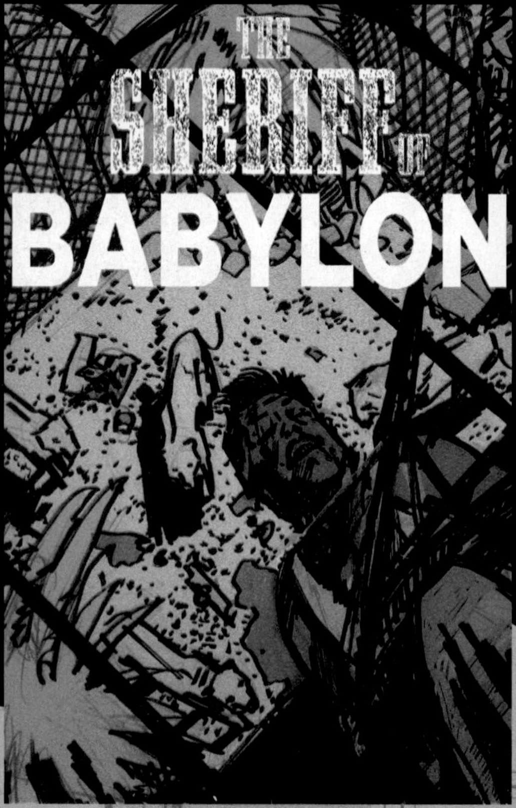
THE SHERIFF OF BABYLON

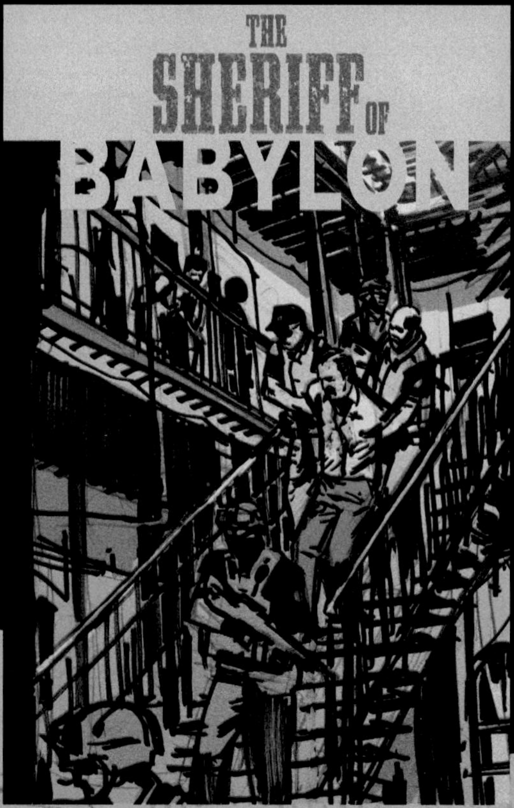
THE SHERIFF OF BABYLON

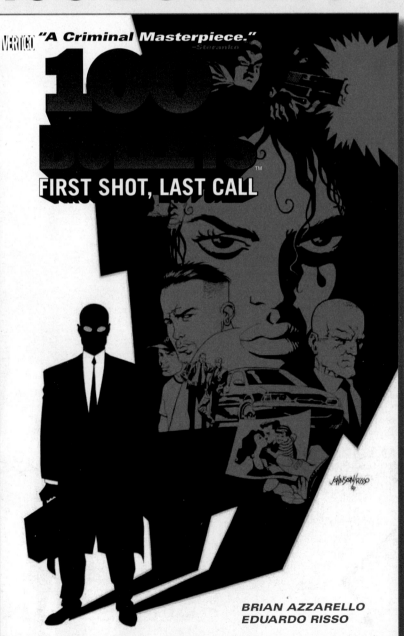

JASON AARON
with R.M. GUÉRA

SCALPED VOL. 4: THE GRAVEL IN YOUR GUTS

SCALPED VOL. 7: REZ BLUES

READ THE ENTIRE SERIES!

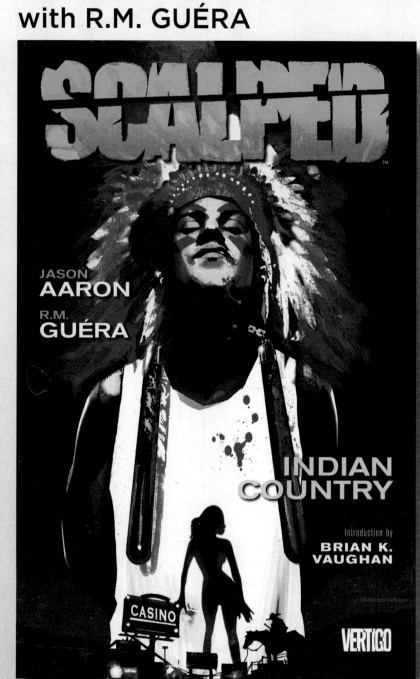

SCALPED

JASON AARON

R.M. GUÉRA

INDIAN COUNTRY

Introduction by BRIAN K. VAUGHAN

CASINO

VERTIGO